L. FRANK BAUM

Creator

of  z

Also by Katharine M. Rogers

The Cat and the Human Imagination:
  Feline Images from Bast to Garfield

Frances Burney:
  The World of "Female Difficulties"

Feminism in Eighteenth-Century England

William Wycherley

The Troublesome Helpmate:
  A History of Misogyny in Literature

L. Frank Baum, 1908.

Katharine M. Rogers

L. FRANK BAUM

Creator

of O *z*

St. Martin's Press New York

Frontispiece from the Library of Congress, LC-USZ62-103206.

Photos following page 144: page 145 top, 145 bottom, 146 bottom, 148 bottom used with the permission of the Alexander Mitchell Public Library, Aberdeen, SD; page 146 top, 148 top from the L. Frank Baum Collection, Syracuse University Library, Department of Special Collections. Used by permission. Page 147 top and bottom from the Moving Image Collections at the Library of Congress.

www.stmartins.com

Library of Congress Cataloging-in-Publication Data

Rogers, Katharine M.
    L. Frank Baum: creator of Oz : a biography / Katharine M. Rogers—1st. ed.
      p.   cm.
    "Works by L. Frank Baum": pp. 291–296
    Includes bibliographical references (p. 297) and index.
    ISBN 0-312-30174-X
    1. Baum, L. Frank (Lyman Frank), 1856–1919. 2. Authors, American—20th century—Biography. 3. Children's stories, American—History and criticism. 4. Oz (Imaginary place) I. Title.

PS3503.A923 Z86 2002
813'.4—dc21
[B]

                                             2002069826

10 9 8 7 6 5 4 3 2

To Ken,
who gave me unfailing support through difficult times

CONTENTS

LIST OF ILLUSTRATIONS

ACKNOWLEDGMENTS

I would like to thank the experts who answered my questions about aspects of Baum's life—Alan Sheff, who explained the probable nature of his heart disease; Myron Karman, who informed me about bankruptcy law; and Bruce Beehler, Roger Klapp, and Mary Weisman, who confirmed Baum's knowledge of birds. The reference librarians at the Library of Congress were, as always, well-informed and helpful. Robert A. Baum, who has inherited his great-grandfather's good will and encouraging spirit, gave me copies of L. Frank Baum's correspondence with his publishers.

INTRODUCTION

All through my childhood, I could go whenever I liked to a wonderful land where I could have a talking lion for my good friend or pick a delicious box lunch from a tree or find a magic word chalked on a loose floorboard that could transform anybody into anything. I might have to pass within arm's reach of a caged giant who was trying to grab and eat me or run the risk of being transformed forever into a piece of bric-a-brac, although I could be sure everything would come right in the end. I would be confronted with problems—vivid, exciting, perilous problems, unlike the routine difficulties of everyday life; then, together with a variety of other children, adults, stuffed dolls, animals, and a robot, we would solve them. I might get to this place by walking down the road in front of my house, which would lead me to a crossroads I had never seen and from there to a city of civilized foxes. And, even though I knew very well that none of these things could happen in the real world I lived in, I believed in them totally as I was reading the Oz books of L. Frank Baum.

In 1958, I became an instructor in a college English department and mentioned these happy memories to the professor who taught children's literature. How surprised and deflated I was to hear that she would not think of teaching Baum, for those who knew the field taught only *good* children's literature. She did not make clear what was wrong with Baum, but it probably had to do with his lack of literary pretensions. Baum narrated his fantastic stories in the matter-of-fact style he would have used for simple reporting; he did not make his authorial presence felt; he let moral or psychological themes emerge as they might. In *Behold the Child* (1994), a scholarly survey of American children's literature, Gillian Avery disparaged Baum partly for his unpolished style, but mostly for blandness and "easy optimism." She took at face value his claim to have excluded anything disagreeable or frightening from Oz and, as a sophisticated English reader, objected to the representation of a world without shadow, unpleasantness, and violence. If she had valued his books enough to read them with attention, she would have found that they include both alarming perils and recognition of human folly and evil.[1]

Only recently have Baum's books been adequately represented in public libraries, although they have sold regularly since he published them. Children have always loved the Oz books, and for some of them the enchantment never faded. Writers such as Alison Lurie, Madeleine L'Engle, and Lloyd Alexander have enthusiastically praised Baum's creation. Perhaps the finest tribute of all is Ray Bradbury's short story "The Exiles" (1950). Bradbury envisions a world in which utilitarian rationalism has triumphed and all fantasy has been banished as unwholesome. Poe, Shakespeare, Bierce, Dickens, and their colleagues have fled to Mars and preserved their fantasy worlds there. But they are pursued by a rocket full of clean-cut scientists from Earth, who burn their books and thereby destroy artists and creations. The last structure to fall is the Emerald City of Oz.

L. FRANK BAUM

Creator

of  z

one

EARLY LIFE: ACTOR, PLAYWRIGHT, OIL SALESMAN, 1856–1888

Lyman Frank Baum was born on May 15, 1856, in a frame house in Chittenango, fifteen miles east of Syracuse, New York. He was the seventh child of Cynthia Stanton and Benjamin Ward Baum. The others were Harriet Alvena (born in 1846), Mary Louise (1848), Benjamin William (1850), and three who had died young. Three years after Lyman Frank, Henry Clay Baum was born. A ninth child lived only until the age of two.

Benjamin was descended from Philipp Baum of Hesse, who settled in central New York in 1748. Benjamin's father had been a prosperous storekeeper, but he lost his money and became a Methodist lay preacher. Benjamin, his oldest son, started life as a barrel maker. He moved to New Woodstock, where he met Cynthia Stanton, the daughter of a prosperous farmer. Oliver Stanton did not consider Benjamin a suitable son-in-law, so the two young people eloped and married in 1842, when both were twenty-one.

The young barrel maker turned out to be an enterprising and astute businessman. Although he suffered periodic reverses and was forced to mortgage or sell property, he always recovered up to the time that he became chronically ill. He embarked on one business after another until he became a wealthy man. By 1850, he was a partner in a pump-vending business in Cazenovia with his wife's brother, as well as being listed in the city directory as a manufacturer of butter and cheese. In 1854, the Baums moved to Chittenango, where Benjamin's sister lived with her husband and their parents. He bought considerable land there, on which he built the family home and a barrel factory. A business directory of 1859 lists Baum Brothers (Benjamin and Lyman), Manufacturers of Tight Barrels (for liquids) and Butter Firkins. In the 1860 census, Benjamin's real estate holdings were valued at six thousand dollars, and "Frankie" was listed among his family members. Lyman Frank had already succeeded in shedding the first name he disliked.

In 1859, oil was discovered in Titusville, Pennsylvania, about two hundred miles from Syracuse. Benjamin recognized a splendid opportunity and joined the crowds who moved in to exploit the oil fields and develop the area. A hundred new wells were drilled every month, ingenious mechanical contrivances were invented, towns and cities were built, "with schools, churches, lyceums, theatres, libraries, boards of trade. There were nine daily and eighteen weekly newspapers published in the region and supported by it."[1]

Benjamin began acquiring oil fields, including a particularly profitable one at Cherry Tree Run, a few miles south of Titusville. He later bought property between Bradford, Pennsylvania, and Olean, New York, where he helped to develop the hamlet of Gilmour and built a hotel and an opera house. In 1860, he moved his family to a handsome house in Syracuse. He was listed in the city directory of 1864 as a "Dealer in Petroleum Oil." But he had other interests as well. He dealt extensively in real estate—city houses and lots, farms, a sawmill with adjacent timberland. He traded stocks and had an office in New York City. He established the Second National Bank in Syracuse in 1863 and was its director or president until 1872. In 1866, he organized Neal, Baum & Company, Wholesale Dry Goods, probably to provide a business for his daughter Harriet's new husband, William Henry Harrison Neal. Benjamin also took responsibility for finding work for his younger brothers, as well as, when the time came, his son Frank.

In 1866, when Frank was ten, his father bought a delightful country estate just north of Syracuse, although they retained their house in the city for two years. Cynthia named the new property Rose Lawn because of the hundreds of rose bushes that grew there. There were also a wide variety of fruit trees and grapevines. The house was large and comfortable, furnished in the dark, ornate style that was fashionable in the 1860s; but it did not have running water.[2] Frank fondly remembered this childhood home and later described it in *Dot and Tot of Merryland*:

> The cool but sun-kissed mansion ... was built in a quaint yet pretty fashion, with many wings and gables and broad verandas on every side. Before it were acres and acres of velvety green lawn, sprinkled with shrubbery and dotted with beds of bright flowers. In every

direction were winding paths, covered with white gravel, which led to all parts of the grounds, looking for all the world like a map.[3]

At the same time, Benjamin bought Spring Farm, eighty acres of dairy land adjoining Rose Lawn, where he raised Jersey cattle and fast harness horses and housed them in a magnificent barn, as well as a 160-acre commercial grain and livestock farm. Frank got his first view of scarecrows, which even then he invested with life. He told a reporter in 1904: "They always seemed to my childish imagination as just about to wave their arms, straighten up and stalk across the field on their long legs."[4] In those days the image was upsetting; Frank had a recurrent nightmare in which a scarecrow chased him but collapsed into a pile of straw just before catching him.[5]

In the late 1870s, Benjamin ran into business difficulties. There was no longer unlimited free enterprise in the oil fields, for John D. Rockefeller had moved in and was increasingly controlling distribution. In 1878, Benjamin organized a group of independent producers to break Rockefeller's grip by building a pipeline from Bradford to Rochester, where the oil could be transferred to tank cars and shipped to refineries in New York and Buffalo; but the Standard Oil Company used its influence with the New York Central Railroad and the state legislature to block the plan. At about this time, Baum also suffered severe losses on the stock market. He had to sell Rose Lawn and his stock farm in 1880, although the family was soon able to buy it back. In 1882, he completed his recovery by discovering some productive oil wells near Olean, New York, and building the Cynthia Oil Works nearby.[6]

Although he had brothers and sisters to play with, Frank spent much of his time daydreaming by himself. He had a defective heart, either congenital or the result of rheumatic fever. This disease, which was then quite common, produces acute illness, which abates but may leave the patient with damaged heart valves; over decades the valves function less and less effectively, although there may be no perceptible effects until the patient develops incapacitating heart symptoms some time between the ages of forty and sixty. This is consistent with Baum's experience: he was sickly as a child, recovered, and led a normal, active life until his late fifties (although extraordinary physical stress did give him chest pain).[7]

Until the age of twelve, Frank, like the other Baum children, was taught at home. At that time the doctors declared him strong enough to attend school, and his parents sent him to Peekskill Military Academy. It seems an odd choice for a dreamy boy with a weak heart; presumably they felt a need to make him more manly. In any case, he loathed the rigid discipline and constantly "complained to my father about the brutal treatment I felt I was receiving at the school." The teachers, he claimed, "were heartless, callous and continually engaging in petty nagging . . . about as human as a school of fish." They "were quick to slap a boy in the face" and beat him with a cane if he "violated in the slightest way any of the strict and often unreasonable rules." Frank spent two miserable years there, but one day, when he was severely disciplined for looking out of the window at the birds while he should have been preparing his lesson, he had a heart attack (probably psychogenic). Thus he proved that he did not belong in military school, and Benjamin took him away. After that Frank was tutored at home. He read voraciously, especially the novels of Dickens, Thackeray, and Charles Reade, whose *Cloister and the Hearth* was one of his favorite books. Perhaps he was already attracted to the theater, for he liked to memorize passages from Shakespeare's plays.[8]

One day when Frank was fourteen, his father took him along to his office in Syracuse, and Frank wandered off and saw a small printing shop. He was so fascinated by watching the old owner work that he lost track of time, and he resolved to become a printer or a newspaper man. Benjamin bought him a small press.[9] There was a fad for amateur journalism at the time, and it was possible to buy a child a press with all the other necessary equipment for something between fifteen and fifty dollars. Once Frank had mastered the techniques and taught them to his younger brother, Harry, they decided to issue a monthly paper.

The first issue of the *Rose Lawn Home Journal,* which is not extant, probably came out on October 20, 1870; more followed on November 20 and on July 1, August 1, and September 1, 1871. The *Journal* was filled with works by Frank and other members of his family, together with pieces drawn from national magazines and books. His father contributed the first installments of a "History of the Oil Company," describing the beginning of the petroleum industry in Pennsylvania. His sister Mary Louise contributed at least two poems, one of which, "To a Spray of Mignonette," he was to reprint and mock in *Aunt Jane's Nieces on Vacation.*

The July 1 issue contains a mock pompous introduction by Frank and Harry, a story by Washington Irving taken from *Salmagundi,* a complimentary letter from "A Neighbor" (perhaps by Frank), riddles and jokes, "To a Spray of Mignonette," a story called "Three Curious Needles" that looks borrowed, verses "By the Editor" on the "Cardiff Giant," and seven advertisements, including one for the dry goods business run by his sister Harriet's husband. "The True Origin of The Cardiff Giant" makes fun of a current hoax that occurred on a farm only eight miles from Rose Lawn, where workmen unearthed a ten-and-a-half-foot stone figure; although it was actually a gypsum statue that a local con artist had buried almost a year before, many people took it for a petrified man from the race of giants described in the Bible, perhaps left behind by the Great Flood, and it had become a major tourist attraction. Already at fifteen, Frank displayed humorous invention in accounting for the giant's location and irony at the expense of credulous, moralizing believers. He and Harry advertised in the *Journal* that they could print "cards, programmes, handbills, letterheads, billheads, etc.; at the lowest prices!" And so they did, especially after Frank got a much better press in 1873. They did job printing, mainly for their uncle's firm.[10] At some point Frank must have begun a novel, for he thanked his sister Harriet for approving it in his inscription to her copy of *Mother Goose in Prose*.

Then Frank was drawn to another contemporary fad, stamp collecting. With his usual enthusiasm, he promptly established a journal, *The Stamp Collector*, a review of the latest stamps with criticism of other amateur papers that dealt with the subject; published an eleven-page *Baum's Complete Stamp Dealers' Directory*; and joined with William Norris, a traveling salesman based in Albany, to form a mail-order business in foreign postage stamps. The *Directory* included advertisements, not only for Baum, Norris & Company, Importing Dealers in Foreign Postage Stamps, and The Young American Job Printing Press, but for *The Empire*, "a First Class Monthly Amateur Paper" published by Baum and Alvord and the Empire Job Printing Office.[11] The young entrepreneur was seventeen. Baum retained a lifelong interest in stamp collecting and had a good collection when he died.

Frank and Harry Baum had pooled resources with Thomas G. Alvord Jr.—a son of the lieutenant governor, who grew up to be a distinguished newspaperman—and announced a monthly journal, *The Empire*, to contain "poetry, literature, new stamp issues, amateur items, etc." Since no issues seem to have survived, this enterprise may never have materialized. The three boys were enrolled in the Syracuse Classical School and are listed in the school catalogue for 1873. Frank left after a year, and this was the end of his formal education.

He had found yet another interest to keep him busy. Benjamin Baum had used some of his oil profits to acquire a string of small theaters in New York and Pennsylvania. Frank could see traveling companies performing there when he accompanied his father on business trips. His Uncle Adam Baum was active in amateur theatricals in Syracuse, and his Aunt Katherine taught elocution professionally. At eighteen, Frank took to haunting the theaters in Syracuse, avidly studying the actors' stage business, speech, and gestures. He approached several managers of traveling companies without success, but finally the manager of a Shakespearean troupe claimed to see promise in this well-dressed and very young man, and accepted him into the company provided he "would equip himself with a complete set of costumes for all the starring roles he might be called upon to take." Frank agreed and the manager drew up a long list. Although Benjamin Baum was suspicious, Frank and his mother managed to persuade him to pay for the lot, on the condition that Frank use a pseudonym, since the name *Baum* was respected in the community. Frank ordered several thousand dollars' worth of the finest velvet and silk garments, trimmed with lace and gold fringe, from a noted New York theatrical costumer. While he waited for delivery, he practiced declaiming Shakespeare.

When the five trunks of costumes arrived, Frank assumed the stage name George Brooks and rushed to join the troupe at Oneida. The manager welcomed him warmly and told him to report to the theater an hour before curtain time. An actor appeared in Frank's dressing room, casually announced that he was to play Romeo and his doublet was torn, and asked whether he could borrow one from Frank. By curtain time almost every man in the cast had had a similar emergency and borrowed an item from Frank. Within a few days, all of his costumes and wigs had been borrowed, and none returned. He was given only a few walk-on roles, and after a few weeks he returned home with empty trunks. Presumably chastened, Frank, in 1875, went to work as a clerk with Neal, Baum & Company, his brother-in-law's wholesale dry-goods store in Syracuse, as his brother had before him.[12]

After acquiring a year or two of practical experience working for Neal, Frank returned to Spring Farm to learn the agricultural business. (The oldest son, Benjamin William Baum, a graduate chemist with a laboratory in Syracuse, was to take over his father's oil investments.) This led to a new enthusiasm—breeding of fancy poultry, which was then a national craze. He formed B. W. Baum & Sons with his father and brother Harry and devoted himself to raising Hamburgs, black chickens with subtly varied secondary coloring. Then he helped found the Empire State Poultry Association in late 1878 and became its first elected secretary, organizing its first two annual fairs in Syracuse—from February 11–18, 1879, and from January 31–February 3, 1880. By this time, chickens from the Baum farm had won many first prizes in shows. At twenty-three Frank must already have impressed people as personable and competent, for when he attended the Seventh Annual Meeting of the American Poultry Association in Indianapolis in January 1880, he was elected to its executive committee.

In March, he founded *The Poultry Record*, a trade journal issued monthly. He took most of his copy and pictures from rival journals, but he did write editorials in which he expressed bold opinions on the fancy chicken trade, occasionally enlivened by clever derision of rival breeders. After nine or ten issues, Baum sold his journal to the *New York Farmer and Dairyman*, which retained him to carry on a column, "The Poultry Yard," beginning in January 1881 and running into April. In May, *The Poultry World*, the leading journal in the field, profiled Baum as "one of our most active and enthusiastic fanciers." H. H. Stoddard, its publisher, commissioned him to write a lengthy article on Hamburgs, which was serialized in the magazine from July to November 1882. Then he reissued it in 1886 (apparently without Baum's knowledge) as *The Book of the Hamburgs, A Brief Treatise upon the Mating, Rearing, and Management of the Different Varieties of Hamburgs.*[13]

Generally speaking, this is a dry, technical manual for fancy chicken breeders, including detailed descriptions of the show points of each variety of Hamburg, advice on breeding to achieve the ideal physical type, and practical instruction on the care of chicks. Baum could never remain impersonal, however, and occasionally his enthusiasm broke through. "Every season and nearly every day unfolds new beauties" in these birds, he declared, "and renders them more fascinating and delightful to his eye. The exquisite symmetry, the novel and shapely rose combs, the snowy and delicate ear-lobes, the tapering blue legs and graceful carriage give them an aristocratic and 'dressed up' appearance." He gave feeling and personality to the Hamburg mother hen, the original ancestor of self-centered Billina in *Ozma of Oz:*

For the first week, perhaps, nearly every old hen is faithful to her little brood, and guards them with that maternal tenderness for which she has been made the symbol of motherly love. But this care soon wearies her, and in a few days she begins to neglect them, marching around in the chill and drenching rains of spring, and dragging her little brood after her through the damp grass, entirely oblivious of their sufferings; and one by one they drop off.

Baum retained his interest in chickens all his life; he kept a flock of Rhode Island Reds in his last home, Ozcot.[14]

While still involved in poultry breeding, Baum found an opportunity to get a genuine start in professional acting. Albert M. Palmer of the Union Square Theatre in New York welcomed and trained new actors. Using the name Louis F. Baum, Frank appeared in a successful play, Bronson Howard's *The Banker's Daughter*, which was first presented on November 30, 1878, and ran for one hundred nights. He probably wrote some pieces for the *New York Tribune* and then, through his father's influence, got a job on a weekly newspaper, the *Bradford Era*. After a year there, Frank returned to the stage. In 1880, his father made him manager of the string of theaters he owned in Bradford, Olean, Richburg, and other towns in the area; he later deeded them to Frank outright.

Frank later recalled that he had trouble getting companies to perform in tiny towns in the oil fields, "So I decided to organize my own company and produce some of Shakespeare's better known plays." Once they "were asked to give a special performance of *Hamlet* in the town hall of a small oil settlement. When we got there we found the hall had no stage—not even a raised platform." They asked the oil workers to cover some sawhorses with planks stacked outside for a building under construction. They did, but since they refused to risk damaging the planks by nailing them, the "stage" was wobbly and the actors had to step carefully. In scene iv, when Hamlet (Baum) started backward on seeing his father's ghost, he dislodged a plank. The poor ghost, blinded by the white sheet draped over him, stepped into the resulting hole and disappeared through the stage. The oil workers thought this was an intentional piece of slapstick and roared with laughter, so "we had to repeat the scene five times before we could get on with the show."[15]

Baum then set about writing original plays more suited to the taste of his audiences. He copyrighted three of them early in 1882: "The Mackrummins" and "Matches," comedy dramas in three acts, and "The Maid of Arran," a melodrama. "The Mackrummins" was never produced and possibly never completed. "Matches" was performed in Brown's Opera House in Richburg, New York, and the Richburg *Oil Echo* of June 3, 1882, praised its humor and Baum's comic acting and lovemaking. It was revived only once, in Syracuse, on May 19, 1883. "The Maid of Arran," however, proved to be a big success. Frank organized a new company to give it a good start. Among its members was Frank's Aunt Katherine, whom Benjamin had persuaded to join the company in order to keep an eye on the young manager and the company's financial affairs.[16]

Baum not only wrote the words and music for "The Maid of Arran" and managed the company, he played the leading role—all under the name Louis F. Baum. He was a tall, very handsome man with dark hair, gray eyes, and a fine baritone voice. He carried himself well and kept himself trim all his life. As "the Fair-haired Stranger," he wore a yellow wig, which his boys found years later in a trunk of costumes and used in acting out spontaneous plays of their own.[17]

The play was based on William Black's popular novel *A Princess of Thule* (1874), in which a dilettante painter from London falls in love with the unsophisticated daughter of the chief of Borva, a remote island in the Hebrides. Frank Lavender romanticizes Sheila as a sea princess and brings her to London as his wife, expecting her to dazzle fashionable society, although his steady older friend Ingram has warned him of the difficulties of transplanting a natural woman into high society. Before long Lavender does become dissatisfied with Sheila's failure to fit in and consequently belittles and neglects her until she is forced to return to her father. Frank is shocked into repentance, renounces living in luxury off his rich aunt, retires to a remote spot in the Hebrides, and works seriously to make his living as a painter. In the end Sheila and Frank are reconciled and settle in Borva.

Baum started with Black's basic situation, but he transplanted Shiela's home to Ireland; and he added some melodramatic turns. He transformed Ingram from an upright civil servant devoted to Shiela (Baum's spelling) and Lavender (Hugh Holcomb in Baum), into a treacherous naval captain who foments discord between them to get Shiela for himself. After Hugh drives her away and then is overcome with remorse, as in the novel, he does not merely renounce luxury and work at his profession; he enlists as a common sailor on a warship in order to make a man of himself. Too late, he finds that Ingram, who betrayed him, is the captain of his ship. Ingram provokes Hugh to strike him and then condemns him to hang. But Hugh is saved by an Irish retainer of Shiela's, and after three hard years of wandering returns to live a happy pastoral life with her in Arran.

The play has only the feeblest hints of humor, proceeding from the Irish retainers and from Hugh's aunt, a self-indulgent lady who claims to be a disciple of Marcus Aurelius. (She was played by Baum's Aunt Katherine.) Rather, Baum's aim, according to the playbill, was "to Ensnare all hearts and leave an impress of beauty and nobility within the sordid mind of man." The play suited contemporary taste, with its Irish setting, melodramatic sentimental plot, and florid language ("That girl has touched a chord in my heart, whose strain I have never heard before. She has the depth of the sea in her eyes, the music of the far off hills, in her voice, and all the brightness and purity of these summer skies lie mirrored in her soul.") Baum also provided impressive scenic effects, especially "the Great Ship Scene," which was "A Triumph of Mechanical Art."[18]

"The Maid of Arran" opened at Baum's Opera House in Gilmour, Pennsylvania. "It was an immediate success," Frank recalled.

> This encouraged me to engage the Grand Opera House in Syracuse for two performances. The first was on May 15, 1882, my twenty-sixth birthday. A correspondent for a New York newspaper sent a favorable account . . . to his editor, and through this notice the Windsor Theater in New York booked us for the week of June 19 through 24. . . . We had a well-filled theater all week. But I soon found that playing the principal part and managing the company, too, had become too much for me. When I asked father what to do, he assigned his brother, John Wesley Baum, to us as business manager for the road tour. It started in Ithaca.

From there they went to Toronto, Rochester, Columbus, and Milwaukee, "arriving in Chicago for ten performances at the Academy of Music beginning October 9. It was my first sight of Chicago, which was very busy and energetic after rebuilding from the great fire." When they returned to Syracuse for the nights of February 14 and 15, 1883, the *Syracuse Journal* reported that both play and performances had been thoroughly polished and improved.[19] The play was never published, however.

During the Christmas holidays of 1881, Baum took time off from his touring company to visit his family, and his sister Harriet invited him to a little party to meet a girl she had met through their Aunt Josephine, the wife of Benjamin's brother Adam. Frank was not enthusiastic, being busy with his stage career and so far unimpressed with girls he knew; but he agreed just to oblige his sister. Harriet told him he might change his mind when he met Maud Gage, the roommate of his cousin Josephine at Cornell University. Maud was "different from the girls you've known around here. Pretty, but independent, with a mind and will of her own. She's twenty years old and lots of fun." As later described by her son Frank Junior, she "had long dark hair, merry mischievous eyes, a slightly retroussé nose and skin remarkably clear and soft." She was taller than average, "had a singularly well-formed figure, and was accounted a beauty." Aunt Josephine introduced them at the party with "Frank, I want you to know Maud Gage. I'm sure you will love her." "Consider yourself loved, Miss Gage," he said. "Thank you, Mr. Baum," she replied; "That's a promise. Please see that you live up to it."[20]

The playful assertiveness was typical of Maud, who had been raised by Matilda Joslyn Gage, a prominent feminist and leader in the campaign for women's suffrage. Mother and daughter were much alike: their strong, square faces expressed determined, forceful personalities. Maud was (according to her hostile son Frank Junior) the "greatly indulged" youngest of the four Gage children.[21] All her life she remained closely attached to her mother, who often lived with the Baums. Frank, too, admired his mother-in-law, whose views were to have significant influence on both his life and work.

Matilda had been raised by her father, a doctor active in abolition and other reform causes, to think for herself and "to accept no opinion because of its authority, but to question the truth of all things." She married Henry Gage, a prosperous local dry-goods merchant, and entered public life at the age of twenty-six, when she attended her first National Woman's Rights Convention at Syracuse in 1852 and delivered a speech arguing that girls must be educated equally with boys and encouraged to be self-reliant and ultimately self-supporting in a business or profession "best fitted to exercise their talents."[22] Her ability was immediately recognized, and from then on, Matilda Gage worked constantly for the women's rights movement—lecturing, writing, researching, organizing, circulating petitions, testifying before Congress. She helped Elizabeth Cady Stanton and Susan B. Anthony found the National Woman Suffrage Association (NWSA) in 1869, and for many years held one or another high office in the association. She was praised for her absolute honesty, "deep sense of justice," and sometimes "appalling frankness of speech."[23] Maud, too, had firm opinions and spoke her mind forthrightly.

Gage's most distinctive contribution to feminist theory was her recognition that organized religion played a key role in oppressing women, at a time when it was generally assumed, even within the women's movement, that Christianity had uplifted their status. In her chapter on "Woman, Church, and State" in the *History of Woman Suffrage* (a book she co-wrote with Stanton and Anthony), she argued that the church oppressed women by teaching that they were created for man, blaming them for Original Sin, preaching self-sacrifice to them, and denying them the right to think for themselves about religion.

Although she rejected traditional religion, Gage believed in the reality of spirit, and she found a basis for her faith in theosophy. What attracted her, as well as contemporaries like Stanton and Thomas Alva Edison, was its claim to provide a rational basis for faith in a spiritual world. Theosophy was a religious faith that was free of superstition and bigotry and compatible with scientific truth: it claimed to incorporate the essential truth that is found in all religions and in science as well. Theosophists believed that they investigated the spiritual world exactly as scientists investigate the physical world; in both cases, the aim was control of natural forces, whether physical or mental and moral, and the methods were the same—"observation of objective phenomena . . . framing of hypotheses . . . repeated experiments to verify deductions, and formulation of results."[24] Theosophy had another powerful appeal for feminists: it denied the reality of any distinctions made on the basis of religion, race, class, or sex. Since the traditional churches actively opposed or at least failed to encourage women's struggles for equality, feminists were drawn to a religion in which they had equal rights. Gage was to be admitted to the Rochester Theosophical Society on March 26, 1885.

Frank's first date with Maud was on Christmas Eve 1881.[25] Within a week after meeting her, he knew that he was seriously interested. But she had other suitors, and they were still just friends when he returned to his theater company and she to her sophomore year at Cornell. On May 15, she saw Frank act in "The Maid of Arran" in Syracuse.[26] Whenever he was free between bookings during the following summer, he returned to Syracuse, borrowed a horse and buggy from his father, and drove the eight miles to her home in Fayetteville. "We were in the front parlor when Maud finally consented to become my wife. Then she asked me to wait there while she told her mother." He could not help hearing what was said in the back parlor. "The old lady told Maud in no uncertain terms that she objected to her marrying an actor who was on the road most of the time, jumping from town to town on one night stands, and with an uncertain future." She would not "have my daughter be a darned fool and marry an actor."

But Maud snapped back, "All right, mother, if you feel that way about it, good bye." When Mrs. Gage demanded what she meant, she replied, "I'm going to marry Frank, so, naturally you don't want a darned fool around the house." "Then Mrs. Gage laughed and said: 'All right, Maud. If you are in love with him and really determined to marry him, you can have your wedding right here at home.' "[27]

Matilda was understandably displeased by the idea of her cherished daughter marrying a traveling actor whose only achievement to date was a trifling melodrama. In addition, she must have been bitterly disappointed that Maud was dropping out of college. Matilda, who had hoped to be a doctor and been denied admission to any medical school, hated to see her daughter throw away her opportunity for higher education. Frank, of course, was not a college graduate, although this was not remarkable in a time when less that 7 percent of children even enrolled in high school.

Before long, however, Frank and his mother-in-law had become good friends. He was extremely likable, and she came to appreciate his gifts. He must have liked and admired her, for within a few years he was committed to feminism and sympathetic to theosophy. When Gage spoke at the national NWSA convention in 1887 and wrote to Maud, "Tell Frank have been very greatly complimented, both as to subject-matter & voice," she clearly assumed that he would share Maud's pleasure in her success.[28]

Maud and Frank were married on November 9, 1882, in the handsome Victorian front parlor of the Gage home by the minister of the Fayetteville Baptist Church. They spent their honeymoon in Saratoga Springs. Immediately afterwards, Frank and Maud headed west with "The Maid of Arran" company for a tour through small cities in the Midwest. The itinerant life must have been hard on Maud. She wrote to her brother Thomas Clarkson Gage from Omaha on November 26 that she liked the life and was "*very, very* happy," but she went on to speak of "dreadful" hotels, and she looked forward to getting to Saint Louis, where they would settle down for a full week. Nevertheless, she closed by advising her brother "to marry at once, and then you will know what it is to enjoy life." "The Maid of Arran" played for three weeks in Chicago in April.[29]

When she became pregnant, Maud insisted on establishing a permanent home where their first child would be born. Frank engaged a new leading man, and they moved into a rented house on Shonnard Street in Syracuse, where Frank Junior was born on December 4, 1883.[30]

The Baum marriage proved to be exceedingly happy, although Frank and Maud did not conform to conventional gender roles for husband and wife. Frank was the sweeter and more compliant partner. Maud's determination and insistence on her prerogative appeared early in their family life. According to an often-told family story, Frank brought home a dozen Bismarks (jelly doughnuts) one day. "Maud bristled and tartly demanded to know whether he was dissatisfied with the food *she* bought and prepared. He assured her he liked her meals, but with a smile, he also liked Bismarks for breakfast." So she served them up to him every morning, although on the third day he suggested they were getting stale. "Maud replied coldly that he had bought them and would have to eat them." They reappeared on the fourth, fifth, and sixth mornings. When he finally protested, "Let's stop this nonsense," she retorted: "You bought them without consulting me, so you will have to eat them. I am not going to have food wasted. But I'll let you off this time if you will promise never again to buy any food unless I ask you to get it." He agreed, and "the affair of the Bismarks" was over. "But it had taught him a lesson he never forgot: that . . . around the house she was the boss."[31]

When the children were born, Frank was a tenderly devoted parent, who would play with his babies for hours and spend "whole evenings rocking" them and crooning lullabies, and was incapable of punishing them. Maud was firm and less demonstrative. The younger Frank's first recollection of his father was of his rushing to comfort him after a nightmare when he was about three. As an old man, Harry, the third son, remembered his childhood love for the smell of tobacco "because it always meant Father was home."[32] Once Frank and Maud found three-year-old Frank Junior sitting with a sharp razor in each hand; and it was his father who quietly distracted the child with a story until he could get the razors away from him. A few years later, Maud severely punished young Frank for falling into a large pan of paste once and then a second time. Over her protests, her husband took a plate of supper to the child's bedroom, told him a story, and watched by him until he fell asleep.[33]

When Robert, the Baums' second son, was very small, he threw the family cat out of the second-story window. Although the cat was not hurt, Mother, "to teach me a lesson, caught me up and held me out the window pretending that she was going to drop me. But it was quite real to me and I screamed so loudly that the neighbors all rushed out and were quite horrified at the spectacle of my mother dangling me out of the window, not sure but that she would let me drop." On a later occasion, he threw a cat into a barrel "and was promptly chucked in myself to see how I liked it." One day years later when Kenneth, the youngest son, misbehaved, Maud told him that his father would punish him when he got home. In order to support Maud's authority, Frank, with great reluctance, gave Kenneth a few half-hearted spanks; but he was too upset to eat his dinner and finally apologized to Kenneth. He refused to spank any of the boys again, so from then on, Maud had to inflict any punishment herself.[34]

Those who knew Frank agreed that he was an exceptionally sweet-natured, easy-going man, whose positive attitude caused others to see the best in themselves and their circumstances. Maud remembered him as "a very kindly man—never angry—pleasant to everyone." Harry characterized his father as "a cheerful, kindly, fun-loving man who loved people, children, and flowers. . . . everyone who knew him loved him for his gentleness, his whimsical humor, and his spontaneous puns which were quite often ludicrous and far-fetched. . . . I recall his saying . . . 'If I had my way, I would always have a young child in the house.' To which my mother . . . replied, 'If I had my way, I wouldn't!' " Frank Junior's tribute was essentially just, despite a bit of worshipful exaggeration: His father

> . . . never looked on the dark side of life; never said an unkind word about any person; never swore or told a dirty story. His sunny disposition, quizzical smile and kindly twinkle in his gray eyes, coupled with irrepressible optimism helped all who knew him to see their troubles in a different and less important light. I am happy in the knowledge that he made this world a better place because he lived in it.[35]

Frank Junior's account of his parents' marriage seems accurate, despite his tendency to exalt his father at his mother's expense. During her long widowhood, Maud would fondly recall that:

...peace and harmony had always graced her home, but those who knew the family best felt this was true only because Frank, from the time of their marriage until his death thirty-seven years later, allowed her to have her own way with the household, the children, and the family purse. Only because of his easy nature and because he remained all those years very much in love with her, was he able philosophically to accept her often unpredictable temper.[36]

Of course, this happy accommodation could not have been reached unless Frank had found much to love in Maud and did not perceive her as repressive or dominating. He was a secure man who did not worry about asserting his masculine authority.

Moreover, Maud was more capable than he of managing the family purse. She had great practical competence, while he could not keep track of his money and was always pursuing specious business opportunities. As Harry said, "Mother was Father's exact opposite. She was serious, unimaginative and realistic—and it was a good thing, too. Father went bankrupt more than once [sic—actually only once] investing in some wild scheme. She finally took control and kept the family solvent."[37] Even Frank Junior had to concede that she managed the household capably through their constantly recurring economic vicissitudes.[38] Her firmness and hardheaded practicality compensated for Frank's tendency to be overoptimistic and careless with money. His softness of heart and consistent agreeableness made him lovable, but they also revealed a bit of self-indulgence. He evaded what he found unpleasant, whether it was disciplining his children or balancing his budget. Although he worked extremely hard at what interested him— whether it was writing, raising flowers, or organizing the annual celebration at his holiday resort—he did not apply his mind to realistic calculation of profit and loss.

For a while the Baums lived comfortably off the continuing profits from "The Maid of Arran," which ran at least through the 1883 season, and from Baum's chain of small theaters. Frank wrote "Kilmourne, or O'Connor's Dream," which was never copyrighted or professionally produced, although it was performed by an amateur group in Syracuse on April 4, 1883. He was to try one more Irish play, "The Queen of Killarney," in 1885; but that never got produced at all. The Baums took an active part in Syracuse social life. Frank acted in at least one amateur performance, the comedy "Dora" at the Syracuse Opera House. Eleven years after they left the city, the *Syracuse Post-Standard* commented that Baum was "remembered by hundreds of friends as a witty and droll but a most enjoyable companion."[39]

As Baum's theatrical career diminished, the family oil business presented a more stable means of support. An advertisement in the *Courier* of July 9, 1883, announced the opening of a store dealing in all types of lubricating oil. (At this period petroleum was used mainly for lubrication and kerosene lamps.) The proprietor was L. B. Baum, evidently a misprint for L. F. It was fortunate that the Baums had this resource, for Frank's theatrical business was about to collapse altogether. Sometime in 1884, his business manager, Uncle John, became ill; and they had to hire a bookkeeper. Maud noticed that the weekly checks were becoming smaller and urged Frank and John to investigate. But Frank was busy writing "The Queen of Killarney," and by the time John was well enough to return to the office, they found the bookkeeper had grossly mismanaged the business; soon thereafter, he disappeared. On top of this, a fire in Gilmour destroyed Baum's theater there, with all the costumes, scenery, and props for "The Maid of Arran" and other plays. The result was that he lost all his realty holdings, including the theaters, production rights to "The Maid of Arran," and more.[40]

Fortunately, a new development increased Frank's oil business. His chemist brother, Benjamin William, invented an improved lubricating oil for wheels and organized Baum's Castorine Company to manufacture and distribute it; he moved the company from Buffalo to Syracuse and appointed his uncle Adam Baum manager and Frank superintendent, a position he held from 1884 to 1888. Evidently this meant head salesman, for Frank's main job was to go on the road to market the new product to owners of drugstores and hardware stores. Castorine was advertised as the best existing axle oil because, unlike tallow or whale oil, it had a consistency like castor oil and would "not gum or chill and is ever ready for use."

For a while the company was successful.[41] But then a series of misfortunes struck. In 1885, the family patriarch, Benjamin Baum (now diminished to "a well-to-do farmer"), was seriously injured in a buggy accident;[42] ultimately he went away to Germany for treatment. Then brother Benjamin also became very sick and died the following February. The father returned from Germany to find that his affairs had been badly administered and his wealth had further dwindled. He moved with Cynthia and Harry, Frank's younger brother, to a smaller house in town, where he died on February 14, 1887. After that, Cynthia and Harry moved out to Spring Farm, where they lived until Harry opened his medical office in Syracuse.

On February 1, 1886, Maud gave birth to her second son, Robert Stanton, in their new house on Holland Street, where they had moved the year before. The childbirth was difficult and caused abdominal infection; Maud contracted peritonitis and almost died. In the days before antibiotics, it was remarkable that she pulled through at all. As it was, she was bedridden for months with a drainage tube in her side. Frank was distraught, for his business required him to be away selling Castorine, sometimes for weeks at a time. He spent every hour he could at home with Maud (and away from business) and moved the family to a rented house so they could be near his sisters.[43]

When Frank's brother-in-law, Clarkson Gage, proudly announced the birth of his daughter, Matilda, on April 22, Frank apologized for not answering him until May 4: "I have so much on hand—with Maud's sickness, business & moving combined." He went on to tease Clarkson about the cares of a father:

> You will now begin to enjoy the felicity of living in earnest. You can awaken a dozen or two times each night and sooth your daughter. . . . You can walk the floor with her over your shoulder, and have a friend point out to you when you reach the store a streak of milky substance down the back of your best coat. You can—but why harrow up our mutual feelings in this way? We are both in boats of similar build, and we should bear our troubles like men. Let us shake hands gently, remove the tear that starts to our eyeballs with a resigned sigh, and forgetting the ills of life, cling only to thoughts of the sweet, innocent child faces that will brighten our lives for years to come, and make us thank God heartily that they arrived at all.[44]

Maud did not recover her health for two years. She solaced herself with frequent visits to her family in Fayetteville. Her sister Julia Carpenter, who was languishing in Dakota Territory, poured intense worries into her diary: "Dear dear Maud has been sick in bed over six months. Poor, poor child. I am almost wild over her—our baby our darling sister. Poor little Robin took all her strength" (August 9, 1886). After a stay in a sanitarium her health improved, but by early November "she was again in bed utterly discouraged with an abscess in her side."[45]

All this while, the Castorine office and factory were neglected. Benjamin William was dead, Frank was on the road selling, and Uncle Adam, who was an invalid, left the business in the hands of a clerk. In the spring of 1888, Frank returned from a sales trip and unlocked the office door to find the clerk dead: he had shot himself after gambling away much of the firm's capital. The business was barely solvent, and ultimately Frank felt there was nothing to do but sell it.[46]

He had to figure out another way to support his family. Perhaps he could find an opportunity in the West. The railroads had opened up Dakota Territory; and cheap land, rich soil, years of good weather, and the prospect of excellent wheat crops had brought many settlers in the late 1870s and 1880s. Henry Gage, Maud's father, owned a sizable farm there and had always been interested in the area.[47] Maud's three siblings had settled in Dakota. Clarkson Gage was one of the founding settlers of Aberdeen in Brown County, laid out in building lots in 1881. Along with two other men from Fayetteville, he operated a successful general store, selling dry goods, notions, groceries, and an unusually good selection of carpets. He was a community leader, who helped to organize an artesian well and irrigation plant and the Aberdeen Building & Loan Association. Maud's sister Helen Leslie Gage and Helen's husband, Charles, also named Gage, moved to Aberdeen in 1887 and invested in property throughout the area, including store buildings on Aberdeen's Main Street. Helen was active in community affairs; she was to become vice president of the Women's Benevolent Society of Aberdeen and to be one of the representatives of the Aberdeen Equal Suffrage Association at the Democratic State Convention in June 1890.

Maud's other sister, Julia Gage Carpenter, and her husband, James D., called "Frank," were less successful. In 1882, they had taken a homestead near Edgeley, about seventy miles north of Aberdeen, in what would become North Dakota. Julia was miserable there: "This is an *awful country*, and I want to live East," she wrote in her diary for January 4, 1884, when the temperature had been 48° below zero in the afternoon. She also suffered from loneliness: "I am *franticly* lonely. Can hardly endure it."[48] Although she acknowledged that her husband was kind and attentive, she could keep herself going only by frequent long visits to her relatives in Fayetteville and Aberdeen. Life for the Carpenters must have been very hard, even though they were not poor. They lived in a twelve-foot-square shanty, where they were confined for most of the winter. Outside was nothing but the vast expanse of prairie, without a hill, tree, or stone to diversify the view. The nearest neighbors were twenty miles away, the nearest town even farther.

Life in Aberdeen, however, was more like that in any American small city that depended for its prosperity on the surrounding farms. Aberdeen had brick stores and hotels and two handsome stone-fronted banks along its Main Street. Although its streets were not paved and became quagmires when it rained or snowed, it had raised sidewalks of wooden planks. It had had telegraphic and electric service since 1886, although the electric supply was so limited that the company was unable to furnish a needed traffic light in 1888. Houses were lit by gas, and there were a few telephones and a good water supply from an artesian well. Aberdeen had a well-established school system, a small public library, and four churches. A large proportion of the inhabitants were business and professional people, forty or more of whom had migrated from Syracuse and Fayetteville; and they re-created in Aberdeen the amenities they were accustomed to. There were many lectures, amateur theatrical and musical programs, and professional performances in the "Opera House."[49] Aberdeen was situated in the fertile James River valley, a rapidly growing area in the northeastern corner of what would become South Dakota. Since three railroad lines crossed there, it had good potential as a distribution center and was, in fact, nicknamed "the Hub City."

In June 1888, Baum visited Clarkson Gage to prospect the situation. The Aberdeen Daily News mentioned his visit and reported that he "finds recreation from the cares of an extensive business [sic] in the fascinating pursuit, amateur photography. Mr. Baum was proficient in the art and during his stay in the city secured a number of fine negatives of Dakota land and cloud scapes."[50] Photography was to be a lifelong interest. In later life he had a darkroom in his basement where he developed and printed his pictures, and he got his boys interested in photography as well.[51]

On his return home, Frank wrote to sound out Clarkson about prospects in Aberdeen. He saw an opening for a high-class variety store, "a Bazaar, selling fancy goods, sporting goods, outdoor games . . . amateur photograph goods, fancy willowware, cheap books and good literature, stationery, toys and crockery specialties, velocipedes . . . etc. Not a 5¢ store, but a Bazaar on the same style as the 'Fair' in Chicago (on a much smaller scale)." He expected that, using one thousand dollars of his own money and one thousand dollars in borrowed capital, he could sell ten thousand dollars' worth of goods in the first year, which would produce an income of fifteen hundred to two thousand dollars. With his usual enthusiasm, he sketched out ambitious plans for promoting his wares by starting a camera club and interesting people in lawn tennis. He would also be on the lookout for investment opportunities. He went on to reveal his discouragement with his present situation in the East, where intense competition "keeps a man down. . . . In this struggling mass of humanity a man like myself is lost." In Dakota, on the other hand, "there is an opportunity for a man to be somebody . . . and opportunities are constantly arising where an intelligent man may profit." "Aberdeen is destined one day to be a good city, and it *may be* a metropolis," so that it seemed like a good idea "to throw my fortunes in with the town."[52]

Despite his record of disappointments, Baum was still determined to pursue success as a businessman, as his father had, and was still confident of finding lucrative opportunities. Although Maud had not liked the western cities she had seen when accompanying Frank with "The Maid of Arran" company in 1882,[53] she would have enjoyed being near her brother and sisters and doubtless welcomed a project that might give the family financial security.

two

FRONTIER STOREKEEPER AND
NEWSPAPER EDITOR,
1888–1891

On September 20, 1888, Frank, Maud, and their two boys arrived in Aberdeen. They stayed with the Clarkson Gages until they were able to move into a house of their own on Ninth Street. On September 25, an advertisement appeared in the *Aberdeen Daily News* announcing that Baum's Bazaar would open on Main Street on October 1, offering "a magnificent and complete assortment of Art Pottery and decorated Table Ware, Bohemian and Native Glass Ware, Parlor, Library and table Lamps, Baskets and Wicker Ware, Toys in immense variety, Latest novelties in Japanese Goods, Plush, Oxidized Brass and Leather Novelties, Gunther's Celebrated Chicago Candies." It occupied the ground floor of a building built and owned by Charles and Helen Gage, who lived in an apartment upstairs. The *Aberdeen Daily News* reported that nearly a thousand people attended the opening, and it complimented Baum on his "artistic" and "elegant" displays of his merchandise. Baum continued to advertise intensively, often with characteristic humor and originality. On October 12, he announced that he had just received "a new poetry grinder," which produced the following when its crank was turned:

> At Baum's Bazaar you'll find by far
> The finest goods in town
> The cheapest, too, as you'll find true
> If you'll just step around.... [1]

The first month's sales were $531.16, very good for the time and place; and Baum was consistently paid in cash.[2]

On November 2, Baum issued a fall catalogue that listed six hundred items. Two weeks later he opened "a branch bazaar at Webster," a small town about fifty miles east of Aberdeen, which he advertised as "Santa Claus' Headquarters." Shortly afterward, however, the ship carrying his stock of holiday goods went down in Lake Huron. He had to reorder hastily before Christmas, while competing businesses profited by his misfortune. Although his financial statement dated January 7, 1889, indicates a $1,029.93 surplus of assets over liabilities, his system of bookkeeping inspired his banker niece Matilda Gage to comment, "bookkeeping does not appear to be one of Mr. Baum's many skills."[3] Baum was doing a brisk trade again by the spring, but, as usual, he could not resist taking on too many activities.

In May 1889, he joined with other businessmen to form the Aberdeen Baseball Club and organize a professional baseball team, the Hub City Nine, which they hoped would stimulate business by advertising the town and bringing people in. In particular, it would increase the demand for sporting goods at Baum's Bazaar. Baum was elected secretary and took on much of the responsibility for hiring and negotiating with players, securing a field, and building a grandstand. By May 30, a field and fine grandstand were ready for the team's first game, with Redfield. Baum's Bazaar supplied the uniforms and equipment on credit. Then Baum led in organizing the South Dakota Baseball League—necessary in order to ensure a season's schedule of games—and became chairman of its executive committee. The *Aberdeen Daily News* provided excellent coverage of the Aberdeen team's activities, probably from releases sent to them by Baum.

The Hub City Nine soon became the champions in South Dakota, and in August, Baum left his store to accompany them on a week's tour of North Dakota, where they also won the championship. However, it was difficult to continue scheduling games, since teams were reluctant to come to remote Aberdeen, and it was too expensive to send the home team to other towns. In the end the club could not pay its way. The first championship season proved to be the last. The team broke up, the club lost $1,000, and Baum was probably never paid the $93.61 due to Baum's Bazaar for uniforms and equipment. He told the *Aberdeen Evening Republican* on October 24 that he did not "want any more to do with base ball. . . . I expended no little time, and worked hard for the success of the organization, but am out both money and time."[4]

Baum's store, financed by loans from friends in the East and by a local bank, had been undercapitalized from the beginning. He had counted on continuing agricultural prosperity, but instead drought and falling prices for wheat were weakening an economy that depended on agriculture. Notices of bankruptcy sales multiplied in the newspapers. Farmers and townspeople could no longer afford art pottery, elaborate toys, and sporting equipment. Increasingly, Baum had to extend credit; some of the bills dragged on and many were never paid. Eventually he was carrying 161 accounts past due, of which he never collected 105.[5] At the same time, his responsibilities were increased by the birth of Harry Neal, his third son, on December 17, 1889.

On January 1, 1890, the Northwestern National Bank of Aberdeen foreclosed on Baum's chattel mortgage and closed down his business. He bravely told the newspapers, "The matter is simply a temporary embarrassment and I hope to effect a settlement in a few days." However, on the eighteenth, "Helen Gage bought 'the stock and good will' of the business for $772.54 at a foreclosure sale and reopened within the month as the H. L. Gage Bazaar." Years later, she wrote that Baum had "let his taste run riot in his choice of the eastern markets" and had set up a store that delighted the cultivated class, but was "too impractical . . . for a frontier town." With a more appropriate inventory, she kept the business running for the next twelve years.[6]

Left with hardly any capital, Baum found an opportunity that made use of his old interest in writing and printing. John H. Drake, whom he had known in Syracuse, was leaving town and eager to sell the weekly *Dakota Pioneer*, which he had established in 1881. It was one of seven weeklies in Aberdeen, in addition to two daily newspapers. This situation was not unusual in the West, where local papers were used to advertise town sites and to publish the notices legally required to finalize ownership of government land. Political parties as well as pressure groups like the Women's Christian Temperance Union (WCTU) had their own newspapers to promote their views and influence. Baum bought the *Dakota Pioneer* on small monthly installments, renamed it the *Aberdeen Saturday Pioneer*, and reduced its subscription price from $2.00 to $1.50 a year. His first issue appeared on January 25, 1890.

It was common for these small local newspapers to be published, edited, composed, and printed by one person, who also had to keep the enterprise afloat by collecting subscriptions and advertising. The task was lightened by the practice of filling many columns with boiler plate; that is, stereotype plates, precast with news, features, illustrations, and advertising. These items would be nationally distributed, as syndicated columns are today. Nevertheless, Baum had to work very hard. As he reminisced twenty-three years later, "I used to go out and rustle up my own ads and set 'em up . . . and when the tramp printer would desert me I would take a fling at the type case, and then I would go out and deliver the papers to my advertisers on a Saturday afternoon so I could collect enough money for a ham sandwich and a cup of coffee."[7]

William Allen White's description of his work on the *Emporia Gazette* in the late 1890s gives a more complete picture of the duties of a small-town editor-publisher: "The Gazette kept me at work twelve hours a day. I was writing the editorials, a good share of the local items, soliciting the advertising, and looking after the subscription books."[8] On the side, Baum did whatever job printing he could get. Moreover, local newspaper editors were expected to take an interest in community affairs. Baum participated in committees organizing events such as the July 4 celebration in 1890, where he also judged the floats and the baby contest.

The *Aberdeen Saturday Pioneer* consisted of eight pages, of which Baum usually wrote a quarter to a half. The rest was filled with boiler plate, advertisements, and legal notices, an important source of income for frontier newspapers. Typically, page one consisted of a long feature, which for most of the run of the paper was an illustrated humorous essay by the syndicated columnist Bill Nye. There were advertisements down the left-hand column and jokes or puzzles down the right. Occasionally Baum printed original material there. Page two gave details, often mere lists, of the proceedings of the state legislature. Page three carried national news, factual paragraphs, and jokes. Three to five editorials appeared on page four, local news and "Our Landlady" on page five. Pages six, seven, and eight were filled with more ready-print features, news, jokes, facts, and fiction, with additional local news on page eight. Baum wrote the editorials and the "Our Landlady" column and compiled the local news, probably using some contributions by others. Nancy Koupal in *Baum's Road to Oz* estimates that Baum purchased pages two, three, six, and seven as boiler plate; he or his workmen would then set the other pages to accommodate editorials, features, and local news and advertisements.[9]

The local news describes an active social and cultural life in Aberdeen, dominated by activities sponsored by the various churches. As in other towns, they vied to devise original types of socials. During the week of January 24, 1891, the Baptists organized a Conversational Social, an ingenious tournament in which people competed to produce the best conversation on a series of given topics, and the Presbyterians held a Zoological Social, in which everyone drew an animal and the others had to guess what it was; the Episcopalians held a more conventional evening of music, cards, and dancing.

The Baums participated actively in these activities; Maud often appears on guest lists of parties. They were both members of Saint Mark's Episcopal Church, although neither seems to have been a committed believer. Frank had been brought up in his mother's Sabbath-observing Methodist household, but he was no longer a churchgoer; indeed, he shared his mother-in-law's suspicions of all organized religion. He told his readers on January 17, 1891, that he contributed regularly to the church "and claim religious freedom in everything else." Nevertheless, Baum was on good terms with the minister and took a leading role in amateur theatricals sponsored by the Ladies' Guild of the church. He directed *Everybody's Friend*, in which he played "Felix Featherly, the victim of his own accommodating disposition"; and, under his old stage name, Louis F. Baum, he played Dr. Daly, the lovelorn elderly vicar in *The Sorcerer*, in June and again in September 1890.

Baum reviewed local amateur performances and the occasional professional performances that came to Aberdeen. His reviews of the amateur concerts, elocution displays, and plays are, as would be expected, sympathetic; but they are not wholly uncritical: he sometimes remarked that a concert was pleasant rather than professional. He devoted loving attention to *The Sorcerer*. On May 24, he noted its progress in rehearsal, and a week later he dilated on its wonderful promise. He gave it a glowing review on June 7: it was "one of the finest amateur performances ever given in Aberdeen," and it had a large, select, and enthusiastic audience. He praised each one of the participants, except for modestly omitting mention of himself.

Every issue of the *Pioneer* included two columns of personal items that would naturally have gratified his readers—guest lists at parties, sicknesses and recoveries, visits and returns home, movings in and out of Aberdeen, new jobs accepted, or developments in local business enterprises. He mentioned that Mrs. Baum and the children had spent the summer in Fayetteville, that he went to Chicago to escort them home, and that the Baum family had moved to a new house. This must have been the second and last house they occupied in Aberdeen, 512 South Kline Street, which still stands.[10]

Matilda Jewell Gage, Clarkson's daughter, recalled visiting the Baums on South Kline Street on Christmas Eve 1890, when she was four. "I was enthralled at the sight inside. In the corner of the living room was the most beautiful Christmas tree, all lighted with candles burning and beside that tree stood Uncle Frank Baum, and in the middle of the room were my young cousins . . . playing. I thought it was the most delightful place I had ever seen. . . . I'm sure I had a tree and many gifts, but I remember how I longed to stay with the Baums. Santa Claus was not merely folklore in the Baum household, for the four boys had plenty of evidence that their father was familiar with the old saint and shared his spirit."[11]

Although most of the local news was social, Baum did occasionally describe useful new enterprises in the community, such as a free school for working girls. He regularly included items that would remind his readers of the woman suffrage campaign that was going on during most of the run of his paper, announcing lectures by suffragists and reporting on their excellence. On October 18, he mentioned that Mrs. Gage, whose accomplishments he listed, was coming to visit her daughter Mrs. Baum, "in time to see equal suffrage triumph in South Dakota."

Support for woman suffrage was certainly the most passionately held conviction expressed in Baum's editorials. There seemed to be a good possibility that women would win the vote in South Dakota, as they had in Wyoming, Colorado, Utah, and Idaho. But when a convention met in 1883 to prepare a constitution for the future state of South Dakota, suffragists sent by the National Woman Suffrage Association, including Matilda Gage, and local women, such as Marietta Bones, were unable to persuade it to omit "male" from the qualifications for voters. The convention compromised by requiring the new state legislature to submit to the voters at the first opportunity, the general election of November 4, 1890, an amendment to strike the word "male" from the article on suffrage.

Local suffragists formed a South Dakota State Suffrage Association in October 1889 and got strong support from the Farmers' Alliance. They asked for help from the National Woman Suffrage Association, which raised money from all over the nation and named Susan B. Anthony to manage the funds and organize the campaign, a back-breaking task because of the sparse settlement in Dakota and the wide distances between towns. But the South Dakota association demanded the money in order to organize its own campaign, and Anthony refused on the grounds that they had not shown her any plan. Finally Bones accused Anthony of misapplying forty thousand dollars in suffrage funds and carried their dispute into the local newspapers—to the glee of the antisuffragists.

In April 1890, Anthony arrived in South Dakota to take charge personally; she set up campaign headquarters in Huron, organizing meetings and speakers and herself speaking almost every night. Her heroic efforts were wasted, however, because her dictatorial style antagonized local workers. Moreover, she opposed them by insisting that the suffrage issue be kept separate from prohibition and from support of the Independent Party, formed when the Farmers' Alliance split off from the Republicans. Unlike the less experienced local women, Anthony recognized the practical consequences of antagonizing the liquor interests and the Republicans, the only major party that might have supported woman suffrage.

Without the support of either major party, there could be no realistic expectation of success for the amendment, although the suffrage lecturers hopefully continued to speak to enthusiastic audiences. And indeed, the results of the election were deeply discouraging. Ida Harper summarized: "Eight months of hard work by a large corps of the ablest women in the United States, 1,600 speeches, $8,000 in money, for less than 23,000 votes" (for suffrage).[12]

Baum involved himself in this campaign from the time he began editing the *Pioneer* in January. When an Equal Suffrage Club was organized in Aberdeen in April 1890, with thirty-four female and thirty-six male members, Baum was elected secretary. Although Matilda Gage was not among the eleven speakers that the National Woman Suffrage Association sent to assist in the South Dakota suffrage campaign, she lived with Frank and Maud for extended periods and undoubtedly imparted her keen interest to them. Many of the national and state suffrage speakers who passed through, including Anthony and Bones, stayed with the Baums or the Gages.

One of Baum's editorials in the very first issue of his paper, on January 25, 1890, was "Equal Suffrage Notes." (The others announced his aims as the new editor and promoted another particular interest that he shared with Matilda Gage, theosophy.) The next week he printed a more substantial discussion of women's rights. After expressing pride in Americans' tolerance for each other's class and national origins, religions, and political parties, he pointed out that we have yet to learn to overlook the difference of sex "and render equal distinction and reward to brains and ability, no matter whether found in man or woman." On February 8, he vigorously rebutted a prominent local woman who declared she did not want the vote. Perhaps this woman has "all the 'rights' at present that her shoulders will bear," but there are women

> ... whose education, intelligence and ambition have prompted them to aspire to a higher condition than that to which the arrogance and injustice of men has heretofore relegated them. They are capable, not only of becoming politicians, but upright, moral and conscientious politicians as well, and from the moment a woman's hand is felt at the reins of government will date an era of unexampled prosperity for our country.... An able intelligent woman will make a better politician than most men, for in a much higher degree is she endowed with refinement, perspicacity and morality.

His essay the following week on the importance of a happy home defied conventional nineteenth-century thinking by placing responsibility on the husband.

> In nine cases out of ten, a happy home depends on the temperament of the "man of the house." A woman is usually so occupied with her household duties and the care of her children that she naturally becomes more or less nervous and irritable, and looks forward to the home coming of her mate as the one excitement that shall relieve the monotony of her daily routine. If he appears sullen, morose and bearish her overwrought nerves give way, and quarrels and bickerings naturally ensue. If he enters the house with a cheerful face, a smile and kiss of welcome and a cheery word her troubles are all forgotten; the latent sweetness in the disposition of the most unsociable woman is involuntarily drawn out, and a pleasant and genial chat restores to her the even poise of her nervous organization.

This editorial both expresses and explains Frank's constant effort to maintain harmony in the Baum household. When Maud was discontented and irritable, Frank did not blame her, as the average nineteenth-century husband would have done, but had the rare understanding to realize that it is very trying to spend every day looking after small children and dealing with household problems on a limited budget. He felt it was his part to support her emotionally by being cheerful and pleasant and paying attention to her wishes.

On March I, Baum strove to make the best of the unfortunate dissension that had arisen between Anthony and Matilda Gage at the convention of the National Woman Suffrage Association in Washington, D.C. Gage, who identified traditional religion as the main obstacle to women's progress, had split from the NWSA to organize the Women's National Liberal Union, dedicated to the separation of church and state and to a wider platform of social reforms. Baum vigorously backed his mother-in-law: "Mrs. Gage is undoubtedly one of the most remarkable women of her age, possessed of the highest literary ability, the brightest thoughts, the clearest and most scholarly oratory, the most varied research and intelligent and diversified pen of any public woman of the past twenty years. . . . Her followers are mainly the most advanced thinkers and the most intelligent and wealthy of the suffrage party." Miss Anthony is "Cast in a commoner mould," although she is an effective leader and "has waged aggressive war for her cause from the beginning." The main point, however, is that all the suffragists should be admired for their "indominatable pluck and perseverance in fighting so bravely a twenty years' war . . . in attacking the government today with the same unflinching zeal and enthusiasm despite their hope deferred."

Through all the dissensions, Baum used the *Pioneer* to keep attention focused on the main point, winning equal suffrage, and maintained admirable evenhandedness among the various factions. He persistently presented the best side of all the suffragists. He found much to like and admire in Anthony and Bones, her principal local opponent; but he sensibly censured both of them for discrediting their important cause by pursuing their feud in public. He agreed with Anthony that the suffragists had more to lose than to gain by allying themselves with the Independent Party, but he criticized her for obstinately insisting that everyone defer to her views. By July 19, however, he gave up on both leaders: he blamed Anthony for disrupting the efficient, harmoniously working local organization and concluded that "South Dakota suffragists have no use whatever for Miss Anthony and very little for Mrs. Bones. The sooner they are muzzled effectively the better for all true friends of the cause."

On March 15, Baum praised enterprising Western women, who, unlike their Eastern sisters, took pride in doing useful work and earning money. Their "independence renders them the more lovable in the sight of all true men. . . . Their bright example stimulates their husbands, brothers and sweethearts to renewed efforts, and their active brains and good judgement are responsible for the success of many a man's business which without their counsel to direct it would be irretrievably involved in ruin." Even now women make an essential contribution to the welfare of households (as Maud's practical business sense sustained the Baums); how much more Western women will accomplish "when they have won their recognition to citizenship and are able to advise and act in the more important affairs of the state."

It is no refutation that the women of the New England states did not want to vote, as an antisuffrage paper claimed. "No, they don't. Neither do they want to do anything else that is useful, helpful, or of benefit to themselves and the State. They simply want to be let alone, to sit in their parlors, wear fine clothes, read cheap literature, talk nonsense and be figureheads in 'Society.' The Western woman is different."

If women indifferent to equal suffrage are useless and frivolous, he wrote on March 29, men opposed to it are "selfish, opinionated, conceited or unjust—and perhaps all four combined. The tender husband, the considerate father, the loving brother, will be found invariably championing the cause of women."

On April 5, he predicted that equal suffrage would win a sweeping victory at the election in November: "It is one of those popular movements which carry all opposition before it, and few voters will choose to thrust aside their chivalry and sense of justice by opposing in the slightest degree the claims of women to full citizenship." Two weeks later, he ridiculed the preposterous statement that women cannot comprehend politics and looked forward to the time when they would discuss politics in a friendly way with their male relatives. For "The mind of woman is more logical than that of man, it is quicker to preceive [sic], more prompt in judgment, more honest in espousing the cause of justice and truth." Baum continued to support the campaign by insisting on its success. On May 31, he hopefully reported: "One by one the newspapers of the state are falling into line with the popular movement that is bound to carry all before it as a whirlwind does the particles of dust in its path."

On June 21, he refuted the antisuffragists' charge that suffragists failed as wives and mothers by pointing to the examples of Elizabeth Cady Stanton and his mother-in-law. Matilda Gage's four children "respect and love her above all other beings on earth." Indeed, there is a natural connection between being a suffragist and being a loving mother and good housekeeper, since one who "has the heart to love her children, the conscience to educate them, the virtue to train them to be moral and useful men and women, the executive ability to become a good housekeeper, and the character to make a pleasant home for her husband and family" would also sympathize with the wrongs of her sex and want them "admitted to full citizenship." "We have yet to hear of one equal suffragist who can justly be accused of neglecting her home and family. The family certainly never consider themselves neglected."

Finally, on November 1, Baum told his readers that their primary duty was to vote for the amendment that would strike "male" from the state constitution. "Let no man who respects justice, no man who respects his family, stay away from the polls. . . . Vote as you would be glad to have your wife or mother vote in case you were a political slave."

On November 8, after woman suffrage was defeated, Baum's editorials are noticeably thin and dispirited. He could say on the subject only that "The defeat of Equal Suffrage will stand as a lasting reproach to the state of South Dakota." His editorials never regained the interest and commitment of the preelection period. Among the few that were distinctive, one attacked the double standard and another insisted that politicians should be constantly mindful of the situation of women. Altogether, feminist editorials, most often on equal suffrage, appeared on almost half of Baum's editorial pages—twenty-eight out of fifty-nine.

Baum's editorials also reflect his personal interest in nontraditional religion and opposition to the organized churches. On his first editorial page, a column called "The Editor's Musings" celebrates "the age of Unfaith"; this does not mean atheism, but "rather an eager longing to penetrate the secrets of Nature" regardless of orthodox religious restrictions. "Amongst the various sects so numerous in America today who find their fundamental basis in occultism," he continued, "the Theosophists stand pre-eminent both in intelligence and in point of numbers. . . . Theosophy is not a religion. Its followers are simply 'searchers after Truth.' " They accept the truth in all religions, including Christianity, but believe that "the truth so earnestly sought is not yet found in its entirety. . . . They admit the existence of a God—not necessarily a personal God. To them God is Nature and Nature God."

Columns such as this might well have provoked criticism; they disappeared for a while, and after they reappeared on October 18, it was always with a self-protective disclaimer: "(. . . This is not the newspaper, it's the man, and if you don't like him you are not obliged to read what he says.)" The column of October 18 openly attacks conventional religion while supporting an enlightened spiritualism. "Fully two thirds" of the American people are unchurched, Baum declared; and this percentage will become greater, because "The people are beginning to think. While everything else has progressed, the Church alone has been trying to stand still," teaching "the same old superstitions, the same blind faith in the traditional bible, the same precepts of salvation and damnation." As "people have been growing more liberal in thought . . . Their reason revolts from" such teachings. However, there is a way to save the "beautiful religion of Christ" and prevent the world from being given over entirely to secularism: the priests must "acknowledge their fallibility . . . abolish superstition, intolerance and bigotry . . . establish the true relations between God and Christ and humanity . . . accord justice to Nature and love and mercy to the All-High . . . reconcile reason and religion and . . . let the people think for themselves." A priest should not think all is well just because his church is filled, his salary is forthcoming, and his congregation do not protest against his precepts. For nine out of ten of his congregation do not come out of devotion, but for policy or fashion. Because "There is a popular and fallacious belief that a church goer is a good citizen," the businessman who wants to sell his wares or attract clients will go to church. Women go to maintain their position in society. "Insincere and indifferent men, fashionable and unthinking women: these are your church-goers." People of intelligence and character are "Studying science," which "we know to be true."

The political issues that most concerned Baum as editor, apart from woman suffrage, were prohibition, support for the Republican Party, the location of the state capital, and promotion of Aberdeen's economic development and faith in its future. (Local newspapers were expected to promote their communities.) Baum supported rigid enforcement of the law against buying and selling liquor in South Dakota (admitted to the Union on November 2, 1889) in order that alcohol would be effectively prohibited and the effects of this measure would be clear. He himself doubted that prohibition would improve happiness or morality, and he believed that it would hurt the economy. But these points could not be demonstrated unless the experiment was fairly tried.

Baum endorsed Republican candidates and carried on a more or less playful running feud with Maj. C. Boyd Barrett, the editor and proprietor of the local Democratic paper. He deplored the defection of the

Farmers' Alliance to form a third party, believing that they were too inexperienced to form an effective political force and would simply weaken the Republicans. But he was more concerned with the competence and honesty of candidates than their party affiliation. Like most Aberdeen businessmen, he promoted Huron for state capital because it was located more conveniently to Aberdeen than the other contender, Pierre.[13]

Although Baum noted the terrible distress in South Dakota on February 1, 1890, he always tried to look on the positive side: on October 25, he triumphed that what was once called the "great American Desert" is now "the wonderful Wheat Belt of the northwest." And so it will continue, because we will have artesian wells to take over in drought years. He repeatedly insisted that people should not be discouraged by the depressed economic conditions to give up and move away, but should remain and invest in Aberdeen. He urged that manufacturing should be encouraged to come in, so the area would not be dependent on agriculture alone, and prodded the city's Commercial Club to be more enterprising in attracting factories and business concerns.

Baum took seriously his editorial responsibility to inform himself on the issues and express firm opinions that could guide his readers. His editorials are interesting and distinctive, and some are remarkably unconventional for a small-town editor who could not afford to antagonize his community. But his most significant writing for the *Pioneer* was the "Our Landlady" columns that appear in almost every issue. The landlady, Mrs. Bilkins, keeps a boardinghouse—a common business in Aberdeen, where there were many transient and unattached men. She volubly holds forth to her three male boarders on everything from local gossip to the most important political issues in the state. She owes something to earlier newspaper characters, Frances M. Whitcher's Widow Bedott (1846) and Benjamin Shillaber's Mrs. Partington (1847), who are also gabby, husband-hunting widows who discuss the social scene with semiliteracy but homespun sense.[14] The closest parallel is Marietta Holley's Samantha Allen, a farm wife who appeared in a series of very popular books from 1873 to 1914. Although she, too, is a comic character who writes in ignorant dialect, she argues vigorously for women's rights, and she argues very well indeed. (Indeed, her arguments are more focused on logically refuting opposing views than are Mrs. Bilkins's. Baum was more interested in Mrs. Bilkins as a character than as a vehicle for ideas.)

Mrs. Bilkins is a richly comic figure as she delivers her opinions about everything in rustic dialect full of malapropisms to three meek male listeners. Her sloppy and stingy (bilking) housekeeping is a constant source of fun. Nevertheless, her outspokenness and interest in public affairs are presented favorably, and her good sense is more evident than her ignorance and gullibility. It guides her to general agreement with Baum's political views, especially on women's participation in politics.

Sometimes Mrs. Bilkins's views unintentionally complement Baum's editorials, as when her naive practicality leads her unawares to supporting his skepticism about the usefulness of church services. The American Sabbath Union was about to hold a convention in a neighboring town, and Baum as editor had expressed his disapproval of its program to strengthen Sabbatarian laws on the grounds that it infringed upon the division between church and state. Mrs. Bilkins approves the Sabbath Union's aim on the grounds that "somebody's got to support these ministers what is gittin' thicker an' thicker every day, or else they'll be obleeged to work fer a livin', an' religion will be at a standstill."[15]

More often, she directly reinforces his views by expressing them in a different way. While Editor Baum bases his opinions on reason and information, Mrs. Bilkins presents the same opinions based on feelings or rough intuitive common sense. The rightness of Baum's position appears self-evident because it is clear even to an unsophisticated person like Mrs. Bilkins. She serves as a burlesque alter ego for Baum when one of the boarders warns her that interesting herself so much in other people's business will damage her chances for remarriage. "Fiddlesticks!" she retorts, "if folks don't like my style they needn't listen to me. I've got to keep busy somehow, an' this 'ere boardin' house don't fully occupy my time."[16] Nor did local Aberdeen issues fully occupy Baum's time; sometimes he had to express his strong personal opinions regardless of consequences. Although Mrs. Bilkins husband-hunts according to stereotype, she attaches more importance to expressing herself on public affairs than to catching a man. Despite her comic failings, Baum liked Mrs. Bilkins's activity, independence, and concern for political issues; and he shared most of her views.

Our Landlady appeared without any formal introduction in the first issue of the *Pioneer*, January 25, serving breakfast to her boarders; we come right in on her restraining the Colonel from using too much butter on his pancakes. She is concerned about the hard times, telling how a poor woman from the country begged the grocery man to trust her for a pint of kerosene and he refused: "It made my heart bleed, that's what it did, and if any o' you boarders had a paid up lately I'd a gin it to her myself." Then she veers off into a string of comically exaggerated examples of the ways various named local citizens are economizing. This semicomic introduction prepares for Baum's serious editorial the following week, when he lamented that people were freezing to death for lack of fuel and censured storekeepers for refusing all credit and men of means for denying loans to farmers to buy seed wheat. Our Landlady is so disgusted by her inability to persuade prosperous men to help the desperate farmers that she resolves to give up any interference in public affairs. Her boarders congratulate her on the grounds that public affairs "should be left to the sterner sex," but far from being persuaded, she sniffs as they file out: "it's the conceit o' men as is the biggest stumblin' block ter universal sufferin' o' women!"[17]

Despite the comic malapropism, it is clear that Baum, who believed that women's influence exerted by their votes would create a more just and humane society, sided with her rather than with her boarders.

Because she is crude, Mrs. Bilkins can speak more plainly than Editor Baum could about those who whine about the hard times in South Dakota.

> Here we are in a country where the sile is richer and deeper than in any other part of Ameriky; where the poor eastern farmers have found peace and plenty, where the bankrupt eastern merchant has found a good trade and a good livin'; where clerks has blossomed into storekeepers and penny-ante men into bankers, an' convicks inter lawyers, . . . Everything they had they owed to good crops an' when the crops went back on 'em they was a pitiful sight. They howl, an' they kick, an' they scream; an' say they'll quit the blasted country an' the Lord forgive 'em for ever comin' here—forgittin' all the time that if they hadn't come they'd probably starved to death 'afore now! . . . If only every man would say "I will do suthin'" instead o' sayin' "why don't somebody else do suthin'?" times would change mighty quick.[18]

She may be an ignorant busybody, but she expresses her author's belief in the value of positive thinking and self-reliance.

Mrs. Bilkins vigorously supported Baum's position on the political cause that meant the most to him, woman suffrage. While he presented rational arguments, she simply assumed she was equal; she felt no need to justify the assumption that she was a citizen just as a man was, because it was self-evident. On March 8, Our Landlady, disgusted with the absence of competent honest candidates, announces that she will run for mayor herself. For Baum, a sensible woman might perfectly well be mayor; for anyone shocked by the idea, he was drawing attention to the desperate need for a better candidate than the incumbent and thus preparing for his editorial of March 15, in which he expressed his hopes for a good man to replace the present mayor.

When a group of daughters of Civil War veterans organized themselves into a drill corps, editor Baum refrained from drawing any implications; but he let Mrs. Bilkins recognize the significance of women playing soldiers. The Aberdeen Guards gave their first performance on May 28, carrying lances topped with red flags and wearing uniforms consisting of red skirts, blue waists with gold braid trim, and red forage hats. In his review, Baum simply praised their "precision of ... manoevers" and "erect and soldier-like bearing." Mrs. Bilkins's review is more lively:

> Now, the time was when the Amazons was celebrated throughout the world as the fiercest lot o' sodjers to tackle there was, an' the men folks was skeert to go near 'em, an' them 'air Aberdeen Guards is built on the same promisin' lines. I tell you, nobody need be 'feered fer the country's safety while them Aberdeen gals is aroun' to see things slide like they orter.

She describes their most impressive drill, in which "Not one o' them thunk anything about their back hair ... Every one was thinkin' o' their country's enemies an' how they'd like to scratch their eyes out."[19] Baum lets her ridicule the amateur soldiers as he would not do in his own person; yet at the same time, he suggests woman's capacity for strength and ferocity. The professionalism of the Aberdeen Guards was to appear in Oz in Glinda's army of girls; the comic aspects suggest Jinjur's army in *The Land of Oz*.

While Editor Baum dutifully supported the Republican Party and its local candidates, he let Mrs. Bilkins express his actual disillusionment with all the politicians. "If there should happen, by any chance to be an honest man left in South Dikoty, what's he goin' ter vote fer?" None of the three parties, she declares: "if he's really honest, he'll jest vote fer ekal suffridge, Bath fer [state] capital, an' ... put the rest of the tickets inter the fire." The massive defeat of the woman suffrage amendment on Election Day prompted Mrs. Bilkins to disgust with the supposedly democratic process that had failed women, which Baum probably felt but would not express so crudely: "Instid o' havin' one king, we've got hundreds, an' they run the government for what money there is in it, an' the people fer what money they can git out of 'em.... I've had enough of politics to last me a life-time, an' if you boarders don't give the sujec' a rest you can find some other boardin' house." (Of course, she has declaimed on politics more constantly than any of them.)[20]

After Our Landlady gave up on politics, her most interesting columns speculate on the technological marvels of the future. The column of January 3, 1891, is a comic extravaganza anticipating the technological magic of Oz and poking fun at Baum's own enthusiasm for inventions and his editorial promotion of artesian wells to solve all the problems of Dakota farmers. On December 16, the *Aberdeen Daily News* had drawn a utopian picture of "The Wonderful Updyke Farm," where power from an artesian well generated electricity that did. all the domestic and agricultural work; they could even extend the growing season by keeping the garden lighted at night.[21]

On January 3, 1891, Mrs. Bilkins visits the Great Downditch Farm, where electricity from an artesian well produces more fantastic wonders. When she presses the bell, the door opens and she is placed in an armchair, which carries her to Mr. Downditch in his study. Electric power not only produces a luxurious meal but places it on the table and causes the table to rise from the floor; afterwards, it lowers the table and washes the dishes. It sends their chairs into a room like the "Oproar House," where a play is performed by electrically powered dummies with phonographs inside them. Baum delights in the wonders he invented, but he also suggests possible dangers in the elimination of all human effort and, consequently, control. In the morning, Mrs. Bilkins remarks that Mr. Downditch must be very nice because he is always smiling, and Mrs. Downditch reveals that "he smiles by 'lectricity." This makes Mrs. Bilkins resolve to keep her thoughts to herself, "fer fear the 'lectricity should get hold o' them." Her apprehension would be more coherently expressed in *The Master Key* (1901), when the boy hero asks the Demon of Electricity, "What right have you to capture vibrations that radiate from private and secret actions and discover them to others who have no business to know them?"[22]

On January 31, Mrs. Bilkins was inspired by Edward Bellamy's utopian fantasy, *Looking Backward,* to dream about Aberdeen in 1895, perhaps because the present was so depressing. The dream reaffirms her and Baum's condemnation of those who fled the city as soon as times became hard. Arriving in Aberdeen by airship, she takes a comfortable room on the sixteenth floor of the new hotel. (In fact, Aberdeen did not get its first "skyscraper" until 1910, and it was only six stories tall.) There she listens to a phonograph (one had, in fact, just recently arrived in Aberdeen), which tells her about Aberdeen, answers her questions, and talks back to her. Aberdeen is now the "Garden o' Eden, the center o' the wonderful irrigated valley o' the Jim [James River]. The most fertile an' productive land in the world surrounds this busy metropolis an' pours its treasures into the city's marts, from whence they are airshipped to all parts of the world and also to Pierre."[23]

In Mrs. Bilkins's final appearance, on February 8, when "She Discusses New Inventions with the Boarders," she reflects first Baum's enthusiasm for technological innovations and then his increasing discouragement and cynicism. Editor Baum had written about a newly invented airship that had had a disappointing trial but still had proved "so successful that the most skeptical cannot longer disbelieve in the ultimate practicability of the invention." Mrs. Bilkins likewise expresses her confidence that the airship can be made to work in the end, just as Howe's sewing machine did. She moves on, however, to less innocent inventions that she has seen in Aberdeen—a bank manager's method for "lettin' his bank bust an' makin' folks think that he's only closin' out an' will pay 'em back their deposits next new years," the saloons' method for "siccin' the prohibitionists onter the druggists an' escapin' themselves . . . oh, there's no end of inwentions, only they don't find a way o' makin' a dime buy a dollar's wuth, ner to give us a crop next year if there ain't no seed in the ground," nor "to pay yer bills when you can't collect a cent to do it with." Baum moves neatly from faith in genuine inventions that promise hope for improving human welfare to worldly cynicism about the eternal inventiveness of human beings in pursuing self-interest through dishonest means to deep disillusionment over the failure of inventiveness to deal with real human misery.[24]

For its first four months, the *Aberdeen Saturday Pioneer* had prospered under Baum's editorship. On May 3, with increasing advertisements, he felt confident enough to expand it to twelve pages. The four added pages were syndicated boiler plate, featuring on page one a long article on Thomas Nast, embellished with seven of his cartoons. On July 5, however, the paper reverted to eight pages (a change not announced until July 12), as it was to remain.

Baum's next extension was a monthly financial journal, the *Western Investor,* which he announced in the *Pioneer* and launched on August 15. He doubtless hoped to profit himself and to help the community by attracting Eastern investors to South Dakota (he criticized the local business community for not being sufficiently enterprising in this regard). He promoted the *Western Investor* in the *Pioneer,* claiming a circulation of twenty thousand. It did so well at first that on October 18 he hired Camilla Jewell to work on the journal, but it disappeared within the next few months. No issues have survived.[25]

After the election on November 8, Baum seems to have lost heart in the *Pioneer.* Almost every cause and candidate he had supported during the campaign had been defeated: the failure of the suffrage amendment was the most painful, but also Pierre had won the contest for state capital and the local Republican slate had lost to the Independents. Baum's editorials on November 15 reflect his depressed state of mind. One hails the National Reform Party on the grounds that "Never in the history of our country has reform been so needed." Another, prompted by the president's Thanksgiving proclamation, is a withering attack on conventional pious thankfulness:

> It's a pretty custom, this Thanksgiving, and the hollowest and most insincere of all the mockeries which usage has accustomed us to. The way we do it is to prepare a better dinner than we can afford, and overload our stomachs to an alarming degree. One man out of a hundred and one woman out of fifty goes to church and hears the minister tell how much they have to be thankful for, and a few sound their own hearts and decide that the blessings which they have attained are very meagre, and are owing fully as much to their own unaided exertions as to the grace of God.

(On November 29, the "Our Landlady" column complemented this editorial by showing Mrs. Bilkins collecting superficial and insincere reasons to be thankful from her boarders.) Despite his gregariousness, his positive thinking, and his frequent endorsement of conventional American and business values, Baum had a sardonic streak that exposed sham and unthinking conformity.

Baum's personal discouragement was aggravated by hard times in

Aberdeen, which became worse and worse. Drought ruined the wheat crop again in 1890. The suffrage lecturer Annie Shaw, traveling around South Dakota by wagon in the summer of 1890, reported that the wagon wheels "sank half-way to the hubs; and in the midst of this dry powder lay withered tangles that had once been grass. Every one had the forsaken desperate look worn by the pioneer who had reached the limit of his endurance."[26] Land that had recently produced twenty bushels of wheat to the acre now produced four. And at the same time, the price of a bushel of wheat declined from over a dollar to forty-nine cents. Farmers could no longer pay interest on mortgages that had seemed like reasonable risks in the boom years; their farms were foreclosed, leaving them with no means of livelihood. Businesses that depended on their customers followed them into bankruptcy. Fear of Indian rebellion further frightened off investors and settlers,[27] and the failure of a prominent local bank deprived local investors of capital. Hundreds of people left the area.

Not only did Baum's subscriptions dwindle from three thousand five hundred to one thousand four hundred, but he often could not collect the money due him. On November 15, he tried to attract subscribers by including one of the magazines published by Harper & Brothers in the price for his newspaper. A large advertisement on top of the editorials column on November 29 offers premiums to Church Societies, Boys, Girls, Everybody to bring in subscribers. With the decline in trade, his income from advertisements decreased, as well as the opportunities for job printing. He could no longer pay his job printer, so he had to do all the work himself. Occasionally, it is true, Baum managed to find humor in his troubles. Once he told an Eastern advertiser who asked him about the circulation of his paper that it had gone from three thousand five hundred to three thousand to two thousand and was now about one thousand four hundred, and that it was "only by the hardest efforts that he prevented the whole lot from going to hell," and the man was so disarmed by Baum's frankness that he continued to purchase space. Baum told the story often in later life; it appears first in a clipping from a Syracuse newspaper of November 11, 1899, and was fictionalized in *Aunt Jane's Nieces on Vacation*.[28]

In December, both editorials and local news got thinner. Advertisements and legal notices occupied a good three-quarters of the editorial page on December 13. On January 17, Baum announced that the *Pioneer* disclaimed any future concern with politics. The "Our Landlady" column in the same issue consists of disconnected bits, and it did not appear at all on January 24. Baum began his report of that week's society events with a dispirited comment that the citizens of Aberdeen should make the most of any teas and parties available to take their minds off "the bleak and uninviting prospects which stare us in the face during the day's scarcely requited labors."

The *Aberdeen Daily News*, also suffering from the hard times, intensified competition with the *Pioneer* by expanding its features and local news. Baum tried to save his paper by transforming it into a twelve-page Sunday paper and increasing his reviews of national journals and books, especially the Harper's magazines that were tied in with *Pioneer* subscriptions. But when the new format made its appearance on February 8, the issue had such obvious deficiencies that Baum felt it necessary to apologize: the *Pioneer* has done its best on short notice, and "We shall try to improve." He pointed out its merits, particularly its expensive syndicated columnists, which still included the humorist Nye, but now added a prominent Brooklyn clergyman. A reprint of his sermon takes up most of page six. In view of Baum's anticlericalism, this looks like a desperate expedient to broaden his readership. The editorials are scrappy bits on several national issues, including the airship recently tried out in Chicago, which set off Our Landlady's pessimistic column on inventions. On February 14, the *Pioneer* went back, without comment, to eight pages.

Baum's spirits must have been further depressed when his reasonable charge that the local school superintendent was incompetent and overpaid provoked an abusive response. In addition, Baum was sick with a tumor underneath his tongue. The issue of February 28 has less than half a column of editorials. The local news is also diminished and includes a notice of Baum's illness, "which must be apology for any imperfections noticed in the *Pioneer*." He reported that he was still sick on March 7, but that he had had the tumor removed and hoped he would soon be better and the *Pioneer* restored. Matilda Gage helped out on March 7 and 14 with feminist articles on women. The editorials on March 21, the last extant issue of the *Pioneer*, do not look like Baum's work; they are on general national topics and are set in different type from the rest of the paper. There is an announcement in the local news that "Mr. Baum has gone East to St. Paul, Minneapolis, and Chicago, which must be apology for any sins of omission noticed in the *Pioneer* this week and next." There is no definite announcement, however, that Baum was giving up the paper.

He wanted to persist, as he had been exhorting others to do; for he had invested much effort and money in Aberdeen, and the hard times might be coming to an end. (They finally did in the mid-1890s.) But at last it did not seem worth the struggle to stay. He needed more steady support for his pregnant wife and three sons and was evidently job hunting in Minneapolis and Chicago. Kenneth Gage, the Baums' fourth and last child, was born on March 24. On April 4, the *Aberdeen Daily News* reported that Baum's health had been "very poor for several months and for this and other reasons he . . . concluded to accept a position on one of the leading dailies in Chicago," where work might be arduous but "is all along one line and is devoid to a large extent of worry and anxiety." Accordingly, he had returned "the plant and good will" of the *Aberdeen Saturday Pioneer* to John Drake, who then sold it.[29]

In later years, Baum explained that he published the *Pioneer* "until the sheriff wanted the paper more than I."[30] Actually, the failure of Baum's newspaper did not necessarily reflect on him as editor or publisher. Even in regions that were not suffering like the Dakotas, more newspapers failed than succeeded, and small newspapers made slim profits; in 1890, all over the United States, the average newspaper's income from advertising, subscriptions, and job printing exceeded basic expenses by only about two thousand five hundred dollars.[31] On the other hand, it must have been bitter to come away from South Dakota with nothing to show for two and a half years of hard work. At thirty-five, Baum had yet to find himself a career.

three

BECOMING A WRITER IN
CHICAGO, 1891–1900

Baum had to recognize that all his efforts and talents were not sufficient to make a success of a small-town newspaper. Still, he had proven his competence as a journalist, and it seemed reasonable that he could put his experience to use by writing for one of the many newspapers in Chicago.

Chicago, America's second largest city, was an exciting place to be in 1891. It was not only a progressive commercial center; it had attracted a large number of artists, architects, writers, and publishers. According to Hamlin Garland, who moved there at about the same time Baum did:

> Chicago was now full in the spot-light of the National Stage. In spite of the business depression which still engulfed the West, the promoters of the Columbian Exposition were going steadily forward with their plans. . . . I believed, (as many others believed) that the city was entering upon an era of swift and shining development. . . . From being a huge, muddy windy market-place, it seemed about to take its place among the literary capitals of the world. Colonies of painters, sculptors, decorators . . . writers . . . were . . . celebrating . . . the changes in thought and aspect of the town. Ambitious publishing houses were springing up and . . . new magazines. . . . I predicted a publishing center and a literary market-place second only to New York, a publishing center which by reason of its geographical position would be more progressive than Boston, and more American than Manhattan.[1]

The World's Columbian Exposition of 1893 was to celebrate progress in the largest world's fair ever held. A complete city was designed and built to accommodate it, so that the new marvels of technology were displayed in a setting that showed what a city could be.

This "White City" was built largely in the classic style, but its planning, integration, and facilities made it seem an ideal of the future.

> Transportation was well planned; the roads macadamized and kept spotlessly clean; the water supply adequate; fire, police, and ambulance stations amply provided; and light, telephone, and telegraphy wires carried in conduits. This small and ephemeral city, into which on some days about three quarters of a million people crowded, represented the best that America could offer—a city intelligently designed for comfort, convenience, and beauty.[2]

The most striking of the marvels demonstrated the possibilities of a great natural force that was just beginning to be exploited: electric power. (This was still exotic for most people—as late as 1907, only 8 percent of American homes were wired for electricity.) At the opening ceremonies, President Cleveland pressed a button that turned on lights over the entire fair site. Electric light enhanced "miles of consumer goods displayed throughout the forty-four acre Manufacturers & Liberal Arts Building, the largest department store the world had ever seen." In the Electricity Building, there was a model home with an electric stove, washing machine, carpet sweeper, doorbell, fire alarm, and lighting fixtures. Two of Edison's latest inventions were on display, an improved phonograph and a prototype motion picture machine called the Kinetoscope.[3]

The Baums were often to visit the exposition, which would have gratified Frank's interest in technological progress and stimulated his imagination. The romantic beauty, as well as the technological magic, of the White City must have helped to inspire the Emerald City of Oz. Its fountains, domes, minarets, spires, and fluttering banners suggested the architecture of the Emerald City. Lit by hundreds of electric lights, the White City could have suggested a jeweled city to Baum as it did to Frances Hodgson Burnett: after dark the White City seemed to be set "with myriads of diamonds, all alight."[4]

Harry Baum recalled one particular family trip to the fair that illustrates Frank's cheerful casualness, which could at times be irritating. He and Maud had arranged to meet for lunch at the Woman's Building in the hope that it would be relatively uncrowded. But when Frank arrived, he could not get in because the princess of Spain was there and everyone wanted to see her. He slipped into the procession that would form the receiving line for the princess and then could not get out of it, so he stood on the line as if he belonged there and enjoyed himself making conversation with his neighbors—until he glanced up to the balcony and saw, "pressed tightly against the rail with a small child clutching either hand . . . a tired and hungry mother staring at him in amazement and anger!"[5]

Meanwhile, Baum had been trying and failing to find work in his chosen career of journalism. As soon as he arrived in Chicago, he applied to the *Tribune*, the *Times*, the *Morning Herald*, the *Daily Journal*, the *Mail*, the *Inter Ocean*, the *Globe*, and the *Daily News*—all without success. Finally he got a job as a reporter and editorial writer on the year-old *Chicago Evening Post* at twenty dollars a week; he was to start on May 1, 1891.[6] He joined the Chicago Press Club—partly to establish useful business contacts, as indeed he was to do, and partly because he was gregarious and enjoyed the society of successful men.

He rented a house at 34 Campbell Park, selecting it because he thought the neighborhood looked warm and comfortable and there were large shade trees and a grassy parkway nearby. It was a modest frame cottage, without running water or a connection for gas. The Baums were to live there for four years. Maud and the boys arrived two weeks later, probably accompanied by Matilda Gage.[7]

On receiving his first paycheck from the *Post*, Baum was dismayed to find that it was a dollar and a half less than he had expected—his salary was eighty dollars per month rather than twenty dollars per week. He was naturally resentful, and Maud kept his resentment lively. It became clear that he would have to leave newspaper work if he was to make a living wage. By the fall he got a job as a china buyer in the Siegel, Cooper & Company department store, having managed to convince them that he knew about china. Actually, his knowledge was acquired by hasty reading in the Chicago Public Library.[8] Siegel, Cooper was a pleasant place to work, but the salary was still low.

Through his work as a buyer, Baum came to know executives of the china wholesale houses, including the sales manager of Pitkin and Brooks, which marketed fine china and glassware throughout the Midwest. Thus he heard of an opening and was given the opportunity to try out for a few months as a traveling salesman, working on a liberal commission. Frank and Maud hesitated to exchange a certain salary for uncertain commissions, and they did not like the prospect of his being away for weeks at a time. But they looked forward to having an adequate income for a change. It is not clear when he started his new job; from June 1893, Matilda Gage's letters refer to regular business traveling.

A letter to his mother, written on the cheap stationery of Galva House, a hotel in Galva, Illinois, suggests that the new job was not yet secure on June 16, 1894. She was evidently recovering from a severe illness, through which she had been nursed by her youngest son, Harry, now a doctor with an increasing medical practice. Frank tells her that his "present job is until April 1st and if everything is satisfactory then, they will keep me the whole year. I am starting in very well, and have not much fear now but what I shall be able to get bread and butter anyhow, altho I'm afraid we cant indulge in many luxuries," including, most likely, going to see her in Syracuse. He thanks her for her kindness in offering him a home but assures her he will not need that. "While I live I shall *somehow* manage to provide for those dependent on me, and I shall never burden you, although I know your love would not consider it a burden."[9]

For some time, "Money was not very plentiful and a penny went a long way." "Red letter days were when father would come home from a sales trip and we would ask for a penny and he would magnanimously hand out a nickel."[10] Baum was constantly trying to increase his income with "side lines." In 1894, he became enthusiastic about a newly invented "nut lock" (now called a lock nut, a nut that will not work loose). He marketed it as he made his sales rounds, but fortunately did not invest any money in its development. Matilda Gage also thought nut locks a promising investment and tried to interest Clarkson in the project. Maud, however, did not share their confidence and kept Frank to his china selling. She contributed to the family income by starting a business based on her love of sewing; she gave lessons in embroidery and lace making, charging twenty-five cents for group and fifty cents for individual lessons. In February 1897, she had over twenty students and had made enough money to buy a rug and other household furnishings. She was still giving lessons a year later.[11]

Frank soon became his firm's leading salesman, partly because he would come back after making a sale to help the merchant arrange the goods effectively so as to sell more, and thus would receive another order.[12] In 1895, the Baums were able to move to a larger and better house in the same neighborhood at 120 Flournoy Street. It had a bathroom and gaslights. They had a large dog, apparently a husky, who would pull the boys around on their sleds. They were able to import a maid from Sweden, who did most of the housework and helped to look after the younger boys; she remained with them for eight years.[13]

Nevertheless, in November 1897, Matilda Gage noted that "times seemed very hard" for the Baums.[14]

Whatever the family's financial difficulties, Frank always managed to create fun in the household. Since one of his sidelines was selling fireworks, he always made the Fourth of July "a wonderful occasion for us, for we had enough firecrackers and other explosives to keep us busy from dawn to dusk. And the night display was the pride of the neighborhood with sky rockets, roman candles, pinwheels, and set pieces galore. People from blocks around would gather in front of our house to watch the display, and mother always breathed a sigh of relief when she got us safely to bed and had counted our fingers and toes to see that they were all there." Life was always exciting around the Baum household. Their family doctor of many years "used to say that when he heard any screaming around our neighborhood he would grab his bag and head out for our house and was always right."[15]

Christmas was even more festive than the Fourth. Harry Baum recalled that the family tree was placed in the front parlor behind closed drapes. Santa—that is, Frank—would come to deck the tree and talk to them from behind the drapes, but though they tried, they never could manage to see him. Frank kept up this custom all his life. His grandson Joslyn recalled Christmas dinners at Ozcot, where everyone waited in the dining room while Frank went ahead into the living room. They would hear him talking to Santa: "Everything ready?... Well, thanks for the presents, Santa. Have a good trip. See you next year!"[16]

Although Baum's income became satisfactory, his work was wearisome and the constant traveling was unpleasant for a man so devoted to his home and family. His sales territory was central and southern Illinois, Iowa, and Missouri. His job involved packing six to ten trunks with samples of fragile china and glassware, which he would ship by railroad to the first stop on his route, where they were carted to his hotel. There he would unpack and display them in a sample room and arrange for visits from local merchants. After getting their orders, he had to repack hundreds of delicate pieces for shipment to the next town.

Already in 1894, Matilda Gage felt he would "fly off" from his job if Maud did not keep him to it. Once, when he was traveling and had not received a letter from Maud for a day or two, he telegraphed that he was coming right home; his dependency prompted his mother-in-law to sniff, "a perfect baby."[17] The situation became urgent when Baum began to suffer gripping chest pains. His heart problem was still mild enough not to cause trouble under normal circumstances— Matilda Gage, who constantly fussed over her own and her family's health, never mentioned it. However, the heavy physical demands of his job brought out symptoms of heart strain. He was advised by a specialist to find less fatiguing work.[18]

During these years, Matilda Gage regularly spent the winter with the Baums, as she had when they had lived in Aberdeen. Her visits were particularly important to Maud when Frank's selling job kept him away for weeks. Frank was evidently happy to have her with them. She wrote to Clarkson, when she was sick in 1897, that Frank had just left on a trip and "came in and kissed me good bye, as he always does. He is very kind to me."[19] In these years, Matilda was occupied mainly with spiritual inquiries and with completing her major book, *Woman, Church and State.* She was convinced the house at Campbell Park was haunted, and various members of the family experienced strange visions and noises there.[20]

To some extent at least, Frank and Maud shared Gage's spiritualist beliefs, which were common among liberal thinkers at that time. Maud apparently dropped out of the Episcopal Church, for she sent her older boys to the West Side Ethical Culture Sunday School, where, Gage noted approvingly, "morality and not religion is taught."[21] On September 4, 1892, Maud and Frank were admitted to the Ramayana Theosophical Society in Chicago. Frank found in theosophy a system of belief that satisfied his reason and at the same time fulfilled his strong spiritual needs. "The spiritual was a living experience" for him, despite his rejection of orthodox creeds, and he had the theosophist's "reverent ... attitude toward all life." According to a clergyman friend, "He had a gospel of his own and he preached it through his books, although you certainly couldn't call them religious."[22] Baum accepted the theosophical beliefs that this visible world is one of many, that life on earth is only one stage in the progress of a soul, and that the good or evil one does in one's lifetime here returns in future reincarnations. He believed that he and Maud had met in earlier reincarnations.[23] The Baums and Gage attended seances in the hope of obtaining objective evidence of the reality of spirits and the afterlife.[24]

Theosophy was to influence the development of Baum's fantasies through its affirmation of a reality beyond the everyday visible world; its vision of a cosmos in which physical and spiritual reality were part of one great whole, filled with beings seen and unseen and governed by the same laws; and its confidence that these laws can be understood through scientific and religious inquiry, which are analogous roads to truth. In theosophic cosmology there are six increasingly spiritual planes above the physical world, which exist around us (generally unseen) and through which souls rise on their way to perfect enlightenment. The lowest spiritual plane, the astral plane, is populated by thoughts, spirits of the recently dead, and "great hosts of natural elementals, or nature-spirits": the elementals of the fire (Salamanders), the air (Sylphs), the water (Undines), and the earth (Gnomes). These intelligences "make all nature a living responsive organism instead of a soulless mechanism." "They are the channels through which work the divine energies in these several fields, the living expressions of the law in each. At the head of each division is a great Being" who directs them. These nature-spirits give form to physical creatures—building up minerals, guiding vital energies in plants, and so forth. They "are the fairies and elves of legends ... charming irresponsible children of Nature," now perceived only by poets and occultists, and occasionally children; but they will eventually be recognized as real.[25]

Baum's imagined world is alive with sylphs (such as the Cloud Fairies in *Dorothy and the Wizard in Oz*), undines (mermaids), and gnomes (nomes). Michael Hearn has suggested that the salamanders appear as "fairies of energy," the Demon of Electricity of *The Master Key* and the Lovely Lady of Light in *Tik-Tok of Oz*.[26] These spirits preside over all forms of life and natural processes. Elflike Ryls nourish the flowers and give them color by putting dyes in the soil, and they are directed by the Master Woodsman of the World in *The Life and Adventures of Santa Claus*. Each type of animal is watched over by a spirit, such as the Fairy Beaver in *John Dough and the Cherub*. Baum's fairies and fairyland are so concretely realized because, as a theosophist, he believed they had spiritual or subjective reality. In his imagined world, which is not sharply distinguished from the world in which we live, divine or at least extraordinary presences are all around, many of whom devote themselves to watching over children and other living things.

Baum's created world, like the theosophical cosmos, is governed by the physical and moral laws of an all-embracing divine order. Animals may kill their natural prey, but only so much as they need to eat ("The Tiger's Eye"). Magic in Oz, particularly in the later books, usually operates in accordance with natural (if hidden) laws. Glinda in her laboratory and the Wizard with his bag of tools conduct their business much like scientists. Conversely, in *The Master Key*, technological marvels in this world suggest magic. In *Tik-Tok of Oz*, the Shaggy Man explicitly connects magic, natural wonders, and science: "All the magic isn't in fairyland . . . There's lots of magic in all Nature, and you may see it as well in the United States, where you and I once lived, as you can here. . . . Is anything more wonderful than to see a flower grow and blossom, or to get light out of the electricity in the air?"[27] In Baum's fantasies, the unseen world that theosophists accepted as real becomes fairyland and the occult knowledge that leads to understanding its laws becomes magic.

Two of the ethical principles Baum promoted in his stories reflect theosophical teaching, although they derived from other sources as well. Baum's heroes consistently solve difficulties by drawing on their own courage and enterprise. Theosophy taught that everyone has latent abilities that can be developed through resolution and effort so as to master oneself and the forces of nature. While a conventionally religious person prays for help, a theosophist "depends upon himself, upon the immediate efficacy of his own knowledge and action."[28] In the same way, Baum's respect and concern for animals was confirmed by theosophy. Annie Besant deplored the mistreatment of animals—slaughtering, sport hunting, and vivisection—that has filled the astral sphere with their hostile, terrified astral bodies, which aggravate their distrust and fear in this world and reinforce our cruelty.[29] In utopian Oz, people are not cruel to animals, and animals are typically friendly and trustful of people. Apart from theosophy, of course, Baum was following his own kindly nature and the fairy-tale convention that it is important to be kind to animals. Actually, according to Maud, Frank was not especially attached to animals in real life, although he was good to them; Maud was the one who loved "them, especially dogs. . . . We always had dogs, good and bad."[30]

Because Gage was living with the Baums while she worked to complete *Woman, Church and State: A Historical Account of the Status of Woman Through the Christian Ages: with Reminiscences of the Matriarchate* (1893), the family must have known and discussed her ideas. This book was the culmination of her lifelong attack upon the patriarchal oppression imposed by institutionalized Christianity, from Saint Paul to the present. It is an impressive piece of research—545 pages based on extensive reading in learned sources.[31]

Gage supported her charge that institutional Christianity is responsible for woman's oppression with a glowing description of a preChristian matriarchy, in which "woman ... was the first in the family, the state, religion"; "never was justice more perfect, never civilization higher than under the Matriarchate."[32] Feminists naturally embraced this idea of an idyllic matriarchal past, for which they could cite respected nineteenth-century anthropologists such as J. G. Wilkinson (*Ancient Egypt*) and J. J. Bachofen (*Das Mutterrecht*). Stanton also promoted the theory.

A conspicuous example of the Church's oppression of women is its persecution of those accused of witchcraft. Gage described this at length, alleging that the Church fabricated and encouraged belief in witchcraft to enrich itself and to keep women down. But she could not resist having it both ways by also using witchcraft as evidence of female wisdom. "We have abundant proof that the so-called 'witch' was among the most profoundly scientific persons of the age." Denied formal education by the Church, woman, "through her own wisdom, penetrated into some of the most deeply subtle secrets of nature."[33]

Gage's association of witchcraft with science accords with the theosophical doctrine that scientific and occult investigations are two aspects of the same process, and her interpretation of magic anticipates Baum's. "Magic simply means knowledge of the effect of certain natural, but generally unknown laws; the secret operation of natural causes ... consequences resulting from control of the invisible powers of nature, such as are shown in the electrical appliances of the day, which a few centuries since would have been termed witchcraft." " 'Magic' whether brought about by the aid of spirits or simply through an understanding of secret natural laws, is of two kinds, 'white' and 'black,' according as its intent and consequences are evil or good, and in this respect does not differ from the use made of the well known laws of nature, which are ever of good or evil character, in the hands of good or evil persons."[34]

Baum's concept of the good witch, explicitly developed in *The Wizard of Oz*, is his most striking borrowing from Gage. Magic in Baum can have good or evil effects, depending on whether Glinda or the Nome King is practicing it, just as the power of electricity in *The Master Key* can be a blessing to humanity or, if it falls into the wrong hands, a curse. Baum was to re-create Gage's matriarchy in Oz.

————

Gage did more than influence Baum's fantasy world, however: it was she who saw where he could at last attain success: as a writer of fantasies for children. She listened to the stories he told his sons and their friends, recognized their quality, and urged him to publish them. By June 1893, two publishers were considering his first book of fairy tales, "Adventures in Phunnyland." He was negotiating with an illustrator, Thomas M. Peirce, his niece's fiancé; and his mother had offered to give him one hundred dollars toward the cost of illustrations.[35] He claimed copyright for "Phunnyland" and a second book, *Tales from Mother Goose*, in a letter dated June 17, 1896. In March 1897, both were making the rounds of publishers.

While he waited, Baum kept trying to find some type of writing that would support his family and relieve him of the drudgery of selling china. If he could not get a regular newspaper job, he could perhaps succeed as a freelance journalist. Since he had to linger for hours in cheap hotels waiting for train connections, he used the time to jot down verses and stories. But for years most of his work was rejected; he kept a sad little account book he called his "Record of Failure." He experimented with comic, sentimental, and supernatural stories in an attempt to discover what he could do and what would sell.[36]

He did succeed in publishing some light verse and stories in the Chicago *Times-Herald*. "La Reine Est Morte—Vive La Reine" (June 23, 1895) caters to current prejudice by lightly satirizing the New Woman, "With her rights and her votes and her bloomers, too!" who is supplanting "the sweetheart fair," with "blushing cheeks" and "eyes that shone so tender and true."[37]

Baum's views on women's progress are more justly expressed in "Yesterday at the Exposition [from the *Times-Herald*, June 27, 2090]," submitted to a contest for the best piece on "Chicago's International Exposition, A.D. 2090." His essay won third prize and appeared on February 2, 1896. A forecast of the future better thought out than those in the "Our Landlady" column, it reflects the same interest in technological progress, as well as in political issues such as women's rights. Ireland is an independent republic, and the President of England is a woman. A new chemical fertilizer causes wheat to grow in fifteen minutes. People convey long-distance messages by thought transference. There is a historical display of ladies wearing long skirts and corsets, and "Many spectators can scarcely believe that so cramped and unlovely a costume was ever universally adopted by women."[38]

On July 12, Baum published verses supporting the Republican presidential candidate William McKinley and his policies of maintaining the Gold Standard and high tariffs.[39] "The Suicide of Kiaros," published in *The White Elephant* in September, is still admired as a powerful story; but, as usual in his serious adult fiction, Baum did not develop character and emotion sufficiently to move and convince. Nor did he deal with the implications of his disturbing plot that lets a murderer get away with his crime.[40]

Then, at last, Baum hit upon an economically viable way to use his skills as writer and editor. From the time he impressed a reporter with the attractive display of his wares in Baum's Bazaar, he had been interested in window dressing. He wrote an article in the May 17 *Pioneer* on "Beautiful Displays of Novelties which Rival in Attractiveness the Famed Museums of the World." He found romance in the merchandise available in Aberdeen stores, which came from "every clime on earth" and was "procured after deliberations, delays, difficulties and even dangers"; and he praised Strauss's harmonious arrangements of neckties and Shaft's artfully careless display of shoes in a parlor. Baum's work as a salesman kept him thinking about techniques for displaying merchandise. The art of window dressing was developing rapidly in the 1890s, facilitated by the improvement in the manufacture of plate glass. Windows could be presented like stage sets.

Baum's idea was to establish and edit a trade journal for window dressers to be called *The Show Window*. This would be a valuable aid for merchants who knew nothing about effective display and had no means of contact with those who did. But he had trouble getting the necessary capital. A letter to his sister Mary Louise Brewster, written from Chicago on *Show Window* stationery on October 3, 1897, expresses his discouragement. Apologizing for not having written before, he tells her:

> I have been more worried than usual about business matters this summer, and have scarcely spend [sic] time to sleep and eat from my business. Writing of all kinds I have been forced to neglect and the result, after all my labours, has profited me but little. I have wanted to quit traveling and find some employment that would enable me to stay at home, and I conceived the idea of a magazine devoted to window-trimming, which I know is greatly needed and would prosper if I

could get it going. I wrote to Mr. Neal [the brother-in-law he had worked for in Syracuse] to loan me the money to start it, but he bluntly refused.

Then a Chicago man promised to back him, but

when the first number was ready to go to press he failed in business and left me just where I started. I have been nearly a month now trying to find some one with money to pick up the enterprise and carry it through, but, although I have got several on the string, have so far been unsuccessful. If once I get it going it will mean 5,000$ a year to me at least.

He does have the good news that *Mother Goose in Prose* "will be out some time this month"; he expects "it to make a success, for it will be beautifully printed and bound." He has "not written any stories lately"; the last he published was "The Suicide of Kiaros," which he sent her.

He goes on to encourage her creative writing.

I liked your verses *very much.* You were always a natural poet and I know have written many beautiful things in that line. But poetry doesn't pay today—especially *good* verse.... *Doggerel* will sometimes command a price, if it is witty and pointed and in humorous lines; but what we know as real poetry is a drug in market. I am glad you got even $5. for your Kitchen article, for that's a *starter*—at least. Don't be discouraged but *keep writing.*

He is glad to hear that her husband, Harry, a New York State tax assessor, "is quite successful now, and that you will be likely to have more means at your command than has latterly been the case.... But the literary work is interesting and will do you good, in any event. I think you ought to be able to write beautiful stories, of a sort that would compel recognition, and I hope you will keep at them." He reports that Maud has not fully recovered from a sickness, but that the boys are all well and attending public school.[41]

Mother Goose in Prose had found a publisher when the Western novelist Opie Read, a fellow member of the Chicago Press Club, introduced Baum to another member, Chancey L. Williams of Way & Williams, publishers who specialized in fine editions. Williams looked at Baum's manuscript in June and accepted it a week later.[42] Soon after, Baum was able to persuade Williams to back his proposed monthly journal,

The Show Window. A Journal of Practical Window Trimming for the Merchant and the Professional. The first issue appeared on November 1, 1897; and he was sufficiently confident of its potential success that he quit his detested selling job. *The Show Window* is practically oriented, consisting of photographs of successful displays, descriptions indicating their themes and explaining how special effects were attained, specific hints about such problems as making a windowful of men's shoes attractive, and notices of new devices for lighting and so forth. Baum wrote much of the material himself but encouraged his readers to contribute photographs and descriptions of their work. Always enterprising in promotion, he proposed a National Association of Window Trimmers of America in February 1898 and was elected secretary at its first national convention in August.[43]

More successful at the theory than the practice of business, Baum explained how proper methods in selling can make all the difference between success and failure. If the show window is arranged with sufficient artfulness, customers will want what they see there whether they need it or not, and the clerk has only to complete the sale. Advertising, Baum had to admit, gave an advantage to the brazen pretender and the shrewd observer of human weaknesses over the honest simple trader: "the merchant who held out improbable and often impossible inducements drew the crowds, proving that the people . . . prefer a glaring uncertainty to a homely and modest surety."[44] This recognition of human gullibility would later give a cynical edge to Baum's fairy tales.

Generally, however, *The Show Window* shows a willingness to exploit people's gullibility for profit that would make any advertiser proud. The Easter issue is unblushingly crass. Next to Christmas, Easter offers the best opportunity for abundant sales, "as it is a time of joy and brightness, of full purses and generous hearts . . . Think of all the bonnets, gloves, laces, shoes, ribbons, silks, satins, and furbelows the ladies will require to 'look sweet' during the Easter sermon. . . . Some one will sell all these things for Easter. What will your share be?"[45] Baum goes on to offer useful pointers on the distribution of artificial Easter lilies, rabbits, and the cross. "The cross is the principal emblem of Easter, and is used in connection with many displays, being suitable for any line of merchandise."[46]

But occasionally the imaginative artist does break through. Baum's editorial in June 1900 declares that making money "is only an incident—a necessary incident—in life" and celebrates "The joy of accomplishing original artistic work." "Window trimming is a bad profession for a man who thinks only of pay day"; it is only right for those in whom it can inspire their "full energy ... best thought ... greatest genius ... truest pleasure." A gifted window trimmer, like a stage designer, can create marvelous effects, comparable to those achieved at the Chicago World's Fair. Baum delighted in analyzing ingenious effects such as the stout ship weathering a storm that advertised the Monarch brand of shirts (that likewise does not founder in the storms of competition). Electric light shining through slits in a revolving wheel produced the effect of lightning, and the ship was tossed through the waves by a rod attached to a revolving wheel below, with different speeds produced by a series of pulleys.[47]

After a slow start, during which time Maud and the two older boys had to help in wrapping and addressing the magazines, The Show Window steadily gained readers and advertisers.[48] Soon it was bringing in a comfortable income. In 1898, the Baums moved to a nicer house at 68 Humboldt Park Boulevard on the North West Side of Chicago. It was a "big two story house on the corner, just a block from Humboldt Park." When Frank Junior finished grammar school, his parents sent him to the Michigan Military Academy. It seems a strange choice, considering his father's misery at military school and the satire on warlike ambition throughout his books. Perhaps the younger Frank insisted on going. In any case, he soon became enthusiastic, wore his uniform at home, and set up a recruiting station in a basement front room. His younger brother Robert and his friends "used to get a lot of fun out of pestering him, calling him a tin soldier and so forth." In another basement room, "father had set up a large foot-power printing press with several cases of type," where he set and printed By the Candelabra's Glare, a collection of his verses. Afterwards Baum let the boys use the printing press, where they did job work and printed a home paper that they wrote themselves.[49]

In 1900, Baum capitalized on the success of his magazine by consolidating its instructions, with some added material, in the form of a book: The Art of Decorating Dry Goods Windows and Interiors: A Complete Manual of Window Trimming, Designed as an Educator in All the Details of the Art, According to the Best Accepted Methods, and Treating Fully Every Important Subject. This is a systematic handbook full of practical advice, such as what sizes of shelving and pillars to keep on hand to construct the framework of displays. It includes loving descriptions of striking, seemingly magical displays that ingenious trimmers designed to draw customers' attention to the window. For example, in one window the upper part of a beautiful young lady lived and moved without a lower part and in another a "Vanishing Lady" disappeared periodically and reappeared with a new hat or shirtwaist. (Both were achieved with live women, pedestals, mirrors, drapery, and, in the second case, an elevator.)

Nevertheless, Baum must have been relieved to announce, in October 1900, that he was resigning from the editorship of his trade paper because "The generous reception . . . of my books for children, during the past two years, has resulted in such constant demands upon my time that I find it necessary to devote my entire attention, hereafter, to this class of work."[50]

He had by this time published six children's books, most recently his "Adventures in Phunnyland," now called "A New Wonderland." Although it took him seven years to find a publisher for this book, Phunnyland was the first fantasy country he created and is interesting as a preliminary sketch for his mature achievements. He had made up its stories for groups of twelve or fifteen children who gathered in the Baum home and made taffy, popcorn, and ice cream to feast on while they listened;[51] and these goodies contributed to his concept of Phunnyland, where the ground is maple sugar, the rain is lemonade, and the snow is popcorn.

The book is a collection of fourteen stories set in a delightful magical valley and unified by recurrence of characters from story to story. The valley has many of the features of Oz: the people do not age or die, and they have no use for money because everything they want grows on trees. In times of crisis, the King calls a council that includes, along with the usual noblemen and the Wise Man, a smart-aleck dog and a donkey made wise by eating schoolbooks.[52] Although the valley is a fairyland, it has connections with modern America: the King and his people play baseball, and the good sorceress Maëtta's castle is adorned with electric lights as well as diamonds. The court is friendly and informal, and people normally feel goodwill toward everyone. Evil deeds are reassuringly reduced by ridiculous motives; a prince plots treason because he is determined to milk his father's ice-cream cow. Yet there are occasional astringent touches that keep Baum's fantasy from the sweet vapidity of many modern fairy tales, as when he points out a consequence of his utopian principles: "It is not much use being a Prince in Phunnyland, because the King can not die."[53]

King Scowleyow, an early sketch for the Nome King, is convincingly evil despite his delightfully ridiculous name. His "people lived in caves and mines and dug iron and tin out of the rocks and melted them into bars," which they sold. He hated the King of Phunnyland "and all his people, because they lived so happily and cared nothing for money." To destroy them, "He put all his mechanics to work and built a great man out of cast-iron, with machinery inside of him. When he was wound up, the Cast-iron Man would roar, and roll his eyes, and gnash his teeth and march across the Valley, crushing trees and houses to the earth as he went."[54] (This creature was based on a real mechanical man that a showman had exhibited in fairs and carnivals in the late 1890s, a suit of armor powered by a steam engine; if it was not properly controlled, "it would keep walking in a straight line, mowing down everything it encountered until it tripped, fell, and became helpless."[55]) The Cast-iron Man is powerfully but not consistently imagined, for he is vulnerable to tickling with a feather and pricking with a pin. There would be no such lapses with Tik-Tok, the Copper Man, in Oz. Like Baum's later Nome King, Scowleyow is the negation of goodwill and happiness, and is associated with the underground and material wealth; he uses his technological knowledge to make an impressive machine capable only of destruction. And, like the Nome King, he reassuringly demonstrates that evil destroys itself.

At its best, "Adventures in Phunnyland" anticipates the humorous nonsense of Oz. In "The King's Head and the Purple Dragon," the King picked a sword from the sword tree to punish the Purple Dragon for raiding his chocolate caramel patch. But dragons are always difficult to kill, especially when they are purple; and the dragon bit off the King's head and swallowed it. "Of course the King realized it was useless to continue the fight after that, for he could not see where the Dragon was."[56] A woodchopper made him a wooden head, which would have been satisfactory if only it could smile. Then the dragon who had disgorged the King's head because the points on his crown gave it indigestion, snapped off the woodchopper's head and replaced it with that of the King. The woodchopper no longer knew who he was, and when he arrived at the palace, the Queen could not tell whether to kiss the King's head on his shoulders or the wooden head on the King's. In this story, Baum first raised the issue of where human identity lies, a theme that he returned to often and later developed far more effectively.[57]

The grave explanation of the King's decision not to fight after he had lost his head and the connection between the dragon's toughness and his purple color amuse by their absurd logic. But details are piled on with the senseless extravagance of a tall tale, and there are irritating lapses in internal logic. Baum's mature fantasies engage sympathy and suspend disbelief because, once one or two impossible premises have been accepted, everything else follows the rules of logic and realism.

These later stories are also strengthened by being centered on a realistic character, such as Dorothy, and located in a clearly defined place. In Phunnyland there is no person from the everyday world, who could anchor and unify the stories and give them plausibility by her realistic reactions to the marvelous events. Phunnyland does not seem like a definite country, but just a nominal site where any imaginable thing can occur. Many of these early stories show clever invention and occasional insights, but they never induce a suspension of disbelief.

Baum announced in his preface "To the Reader" that no one was "expected to believe" these stories; "they were meant to excite laughter and to gladden the heart," to appeal through marvels and nonsense rather than through insights into real life. Actually, as he was to show in his Oz books, an appearance of credibility is perfectly compatible with joyful humor, and marvelous adventures with shrewd realistic observations. Although Baum claimed in his second sentence that he was still a child himself, he was subtly patronizing his readers when he disclaimed realism on the grounds that "It is the nature of children to scorn realities, which crowd into their lives all too quickly with advancing years. Childhood is the time for fables, for dreams, for joy." Children require realism as well as wonder: they tend to be literal-minded, and they have a clear sense of logic and probability. As Royal Historian of Oz, Baum was never smartly superior to his material: he narrated events seriously, just as if they were real rather than fantastic.

Actually, he developed this other aspect of his imagination in his first children's book to appear—"Tales from Mother Goose," published in 1897 as *Mother Goose in Prose*. As "Phunnyland" was filled with exuberant fantasy, *Mother Goose* showed his concern with making his stories believable. Harry Baum told how the younger children would raise questions as they read *Mother Goose*—how could a man scratch his eyes in? and so forth. "Father made up little stories to explain these strange happenings to us," and the result was *Mother Goose in Prose*.[58] Baum faithfully followed all the details given in the rhymes, as a child would demand; and yet he plausibly grounded the absurd circumstances by developing background and motivations that a child could accept as probable. Treating the nonsense verses with respect, as if they were real, produces a fresh point of view and even occasional insights into the actual world.

In the best of the stories, "Three Wise Men of Gotham" (who went to sea in a bowl), Baum combined truth to the rhyme, quasirealistic motivation for the characters, and his characteristic mockery of intellectual pretentiousness. Two old men in a village found they could "earn money without working" by setting up as Wise Men. They were not actually wise, of course; but by displaying their pure white beards and piercing eyes, walking slowly and majestically, and saying as little as possible, they succeeded in impressing their neighbors. When a third pretender appeared, the first two, "knowing themselves to be arrant humbugs," realized they had to defend their position by engaging him in disputation. After the people gathered around "to hear the words of wisdom that dropped from their lips," one Wise Man put forth his reasons why the world must be flat, and the other two demonstrated their superior wisdom with arguments for equally absurd conflicting theories. They agreed to settle the question by sailing to the outermost edge of the ocean and went out in a bowl because the boats were all out fishing.[59] With Baum's help, a child can have the delight of seeing through adult pomposity.

"The Woman Who Lived in a Shoe" is sympathetically characterized as a hard-pressed grandmother who had counted on spending her latter days in peace and comfort but instead had to raise sixteen grandchildren and managed to do a good job of it. The last tale, "Little Bun Rabbit," is not based on a nursery rhyme and is noteworthy for introducing a nice little farm girl in a sunbonnet named Dorothy, who is so congenial with animals that she can understand their language.

Way & Williams produced *Mother Goose* handsomely. They hired Maxfield Parrish, already a well-known poster artist, to illustrate it with fourteen black-and-white drawings and a full-color illustration for the cover. This set a precedent. Every one of Baum's children's books was richly illustrated, often with color plates as well as line drawings. In 1914, Baum's publisher, Frank Reilly, reminded him that a Baum children's book cost $0.25 to produce and sold for $1.25, while the average novel cost $0.18 to produce and sold for $1.55.[60] Despite its handsome appearance and its originality, *Mother Goose* was only moderately successful. Still, it sold well enough that Williams planned to publish "Phunnyland"; but unfortunately his firm failed in the following year.

Frank inscribed Maud's copy of *Mother Goose in Prose:* "One critic I always fear and long to please. It is my Sweetheart. . . . I hope this book will succeed, for her sake, for we need the money success would bring. But aside from that sordid fact I care little what the world thinks of it. The vital question is: What does my sweetheart, my wife of fifteen years, think of it?" He wrote to his brother, Harry: "I send you this book in memory of the days when, occupying the same bed, contending for the same pleasures, following much the same pursuits; studying together, playing together—aye, fighting together—but always animated by an honest, brotherly love, we came to the crossways of life and stepped out upon divergent paths to emerge *men* instead of *boys*. The old life, so sweet to remember, is now left far behind, and all, *save the love*, has become a dream of the past."[61]

In his sister Harriet's book, he credited her with being the one "who first encouraged me to write. Years ago you read to father an incomplete 'novel' which I, in my youth and innocence, had scribbled; and you declared it was good. Therefore, when I inflict these pages upon you— for I shall expect you to read them!—you have but yourself to blame for this sad result of your past rashness." He wrote a particularly touching inscription in Mary Louise's presentation copy:

> When I was young I longed to write a great novel that should win me fame. Now that I am getting old my first book is written to amuse children. For, aside from my evident inability to do anything "great," I have learned to regard fame as a will-o-the-wisp which, when caught, is not worth the possession; but to please a child is a sweet and lovely thing that warms one's heart and brings its own reward. I hope my book will succeed in that way—that the children will like it. You and I have inherited much the same temperament and literary taste and I know you will not despise these simple tales, but will understand me and accord me your full sympathy.[62]

What a fortunate change of direction!

Matilda Gage must have been pleased to see the result of her advice to Frank. She was too sick during the winter of 1897–98 to speak at the fiftieth anniversary convention of the National American Woman Suffrage Association, as she had planned; but she wrote an address from her sick bed in the Baums' house that was read at the convention and highly praised. In March, she had a fatal stroke. Maud missed Matilda dreadfully; she wrote to her sister Helen two months afterward that she could hardly bear her loneliness: "She was so thoughtful of me [,] so worried when I fell ill. I feel as if I had lost all that especially care about me. Frank is good and kind, but he is different from Mother, and I do want her so."[63]

The women in the Gage family remained warmly attached all their lives. The families often visited each other for extended periods. Julia Carpenter could forget her chronic illnesses and complaints only in the company of her mother and sisters. Robert Baum spent several summers with the Carpenters in Edgeley, North Dakota; and in 1898, his father was with him from July until September. During part of this visit they camped out rather luxuriously in the hills where Frank Carpenter was putting up hay, with a cooking shanty on wheels, two portable rooms, and a portable bath. The Carpenters' son Harry, who was Robert's age, was almost like a brother to the Baum boys; and Harry idolized his Uncle Frank. Maud's three nieces—Magdalena Carpenter, Matilda Jewell Gage (Clarkson's daughter), and Leslie Gage (Helen's daughter)—were like the daughters the Baums never had. Maud was so fond of Magdalena, whom she thought was most like herself, that she wanted to adopt her. She pointed out that she and Frank could give Magdalena all the advantages the Carpenters could not, but Julia would not hear of it.[64] Harry Carpenter and the girls made frequent long visits to Chicago and to the cottage the Baums were to buy at Macatawa Park, an attractive resort on Lake Michigan. Matilda came to see the World's Fair in 1893.

Late in 1897, Read introduced Baum to William Wallace Denslow at the Press Club, and they became close friends. Denslow, who was the same age as Baum, was a very successful newspaper artist and designer of posters and book covers. Because he signed his pictures with a seahorse, he came to be known as "Hippocampus Den." Denslow was a gregarious, popular man, although he was also sardonic and derisive. One of his most famous pictures showed a skull crowned with laurel, with the caption "What's the Use?" He suggested that Chicago's coat of arms be "a sluggish sewer with two branches, a Hog Rampant on a field of orr [or], supported by two shorn lambs." Eunice Tietjens described Denslow as "a delightful old reprobate who looked like a walrus."[65] Although Baum and Denslow were temperamentally quite different, Denslow's cynicism would have appealed to the sardonic streak in Baum.

Baum was too busy with *The Show Window* to do much original work in 1898, apart from a few stories and verses.[66] But he did collect his verse in *By the Candelabra's Glare*, a beautiful little book that he printed and bound himself and got eight artist friends to illustrate, including Denslow, who was to illustrate three of his books; his sister Harriet's son-in-law Peirce, who did not illustrate "Phunnyland" but was to do *Daughters of Destiny*; and Ralph Fletcher Seymour, who was to hand letter *Father Goose* and decorate *American Fairy Tales*. Baum recompensed Denslow for his two pen and ink sketches by hiring him to draw the cover of the November 1898 *Show Window*.[67]

Baum published his book himself in a limited edition of ninety-nine copies for his friends. He dedicated it to his friend Harrison H. Rountree, a cheerful, optimistic businessman, brother-in-law of his publisher Williams. The verses, Baum freely admitted, were not remarkable. The first describes how, when he cannot sleep, he writes verses "By the candelabra's glare." Actually, he confesses in a note, he wrote by gaslight, but after his friend Mr. Costello designed him a cover with a candelabra, he "wrote the verse to give the cover countenance." The opening sections consist of love poems suggestive of greeting cards and "Cycling Verse," on subjects such as girls intentionally falling off their bicycles so that men will catch them in their arms. Baum included "La Reine Est Morte—Vive La Reine" from the *Times-Herald* and "Two Women," a dialogue that considers the feminist issue more thoughtfully. Woman New proclaims her wide interests and accomplishments, Woman Old celebrates the value of wife and motherhood; each is convinced the other is missing out on what is most important and has failed to understand woman's true nature and function; Baum does not commit himself but ends with the question, "which was right?"

"Nance Adkins," which Baum reprinted from the *Aberdeen Saturday Pioneer* of March 1, 1890, is a touching story of a good farm wife who secretly applied for seed wheat when her husband was too proud to do so, and thereby saved the family from starvation. In "The Heretic," an attack on conventional Christianity, the heretical speaker shows himself better than the pious deacon who tells him he will go to hell. While the heretic always tries "To help my feller man," the deacon drove a starving father from his door, prompting the heretic to declare, "This selfish Christianity/Ain't good enough fer me!" The final section of the book consists of puerile children's verses, some of which, such as "Who's Afraid?", were to reappear in *Father Goose.*

Baum inscribed copy five to Mary Louise with verses explaining why "verse-mongers" print their own books to delight/annoy their friends and suggesting that she print a book herself. The inscription on copy three, to "My darling Mother," shows affection but some distance between them: "I hope you will like these little stories in verse. My favorite one is 'Nance Adkins.' You must remember, in reading 'The Heretic' that it is the heretic himself who is speaking, and that he only finds fault with *selfish* Christianity, which I am sure, dear, that *you* do not approve of."

Baum's mother was pained by her son's disregard for conventional religion, for she was a devout Methodist who had reared her children with strict observance of the Sabbath. He liked to tease her with fictitious biblical citations. Once when she accused him of telling her an untrue story, "he replied at once, with a straight face, 'Well, Mother, as you know, Saint Paul in his Epistle to the Ephesians said, "All men are liars." ' " She thought gravely a moment and then told him he must be wrong, for she did not recall that quotation. Nevertheless, despite having "been fooled many times before," she could not resist getting out her Bible and looking up the imaginary verse.[68] Baum does not seem to have been very close to his mother, in contrast to his relationships with his siblings and Matilda Gage. Although she lived until 1905, he never dedicated a book to her. Their differing religious values might have been one of the factors that kept them apart. Matilda Gage found Cynthia Baum intolerable, writing from the Baums' house some time in 1896, "Mrs. Baum is here for six weeks or so and behaves like a child. She is terrible;—saps my vitality [.] I wish I could get away while she is here."[69]

One Sunday Cynthia Baum was visiting the Baums at Flournoy Street when Frank was attending the Cubs baseball game at their stadium nearby, as he regularly did when he was in town. She heard the loud cheers and boos from the ballpark and inquired disapprovingly about the unseemly noise on the Sabbath. Robert blurted out, "That's Daddy, yelling at the baseball game!" "There was stunned silence. Maud was embarrassed. The elder Mrs. Baum was shocked. That evening she lectured her son . . . and after that he passed up Sunday baseball whenever she was a visitor."[70]

Baum and Denslow decided to collaborate on a book that would combine old and new verses by Baum with illustrations by Denslow. Baum started off with an amusing conceit: because "Old Mother

Goose became quite new,/And joined a Woman's Club," poor Father Goose was left at home to amuse the children with his songs. Some of his verses imitate the simplicity of Mother Goose rhymes, such as one that describes "our friend the clock" who softly sings "Tick-Tock!" all day. Others exploit nonsense more self-consciously than Mother Goose ever did:

> Did you ever see a rabbit climb a tree?
> Did you ever see a lobster ride a flea?
>   Did you ever?
>   No, you never!
> For they simply couldn't do it, don't you see?

Baum and Denslow developed *Father Goose* together. Denslow found inspiration for comic illustrations in Baum's verses, and sometimes Baum invented verses to fit pictures Denslow drew. "One evening Baum casually mentioned that he had written a verse about an 'ostrich dance,' and Denslow quickly sketched an ostrich dancing with a little girl wearing ostrich plumes. Baum's initial conception was of an awkward fellow who moves like an ostrich, but Denslow's drawing was so charming that he scrapped his original verse and wrote a new one."[71]

Denslow's pictures are both stylish and humorous. Moreover, he did not merely draw illustrations for the verses; he arranged pictures, color, and text to make an artistically unified page, so that the book resembled "a series of art posters bound together." Even measures undertaken to save expense added to the attractiveness of the volume. Baum and Denslow persuaded their friend Ralph Fletcher Seymour to hand letter the verses to save printing costs. Their limitation of the color scheme to yellow, red, gray, and black inspired Denslow to interestingly creative use of a limited palette. This was by far the best work that Denslow had produced, and Baum fully appreciated it.[72]

By early 1899, they were ready to look for a publisher; and in March they registered two possible titles at the copyright office. They agreed to share the royalties equally. Nevertheless, Denslow prepared a cover with his name in big letters and Baum's in smaller ones. He had to be persuaded to re-letter the cover so as to give Baum equal credit. They approached the publisher George M. Hill, who specialized in cheap reprints of standard novels; he was not enthusiastic about the project, but he agreed to print and bind the book if Baum and

Denslow would pay the entire cost of publication. Later he saw some possibility of profit and invested some of his own money. In the final agreement, Baum and Denslow were to pay for the lavish illustrations, supplying "all the plates for the pages, cover, and even advertising posters," while "Hill would handle the other expenses, including binding, paper, and distribution." According to his son Harry, Baum was still not prosperous enough to cover his share of this cost and must have borrowed the money.[73] The book appeared in September.[74] Frank inscribed Maud's copy: "To my old chum ... with the hope that she will find this book instructive and elevating and will remember me as the goose who wrote it."[75]

It proved to be an outstanding success. By the end of the year, it had sold 75,500 copies. Baum's undistinguished verses appealed to children and to adults as well. The *Times-Herald* of September 17, 1899, found "a quaint funniness about this new Goose book ... the oldest and wisest heads will read it and laugh till the tears trickle." *The Home Magazine* said that "Many of Mr. Baum's verses will linger in the minds of the little ones and cling to them, probably, when they are old and gray." The reviewers were also, with greater justification, impressed with Denslow's illustrations, especially as a handsomely illustrated children's book was then a novelty in America.[76] According to Frank K. Reilly, then working in Hill's firm, *Father Goose* got "free publicity in the newspapers—because we had something absolutely new." In addition, Baum and Denslow got their friends in the Press Club to publish news items about the book. Ike Morgan showed it in two Christmas cartoons in the Chicago *Times-Herald* in December 1899.[77]

The Denslows hosted a New Year's Eve party at Rector's Restaurant at the end of 1899, to which they sent invitations decorated with *Father Goose* characters to the Baums, George Ade, Ike Morgan, and other close friends. Baum wrote in the Denslows' guest book:

> Our Den once made a picture—"What's the Use?"
> Which filled us with dejection and with sorrow
> And then he illustrated Father Goose—
> That he who sighed today might laugh tomorrow
> Which proves the use of Father Goose
> And makes me bold to mention
> There's no excuse for "What's the Use?"—
> A Misanthrope's Contention.

The Denslows gave a similar party on New Year's Eve in 1900, and Baum wrote in the guest book: "the new Century looks upon many artists—but only one 'Den' [here he sketched a seahorse] God bless him! May his pencil never lose its point or his hippocampus its alert and valiant expression."[78]

However, the conflict over who should get primary credit for their joint productions remained unresolved. When the *New York World* commissioned Denslow to draw a full-page picture based on *Father Goose*, Denslow did not share his payment of one hundred dollars with Baum, the co-owner of the copyright; and when the comic page appeared in January 1900, it listed Denslow as the "famous creator of 'Father Goose,' " without mentioning Baum. On a second comic page, which appeared that summer, both names did appear as collaborators on *Father Goose* and the forthcoming *Wizard of Oz*. Baum retaliated by identifying himself as "the original 'Father Goose' " when he published *American Fairy Tales* in several newspapers the following winter and later in book form.[79] Nevertheless, Baum and Denslow cooperatively capitalized on the success of *Father Goose* by contracting with Alberta N. Hall (later Burton) to write music for twenty-six of the verses; and Hill brought out *The Songs of Father Goose, for the Home, School and Nursery* in June 1900. It "made money, which was all that it was expected to do." Royalties were divided among Baum, Denslow, and Hall.[80]

Meanwhile, on January 20, 1900, Baum registered the title of *The Army Alphabet* at the copyright office. This picture book was a joint venture with two artist friends, consisting of verses by Baum, illustrated by Harry Kennedy and hand lettered by Charles Costello. They signed a contract with Hill on April 7, and Hill issued the book to coincide with the national encampment of the Grand Army of the Republic held in Chicago that summer. A matching volume, *The Navy Alphabet*, followed.[81] They are both handsome books, but the verses are too plain and simple to appeal to adults, and the illustrations lack the distinctive style of Denslow's. Both sold poorly.

After Way & Williams went out of business, their successor, H. S. Stone and Company, agreed to publish "Adventures in Phunnyland"; but they failed to get an illustrator. Armed by the success of *Father Goose*, Baum took the manuscript away to Robert Howard Russell in

New York, who published it in October 1900, as *A New Wonderland*. It was illustrated with self-conscious cuteness by Frank Ver Beck, but Baum preferred his work to Denslow's.[82]

The *New York Herald* of October 7, 1900, praised Baum's "humor and inventiveness . . . With a grave air he spins the most impossible yarns," although he is not "such a master of nonsense as Lewis Carroll." The reviewer shrewdly pointed to the failings of this early work, mechanical repetition of effects and lack of "the underlying logic which in a sort of wrong-headed way seems to justify the most bewildering of Carroll's fabrications." But, the reviewer concluded, "Mr. Baum is not Carroll, indeed, but he is Baum, and Baum is a very satisfactory personage in himself."[83]

A long letter to his brother Harry in Syracuse, written from Frank's home on Humboldt Park Boulevard on April 8, 1900, gives a fascinating picture of Frank Baum's situation and aspirations on the eve of his first real success. Frank Junior (then sixteen) "has controlled his anguish at the uncertainty of an appointment to Annapolis, and decided that West Point would do just as well and that he will be lucky if he gets either." All the boys have grown so that

> . . . I sometimes think I must be a kid no longer, when I behold the stalwarts around me and hear them call me 'dad.' There's a mistake some where, for I have failed to grow up—and we're just 5 boys together. The young 'uns are all great readers, but Frank is the only one with strongly developed military ambitions. Rob fills the house with electric batteries and such truck and we are prepared to hear a bell ring whenever we open a door or step on a stair. The other two have not yet developed a fad.

Frank reports that Mame (Mary Louise) and Henry Brewster visited and forgot their cares during their visit, and that he intends she shall come every year.

> I miss the friends at times. Here I have many acquaintances, but, outside my home, no intimates. I do not make friends easily, nor does Maud. Her brother often visits her and occasionally her sisters from Dakota come; but it has been a long time since one of my own family was here, and I could scarce bear to have Mame out of my sight. I wish more of you could come, and oftner.

He will "probably . . . make Chicago my home," as "The boys have grown up here and Maud likes it" and "is nearer her family, and her wishes are the most sacred."

However, he will "be able to go home oftener if I am successful."

> The financial success of my books is yet undetermined and will only be positively settled after the coming fall season. We only had three months sale of "Father Goose," and tho it made a hit and sold plenteously we cannot tell what it's [sic] future may be. . . . I have been grateful for it's [sic] success. The money has been a pleasure to us and my work is now sought by publishers who once scorned my contributions.

Harper Brothers, Scribner's, Appletons, Lothrops, and the Century have all approached him. "This makes me proud, especially as my work in Father Goose was not good work, and I know I can do better. But I shall make no contracts with anyone till next January. If my books succeed this year I can dictate terms and choose my publishers. If they fall down I shall try to discover the fault and to turn out some better stuff." He reports that *The Songs of Father Goose* will appear on June 1. He is fairly confident that *The Army Alphabet* and *The Navy Alphabet*, "wonderfully illustrated by Harry Kennedy" and scheduled to appear in May and August, will "catch on." He is delighted with Frank Ver Beck's illustrations "for my Phunniland book," to appear as "A New Wonderland" on July 1.

> Then there is the other book, the best thing I ever have written, they tell me, "The Wonderful Wizard of Oz." It is now in the press and will be ready soon after May 1st. Denslow has made profuse illustrations for it and it will glow with bright colors. Mr. Hill, the publisher, says he expects a sale of at least a quarter of a million copies on it. If he is right, that book alone solves my problem. But the queer, unreliable Public has not yet spoken. I only need *one* hit this year to make my position secure, and 3 of these books seem fitted for public approval. But there—who knows anything? I'm working at my trade, earning a salary to keep my family and holding fast to a certainty until the fiat has gone forth.

(He was to continue laboring on *The Show Window* for six months.) He closes by congratulating Harry on "winning fame and love daily, and some money—but not enough," expressing confidence that that too will come in due time, and telling him that he and Maud will go to Syracuse on May 10 to be with him on his birthday.[84] (In fact, Harry became a distinguished dermatologist.) Frank and Maud did stop in Syracuse on their way back from New York, where Frank had read the proofs of *A New Wonderland*.[85] As the branches of the Baum family became more prosperous, they visited each other regularly.

four

THE WONDERFUL WIZARD OF OZ, 1899–1900

In April 1900, *The Wonderful Wizard of Oz* had just gone to press with its final title. It was, as Baum told his brother, by far the best thing he had ever written. At the age of forty-four, he had at last found his vocation and learned to make the most of his talents and experience to produce a great imaginative work. He developed the stories he had been telling children for years into an extended, significant narrative, which brought together the exuberant fantasy and nonsensical humor of *A New Wonderland* and the attention to logic and realism of *Mother Goose*. He deepened his child's story with adult speculations about identity and appearance and reality. And he made good use of his own experience—of Matilda Gage's discussions of matriarchy and magic, of the illusions created by window dressers, of the grim lives of farmers trying to grow crops on drought-stricken prairies. Dorothy's little house in its vast empty setting closely resembled the one in which Maud's sister Julia became increasingly desperate.

Opening his fairy story with a grim naturalistic picture of a poor midwestern farm showed striking originality. In four simple paragraphs, he conveyed the vastness of the prairie, its lack of trees, its drought, its loneliness, its liability to cyclones, and the effects of these conditions upon those who lived there. At the same time, he set up a wonderfully effective background to contrast with Oz.

"Dorothy lived in the midst of the great Kansas prairies, with Uncle Henry, who was a farmer, and Aunt Em, who was the farmer's wife. Their house was small, for the lumber to build it had to be carried by wagon many miles. There were four walls, a floor and a roof, which made one room; and this room contained a rusty-looking cooking stove, a cupboard for the dishes, a table, three or four chairs, and the beds." Then, after two sentences explaining the cyclone cellar:

When Dorothy stood in the doorway and looked around, she could see nothing but the great gray prairie on every side. Not a tree nor a house broke the broad sweep of flat country that reached the edge of the sky in all directions. The sun had baked the plowed land into a gray mass, with little cracks running through it. Even the grass was not green, for the sun had burned the tops of the long blades until they were the same gray color to be seen everywhere. Once the house had been painted, but the sun blistered the paint and the rains washed it away, and now the house was as dull and gray as everything else.

When Aunt Em came there to live she was a young, pretty wife. The sun and wind had changed her, too. They had taken the sparkle from her eyes and left them a sober gray; they had taken the red from her cheeks and lips, and they were gray also. She was thin and gaunt, and never smiled, now. When Dorothy, who was an orphan, first came to her, Aunt Em had been so startled by the child's laughter that she would scream and press her hand upon her heart whenever Dorothy's merry voice reached her ears; and she still looked at the little girl with wonder that she could find anything to laugh at.

Uncle Henry never laughed. He worked hard from morning till night and did not know what joy was. He was gray also, from his long beard to his rough boots, and he looked stern and solemn, and rarely spoke.[1]

In language that seems absolutely artless and direct, Baum makes us see the harsh physical setting, the poverty, and what happens to people trapped in an unceasing battle with nature. *Gray* moves from a physically descriptive term—conveying the appearance of the landscape in a single word—to one that expresses human joylessness and loss of hope. The simple statement that Toto "was not gray" and saved Dorothy "from growing as gray as her other surroundings"[2] tells us better than any labored psychological analysis that animals refresh us by their happy freedom from human cares and apprehensions. The surface is simple—plain words, straightforward sentences, concrete images—but the content is far from simple-minded.

Although Baum limited his details to those a child can understand, his description is as powerful as those of the realist Hamlin Garland, whose family left Iowa to settle near Aberdeen. After repeated years of drought, nearly everyone Garland saw, "even the young men, looked worn and weather-beaten and some appeared both silent and sad. Laughter was curiously infrequent." His cheerful little sister Jessie "admitted that something gray had settled down over the plain." "No green thing was in sight, and no shade offered save that made by the little cabin. On every side stretched scanty yellowing fields of grain."[3] Garland's story "A Branch Road" tells how a young man returns after seven years to see his former sweetheart, now a wife still in her twenties, and finds her "worn and wasted incredibly. The blue of her eyes seemed dimmed and faded by weeping, and the old-time scarlet of her lips had been washed away."[4]

It took courage to start a child's story so naturalistically. Garland had been abused for his "false interpretations of Western life." Critics produced statistics to show that farmers owned pianos and Brussels carpets and that tilling the prairie soil was "the noblest vocation in the world"—even though corn then sold for eleven cents per bushel and all the bright boys and girls were leaving the farm.[5] The nation still wanted to idealize the rural Midwest as the site of traditional American values.

Perhaps Baum avoided placing Dorothy in South Dakota, the grim area he knew intimately, in order to spare the feelings of his Gage relatives still living there. It was appropriate to move her to Kansas, where conditions were similar, because the Kansas editor William Allen White had recently lambasted his state's poverty and hopelessness in an editorial "What's the Matter with Kansas?" This editorial was highly praised and widely reprinted, so it gave Kansas a particular topical interest.

In *The Wizard* Baum first perfected the tone that distinguished all his best fantasies, a tone that is authentically childlike without sinking into simple-mindedness. He entirely avoided self-conscious adult mannerisms such as writing down from a position of superior sophistication or conjuring up the mysterious, poetic atmosphere that adults assume is appropriate to fantasy. Instead he told his story as a child would experience it, grounding it in a child's understanding of reality. Both Kansas and Oz are presented in a matter-of-fact way; Dorothy takes things as they come, without speculating about them; she reacts, interprets, and judges with a small child's simplicity. Baum retained enough of his childish self to give him wonderful insight into children's understanding and feelings. The distinctive colors of the countries of Oz, for example, reflect a child's preoccupation with favorite colors and a child's possible misinterpretation that the colors on maps represent the actual colors of the various countries.[6] At the same time, Baum did not literally come down to a child's level; he managed to incorporate sophisticated humor and philosophical interests into his text without falsifying the child's plain, direct view of things.

Dorothy is not highly individualized, which makes it easier for readers to identify with her. Even her age is not specified. Hearn plausibly calculates (on the basis of a hint in *The Tin Woodman of Oz*) that she must have been five or six when she first visited Oz, and Denslow drew her as a child of that age. She is remarkably self-possessed and skilled for a six year old; consider how efficiently she organizes the Winkies to rescue the Scarecrow and the Tin Woodman after the Witch of the West is dead. Her method, however, is one a child can understand: "she chose a number of the Winkies who looked as if they knew the most, and they all started away."[7]

It is not necessary to know Dorothy's age or physical appearance. What is important is her realistic consciousness, which validates the marvelous events, and her admirable character, which provides a role model. She is kind, responsible, self-reliant, brave, sensible, honest, self-confident, yet unpretentious—just what a child would like to be and what she ought to be. She has clear ideas of what is right and true, and calmly holds to them regardless of what older and stronger people say. She believed that she must obtain the Wizard's help to get home, and so she quietly insisted on seeing him, knowing it was a reasonable request, even though no one had ever thought of seeing him before. Even when she was being carried off by a cyclone, she had the presence of mind to realize that "hours passed and nothing terrible happened," so "she stopped worrying and resolved to wait calmly and see what the future would bring."[8] By presenting her reaction as the only sensible, logical one, Baum gave an implicit lesson in how to face unfamiliar situations.

Through Dorothy, Baum shows his child readers their capacities and reassures them that they can meet challenges, without ceasing to be polite and considerate. As Roger Sale points out, the children in European fairy tales tend to be potential victims of ogres, witches, or stepmothers and are seldom "presumed to be naturally adequate." Since Baum's protagonists are capable, "he can let them carry on, without his intervening as narrator."[9]

Boy readers do not have trouble identifying with Dorothy, because she has qualities they admire and adventures that engage them. But she is a particularly helpful example to girls. In contrast to the usual situation in fairy tales, where female characters must be assisted by males and find validation through a lover or father, Dorothy is independent: she deals with adventures on her own and achieves her ends—overcoming evil obstacles and returning home—through her own strength of character, common sense, and exertions. Moreover, she helps three male characters to become complete human beings (or lions). Her example even inspires the Wizard to leave his secluded palace for a healthier normal life in Omaha. Fantasy can provide opportunities that real life (or realistic fiction) does not, especially for girls—opportunities for children to use their own understanding and strength to deal with whatever problems life or adult demands present.

Knowing only Kansas, Dorothy marvels at the rich greenery, flowing streams, and prosperous farms of Oz; but actually it is only a slightly heightened version of inviting rural parts of the United States, such as Baum's home area around Syracuse. Unlike Mo, Oz is governed by the natural laws we know: "The rain, the streams, and the rivers are only water...nothing grows on the trees and bushes but fruits, nuts and berries [until later books]...the Yellow Brick Road falls into disrepair when it is not taken care of."[10] The general friendliness, of Dorothy and her companions and of most of the people they meet, is that of rural America at its best. Ideologically, the settled parts of Oz are close to the pastoral Midwest (Iowa rather than Kansas or the Dakotas), idealized by many writers of the time as a happy medium between wilderness and urban-industrial evils. This was a place where hard work could be counted on to produce comfortable prosperity, and the traditional American traits of self-reliance and egalitarianism flourished. Stephen Dale, a New York journalist, wrote in 1904 of the Midwest: "There is a notable absence of pretense, a willingness to be thought poor if they are poor and an equal willingness to be known as rich when rich.... Every man who approaches a stranger is taken to be honest until he proves himself to be otherwise."[11] As Alison Lurie deftly put it: "Oz itself can be seen as an idealized version of America in 1900, happily isolated from the rest of the world, underpopulated, and largely rural, with an expanding magic technology and what appear to be unlimited natural resources."[12]

The essential distinction between idealized America and Oz is that "the Land of Oz has never been civilized."[13] That is why witches practice magic there, animals talk, and scarecrows are alive. Civilization in this context suggests the social conventions that limit imaginative possibilities by defining what is real, prescribing roles, and controlling nature. Nature in Oz, however, is not necessarily benign: it includes ferocious hybrid beasts and poppies so potent they can put animals to sleep forever as effectively as morphine can in our world.

Untamed nature had particular symbolic importance at this time because the Superintendent of the Census had officially announced, in 1890, that the frontier had closed. This was not strictly accurate geographically, but its psychological implications were profound: the uncontrollable, unknown, unpredictable area of the country had been tamed, and Americans' opportunities for adventure were henceforth limited. In a famous lecture prompted by the announcement, "The Significance of the Frontier in American History" (1893), the historian Frederick Jackson Turner defined the frontier as "the meeting point between savagery and civilization." He argued that the frontier experience was the primary factor in shaping American character and institutions. This experience developed the qualities on which Americans pride themselves—individualism, independence, practicality, inventiveness, disregard for forms and hierarchy, idealism, and optimism.[14] These are the qualities that distinguish Baum's thoroughly admirable American characters.

North America had been "civilized" from Atlantic to Pacific, but Oz was unknown and untamed. In *The Wizard* and subsequent books, it provided a never-ending source of exciting new countries for the protagonists to explore. Oz is wonderful because it constantly offers unexpected happenings and adventures unlimited by the actualities of daily life. Although it later became a utopia, in *The Wizard* Oz is utopian only to the extent that people are normally nice, good is reliably more powerful than evil, and perseverance and good sense always bring success. When we first see Oz, bondage is widespread, people age and die, goods are bought and sold, there are prosperous and seedy areas. The country is ruled by a tricky politician (who will leave it to a stuffed man), and the court is filled with richly dressed courtiers who "had nothing to do but talk to each other, but . . . always came to wait outside the Throne Room every morning."[15]

Warren Hollister identifies the outstanding merit of *The Wizard of Oz* and its successors as the believability of the fantastic world; Oz has a seeming reality not found in more artfully described fantasy lands. Therefore the books can give children the "experience of going into another universe where everything is brighter and more fragrant, more dangerous and more alive—a world of intensely satisfying unexpectedness—a real journey."[16] The cyclone that takes Dorothy to Oz is at once a typically American phenomenon and a force so unfamiliar to most readers that it borders on the supernatural. Thus Baum can ease into fairyland without our noticing it: Dorothy's house is seized up by the cyclone with her inside (definitely possible), she survives because the house is at the still center of the cyclone (sounds plausible), the house lands (as sometime it must) in a country that turns out to be magical. Baum's calm, matter-of-fact style continues unchanged from Kansas to Oz, suggesting that both are, of course, real. Dorothy first realizes she is in a very strange country when the nice old woman who is talking to her announces, to the child's horror, that she is the Witch of the North. But she goes on to explain that she is a good witch.

Baum got his concept of good witches (which upsets fundamentalists to this day) from Matilda Gage. He agreed with her that magic was simply a form of knowledge and that witches (and sorcerers) were people with extraordinary knowledge, who could use it for good or ill, depending on their character. Because only the female witches have real power, Oz is a matriarchy. The only male leader and magic worker is a humbug, who cannot really accomplish anything. The whole story is organized around the witches: the Witch of the North, who sets Dorothy on her way, the Witch of the South, who resolves her problem at the end, and the Witch of the West, who is the major antagonist.

As in traditional fairy tales, powerful witches represent the all-powerful mother, and wicked ones represent the bad mother. Baum gives Dorothy the opportunity, enviable to any child, of killing the bad mother without guilt. Her first "act" in Oz is to kill the Wicked Witch of the East, but since she does it accidentally, she can remain "an innocent, harmless little girl."[17] Later she will become justifiably angry at the Wicked Witch of the West and destroy her by throwing a bucket of water over her—and still remain innocent because she had no idea that water would melt her.[18] The witches of the North and South, of course, are the kind, protective, helpful good mother.

Wonderful as Oz is, Dorothy is eager to get back to her aunt and uncle. As any child knows, the security and love of home and family are more important to a child than anything else. Presumably we may hope that Kansas is not quite so gray at the end as at the beginning: Uncle Henry has found the resources to build a new house,[19] and Dorothy will always have the imaginative possibilities represented by Oz. Oz affirms the validity of the imaginative life that will preserve Dorothy from becoming gray like her surroundings.

Although the Witch of the North talked to Dorothy like an ordinary helpful old lady, she left her by simply whirling around and disappearing. Dorothy, knowing the ways of witches, was not surprised; but

Toto "barked after her loudly enough when she had gone, because he had been afraid even to growl while she stood by."[20] Toto, an entirely natural dog in a land of humanized animals, contributes contrast and authenticity to the story.

The fantasy is constantly anchored with realistic detail. We are kept informed when and what Dorothy eats and what she feeds to Toto. Like the responsible child she is, she locks the door when she leaves her house. The Wizard's plan for getting her and himself home in an ascension balloon is credibly worked out. We see Dorothy sewing strips of silk together to make a big bag and the Wizard painting it with a coat of thin glue to make it airtight.[21] He explains that there is no suitable gas (hydrogen) in Oz, but they can use hot air, although it is not so good because if it cools the balloon will come down. Because of such details, and because Baum's descriptions of fantastic characters and events are as clear and forthright as his description of Kansas, Oz is a land children "can not only dream of but completely visualize, enter into, and enjoy."[22]

Scarecrows were still common in cornfields in Baum's day, and farmers often took pride in making and dressing them. The Tin Woodman also had a basis in real life: a dummy of metal parts, with a washboiler for a torso, stovepipes for limbs, the underside of a saucepan for a face, and a funnel hat, which Baum had created for a hardware store window display.[23] Like the Scarecrow, he is brought convincingly alive by being concretely realized; he cannot move until Dorothy and the Scarecrow oil and work his joints one by one.

Dorothy is surprised when the Scarecrow winks at her. But with her characteristic calm acceptance of the most unexpected happenings, she takes him down from his pole when he asks her to and is soon walking and conversing with him. He explains that he knows nothing because he has no brains, which seems logical, but as we shall see is fallacious; his problem is that he has no experience. As soon as he is created, he has a consciousness, comparable to the tabula rasa that philosophers have used to describe the undeveloped human mind. He begins to take in information as soon as he has working ears and eyes and to build it into interpretations. As the story goes on and he gains experience, he becomes very intelligent; in chapter 7, for example, he is the one to figure out how to cross gulfs and escape the Kalidahs.

One reason why Baum's best children's tales never seem simpleminded is that he deals with genuine intellectual questions. Although presented in the form of simple concepts in plain language, the questions themselves can interest children of all ages and adults as well. The Scarecrow's quest (and those of the Tin Woodman for the capacity to love and the Cowardly Lion for courage) raise searching questions about the nature of these complex qualities. It is easy to see the characters' naïveté, but Baum also raises doubts about definitions conventionally accepted as adequate. The Scarecrow cannot understand why Dorothy should want to leave beautiful Oz to return to gray Kansas, and Dorothy explains that if he had brains, he would know that home is best, however dreary it may be. He responds that if the heads of flesh and blood people "were stuffed with straw, like mine, you would probably all live in the beautiful places, and then Kansas would have no people at all. It is fortunate for Kansas that you have brains."[24] Baum (who moved all over the United States in search of better places) slyly leaves us to wonder whether it is their brains that keep people from leaving home, and if so whether brains are an advantage.

Because the Scarecrow has human consciousness, he assumes he is a man. And of course Baum presents him as one, implying that his painted face and straw stuffing are inconsequential. Similarly, the Tin Woodman is defined by his consciousness of himself, which is based on his memory of the experiences he accumulated through life (according to John Locke's theory). Thus he remains the same man even though his body parts have been replaced one by one with tin. As he explains in a later book, "A man with a wooden leg or a tin leg is still the same man; and, as I lost parts of my meat body by degrees, I always remained the same person as in the beginning, even though in the end I was all tin and no meat."[25] It is analogous to a problem posed by ancient thinkers: if a ship's parts wear out one by one and are replaced, is it the same ship when all have been replaced? Baum's belief in reincarnation must have intensified his interest in this question, since that doctrine presupposes some sort of continuing consciousness independent of the physical body; a person somehow remains the same even though s/he acquires a different body and brain in each incarnation.[26] The only difference between the flesh and the tin woodman is that he no longer loves his fiancée because he no longer has a heart—or at least he thinks that is the reason.

Baum gets much fun from the obsessions of the Scarecrow and the Woodman with what they believe they lack. The Tin Woodman suggests the Lion's lack of courage might result from heart disease and fatuously regrets that his lack of a heart prevents his ever having this experience (one Baum himself knew all too well). The Scarecrow reveals the silliness of his obsession when he wistfully asks the Lion if he has brains, to which the beast sensibly replies, "I suppose so. I've never looked to see."[27] The Lion, lacking human self-consciousness, never gets as silly as they do.

The constant reiteration of the words *brain, heart, courage* forces the reader to think about the difference between the outward signs of qualities and what they really are. If you feel tenderly for others, you do not need a heart in your chest; if you act bravely whenever courage is called for, it does not matter that your heart beats fast when there is danger.

Baum raises another question of appearance and reality when the travelers reach the Emerald City. The Guardian of the Gate locks green spectacles over their eyes, "Because if you did not wear spectacles the brightness and glory of the Emerald City would blind you." The Wizard ordered that they be locked on when the city was first built.[28] When the travelers get inside the city, they find that even the sky, the sun, and the people's skins are green—a hint that the color resides in their glasses rather than in what they see. This is confirmed when they remove their glasses and see that Dorothy's apparently green dress is really white. Fakery with green glasses recalls an old rural joke, which Baum had repeated in "Our Landlady": a farmer in a drought-blighted area puts green glasses on his horses so they will accept wood shavings as grass.

At the same time, however, the city is genuinely splendid, built all of marble and emeralds. Thus the Emerald City is both wonderful *and* fake, just like the White City of the Columbian Exposition. The White City was not real in the sense of being a permanent, workable city where people could live; its impressive buildings and statues were not made of marble, but of staff, a composition of plaster with cement and fibre added. But it was a vision of what an ideal city could be, and ideals have their own reality and significance. In the same way, the total greenness of the Emerald City—the exact opposite of the *gray* of Kansas and Nebraska—fulfills people's need for an ideal even if it is not altogether what it seems.

The humbug Wizard is a quintessentially American figure placed in the middle of fairyland. He first appears (to Dorothy) as an enormous Head, thus supporting his reputation as a sorcerer who can take any form he chooses. The disembodied Head understandably terrifies her, but it was a common illusion performed by magicians in American sideshows. In relating the episode, Baum artfully planted clues as to the

Head's true nature: its eyes roll so very conspicuously, while the rest of it (except the mouth) does not move at all. Its answer to Dorothy's request suggests a Gilded Age American rather than a mighty sorcerer: "You have no right to expect me to send you back to Kansas unless you do something for me in return. In this country everyone must pay for everything he gets."[29] This strikes an intentionally jarring note in a country where requests for help are met as a matter of course.

The Wonderful Wizard is ultimately exposed as a clever little showman from Omaha, who impressed the uncivilized people of Oz with cheap nineteenth-century American tricks in the same way that Mark Twain's Connecticut Yankee amazed the people of Arthurian England. The Wizard was drawn from two conspicuous American types, showmen like P. T. Barnum, who gloried in fooling the public, and popular politicians, who did the same thing more subtly. Barnum was famous for the bold impostures that he not only devised but got away with. The people loved his American Museum, where a picture outside promised a beautiful eight-foot mermaid, half woman and half fish, while inside they found the preserved head of a monkey attached to the dried body of a fish. Barnum entertained visitors to his home, an exotic Oriental-style mansion, with the illusion of the disembodied head. He candidly recounted such deceptions, with precise details, in his best-selling autobiography, *Struggles and Triumphs* (1854). He proudly called himself a humbug, and newspapers often wrote about "the marvelous, wonderful wizard P. T. Barnum."[30] The Wizard's explanation of his creation of the great Head and other apparent magic also reflects Baum's own fascination with special effects. He was writing *The Show Window* at the same time as *The Wizard*. He had proudly advertised the Great Ship Scene in "The Maid of Arran," and he enjoyed devising elaborate scenic effects for all his subsequent shows.

The Wizard describes himself as a ventriloquist and a balloonist, familiar figures to anyone who attended the circuses that traveled all over the United States in Baum's time. The balloonist advertised the arrival of the circus by going up in a captive balloon, which would be visible for miles against the prairie skies. If the rope holding him to the ground broke, he could be carried away by the wind. Barnum and Bailey's balloonist, Washington Donaldson, who was also a magician and ventriloquist, disappeared in a storm over Lake Michigan in 1875 and was never seen again.[31]

The Wizard's ventriloquism—that is, his different voices for different occasions—his failure to deliver on his promises, and his supplying the people "with colored glasses that make life greener than it really is"[32] are the tricks of a politician. The Wizard came from Nebraska like William Jennings Bryan, the most charismatic politician of the time. When the Wizard reappears in *Dorothy and the Wizard in Oz*, we learn that Bryan's father was a politician and that he himself used to be with Bailum and Barney's circus.

Throughout Baum's work there is a characteristically American skepticism about the authority and superiority of leaders and a characteristically American faith in the capacity of ordinary people to govern themselves. The mighty ruler of Oz is a humbug without real power who has usurped the throne; he is unmasked by four unpretentious private citizens. Rulership in *The Land of Oz* is contested between two undeserving and incompetent candidates. In *Queen Zixi of Ix*, the throne of Noland goes to the forty-seventh person who happens to pass through a gateway, a child who lacks judgment to rule. In *John Dough and the Cherub*, the people of Hiland and Loland are so desperate for a ruler that they hand over the throne to a gingerbread man. Leaders gain their position not through ability, public spirit, or divine right, but shrewd opportunism (the Wizard), selfish aggression (Jinjur), or chance (Bud and John Dough).

Although the humbug Wizard cannot solve Dorothy's objective problem, he does satisfy her companions. He spells out what Baum has been implying all along—that the material brains the Scarecrow longs for are merely an emblem of experience and the intelligence to use it, that the Lion already has true courage, which is "facing danger when you are afraid." But when they persist, he agrees to give them what they want. He delights the Scarecrow with some bran-new brains, made of bran and mixed with pins to make him sharp. (Baum controlled his love of puns in *The Wizard*, but overindulged it in other works, especially his musical plays.) The Wizard obliges the Lion by giving him some courage out of a bottle (a sly reference to Dutch courage). Here Baum is not satirizing humbuggery, but the gullibility that encourages it. How, the Wizard asks himself, "can I help being a humbug . . . when all these people make me do things that everybody knows can't be done?"[33] As Baum had suggested in *The Show Window*, it may be wrong to mislead people, but the wrong is almost justified by their folly in demanding to be promised gratification of impossible wishes.

The results reinforce Baum's point that what the three receive is worthless. "The Scarecrow told them there were wonderful thoughts in his head; but he would not say what they were because he knew no one could understand them but himself."[34] Obviously these incommunicable thoughts are less valuable than the problem-solving intelligence he has been demonstrating all along. The Tin Woodman feels that his silk heart is kinder and more tender than his original one, but he is still indifferent to the girl he had loved as a man. The Lion is delighted to have become fearless, but his behavior remains as it always was.

Yet in a way the Wizard has helped the three friends, for they believe he has, which amounts to the same thing. He has given them the self-confidence to recognize their own worth. In the same way, he has been a good ruler, even though he became one under false pretenses. After he left, the people remembered him lovingly because he built the beautiful Emerald City for them; it does not really matter that they did the actual work themselves. Baum makes us question the distinction between what is "objectively" true and what is believed to be true, just as he blurs the distinction between the magical worlds he describes, which are real in our imaginations, and the everyday world in which we actually live.

Baum had been developing ideas for *The Wizard of Oz* for several years in stories he told to the local children. After the family moved to Humboldt Park Boulevard, where for the first time Frank had a den for himself, he began writing down the stories as "The Emerald City." He wrote with his left hand in soft pencil on a pad on his knee, sitting in a leather-upholstered armchair with first one leg and then the other draped over its arm. His handwriting was so legible that the book was typeset from his longhand copy. He was to keep the last pencil stub, frame it, and hang it on the wall of his study in Hollywood, labeled "With this pencil I wrote the MS. of *'The Emerald City.'* Finished Oct. 9th, 1899."[35]

Shortly after he began writing, Baum showed his manuscript to Denslow. They worked together in Baum's den, while Baum chain-smoked cigars and Denslow puffed on his pipe.[36] They would discuss the story; then Denslow made sketches, which might have helped Baum to develop his plot and characters. In an interview of 1904, Denslow implied that the Cowardly Lion was a joint creation. Probably in the spring of 1899, Baum and Denslow signed a contract to create " 'The City of Oz' or some other appropriate name."[37]

Denslow's illustrations certainly enhanced the originality and seem-

of each mouse and the other end to the truck. Of course the truck was a thousand times bigger than any of the mice who were to draw it; but when all the mice had been harnessed they were able to pull it quite easily. Even the Scarecrow and the Tin Woodman could sit on it, and were drawn swiftly by their queer little horses to the place where the Lion lay asleep.

After a great deal of hard work, for the Lion was heavy, they managed to get him up on the truck. Then

The Wonderful Wizard of Oz. The field-mice pull the Cowardly Lion out of the deadly poppy field. W. W. Denslow

ing reality of the finished book. His use of color in the plates is particularly attractive, creating a distinctive harmony with a limited range of related colors, determined by the relevant region of Oz. Plate XXXIV, "The Monkeys wound many coils around his body," is suffused with Winkie yellow, with a background of yellow sky and yellow-green grass with buttercups, an orange Lion, and brown monkeys. Denslow often enhanced the total effect by incorporating his pictures into the text, as in chapter 9, where the field mice pull the wagon on which the

the Queen hurriedly gave her people the order to start, for she feared if the mice stayed among the poppies too long they also would fall asleep.

At first the little creatures, many though they were, could hardly stir the heavily loaded truck; but the Woodman and the Scarecrow both pushed from behind, and they got along better. Soon they rolled the Lion out of the poppy bed to the green fields, where he could breathe the sweet, fresh air again, instead of the poisonous scent of the flowers.

sleeping Lion lies and the Scarecrow and the Tin Woodman push from behind. The Lion and wagon occupy the top of page 105, while the mice stream across the bottom of page 104. Green grass and bushes appear behind the text, for the travelers are near the Emerald City. The picture also shows Denslow's skill at drawing comic animals with human expressions, especially the dead-to-the-world Lion and the dignified Queen of the Field Mice. The Scarecrow actually looks as if he is both stuffed with straw and exerting muscle power. It is concrete visualizations like this that made Denslow feel he had jointly created the fantastic Oz characters.

By the fall Baum and Denslow had enough chapters and drawings to present to Hill. He agreed to publish the book as he had *Father Goose,* with Baum and Denslow supplying the plates and Hill paying all other costs. The author and illustrator were to share equally the 12 percent royalty payments, each receiving $0.09 for every copy sold at the list price of $1.50. However, Hill rejected their current title, "The Emerald City." By November 17, it had become "From Kansas to Fairyland." Denslow prepared a drawing for the copyright notice with the date 1899, probably hoping that it would be published in time for Christmas. But Hill decided to wait until he knew the public's reaction to *Father Goose.* As its sales mounted, Hill became more confident; and on January 15, 1900, he paid each man a $500 advance on their royalties. Three days later, Baum and Denslow jointly copyrighted their book as "The Land of Oz." Denslow prepared a title page with this title, but Baum still wanted something more eye-catching. "In early March Denslow pasted a paper label with Baum's final decision over the title page drawing, and the book went to press as *The Wonderful Wizard of Oz.*"[38] Baum dedicated it "to my good friend & comrade, My Wife."

Advance copies were available in May, when Baum presented an unbound copy to his sister Mary Louise during a visit to Syracuse. Hill received over 5,000 orders for the book during the summer. Officially published in September, it was an instant success, selling over 37,672 copies in fifteen months. This meant that each man got, in addition to his advance, a royalty payment of $1,423.98 on November 30 and $1,966.55 by the end of 1901.[39] Even so, *The Wizard* was not so immediately successful as *Father Goose,* which was still the best selling Baum-Denslow title when the Hill company went bankrupt in February 1902.[40]

Baum did not immediately recognize the success he had created. According to a family story related by Frank Junior, Maud asked Frank to go to Hill and request an advance on his royalties to help with Christmas presents for 1900. Baum demurred, thinking it unprofessional to ask for royalties before the customary semiannual payment in January. She insisted; he went to Hill's office, diffidently asked for whatever royalties had accumulated, and pocketed the check without looking at it. When he got home and handed her the check, they were both struck with astonishment at the amount—$3,432.64![41] Frank Junior garbled the numbers in his account, and his brother Harry later doubted its details. Harry did, however, recognize what it revealed about the relationship between Frank and Maud. Father protested, but Mother "felt that she needed some extra money, and, after further discussion, Father, as usual, did what Mother asked."[42]

According to Frank Junior, the name Oz came to his father as he was telling a group of children about Dorothy, the Scarecrow, and the Tin Woodman on May 7, 1898. When a child asked him where these adventures were taking place, he glanced at his file cabinet, noticed that the last drawer was labeled O–Z, and replied, "Oz." He remembered the exact date because there was a newspaper in the room that headlined Admiral Dewey's victory in Manila. However, this anecdote did not surface until April 1903 (and then without any precise date) in a Bobbs-Merrill press release announcing its reissue of *The Wizard.* Furthermore, Baum was known to make up good stories for interviewers. According to his nephew, Henry B. Brewster, he "always liked to tell wild tales, with a perfectly straight face, and earnestly, as though he really believed them himself, and he may have. . . . Frank Baum was one of the most imaginative of men. There was nothing wrong, but he did love to 'Fairytale,' or as you might say, tell 'white lies.' " In the absence of earlier evidence, most scholars do not credit the story. Jack Snow suggested that *Oz* might represent *Ahs* of wonder, and there have been other, less likely speculations.[43] It could be that Baum merely thought up a distinctive and amusing name, and it has no more meaning than his other monosyllabic names for countries, Ev, Mo, and Ix.

The name Dorothy, however, was not chosen by chance. Although Frank Junior insisted that Baum selected the name simply because he liked its sound and had thought of it for the daughter he longed to have, and that he did not even know any girl or woman with that name when he wrote *The Wizard,* this was only technically true. Actually there had been a cherished Dorothy in the family—a particularly enchanting baby born to the Clarkson Gages, who had died in 1898 at the age of five months and to whom Maud had been deeply attached.[44] The character of Dorothy may well have been inspired by Maud's favorite niece, Magdalena Carpenter, a bright, delightful child living with parents depressed by their grim environment.

The Wizard of Oz was widely reviewed, by at least 202 publications, and generally praised. Reviewers noted the book's use of realistic American material and its appeal to adults as well as children. On September 8, 1900, the *New York Times* reviewer judged that it was "ingeniously woven out of commonplace material." Although the adventures and dangers of Dorothy and her companions recalled those of traditional English fairy tales, Baum's tale had humor and "stray bits of philosophy," as well as "several new features and ideals of fairy life," such as the scarecrow and the humbug wizard. The October *Kindergarten Magazine* praised Baum for making Dorothy's "impossible" companions both real and lovable. Moreover, "Delightful humor and rare philosophy are found on every page." A Philadelphia newspaper reviewer predicted that the book's "philosophy and satire ... will furnish amusement to the adult and cause the juvenile to think some new and healthy thoughts. At the same time it is not objectionable in being too knowing." Reviews in the *Dial* (December 1) and the *Chicago Evening Post* (September 21), on the other hand, gave credit to Denslow more than Baum for the book's success; the *Dial* reviewer actually denied originality to Baum.[45]

In his introduction to *The Wizard*, Baum drew attention to what he saw as the distinctive features of his new type of fairy tale: "the stereotyped genie, dwarf and fairy are eliminated, together with all the horrible and blood-curdling incident devised by their authors to point a fearsome moral to each tale." His book "aspires to being a modernized fairy tale, in which the wonderment and joy are retained and the heart-aches and nightmares are left out." Fortunately for the dramatic impact of his story, he did not exactly follow these precepts.[46]

Baum used a traditional fairy-tale plot: his protagonist is removed from her normal setting and has to find her way back; she meets and helps three creatures, who in turn help her to reach her goal; she is befriended and opposed by witches, good and bad, who work magic by familiar methods. But he reinterpreted these traditional elements to make them new.

Baum did avoid the horrors of the Grimms' fairy tales, but he included frightening and heartbreaking things in *The Wizard*. The Wicked Witch of the West, who sees our four friends miles away from her castle and sends her flock of crows to "peck out their eyes and tear them to pieces,"[47] is an evil nightmare figure. Although characters in the Oz world are normally friendly and helpful, all the Oz books have genuine villains. However, Baum almost always took care to prevent them from being too frightening. The witch is reduced by the way Denslow drew her (a squat figure in pigtails, wearing a man's jacket and spats and carrying an umbrella), by the prosaic way she persecutes Dorothy (making her do general housework), and by the limitations on her power (she cannot harm Dorothy because she cannot overcome the protection of the good witch's kiss, and even Toto gets away with biting her).[48] Baum's wicked witches and the Nomes of later Oz books contrast strongly with such creatures as George MacDonald's goblins (in *The Princess and the Goblin,* 1872), another small underground race with evil intentions who are not humorous at all and who present a serious threat to the good characters. Not just in his happy endings, but throughout his stories, Baum reassures us that "the Power of Good . . . is greater than the Power of Evil."[49]

Many a child will weep over the Lion who could not run quite far enough to escape from the deadly poppy field, but

> . . . had given up, at last, and fallen only a short distance from the end of the poppy-bed, where the sweet grass spread in beautiful green fields before them.
>
> "We can do nothing for him," said the Tin Woodman, sadly; "for he is much too heavy to lift. We must leave him here to sleep on forever, and perhaps he will dream that he has found courage at last."[50]

However, Baum can always be counted on to avoid lasting heartaches by contriving a rescue. Using the traditional theme of little animals unexpectedly helping stronger ones who have been good to them, Baum has the Field Mice repay the Tin Woodman for saving their Queen's life by saving his friend the Lion. But they go about it with typical Baumian contrivance: the Tin Woodman builds a wagon, the Scarecrow asks each mouse to bring a piece of string, he hitches them to the wagon, and they pull the Lion out of the poppy field.

Baum renounces punitive morality devised "to point a fearsome moral," and he never preaches directly; but throughout the book he implicitly teaches kindness, helpfulness, courage, and responsibility. Dorothy is happy to help the Scarecrow by taking him along to see the Wizard, the two of them welcome the Tin Woodman to join them, and then the three welcome the Cowardly Lion; each addition promptly repays their helpfulness by contributing something to the success of the journey, according to his particular capacities. Here, as in all his works, Baum unobtrusively teaches a wholesome practical morality through examples, emphasizing the virtues that are understandable and recognizably valid to children. Knowing that children demand justice, he enforces it in his books: good deeds are rewarded and bad ones penalized, although usually with leniency.[51]

Years later, Baum further developed his ideas about fairy tales in an interview he gave at his summer home in Macatawa to a reporter from *The Advance,* the journal of the Congregational churches, printed on July 22, 1909. He repeated that stories for children should exclude "the tragic and the dreadful" and added that romantic love was not an appropriate theme for appealing to the imagination of children. He went on to explain that developing imagination, the capacity to envision what does not exist in the everyday world, was the essential function of fairy tales, a key idea that he reiterated throughout his career. Imagination is "one of the greatest factors and forces in human progress. Stunt, dwarf, or destroy the imagination of a child and you have taken away its chances of success in life. Imagination transforms the commonplace into the great and creates the new out of the old. No man ever made a new invention or discovery without imagination, and invention and discovery have made human progress."[52]

In *The Advance* of August 19, Baum defined his critical standards more precisely in an essay on "Modern Fairy Tales." Although he admired Andersen, he preferred Lewis Carroll because Alice appealed to children more "than any prince or princess that Andersen ever created. The secret of Alice's success lay in the fact that she was a real child, and any normal child could sympathize with her all through her adventures." Although the story is bewildering, for it has "neither plot nor motive in its relation," "Alice is doing something every moment, and doing something strange and marvelous, too; so the child follows her with rapturous delight." He urged parents to select "modern, up-to-date fairy tales" that would "feed the imaginative instinct of the little ones and develop the best side of child nature," and to "see that the story is not marred by murders or cruelties, by terrifying characters, or by mawkish sentimentality, love and marriage," as well as long passages describing the beauties of nature, which children do not yet appreciate. Giving children literature they cannot comprehend will simply destroy their pleasure in reading: "What they want is action—'something doing every minute'—exciting adventures, unexpected difficulties to be overcome, and marvelous escapes." "The children know very well that fairies and fairylands are apart from human life, even if they believe for a time that such things really exist. The myth concerning Santa Claus deceives few modern children, but delights them all."[53]

It is clear that Baum followed these principles in his own fairy tales. He put his finger on the qualities that make Alice appealing, which are those she shares with his protagonists: she is a real child, who is constantly having exciting adventures and handling difficulties. It doubtless increased Baum's appreciation that this active, thinking hero is, like his own, a girl. Like Carroll, Baum looked at his world from the child's point of view. Both Dorothy and Alice are faced with unfamiliar situations that they cannot understand; both are unfailingly sensible and right-thinking in face of arbitrary, incomprehensible behavior by more powerful adults.

The significant difference is that Dorothy is able to make sense of the confusing world she is plunged into and to influence it: people listen to her, and she can act effectively and resist unreasonable authority; her good sense and resolution win the success they deserve; she overcomes all obstacles in her path and gets home. Alice, on the other hand, is always subject to forces she cannot comprehend or control: she is ordered around, expected to follow rules she cannot know, bombarded with questions she cannot answer, driven in directions she has not chosen. This may be why Baum criticized Carroll's plots as bewildering. Baum's fantasy of an idealized world reassures children that they can solve puzzles and overcome difficulties. Carroll's gives exaggerated, concrete form to the frustrations children face in their everyday lives.

Baum's insistence that literary forms should be modernized to fit present-day American readers was common among his Chicago contemporaries. In *Crumbling Idols* (1894), Hamlin Garland demanded "a characteristic American literature" that embodied the present time with sincerity and truthfulness and had "such quality of texture and background that it could not have been written in any other place or by any one else but a native."[54] Baum's friend Ralph Fletcher Seymour noted that the artists who gathered in Chicago from the 1880s "recognized the brand of living in their neighborhood as peculiarly American, and undertook to translate their understanding of its beauty and meaning into art forms. They believed that art which would interest those around them would have to be expressed in terms of a home-grown, native art" and therefore turned away from "European, eastern or conventional rules [and models] for guidance in saying what they wanted to say."[55]

Although Baum emphasized modern time rather than American place in his critical statements, the details and ideals of *The Wizard of Oz* and most of his other stories are distinctively American (and, as such, contrast strikingly with the very English Alice books). Hierarchy is unselfconsciously ignored, whether it is the hierarchy of social class, gender, age, or species: Dorothy, quietly conscious of her worth, speaks forthrightly to the Witches and the Wizard and recognizes the equality of a Scarecrow and a Lion. Everyone is listened to with respect, and they work out problems together. And, in accordance with characteristic American optimism, all the problems do get solved by effort and practical sense.[56]

five

SUCCESSFUL AUTHOR,

1901–1903

Baum now recognized that his vocation was writing fairy stories, but not, evidently, that in *The Wizard of Oz* he had found the perfect expression of his distinctive style and imaginative vision. He had not thought of *The Wizard* as the first book of a series, but as a free-standing fairy tale brought to its logical conclusion. The "Author's Note" to *Dot and Tot of Merryland*, his next book, implies that he was following up the success of *The Wizard* by writing another (unrelated) fantasy for children. *Dot and Tot*, written for younger children and set in a different fairyland, is very different from *The Wizard*. Baum's other fairy stories of 1901, *American Fairy Tales* and *The Master Key: An Electrical Fairy Tale*, show equally different approaches to the same genre.

Dot and Tot of Merryland truly puts in practice Baum's principle of avoiding heartaches and nightmares in children's stories, perhaps because it was directed at a younger audience. Consequently we feel the want of the constant exciting adventures he himself recognized as necessary. It is an insipid string of fantastic descriptions, lacking narrative drive and dramatic tension.

Dot, daughter of a wealthy banker, goes to stay at Roselawn, which has the name and appearance of the author's fondly remembered childhood home. She meets Tot, the gardener's son, who speaks tiresome baby talk (which nineteenth-century American children's authors found irresistibly endearing); they go off in a boat on the river and are carried through a tunnel to Merryland, seven valleys connected by the river. The only hint of drama comes in the fourth valley, peopled by dolls and ruled by a lovely wax doll who is also a fairy. She normally keeps her doll subjects asleep, and when at Dot's request, she wakens them, they become impossibly naughty and unmanageable until the Queen puts them to sleep again with her magic wand.

The sixth valley contains wind-up toys, which are kept wound by Mr. Split, who splits into two halves so he can do twice the work. In this state he can speak only the left or right half of each word, depending on which half of him is talking; when he hooks his halves together, he speaks coherently. He was presumably intended to convey something about split versus integrated personality, but his significance is not developed. The book did not sell very well, and Baum turned to a more sophisticated audience.

In the *American Fairy Tales*, he aimed to Americanize the fairy tale, not by introducing familiar life into fairyland, as in *The Wizard of Oz*, but by putting magic and fairies into contemporary American settings. In such settings, however, the magic is blatantly inappropriate and implausible. Why should we believe that an old trunk in the attic of a house on Prairie Avenue, Chicago, contained three Italian bandits who ran out when it was opened and ransacked the place? Moreover, the contemporary setting tempted the author to make topical wisecracks aimed over children's heads; these further undermine credibility and introduce a jarring worldliness. The little girl who opened the bandits' box suggests that in Chicago they can use their skills as politicians.[1] Obviously a child would not be so sophisticated about political corruption. Because the stories fail to suspend disbelief, they do not evoke wonder or joy. In most of them, the author diverged from his usual practice by undermining his effects with a knowing, superior tone.

Two of the stories are plausible and moving because Baum took the trouble to work out a basis for the supernatural happenings. "The Enchanted Types" is his first published story to use his theosophically inspired mythology of nature spirits—fairies, knooks, and ryls that preside over and help mortal creatures. One night a well-meaning knook wanders into a millinery shop and is pained to see a case of hats each decorated with a stuffed bird, for "knooks are the especial guardians of birds, and love them dearly." He opens the case and calls to them to fly out, and so they do; for, "stuffed or not, every bird is bound to obey a knook's whistle and a knook's call." The next day, however, he is dismayed to find that he has ruined the milliner's business. He asks the birds to return, but they justifiably protest: "If it were the fashion to wear knooks perched upon women's hats would you be contented to stay there?" The situation is resolved when the knook enchants the newspaper types and editors to convince women that it is no longer fashionable to wear birds on hats. Baum ingeniously adapted the theosophical belief that advanced souls in heaven—"wise little immortals" such as knooks, in the context of the story—inspire humans on earth to enlightenment and philanthropy.[2]

"The Dummy That Lived" is a touching story, more characteristic of Andersen than Baum, about a wax mannequin brought to life by a mischievous ryl. She comes to consciousness like the Scarecrow, but because this is America rather than Oz, she cannot fit in or be accepted by humans, and she is destroyed.

Hill commissioned these stories from Baum and arranged for their weekly syndication in the *Chicago Chronicle*, the *Cincinnati Enquirer*, the *Boston Post,* and at least two other newspapers from March 3 to May 19, 1901; in October, he published them in book form, with illustrations by Seymour, N. P. Hall, Harry Kennedy, and Ike Morgan.[3]

In 1908, Bobbs-Merrill brought out a new edition of *American Fairy Tales,* with all the stories slightly revised and three new ones added: "The Ryl" and "The Strange Adventures of an Egg," sentimental tales that had previously appeared in newspapers, and "The Witchcraft of Mary-Marie." The last is a charming tale of a nice girl who learns witchcraft because it is her only available means of making her living. Baum wrote a new "Author's Note," in which he spelled out his aim of writing contemporary American fairy stories: "If fairies exist at all— and no one has yet been able to prove that they do *not* exist—then there is no good reason why they should not inhabit our favored land as well as the forest glades and flowery dales of the older world across the water." He aims "to offer our wide-awake youngsters modern tales about modern fairies" that "bear the stamp of our own times and depict the progressive fairies of to-day." It sounds like a fine program, but Baum did not consistently pursue it. "The Witchcraft of Mary-Marie" is a traditional fairy tale set in a magic country.

While Baum was completing his *American Fairy Tales,* Bowen-Merrill of Indianapolis, a more prestigious publisher than Hill, approached him for a full-length fairy story. He did not want to compete with his own forthcoming *Dot and Tot,* but he agreed to write an entirely different kind of story and produced one of his most interesting experiments, *The Master Key: An Electrical Fairy Tale, Founded upon the Mysteries of Electricity and the Optimism of its Devotees. It Was Written for Boys, but Others May Read It* (1901). The book is actually science fiction, inspired by his teenage son Robert's delight in electrical contrivances and dedicated to him. Rob made many things in his large attic workshop, he wrote in his autobiography: "My parents really must have been quite lenient with me, because I bored holes all through the house and installed wires to operate my various gadgets . . . when I wanted privacy in my room, I got it by . . . installing a wire from a spark coil and battery to the inside handle of my door," which administered a shock to anyone who turned the handle. He also rigged up an apparatus that turned on the gaslights by pushing a button to set off an electric spark and an annunciator that dropped a sign into the kitchen to alert the cook to start his breakfast when he pushed a button in his room.[4]

With his wonderful ability to find magic in everyday experience, Baum personified the natural force of electricity as the Demon of Electricity and heightened the possibilities of what it could do. Electricity was tremendously exciting and new in 1901: Edison was exploring applications that would have been magic a generation before, and no one could be sure about its destructive potentialities. Charles W. Eliot expressed the awe people felt: "Electricity" is "carrier of light and power; devourer of time and space; bearer of human speech over land and sea; greatest servant of man—yet itself unknown."[5]

The hero of *The Master Key* is named Rob, and his family, which has Matilda Gage's maiden name of Joslyn, is loosely modeled on the Baums. The fictitious Rob has wired the house like his prototype:

> There were bells, bells, bells everywhere, ringing at the right time, the wrong time and all the time.

His mother became fed up,

> but his father was delighted with these evidences of Rob's skill as an electrician, and insisted that he be allowed perfect freedom in carrying out his ideas. "Electricity," said the old gentleman, sagely, "is destined to become the motive power of the world. The future advance of civilization will be along electrical lines. Our boy may become a great inventor and astonish the world with his wonderful creations." "And in the meantime," said the mother, despairingly, "we shall all be electrocuted, or the house burned down by crossed wires . . ."

But, as Maud must often have done, "Mrs. Joslyn sighed. She knew remonstrance was useless so long as her husband encouraged the boy, and that she would be wise to bear her cross with fortitude."[6]

One day Rob is determined to light up a toy palace with electric lights. He crosses and recrosses wires, adding more and more power, until he produces a blinding flash of light and evokes a curious Being. He has unawares "touched the Master Key of Electricity" and thereby summoned the Demon of Electricity, who must "obey the commands of any one who is wise and brave enough—or, as in your own case, fortunate and fool-hardy enough—to touch" the key. The Demon has been longing to be called, since he had despaired that any Earth people would be able "ever to master the secret of electrical power." Even Edison's "inventions are trifling things in comparison with the really wonderful results to be obtained by one who would actually know how to direct the electric powers instead of groping blindly after insignificant effects."[7]

Having struck the Master Key, Rob may demand and get from the Demon three electrically powered gifts per week for three weeks. The first gifts are a box of tablets each of which will nourish his body for a whole day, a tube that will stun any attacker for an hour and thus prevent violence (which is wrong even in self-defense), and a machine that looks like a wristwatch and will transport him by means of electromagnetic currents. Rob uses his gifts on some frivolous adventures with cannibals and pirates, for which the Demon rebukes him. The Demon's next three gifts are a garment that will repel any missile, a Record of Events in the form of a small flat box that can show him anything that is happening anywhere (like television news), and a Character Marker, a pair of spectacles that will reveal people's real nature despite appearances—good or evil, wise or foolish, kind or cruel. With these six gifts, Rob is equipped "to astound the world and awaken mankind to a realization of the wonders that may be accomplished by natural forces."[8]

At first Rob is thrilled with his powers and looks forward to impressing everyone. But then he begins to think about consequences, and he resists the temptation to apply the Character Marker to his family. "They were his nearest and dearest friends on earth, and in his boyish heart he loved them all and believed in their goodness and sincerity. The possibility of finding a bad character mark on any of their familiar faces made him shudder, and he determined then and there never to use the spectacles to view the face of a friend or relative."[9]

Rob takes off on another trip, during which he uses his spectacles to save himself from a French scientist who means to kill him to steal his gifts, saves the French Republic, and has other melodramatic adventures. On his way home, however, he feels homesick and depressed, perhaps "because he was born and reared a hearty, healthy American boy, with a disposition to battle openly with the world and take his chances equally with his fellows, rather than be placed in such an exclusive position that no one could hope successfully to oppose him." He descends in the "most wonderful and cosmopolitan city" of Chicago, where he meets a businessman who proposes they exploit Rob's gifts to make exorbitant profits and tries to kill him when he does not cooperate.[10] His encounters with the scientist and the businessman alert Rob to the danger of technology falling into the wrong hands. Ironically, the Demon had complained because he had to offer his gifts to a child instead of a knowledgeable adult.

When Rob returns home, the Demon offers him his next three gifts, the first of which is an Electro-Magnetic Restorer that will cure any disease and even restore the dead to life if the blood has not yet chilled. But Rob indignantly refuses it and returns the other gifts. What right have people to see records of others' lives? he asks. The tablets are unnatural because Nature gave us a sense of taste to enjoy food. The use of the Character Marker is "mean and underhanded." The Demon assures him that the Electro-Magnetic Restorer "could not possibly do harm," but Baum evidently foresaw the dangers of medical advances that can prolong life indefinitely. Humanity is not yet ready to use unlimited power properly. The Demon retorts that readiness would have come sooner if Rob had used his powers wisely. " 'That's just it,' answered Rob. 'I'm *not* wise enough. Nor is the majority of mankind wise enough to use such inventions as yours unselfishly and for the good of the world. If people were better, and every one had an equal show, it would be different.' "[11] Rob is relieved when the Demon leaves him.

The Master Key presents Baum's characteristic linkage between magic and technology from the scientific side. As Oz magic is often an extension of technology, the potential advances in technology presented here have the appearance of magic. The nutrition tablets resemble Professor Wogglebug's Square Meal Tablets; the wristwatch-traveling machine, the Magic Belt; the Record of Events, Ozma's Magic Picture or Glinda's Book of Records. Human beings here are not yet capable of handling the enormous powers of technology, which can be used for good or evil; even in Oz, magic must be controlled by wise and public-spirited rulers. Baum's preface suggests that someday the impossible wonders offered by the Demon will become familiar everyday devices, and in the end Rob supposes that someday humanity will have developed sufficiently to be able to use them wisely.

The Demon is a theosophical elemental, who, like other Baumian immortals, is frustrated with the inaction of his spiritual world and wants to be involved with striving humans. The story enforces the theosophical teachings that "all things are regulated by exact laws of nature" and that humans can accomplish wonders if they once understand these forces.[12]

The book was deservedly successful: it went through two or probably three printings during its first two years. On the flyleaf of the copy Frank presented to Robert, he credited his inspiration to Robert's experiments and continued: "The book has been so well received that I am sorry, now, I did not end it differently and leave an opening for a sequel."[13]

For his next children's story, *The Life and Adventures of Santa Claus* (1902), dedicated to his son Harry, Baum tried out still another mode. He fleshed out folk material as he had in *Mother Goose in Prose;* but in addition he set it in a context of moral teaching and nature mythology derived from theosophy. Santa Claus appealed to Baum as a secular saint, who did much good and was in touch with the spiritual world and yet was not connected to organized religion. Baum had used the opportunity of his pre-Christmas issue of the *Pioneer,* December 20, 1890, to dwell gleefully on the holiday's pagan origins in the winter solstice and to trace Santa Claus to the ancient German Yule Feast.[14]

Baum placed Santa Claus in a traditional fairy-tale context, using a slightly elevated, archaic style. He worked out his own elaborate nature mythology, inspired by the theosophical vision of a physical world infused with spiritual presences and governed by the laws of Nature. His story opens in the Forest of Burzee, timeless home of the immortals who preside over the natural world. The Nymphs look after the trees, the Ryls nurture and color the flowers, the Knooks guard and manage the animals, and the Fairies watch over humans. These beings are ruled by Ak, the Master Woodsman of the World.

Immortals, who do not age and suffer themselves, are not supposed to help humans directly, for "Suffering, in moderation, is the natural lot of mortals." In Baum's fable, Ak finds an abandoned baby, and the wood-nymph Necile, weary of the static perfection in which she exists and longing for something to care for, begs to adopt him. She is allowed to raise young Claus, who grows up surrounded by pure, loving influences and is therefore wholly good. He is in total harmony with the immortals and therefore with Nature, talking with the animals and building his house with fallen trees to avoid cutting into living ones. When he leaves the forest for the first time and realizes that the world is full of suffering people, he is seized by a longing to help his fellow mortals; and so he must go out into the world "to take my part in the endless struggle to which humanity is doomed." His special mission (like Baum's own) is to make the children happy; he invents toys and gives them away, and at the end, with the aid of volunteer reindeer, is distributing toys all over the world on Christmas Eve.[15]

Despite several references to the suffering in the actual world that makes Claus's altruism needed and meaningful, Baum's fable is a little too bland and sweet. The language is sometimes mawkish, as in the constant idealization of "the little ones" and the name Bessie Blithesome. Claus's goodness becomes cloying, as he is not only infinitely benevolent, but invariably merry. He should be, of course, since he has no obstacles or dangers to deal with, being always protected by the immortals. Evil is present, but totally unconvincing. The Awgwas hate Claus because he keeps the children happy and good, but they haven't a chance against him. "The Battle Between Good and Evil" has a foregone conclusion, for no more convincing reason than the narrator's declaration that "it is the Law that . . . the powers of Good can never be overthrown when opposed to Evil."[16] Thorns and fairy wands demolish goblins and dragons without the slightest difficulty.

A later story on this theme, "A Kidnapped Santa Claus" (published in the *Delineator* for Christmas 1904), presents a less rosy view. The Daemons of Selfishness, Envy, Hatred, Malice, and Repentance hate Santa because he makes children so happy that none pass through their caves. So they kidnap him on Christmas Eve. He is soon released by an army of good immortals, but he tells them that "It is useless to pursue the Daemons," who "have their place in the world, and can never be destroyed."[17]

Once committed to a career in creative writing, Baum thought about his old love, the theater. Among other projects, he accepted Edith Ogden Harrison's proposal to help her turn her successful book *Prince Silverwings and Other Fairy Tales* (1902) into an extravaganza. He probably completed the script late in 1903. The play was scheduled for production in the summer of 1904, but a disastrous theater fire in December 1903 caused the mayor (Harrison's husband) to close all the theaters in Chicago; "Prince Silverwings" could not open there and never was produced.

When the play failed of production, Baum thriftily used parts of it in his own books. The play opens with Charminia, Queen of the Fairies, sending members of her band to find and comfort mortals in distress, as Queen Lulea in *Queen Zixi of Ix* will send a fairy to give the magic cloak to the most unhappy mortal she can find. The Storm King's favorite daughter has been stolen, and Silverwings and other characters go to search for her in the volcano ruled by Kwytoffle, the Gnome King, who threatens to throw them into a furnace. He is infuriated by beans, which were to be replaced in *Ozma of Oz* by the more meaningful symbol of eggs. Similar searches for a prisoner in the Gnome King's dominions were to occur in three Oz books. The Cloud Maidens, inventions of Harrison, were to reappear in *Dorothy and the Wizard in Oz* and be developed in Polychrome, the Rainbow's Daughter.[18]

Baum used the lovely name Kwytoffle in the fairyland he was developing at this time in *The Enchanted Island of Yew* (1903), which he dedicated to his son Kenneth. More favorably disposed to technological progress than most fairy-tale writers, Baum celebrated technological advances in the later Oz books as analogous to magic and equally wonderful. But in the first chapter of *Yew* he took the obvious traditional view that the two worlds are opposed: what humans have gained in capacity to deal with life's practical problems, they have lost in contact with nature and the world of imagination.

> In the old days, when the world was young, there were no automobiles nor flying-machines to make one wonder; nor were there railway trains, nor telephones, nor mechanical inventions of any sort to keep people keyed up to a high pitch of excitement. Men and women lived simply and quietly. They were Nature's children, and breathed fresh air into their lungs instead of smoke and coal gas; and tramped through green meadows and deep forests instead of riding in street cars; and went to bed when it grew dark and rose with the sun.

In the days before people could work their own magic with technology, fairies would help them and often show "themselves to those they befriended."

"So people knew fairies in those days . . . and loved them, together with all the ryls and knooks and pixies and nymphs and other beings that belong to the hordes of immortals. And a fairy tale was a thing to be wondered at and spoken of in awed whispers; for no one thought of doubting its truth." In "our busy, bustling world," the fairies are mostly unseen and unthought of; and our storytelling has declined.[19]

Yew has a traditional fairy-tale society, with knights and castles, as well as fairies. A fairy, bored with the perfection of a life without folly, struggle, and excitement, gets herself transformed into a mortal—a male one, because only boys were allowed to have adventures in the old days. Her adventures as Prince Marvel involve the traditional bandits, dragon, and evil magician; but all are touched by Baumian comedy. Prince Marvel easily knocks out all fifty-nine bandits, ties them up, and lays them in a row to be hanged. But he cannot proceed because their chief, Wul-Takim, convinces him that he should not hang honest men, and the thieves have all reformed. It seems that Marvel has been outwitted by slippery logic, but actually his forbearance proves to be wise. He tells his squire that, "If we mistrusted all who have ever done an evil act there would be fewer honest people in the world,"[20] and, sure enough, the thieves rush to help him when he calls for them. The Royal Dragon of Spor fails to breathe fire because his inner fire has gone out and his keepers are out of matches; he complains bitterly of rheumatism and refuses to fight Marvel because he suspects the Prince is Saint George in disguise. The magician Kwytoffle keeps everyone terrified by threatening to transform them into grasshoppers, but he turns out to be a humbug like the Wizard of Oz.

In the land of Twi, where everything exists in double form, Baum probes the issue of split and integrated personality that he had raised with Mr. Split in *Dot and Tot.* The ruler, the Hi Ki, is twins like everyone else, with identical minds as well as bodies. When she/they is deciding on Marvel's fate, he performs a spell to give them independent minds; and the results are disastrous. The good feelings go to one of them and the hostility to the other; they look at each other for the first time and resolve to fight until one conquers the other. Only when Marvel reunites the two half-personalities can the Hi Ki be restored to happiness and goodness. The double nature of the Twis also serves as a symbol of disturbing conformity. "Two people would always look at two [identical] pictures at the same time and admire them in the same way with the same thoughts." The Twis are alarmed by anyone who thinks or feels as an individual, for they cannot even conceive of a single independent identity: "There is no such word as 'one' " in their language.[21] In their view, *singular* can only mean deviant from normality.

At the end of the story, the people of Yew become civilized, "and they no longer robbed or fought or indulged in magical arts, but were busily employed and leading respectable lives." They no longer have fairy knights among them, but they also need not worry about mirrors like the Red Rogue's that catch the spirit of anyone reflected in them. As Baum had implied in *The Wizard of Oz*, "civilization" promotes predictable order and control of life by technological advances. A civilized country cannot tolerate the imaginative possibilities of fairyland, whether wonderful or terrifying. Civilization undoubtedly signifies advance, but there is something to regret, too.[22]

Baum had bad luck with his first few publishers. Way & Williams had accepted "Adventures in Phunnyland" and gone out of business before they could publish it. The George M. Hill Company went into bankruptcy in February 1902, two months after announcing *The Life and Adventures of Santa Claus*. The receiver seized the company's production plant, sets of plates and books in process, and the rights to its juvenile titles, including the Baum-Denslow books; he also held onto the plates that were their personal property. Not only did their royalties stop, but they could not get hold of their own plates to take them to another publisher.

Bowen-Merrill, publishers of *The Master Key*, brought out *Santa Claus*; and in September 1902, they bought the plates of and rights to *The Wonderful Wizard of Oz*, as well as all of Baum's other children's books. On July 15, 1903, the company, later Bobbs-Merrill, published its first edition as *The New Wizard of Oz*, so titled to avoid confusion with the currently running hit show of "The Wizard of Oz." It was slightly less lavish than the original edition, with sixteen rather than twenty-four color plates; and later printings economized further by dropping more of the illustrations. Bobbs-Merrill also reissued *A New Wonderland* as *The Magical Monarch of Mo and His People*; Baum revised his text, mainly his opening chapter, to give his Wonderland the catchy, distinctive name Mo (comparable to Oz).[23] It was dedicated to his brother, "the Comrade of my boyhood days Dr. Henry Clay Baum." In the next few years Bobbs-Merrill reissued most of Baum's early books, including the new, enlarged edition of *American Fairy Tales*. They published *The Enchanted Island of Yew*, Baum's only original story of 1903.

In addition to his fairy stories, Baum was now devoting much of his energy to theatrical projects. Having demonstrated his flair for humorous writing, he decided to try musical comedy rather than melodrama. Through Ike Morgan, he met Paul Tietjens, a musician who hoped to make his name as a comic opera composer and thought "Baum would

be just the man to write the libretto and Denslow could design the costumes, etc." Tietjens approached Baum in March 1901 and, by playing
him some music he had composed, persuaded him to make up a plot.
Four days later, Tietjens received a plot for a comic opera called "The
Octopus" or "The Title Trust," which he found "one of the funniest
things I have ever run across." They worked together on the words and
music, which included a bass solo for Gripem Harde, "I am a great
promoter," and two songs that would later be used in their extravaganza "The Wizard of Oz": "Love Is Love" and "The Traveller and
the Pie." By May, Baum was trying to find a producer in Chicago; when
that failed, he made a trip to New York, again without success. By June,
Tietjens felt that Baum was "losing interest and hope in the opera, for
he speaks of how much better our second opera ought to be."

After Baum went off to spend the summer at Macatawa, Denslow
suggested a musical show of *The Wizard* to Tietjens. Baum invited the
Tietjenses to Macatawa, where they spent a pleasant two weeks and
projected another comic opera, "King Midas." But Tietjens thought a
dramatization of *The Wizard* would be their "best chance for an immediate production." Baum was reluctant at first, for he did not want to
share royalties with Denslow; but he did write a scenario, and Tietjens
started on the music. He quickly wrote what proved to be the hit song
of the show, "When You Love, Love, Love." Denslow set about finding
a producer.[24]

During the summer, Baum, Tietjens, and Denslow would meet at
Baum's cottage at Macatawa to work together on the libretto, music,
and costumes and scenic effects. (Denslow, who had theatrical experience, was in charge of the latter.) They would cut "up like a bunch of
school boys," Robert Baum recalled in his autobiography. Tietjens
"would pound out a piece on the piano and father would sing the
words or perhaps do a tap or eccentric dance, accompanied by the ferocious looking Denslow, who was a thick set man with a heavy 'walrus'
mustache and looked like a brigand. It was better than a vaudeville
show to us boys."[25] Unfortunately this genial harmony fell apart when
the three partners began to dispute about their respective contributions
and proper share of the royalties. They had originally agreed to divide
them equally, but when the time came to draw up the contract,
Denslow proposed to reduce Tietjens's share to one-fifth, so that he
and Baum would get two-fifths apiece. Tietjens retaliated by threatening to pull out of the project unless Denslow's share was reduced so
Tietjens would get a half. Finally Baum persuaded him it would be bet-

ter to let Denslow have a third than abandon the project, and they returned to the original agreement. Baum and Tietjens copyrighted the scenario in September 1901.[26]

Baum planned an extravaganza modeled on the British Christmas pantomime, with the traditional fairy-tale plot, topical jokes and wise-cracks, spectacular scenery and stage effects, a big chorus of pretty girls, a man dressed in animal costume, and the whole thing tied together by a comic team consisting of a straight man and an extrava-gant clown. Baum fitted these elements into the plot of his book. The Scarecrow would be the star comic, the Tin Woodman the straight man, and the Lion the clown in an animal suit. Act I dramatizes Dorothy landing in the Munchkin country, rescuing the Scarecrow and the Tin Woodman, and meeting the Lion; it climaxes with Dorothy and the Lion falling asleep among the Deadly Poppies, represented by chorus girls. The Lion is rescued by field mice, as in the book (Baum does not suggest how this might be staged). Act II is set in the Emerald City and the Wizard's Throne Room. Act III represents several of the adventures in the Quadling country: the travelers are attacked by the Fighting Trees (men in tree suits) and taken by the Winged Monkeys to the palace of Glinda, who sends Dorothy home. Baum provided Glinda with four counselors—the three humbug wise men from *Mother Goose* plus another named Chumpocles.

In some places Baum followed the dialogue in his book quite closely, although he loaded it with puns and wisecracks. Dorothy tells the Scarecrow, "I have seen many a man without brains, but you are the first one I ever met who would admit it." The Scarecrow answers, "I might as well own up to it, because people will get on to me sooner or later, and want me to go to Congress." There are some clever songs, such as Dorothy's, "Oh, I long to be in Kansas,/Where the flowers and blizzards blow . . . There's a prairie big and wide/And there's little else beside." Most of the songs are mediocre, however. Baum's "The Scare-crow" is painfully inane compared to "If I Only Had a Brain" in the 1939 movie musical. Baum did drag in one "topical"—that is, totally irrelevant—song, "The Traveller and the Pie" from the old "Octopus" script.[27]

Baum sent his play to the producer Fred R. Hamlin, who saw possi-bilities, particularly in Baum's idea of making the Scarecrow and the Tin Woodman the comic team. But although Baum had sophisticated his style in the script, Hamlin did not consider it sufficiently worldly and called in Julian Mitchell, an experienced director. Mitchell worked for many unhappy weeks first with Baum and then with Tietjens, and transformed their show into a conventional extravaganza. The focus moved from Baum's story to the star comics Fred Stone (the Scarecrow) and David Montgomery (the Tin Woodman), who did routines that worked for them regardless of whether they fitted into the plot. After the comics, the most important element was production—devising decorative routines for the chorus and thinking up stunts and tableaus. Palace plots and revolutions were added because melodramatic Graustarkian plays had recently been hits. Dorothy became a young woman, suitable for romantic attachments, and Toto became Imogen the cow, who could be played by a human clown. The Wizard was turned into an Irishman or other ethnic comedian, his ethnicity varying from city to city. Mitchell discarded all but eight of the Baum-Tietjens songs, then bought and arbitrarily introduced twenty new songs that had nothing to do with the story.[28] Even more changes were made later, for musical comedies were completely revised during the course of rehearsal, and jokes and comic routines were added and replaced during the show's run to keep it fresh.

The resulting extravaganza was not a dramatization of *The Wizard of Oz*, but a hodgepodge of spectacular effects, comic romantic entanglements, slapstick routines, puns and wisecracks. After a tableau of a Kansas farm and a cyclone, Dorothy arrives in Munchkinland. There she finds Locusta, the Good Witch of the North, Cynthia, a Lady Lunatic who has lost her reason because a Wicked Witch has transformed her fiancé, Nick Chopper, into somebody else, and the Poet Laureate, Sir Dashemoff Daily, who promptly falls in love with Dorothy. He announces that the cyclone also brought Pastoria, the rightful king of Oz, whom the Wizard had sent away in his balloon. Pastoria has been working as a streetcar motorman in Topeka and is now leading a revolution to get his throne back; he is followed by Tryxie Tryfle, his fiancée, who was a waitress in the railroad station. Dorothy is eager to return to Kansas with Imogen because "poor Father will miss" them so. Imogen was "the only thing to prove he ran a dairy. Now he won't be able to mix up any more milk until I get back with the key to the plaster of Paris barrel."

After Dorothy brings the Scarecrow to life and they rescue the Tinman, the three sing "When You Love, Love, Love," which celebrates love ("There is nothing so divine, there is nothing half so fine,/As the gladness of your madness when you love, love, love"). A cynical conclusion was added to Baum's original song: "But though of love you gaily sing/'Twill turn your heart quite stony,/To end the whirl and find the girl/Is seeking 'Alimony.'" The act ends with a spectacular and much admired scene in the deadly poppy field, in which rescue by the field mice was replaced, for practical reasons, by the Snow Queen blighting the poppies (thirty or forty chorus girls) with a snowstorm.

In the second act, set in the throne room in the Emerald City, the Wizard grants the Scarecrow's and Tinman's wishes. Pastoria exposes the Wizard as a fraud and takes over the kingdom. Act III abandons Baum's story altogether. Pastoria's soldiers arrest the Scarecrow and Tinman as rebels and hoist them up in a cage. Dorothy rescues the Scarecrow by letting the Tinman cut him up and pass him through the bars; then they put him together on stage, in another famous special effect. The Lady Lunatic gets the Tinman to play the piccolo and thereby recognizes her lost fiancé Niccolo. Ultimately Locusta sets all things right.[29]

The show was an enormous success. Baum took enthusiastic curtain calls on June 16, 1902, when it opened at the Grand Opera House in Chicago, where it remained for fourteen weeks. It played to 185,000 people and grossed $160,000—sensational figures for that time. Then the show went on the road West and into Canada, returned for two weeks to Chicago, and in January 1903 opened in the Majestic Theater in New York. This location, twenty-five blocks north of the theater district proper, indicates that managers did not believe "The Wizard" would appeal to the more sophisticated New York audience. But it filled the house for two seasons. Meanwhile, road companies multiplied. Altogether, "The Wizard" ran for over eight years. It was a major theatrical event.[30]

On Christmas Eve 1905, "The Wizard of Oz" was revived in Chicago with Montgomery and Stone. Amy Leslie, a prominent Chicago critic, praised it highly, especially a Cherokee dance and pantomime for Stone and a football song and dance for Stone and Montgomery. Leslie was still enthusiastic when it was revived in 1908 with new numbers acquired on the road, although Montgomery and Stone had left the show in 1906.[31] The royalties that Baum and Tietjens each received from "The Wizard" have been estimated variously at ninety thousand dollars or one hundred thousand dollars.[32]

At first Baum was outraged at what had been done to his book, but the success of the show reconciled him. He published a letter in the

Chicago Tribune on June 26, 1904, to contradict rumors that he was dissatisfied with the show. "I acknowledge that I was unwise enough to express myself as dissatisfied with the handling of my play on its first production. . . . Few authors of successful books are ever fully satisfied with the dramatization of their work." After Mitchell declared the manuscript "would never do . . . for stage usage," Baum tried unsuccessfully to rewrite it, and then Mitchell took over: "The original story was practically ignored, the dialogue rehashed, the situations transposed, my Nebraska wizard made into an Irishman, and several other characters forced to conform to the requirements of the new schedule." But it "is not true" "that I was heartbroken and ashamed of my extravaganza when it was finally produced," although he did "protest over several innovations." "Mr. Mitchell listened to the plaudits of the big audiences and turned a deaf ear to my complaints . . . after two years of success for the extravaganza . . . I now regard Mr. Mitchell's views in a different light. The people will have what pleases them, and not what the author happens to favor." "My chief business is, of course, the writing of fairy tales," he concluded; "but should I ever attempt another extravaganza, or dramatize another of my books, I mean to profit by the lesson Mr. Mitchell has taught me, and sacrifice personal preference to the demands of those I shall expect to purchase admission tickets."[33]

From one point of view, the success of "The Wizard of Oz" extravaganza did more damage to Baum's career and peace of mind than any disaster that befell him. Because it brought him so much fame and profit, it confirmed his infatuation with the stage. "He spent the rest of his life trying to replicate the show's amazing success."[34] It prompted him to write an extravaganza based on *The Land of Oz* in 1905, which was a humiliating failure; it tempted him to produce the Radio Plays of 1908, which sent him into bankruptcy, and to undertake the Oz Film Manufacturing Company, which fruitlessly exhausted his waning energies in 1914. Because "The Wizard" was a shoddy piece of work that perfectly met public taste, it encouraged Baum to lower his standards of humor and abandon all originality when writing for the stage. For, as he spelled out in his letter to the *Tribune*, he had learned it was silly not to cater to public taste, however inane and debased it might be. Even some of the later Oz books were damaged by the inferior standards that Baum considered appropriate to dramatic writing.

The extravaganza had a few minor effects on the future development of Oz. Dorothy got her last name there, because she arrived in a Gale (cyclone). The pre-Wizard history of Oz as given in *The Land of Oz* was originally worked out in the show; Pastoria, the former king of Oz, was actually invented by Mitchell rather than Baum.[35] The Tin Woodman acquired the name Niccolo Chopper in the show, which became the more appropriate Nick Chopper in *The Land of Oz*.

Continuing dissension over each man's share in creating the original *Wonderful Wizard of Oz* precipitated a final breach between Baum and Denslow. Denslow thought he deserved a large share of the royalties from the show because he was half-owner of the copyright of the book, while Baum maintained that Denslow had had no part in preparing the story for the stage. Denslow, for his part, claimed credit for originating the characters of the Scarecrow and the Tin Woodman in the play on the grounds that he had designed their much-praised costumes. The two men had always differed in tastes: Denslow liked to celebrate with bohemians in his studio, while Baum preferred quiet evenings at home with his family. The failure of their publisher, Hill, and Denslow's move to New York in 1902 confirmed their separation.

In the next few years, Denslow tried to capitalize on "The Wizard" 's success with picture books and illustrated stories in newspapers. Shortly after "The Wizard" opened in New York, Hill's successors issued a pamphlet, *Pictures from the Wonderful Wizard of Oz* by W. W. Denslow, with a story by Thomas H. Russell, which made no mention of Baum. Denslow himself wrote and illustrated a collection of short stories, *Denslow's Scarecrow and the Tin-Man* (1904); and in December he instituted a "Scarecrow and the Tin-Man" comic page in imitation of Baum's similar newspaper series, "Queer Visitors from the Marvelous Land of Oz." His drawings are better than those of Baum's illustrator, Walt McDougall; but his stories are inane, and the series lasted for only fourteen installments.

By this time Baum and Denslow were no longer speaking, but Baum was induced to collaborate with Denslow and Tietjens on a dramatization of *Father Goose*. They signed a contract to divide the profits equally, and Baum and Tietjens wrote it during the summer of 1904. It was never produced.[36] Judging from the two men's characters, it seems likely that Denslow was mainly responsible for the breakup. He was touchy and hot-tempered, inclined to distrust people and to see the world as conspiring against him. His three marriages failed, and he quarreled with each one of his successive professional partners.

While he continued to write stories for children, Baum was determined to follow up on "The Wizard" 's success with another musical comedy. He set to work planning and writing four additional musical comedies and a children's fantasy play with different collaborators. None of these were to achieve production. In September 1902, he copyrighted the comic opera "King Jonah XIII," with music by Nathaniel D. Mann; in March, 1904, Mann was still unsuccessfully trying to find a producer for it in San Francisco.

Baum worked for several years with his friend Emerson Hough, a fellow member of the Chicago Press Club and a popular novelist also published by Bowen-Merrill, on a series of ideas for musical comedies. On July 22, 1903, Baum wrote to Hough from Macatawa that an agent was trying to find a producer for their joint effort "Montezuma" (based on an old play of Hough's, with music by Mann) in New York. By March 28, 1905, Hough and Mann agreed that "Montezuma was no go," although the project lingered on for another year. On March 15, 1904, Baum encouraged Hough to keep working on another project, "The Maid of Athens," which they had copyrighted in 1903: "Keep scratching out lyrics. And I'll do the same." On July 18, Baum wrote from Macatawa to Hough in Chicago to warn him that a new play by George Ade used a college setting and might damage the chances of "The Maid of Athens," and to urge him to get all the newspaper publicity he could for their play. (Hough, less sanguine, suggested on July 26 that instead they try to sell Ade their interest in the college plot.)

On January 13, 1905, after indicating (untruly) that "Father Goose" had been accepted for production, Baum mentioned a new collaborative effort, "The King of Gee-Whiz" or "The Son of the Sun," which was probably developed from "Montezuma." When he and Hough were unable to find a producer, they thought they might create a demand for their story by publishing it. But their hopes for getting it syndicated in newspapers came to nothing, and Reilly & Britton could not bring it out promptly as a book. Hough then published it as a short story in *Everybody's Magazine*, but he and Baum still hoped to publish it collaboratively as a book; Baum even wanted to make a book of "Montezuma" as well.

Neither book nor comic opera had materialized, however, by January 1906; and on January 27, the Baums were leaving for a five-month tour abroad. Hough, who had given up hope of a theatrical production and was impatient to capitalize on his material, tried to persuade Baum to make over his interest in the story before he left so that Hough would be free to develop it as a book (January 6). On January 8, Baum reluctantly agreed to do so, provided Hough returned to him exclusive use of the three ideas he had contributed; he protested that he had worked hard to place the play and in fact was going to present it to two producers in New York before he sailed. Hough replied with some asperity on January 11 that he thought Baum had not wanted to go on with "Gee Whiz," that he did not want to prolong a partnership "where both sides cannot feel satisfied," and that one of the ideas Baum claimed was actually Hough's; nevertheless, if Baum was still willing, Hough would like to keep on working with him to place "Gee Whiz." Meanwhile, he had started work on the "Gee Whiz" book; and on January 15, he urged Baum to specify what parts of the material he considered his property.

Baum replied on January 18 from Syracuse, where he was stopping on his way to New York, that he was still "quite confident that he could place" "Gee Whiz" for production the following summer. As for Hough's "Gee Whiz" book, Baum was still worried about use of his ideas and evasively assured Hough that he had plenty of material without using anything they had produced collaboratively. Hough published *The King of Gee-Whiz* that year, having evidently satisfied Baum's objections. Meanwhile, Baum suggested, writing from Egypt on February 22, that they might partly underwrite the show themselves, each contributing a third, which would cost "only $3,000 to $5,000 each." On March 8, Baum was still determined to place the show on his return to the United States. This is the last we hear of it.[37]

The surviving synopsis of "The King of Gee-Whiz" makes one wonder why Baum and Hough spent so much time and effort on it. Lt. Arthur Wainwright lands on the tropical island of Gee-Whiz and saves his life by enthralling the king by blowing soap bubbles; unfortunately he has only one bar of soap. More Americans arrive, including a fat missionary, and the king has him boiled down into soap. But he miraculously revives in the third act, springing from the pot to announce that he is, in reality, Sherlock Holmes returning, as Doyle had revived Holmes in "The Adventure of the Empty House" (1903). This act is set in the Radiant Valley, full of gold that turns into lead when venal characters touch it, but back into gold when the true lovers do.[38]

Baum and Hough's other surviving effort, "Maid of Athens," which exists in the form of a rough scenario, shows the potential for an amusing show. The story is set at a coeducational state university (then a novel institution) that is infatuated with football. The hero, the sophomore Spartacus Smith, is courting Dora Jones of Athens, Ohio, an avid sports fan. She tells him he must win tomorrow's game for Illiana University, and he, knowing himself inadequate, wishes the classical Spartacus could give him pointers and falls asleep before his namesake's statue. He wakes in ancient Athens, where the first Spartacus helps him.[39]

Yet another show, "The Whatnexters," is mentioned among Baum's theatrical projects at this period; but this may actually have been one of his little jokes. His son Frank never heard him mention such a play and suggested he might have simply tossed off the title when reporters were badgering him about his next project.[40] Along with all his collaborative projects at this time, Baum was writing the "The Woggle-Bug" extravaganza on his own, conducting difficult negotiations with its producer, and facing the ultimate failure of the show.

Regardless of these frustrations in his theatrical projects, Baum now received dependable royalties from his children's books and large continuing profits from "The Wizard of Oz" extravaganza. At last the family could enjoy secure prosperity. Apart from the increase in income, Maud had now taken charge of the family's financial affairs. Already in 1899, in a contract witnessed by the Denslows on November 17, Frank had transferred to Maud all rights of his books—*Mother Goose in Prose, Father Goose*, "The King of Phunniland" (*A New Wonderland*), and "From Kansas to Fairyland" (*The Wizard of Oz*)—for which she paid him one thousand dollars.[41] By 1901, according to a newspaper interview, she kept the accounts, negotiated Frank's contracts, collected his royalties, and acted "as a 'guardian angel' in general." When he bought shares in a copper mine in 1904, he put the stock certificates in Maud's name.

At forty-five, Baum was "a young man of splendid physique, with a handsome head, a fine, strong face, brown eyes and hair." He "is exceedingly well groomed, a brilliant conversationalist; in fact, an ideal society man. It is seldom one finds combined in one man, and especially a handsome man, all the manly virtues, but Mr. Baum is a loving husband and father, a staunch friend, an indefatigable worker and a money-maker, in spite of the fact that he is a successful author."[42] Maud confirmed Frank's care about dressing well; in his prosperous later years he "always had his suits made by the best tailor in Los Angeles" and "had many changes."[43]

In 1903, the Baums moved into a large, two-story house on the South Side of Chicago, at 3726 Forest Avenue (now Giles Avenue) near the lake front in "a very swanky neighborhood." They still did not have electric lights, but they got their first telephone. Maud and Frank moved Rob from public school to a private school, Lewis Institute, and then away to the Michigan Military Academy in 1903, because it enforced stricter discipline, he suspected. Actually, he "was quite thrilled at going, because my brother Frank . . . had just graduated."[44] At least three of the four Baum sons attended this academy, although only Frank Junior went into the army. They all grew up to be tall and handsome like their parents. When they were grown, Frank told an interviewer, "I've got twenty-four feet, four and a half inches of boys myself. Four of them, and every one over six feet."[45]

On pleasant summer Sunday afternoons, the whole family would bicycle to Humboldt Park for a picnic lunch and a band concert. In the winter they went to the North Side Turnverein Hall to hear an orchestra of forty to fifty German musicians. Often they had musical evenings at home. Frank would "sing popular songs and accompany himself on the old square piano while the boys and Maud joined in with violin and mandolins. . . . At his urging, each of his sons learned to play some instrument, even though none ever became more than a fair performer. For an hour or more the family orchestra would play." Then the boys would go to bed, and Frank would write while Maud sewed.[46]

Maud's niece Matilda Gage often visited from Aberdeen. When she was about seventeen, she spent the summer with the Baums and sat in a box with Frank at "The Wizard of Oz." The audience called for "the author," he stood up and bowed, and she was thrilled. Frank regularly sent her his latest children's book at Christmas, starting with *Mother Goose in Prose*, even though she was too old for them. In 1903, he delighted her with a gift of five dollars, a larger sum than she had ever had, "to be spent *entirely* for nonsense, and by *you*. Not a sensible thing must be bought with it." She was enthralled with the elegance and lavishness of the Baums' lifestyle. "They represented to me something that I knew nothing about, I was thrilled with the things they did, their food, the household, everything." She spent weekends with them in

Chicago during her two years at Northwestern University. In 1905, when she had to produce a short story for her English A class, Baum reeled off "The Man with the Red Shirt"—a mediocre effort from Baum, but it got her an A.[47]

The Baums became prosperous enough to buy a cottage at Macatawa Park, reached from Chicago by an overnight steamer that ran daily during the summer months. Frank had first heard about Macatawa through friends at the Chicago Athletic Club and had visited it in the summer of 1899. For the following two summers, the Baums rented a cottage there. Frank made a sign for it like the other cottagers, but instead of choosing a cliché like Kum-Inn, he named it "Hyperoodon rostratus," after a bottle-nosed whale whose skeleton had caught his eye in the Field Museum.[48]

Then in 1902, delighted with the natural loveliness and congenial neighbors, they bought a cottage overlooking the lake. Because it was paid for largely by royalties from *Father Goose*, Frank named it "The Sign of the Goose." He made a sign with this name, adorned with a white goose copied from Denslow's drawing on the front cover, and hung it on the front porch. The family would move to Macatawa as soon as school was out and return to Chicago just before it opened in September. (In 1902, Frank Junior would have been nineteen; Robert, sixteen; Harry, thirteen; and Kenneth, eleven.) The Baums bought a twenty-five-foot mahogany motor launch and, in 1905, an early model Ford. Cars in those days were partly made to order, and Rob had carefully selected the engine and observed the assembly of the car at the Ford factory in Detroit.[49]

About the time the Baums bought their cottage, Frank suffered an attack of Bell's palsy, a paralysis of the muscles on one side of his face. On his doctor's recommendation, he gave up writing for some months and occupied himself with light manual work. The new cottage provided a perfect opportunity. Frank made the furniture for the living room, including two large rocking chairs with sides consisting of outlines of geese painted in white enamel, which he upholstered in tan leather fastened with decorative nails that had brass geese as heads, cast for him by his friend Harrison Rountree, the president of a brass foundry. Frank commissioned a stained-glass window with a white goose on a green background and stenciled a broad frieze of green geese around the white walls.[50] Although no one ever taught him craftsman's skills, Maud recalled, Frank "could do anything with his hands always."[51]

Paul and Eunice Tietjens rented a cottage at Macatawa in 1904 so that he and Baum could work on "Father Goose."[52] Eunice recorded in her autobiography that Baum

> ... was a character. He was tall and rangy, with an imagination and a vitality which constantly ran away with him. ... Constantly exercising his imagination as he did [writing so many books], he had come to the place where he could honestly not tell the difference between what he had done and what he had imagined. Everything he said had to be taken with at least a half pound of salt. But he was a fascinating companion.
>
> He was never without a cigar in his mouth, but it was always unlit. His doctor had forbidden him to smoke, so he chewed up six cigars a day instead. There was one exception ... Before he took his swim in the lake in the afternoon he would light a cigar and walk immediately into the water. He would solemnly wade out till the water was up to his neck and there walk parallel to the shore, moving his arms to give the impression that he was swimming. When a wave splashed on the cigar and put it out he at once came in and dressed.
>
> His house was full of the most remarkable mementos of the time when it had been necessary for him "to rest his brain," following a stroke of facial paralysis.

She describes his furniture and other handicrafts and concludes:

> Because all this had not rested his brain enough, he had made an elaborate piano arrangement of Paul's music for *The Wizard of Oz*— though he was no musician it was pretty good—had then figured out the system by which pianola records were made and had cut a full-length record of this arrangement out of wrapping paper! This seems to have done the trick, and he was presently back at work.[53]

And Baum did work, wherever he was. Although he "did less writing at Macatawa than in Chicago,"[54] he developed theatrical projects and continued to work on his books in progress. He also spent much time answering the large numbers of letters he got from children. "Not a day passes," he told an interviewer in 1904,

> but I get a letter from a child. They come sometimes singly, sometimes in batches of fifty or a hundred. Entire classes ... have written

to me. I answer every one personally. When I was a child I know how, if I had received a real letter from an author whose book I'd read, I would have been the happiest boy alive. And if I am to do any good in the world my highest ambition will be to make children happy.

Harry confirmed this account: "There might be some delay ... but each letter received an individual reply. Quite frequently, the children made suggestions in their letters or wanted to know more about some incident, and these were always acknowledged and explained."[55]

The Baums led a very active social life at Macatawa. In addition to their many local friends, the Carpenters visited regularly and Maud's three nieces would spend summers there. Maud recalled that there was "always someone coming to the house who wanted to meet" Frank. He "enjoyed a good game of cards—liked to go over to the Yacht Club. Made a wonderful Welsh rabbit. Was always having people at the house in the evening, which ended up with one. One summer he ordered 100 lbs. of cheese sent over. We also made many trips by auto in Michigan."[56]

Harry Baum recalled

most pleasant memories ... of family gatherings around the dining table where fun, jokes, atrocious puns, and even learned discussions flowed fast and furiously. My three brothers and I were home from various schools and, when the family was together around one large table, Mother often said that there were five boys to gang together against her instead of four.... To settle the frequent points of dispute which arose, a small shelf was built in the dining room where a dictionary, a single-volumed encyclopedia, and an atlas were kept for quick, convenient reference and decision. We had a good time always. When Father made an especially far-fetched pun, we would all laugh uproariously and then reach out our hands to him for any loose change as a reward for laughing.

One of these jokes has been preserved: "Why is Ken's hair like Heaven?" Answer: "There is no parting there."[57]

Frank took an active part in organizing Regatta Week, the big event of the season, which took place in August. It featured an annual Vaudeville Entertainment at the Yacht Club, which, on Saturday, August 16, 1902, started with a performance of the Lake Front Mandolin Club, whose seven members included Robert Baum, F. Joslyn

Baum, and L. F. Baum.[58] Baum contributed a song and dance to the program on August 27, 1904.

Baum published a "rhapsody," "To Macatawa," in the *Grand Rapids Sunday Herald* of September 1, 1907, that concluded: "Where else, in short, is found so nice/An imitation paradise?"[59] There was only one problem with this paradise: two charming scoundrels, Fred K. Colby and E. C. Westervelde, were the park's chief stockholders and controlled all its services. They collected money whenever the cottagers put in a telephone, had their groceries delivered from the local store, or went to Chicago using the only available ferry. Furthermore, the two exploiters had let the boardwalk and the electrical and sewage systems fall into ruin. In 1906, Basil P. Finley, an attorney from Kansas City, arrived and organized the cottagers to wrest control of their colony from Colby and Westervelde.[60]

Baum genially satirized "The War of the Cottagers" in a roman à clef that he called *Tamawaca Folks* and privately published under the name John Estes Cooke in 1907. Colby and Westervelde appear as Wilder and Easton, and Finley as Jarrod. Baum claimed in his preface that it was all written "in a spirit of broadest good-fellowship," and apparently even Colby was not offended by being represented as "the pirate of Tamawaca." Among the cottagers that Jarrod organized to dispossess the two cheats was "our distinguished author," Mr. Wright (Baum himself), who "was stubborn, loud-mouthed and pig-headed, and wanted to carry everything with a high hand, the way they do in novels. He had about as much diplomacy as a cannon-ball." Baum playfully inscribed his son Frank's copy: "Nobody knows who wrote this book but me—and I wish I didn't."[61] Actually, everyone soon guessed the author.[62]

six

REILLY & BRITTON'S STAR
AUTHOR, 1904–1907

After the Hill Publishing Company failed, two of Hill's former employees, his production manager, Frank K. Reilly, and his head salesman, Sumner C. Britton, formed their own company. They needed an established author for their first trade list in 1904, and Baum was dissatisfied with Bobbs-Merrill's promotion of his books. He later complained to Hough that their "royalty returns were positively laughable," only $1,264.10 on all his books for July through September 1904.[1]

Baum would be the most distinguished author on Reilly & Britton's list, while he was just one among many at Bobbs-Merrill. They approached Baum for a book, and he proposed a sequel to *The Wizard of Oz*, tentatively entitled "His Majesty the Scarecrow." They signed a contract on January 16, 1904. This time Baum took care to protect his property in case the firm should fail; the contract provided that he could purchase the printing plates for his book and that publishing rights would revert immediately to him.[2] Because two companies of "The Wizard" were touring the country, Reilly & Britton suggested the new book capitalize on the show's success with the title "Further Adventures of the Scarecrow and the Tin Woodman." Baum protested because *Denslow's Scarecrow and the Tin-Man* had just been announced. Finally, when the publishers had to have a title for their salesmen, they discussed the problem with Baum over lunch, and he came up with *The Marvelous Land of Oz*, retaining the publishers' title as his subtitle.[3] Shortly after publication, this was shortened to *The Land of Oz*.

Baum's relationship with his new publishers proved highly satisfactory. They exerted themselves to promote his books; occasionally they made constructive criticisms of his manuscripts, to which he responded graciously. Reilly & Britton never became a prestigious

firm—their two most prominent authors were Baum and the sentimental versifier Edgar Guest. This limitation may have diminished
Baum in the eyes of critics and book review editors, but it had no
effect on his enthusiastic readers, who were always his main concern.
After 1905, Reilly & Britton published all of Baum's new books for
children and adolescents. (The firm became Reilly & Lee in 1919.)
The Reillys and the Brittons also became personal friends of the
Baums and visited them several times at Macatawa. The Brittons
were close friends. Most of Baum's letters to his publishers were sent
to "Brit," while those to Reilly were addressed to "Mr. Reilly"
through 1916. He felt "affection" for Britton "and admiration for
Reilly."[4]

Although it marks a return to Oz, *The Land of Oz* is very different
from *The Wizard of Oz*. There is no interplay between the fantasy world
and the everyday world, for all the action takes place in Oz (apart from
a brief excursion to an unspecified place outside).[5] Baum did, however,
introduce his typical homely details into fairyland: the wonderful Powder of Life comes in an old pepper box with a label written in pencil.
He maintained the careful attention to detail that keeps his fantasy
believable. The Tin Woodman cannot unscrew a box with his stiff fingers, nor can the Scarecrow pick up a pill with his clumsy padded ones.
The central human character is a mildly mischievous boy, Tip. The
story is loosely plotted, without a quest or other clear narrative aim. It
is tied to the earlier book principally by the characters of the Scarecrow
and the Tin Woodman.

Baum did invent two new and delightful odd characters, Jack Pumpkinhead and the Highly Magnified and Thoroughly Educated Woggle-
Bug. Jack may be stupid, as his name implies; but he often shows the
plain sense that Baum liked to associate with unpretentious modesty, as
well as a dignity that belies his comic awkwardness and perpetual grin.
His first words, when he heard Tip laugh at him, were, "I hope you are
not reflecting on my personal appearance." When Tip animated the
Saw-Horse and became angry that the animal did not stop when he
shouted, "Whoa!" Jack pointed out that the horse had no ears and suggested Tip make him some.

"That's a splendid idea!" said Tip. "How did you happen to think
of it?"

"Why, I didn't think of it," answered the Pumpkinhead; "I didn't
need to, for it's the simplest and easiest thing to do."[6]

As Edward Wagenknecht has pointed out, Baum almost certainly drew inspiration for Jack Pumpkinhead from Nathaniel Hawthorne's "Feathertop." In Hawthorne's story, the witch Mother Rigby made a scarecrow with a body of sticks and a pumpkin head, dressed it in tattered finery, and on a whim brought it to life and named him Feathertop. With the same magic, she gave him a fashionable appearance, although of course he continued to lack both a brain and a heart. He impressed all the townspeople with his manners and polite conversation and was making good progress courting a girl until they both happened to look into a mirror. There the fashionable gentleman saw himself for what he really was—a scarecrow; this self-knowledge gave him human feelings, and in despair he collapsed into a lifeless pile of sticks. Baum skillfully turned this theme to comedy. Like Feathertop, Jack is touching because his absurdity and inadequacy are united with human feelings; but in the benign world of Oz, he can be accepted for what he is by himself and others.

The idea that a mirror reveals truth concealed from the world by a specious appearance was to be a major theme in *Queen Zixi of Ix*, where Zixi was tormented like Feathertop by the truth she saw in a mirror. Her torment is silly rather than tragic, however, because confrontation with the truth does not actually damage her self. Only in his atypically wistful "The Dummy That Lived" did Baum retain the emotional tone of Hawthorne's story.

Baum's Woggle-Bug owed his existence to lucky chance. As Baum related in an interview in the *Philadelphia North American* (October 3, 1904), a little girl playing in the sand on Coronado Beach picked up a sand crab and asked him what it was. He answered, "A Wogglebug"— "the first term that popped into my head." The child was delighted with the word, and so was Maud when Baum mentioned it to her that evening; she "told me I should put the Wogglebug in *The Marvelous Land of Oz*. The book was one third written and Jack Pumpkinhead was the hero, but I brought in the Wogglebug right away. After that H. M. Wogglebug, T. E., was the hero and has become my most popular character."[7]

It was clever to satirize intellectual pretentiousness through a big bug, although the Woggle-Bug would be more satisfying if he were anatomically closer to a real insect. Baum could have made humorous use of an insect's six limbs (and in fact was to do so in later short stories about the character). The Woggle-Bug's permanent magnification is so neatly worked out that it is almost plausible.

In an engaging bit of self-mockery, Baum made the Woggle-Bug an inveterate punster. The Woggle-Bug insists that punning proves one's education and "thorough command of the language," but his companions sternly restrain him; even the Saw-Horse snorts, and Jack covers his mouth with his hand because he cannot change his carved smile to a frown. When the Woggle-Bug cannot resist making another pun because it seems so new and original, Tip represses him by assuring him that it had been discovered years ago: "An educated Woggle-Bug may be a new thing; but a Woggle-Bug education is as old as the hills."[8]

Jack's modesty contrasts with the pretensions of most of his fellow characters. After a housemaid easily fooled both Jack and the Scarecrow into thinking they could not understand each other when in fact they were speaking the same language, the Scarecrow rebuked Jack for trying to think: "For unless one can think wisely it is better to remain a dummy—which you most certainly are." Jack meekly agreed, but obviously he was not the only dummy.[9] The Scarecrow and the Tin Woodman constantly plume themselves on the wonderful brains and heart the Wizard gave them, as does the Woggle-Bug on the profound learning he acquired by listening to the lessons in a country schoolhouse. Each seizes every opportunity to declare the supreme importance of his particular gift. Jack does not boast, but he reveals equal self-centeredness in his obsession with the nature of pumpkins. Each new experience prompts a worry about whether water injures pumpkins? or sunshine? or stinging bees? Recurrently they join in a comic chorus of self-absorption:

> "I place 'T.E.'—Thoroughly Educated—upon my cards; for my greatest pride lies in the fact that the world cannot produce another Woggle-Bug with a tenth part of my own culture and erudition."
>
> "I do not blame you," said the Scarecrow. "Education is a thing to be proud of. I'm educated myself. The mess of brains given me by the Great Wizard is considered by my friends to be unexcelled."
>
> "Nevertheless," interrupted the Tin Woodman, "a good heart is, I believe, much more desirable than education or brains."
>
> "Could seeds be considered in the light of brains?" enquired the Pumpkinhead, abruptly.[10]

Baum loved Dickens, and the influence of Dickens's broad-brushed humorous characterization of eccentrics is particularly apparent in this book.

The Land of Oz opens with a detailed description of Tip's construction of Jack, gratifying a child's love of seeing how things are made. The creation of the Gump, when Tip and his friends must build a flying machine to escape from a besieged palace, is more challenging. (*Gump* was a slang term for a fool, current between 1865 and 1920.) They must figure out how to construct it from unpromising materials—the stuffed head of a Gump (a sort of elk), two sofas, four large palm leaves, lengths of clothesline, and a broom. Then they must animate it with an insufficient amount of the Powder of Life. Their ingenious problem solving makes absorbing reading.

The minute the Gump comes to life, it reveals a distinct personality. Recognizing that it is no longer a real Gump and therefore "cannot have a Gump's pride or independent spirit," it resigns itself to becoming the party's servant and carrying them through the air. Indeed, "I greatly prefer to navigate the air. For should I travel on the earth and meet with one of my own species, my embarrassment would be something awful!"[11] Things readily come to life in Baum's world, and whatever is alive has feelings and expresses them.

The revolt of Jinjur and her army of girls is hard to reconcile with the enlightened feminist views Baum proclaimed in the *Aberdeen Saturday Pioneer* and implied in many of his stories. He certainly appears to be belittling the woman suffrage movement. When Jinjur, sitting on the throne eating caramels, declares that "The throne belongs to whoever is able to take it" she echoes the epigraph to volume II of the *History of Woman Suffrage* (coedited by Maud's mother): "The world belongs to those who *take* it."[12] The girls are armed with knitting needles, but confidently expect that men will not fight them because they are all pretty. They wear colorful uniforms like the Aberdeen Guards and express the absurdly exaggerated ferocity that Mrs. Bilkins attributed to that group. They want to overthrow male rule because it is now women's turn to rule, because they would rather spend their time gossiping than washing dishes, because they want to seize all the jewels in the Emerald City to adorn themselves. The bold girl soldiers run in terror from a dozen mice. They are selfish and silly and have no legitimate grounds for complaint. The most complacent male antisuffragist could say no worse.

The most likely explanation is that Baum had a stage production in view when he wrote *The Land of Oz:* the girl army would provide attractive business for the chorus girls, and the burlesque of a current unpopular cause would pander to the prejudices of a conventional audience, which Baum had accepted as necessary in popular theater. Probably he was so taken with the idea of a theatrical success that he simply did not recognize as he should have that he was belittling a serious issue. Perhaps, too, he was recalling the selfishness and frivolity that had exasperated him when he saw suffragists damaging their own cause in South Dakota by shortsighted infighting.

Baum's possible motives are less important than the ways in which he qualified his attack on female rebels and female rule. The problem with making men do all the housekeeping and child care is not that this work is demeaning to male dignity but that men are broken down by work that women manage easily. Nowhere is it suggested that men are wiser, stronger, or better fitted to rule than women. The Scarecrow and the Tin Woodman are not more efficient or responsible rulers than Jinjur and cannot stand against her until they get the support of the Sorceress Glinda. Glinda demonstrates that female power can be good and wise, and she is supported by an army of girls that is effective, properly armed, and well trained. The situation is hopelessly disorderly until Glinda takes charge and restores the rightful ruler, who will rule Oz well, in contrast to her male predecessors.

The happy transformation of the boy protagonist into a girl is another statement that girls are at least equal to boys, as well as an expression of Maud and Frank's never-fulfilled longing for a daughter. Tip automatically protests against the proposed change, assuming boys are superior and knowing they were more apt to have adventures and fun; and after his transformation she insists she is the same person as always. Jack Pumpkinhead probably speaks for Baum when he qualifies, "Only you're different!"[13] Girls are not the same as boys, but they are not inferior, and basic identity is not determined by sex.

To illustrate the book, Reilly & Britton hired John R. Neill, a young but established newspaper illustrator who could draw both realistic and comic pictures. They were impressed by Neill's ability as "a painter of grotesques, of which he has produced a long series, each conception being peculiarly quaint and humorous. His illustrations are ... clear and suggestive in line; and his use of detail is effective in the extreme." From then on, he illustrated most of Baum's children's books. Neill would spend about a month on an Oz book, making about 150 drawings. He was paid six hundred dollars, plus an additional royalty of one penny per copy from *Ozma of Oz* on. Made wary by his unpleasant experience with Denslow, Baum had resolved never to let another artist share the copyright on his characters; he was still nursing his resentment in 1915, when he reiterated this resolve to his publishers.[14]

Neill was never a personal friend of Baum's, as Denslow had been. Baum's successor, Ruth Plumly Thompson, described Neill as an "altogether delightful person . . . a live and mischievous leprechaun";[15] but Baum knew him only through their business connection and met him only a few times. Neill lived far away in Philadelphia. Reilly & Britton would send him a copy of Baum's manuscript; he would send sketches to the publishers for approval, and then he would finish the pictures. Neill's illustrations are rather stiff and blockish in *The Land of Oz*, possibly in imitation of Denslow. They would become more decorative and flowing in later books. Some have a romantic beauty, which is at least as important to children as humor. Although Denslow had a more distinctive style, most lovers of the Oz books prefer Neill's illustrations as more true to Baum's text.

The Marvelous Land of Oz: Being an Account of the Further Adventures of the Scarecrow and Tin Woodman and Also the Strange Experiences of the Highly Magnified Woggle-Bug, Jack Pumpkinhead, the Animated Saw-Horse and the Gump appeared on July 5, 1904. It received only about half as many reviews as *The Wizard*, but they were generally favorable. A particularly perceptive one appeared in the *Cleveland Leader* on November 6. After praising Baum's "invention and humor," the reviewer pointed out that the fantasy succeeds "because Mr. Baum himself believes in his work and delights in it. . . . A man must have the child heart to write for children. This does not imply that his intellect should be childish." The reviewer noticed that "part of the book, and that the least enjoyable, has been written with a view to the stage. General Jinjur and her soldiers are only shapely chorus girls."[16]

Reilly & Britton went all out to promote *The Land of Oz*—both to renew interest in Oz and to make a hit of the first book published under their name. They distributed many copies of the *Ozmapolitan of Oz*, supposed to be the newspaper of Oz, which includes news about ex-General Jinjur and other characters in *The Land of Oz*, together with a glowing notice of the book.[17] It also reports that the Scarecrow, the Tin Woodman, Jack Pumpkinhead, the Woggle-Bug, the Saw-Horse, and the Gump will be visiting the United States.

On August 18, 1904, wireless bulletins from outer space began appearing in the *Chicago Record-Herald*, the *Philadelphia North American* and other newspapers to announce that a peculiar flying machine was heading toward Earth. The machine was identified on August 28, 1904, on the front page of the Comic and Children's Section of the newspapers. This was the introduction to a series of twenty-six stories (more American fairy tales) called "Queer Visitors from the Marvelous Land of Oz," which appeared every Sunday until February 26, 1905. They filled a comic page—a slight story by Baum about the visitors' adventures and mishaps in the United States, profusely illustrated by the cartoonist Walt McDougall. Through 1904, each story ended with a question and a clue; the Woggle-Bug gives the answer, but it is not printed in the story. There was a contest, with five hundred dollars in prizes every month, for answering the question: "What did the Woggle-Bug say?" The series was further promoted by Woggle-Bug buttons, postcards, and a nonsense song with this title, with words by Baum and music by Tietjens. The prominence and sympathetic presentation of the Woggle-Bug in these stories served to publicize the coming show that went by his name.

Most of the stories mechanically juxtapose magical characters and everyday American life: either the Ozians are puzzled by something ordinary in America, or they create excitement with a bit of magic. Some express typical Baumian themes, like the parallel between magic and technological invention. "In their own fairyland they accomplish things by simple magic which we have to accomplish by complicated mechanical inventions. It is not a strange thing to them to bring a wooden Saw-Horse to life by means of a magic powder; but an automobile (which is even more wonderful than a living Saw-Horse) filled their simple minds with wonder."

In another story, Maud Baum's method of punishing cruelty to animals becomes more dramatic when heightened by magic: the visitors reform a boy who tormented a stray cat by putting him into the cat's body for a day and a night.[18] When the series ended, Reilly & Britton issued *The Woggle-Bug Book* (March 1905), with pictures by Ike Morgan. It reads like a drawn-out version of one of the weaker "Queer Visitors" tales, with its plot turning on a lame joke that was to be a major theme in *The Woggle-Bug* show: the Woggle-Bug falls in love with a loud-checked dress he sees on a mannequin in a shop window and pursues it as it passes from one woman to another. The wearers are a series of ethnic stereotypes. Nevertheless, Baum thought well enough of his work to inscribe a copy to his brother Harry: "a grand physic if taken in small doses." It sold well, though it soon went out of print.[19]

Baum had claimed in his "Author's Note" that he wrote *The Marvelous Land of Oz* in response to the pleas of children for "something more" about the Scarecrow and the Tin Woodman. But the success of the "Wizard" extravaganza, which was still running strong with Stone and Montgomery, certainly contributed to his decision to return to Oz. In addition to referring to their roles in his subtitle, Baum dedicated his book to them and had their photographs in costume on the endpapers. The frivolous treatment of the suffragists can best be explained as designed for success in popular theater aimed at adults. A girl army in picturesque uniforms could repeat the precision drills by the Wizard's Girl Guards that had been much admired in the stage "Wizard." The evil witch Mombi's attempt to block the travelers' progress by surrounding them with sunflowers with girls' faces prepared for a reprise of the deadly poppy scene in *The Wizard.* Tip's transformation into a girl was a common stage effect in pantomime, where the leading boy was played by a girl and reverted to her proper sex at the end. Even the arrangement by which Tip was concealed by pink curtains to emerge as Ozma anticipated the stage effect in the forthcoming show.

But when Baum approached Montgomery and Stone, they declined, fearing to get fixed in their roles as Woodman and Scarecrow. So Baum dropped these characters from his play, replacing them with the Woggle-Bug and Jack Pumpkinhead as the comic team in the show now called "The Woggle-Bug."

In the Prologue, Tip makes Jack Pumpkinhead and Mombi brings him to life. In Act I, the magnified Woggle-Bug steps off a projection screen and has a lengthy humorous dialogue with the Professor, in which he displays what he has learned in the schoolroom, with many malapropisms. Prissy Pring enters with other rustic girls, looking for Jinjur and her army of revolt. The Woggle-Bug admires the gorgeous checks of Prissy's dress: "I'd like to cash in on those checks." (Bad puns, rightly derided in *The Land of Oz*, are supposed to be hilariously funny in the show.) Jinjur appears and announces: "With a great army of gallant milkmaids and scullery ladies I am about to march upon the City of Jewels to wrest the power . . . from the tyrannical regent, and rule the nation in the exclusive interest of my sex." The Woggle-Bug joins her army to be with Prissy's gown. In the next scene, Tip arrives with Jack Pumpkinhead before the City of Jewels and reveals that he has dreamed he is Princess Ozma. Mombi appears in Prissy's dress, and the

Woggle-Bug falls in love with her; meanwhile Jack falls in love with Prissy. Jinjur's army captures the city and takes Tip, Jack, and the Woggle-Bug prisoners.

Act II shows Jinjur and her army eating fudge and playing cards. They bring in Dinah the cook, a comic stage darky, so Mombi can tell her how to cook Jack and the Woggle-Bug, who immediately falls in love with Dinah because she is now wearing the dress. Tip and his friends construct and escape in the Gump. They land in a field of chrysanthemums (the chorus girls), who block them from leaving; the Woggle-Bug raises a flood that drowns them. In Act III, the sorceress Maëtta straightens everything out.[20]

On November 15, 1904, Baum signed an agreement with Henry Raeder, a Chicago theatrical producer, to present a complete libretto of "The Woggle-Bug" by March 1, 1905, and to make any revisions that might "be deemed advisable." Raeder would produce it on or before July 1, 1905, in "a first-class manner with all the appropriate scenery, costumes, and properties." He would choose the composer, but Baum would be consulted on the stage manager and the principal players. Baum's royalty was to be 3 percent of the first six thousand dollars of weekly gross receipts, 4 percent of the next one thousand dollars, and five percent of all over that. If "The Woggle-Bug" proved successful, Raeder's company would produce a second musical written by Baum in 1906; and if that succeeded, a third one in 1907. Probably because Raeder failed to get financial backing for the show, Baum got this contract annulled in March. He then signed another contract, bringing in another man, although Raeder remained in charge and engaged the composer, Frederic Chapin.[21]

"The Woggle-Bug" opened at The Garrick Theater in Chicago on June 18, 1905. The reviews were devastating. The *Tribune* said it was "only a shabby and dull repetition of a cheapened *Wizard of Oz*. The book is the weakest portion of the new offering. It contains virtually no story whatever and witty lines are almost totally lacking."[22] The script *is* awful, trying unsuccessfully to appeal to adults as well as children. All that could be praised were some impressive special effects—the magnification of the Woggle-Bug, the attack by Jinjur's army on the city, and the flooding of the chrysanthemum girls.

On June 25, Baum wrote to Hough that he "collapsed last week from the strain and worry" and came to Macatawa "in a used-up condition. But the rest has helped me and I'll get back to Chicago the middle of this week to get our new comedians started." He blamed the failure of the show on the deficiencies of the two leading comedians, but even after Fred Mace, the Woggle-Bug, was replaced and the production revised, the public stayed away. Raeder could not pay salaries and bills in July. The Garden City Calcium Light Company took back their electric lights, which were essential to the special effects, on July 12. After one embarrassing performance without them, the show closed on July 13. Probably Baum did not lose money of his own, but the failure of his creation was humiliating.[23]

It is hard to understand today the enormous contrast between the receptions of "The Wizard of Oz" and "The Woggle-Bug": the plot of the later show is not much more inconsequential, nor are its jokes and comic routines much more witless. Probably "The Woggle-Bug" failed because it lacked the star power and directorial expertise that largely accounted for "The Wizard"'s success and because Baum repeated almost mechanically the successful novelties of the earlier show. Instead of capitalizing on its success, as he had hoped, he invited unfavorable contrasts with a hit that was still running.

For the next three years, Baum devoted all his energies to fiction, producing successful books for children, adolescents, and even adults. The royalties from his books, together with continuing royalties from the "Wizard of Oz" show, made the Baums so prosperous that they could maintain a home in Chicago and their cottage at Macatawa while spending several months of every year traveling. In February and March of 1904, they toured the Southwest, going through New Mexico and Arizona and up the California coast from San Diego to San Francisco. Near San Diego, they visited the utopian theosophical community at Point Loma and also got their first view of Coronado, a beautiful spot across the bay from San Diego, where the view included a "broad stretch of orange and lemon groves, hedged with towering palm trees; Santa Catalina and the Coronado Islands; the blue Pacific rolling in front and rugged Loma with its rocky cliffs behind."[24] Baum told an interviewer in February 1904 that "those who do not find Coronado a paradise have doubtless brought with them the same conditions that would render heaven unpleasant to them did they chance to gain admittance."[25]

The Baums stayed at resort hotels, of which their favorite was the palatial nine-hundred-room Hotel del Coronado, "with its hundred towers and gables." Its builders in the late 1880s had aimed to make it "the talk of the Western world" and "a cultural oasis of European charm and cuisine" in a relatively unsophisticated area.[26] The result was a hotel so luxurious and elegant it could set a standard for palaces in Oz. The Baums returned each of the following six winters, except when they were abroad in 1906.

Morgan Ross, the manager of the Hotel del Coronado, became a close personal friend. In 1907, Baum and other guests presented him with a gold watch, together with a speech by Baum: "the guests of this hotel are very indignant. It is scarcely necessary to draw your attention to our cramped and confined quarters; to the lack of consideration on the part of the management; to the dust and dirt everywhere prevalent. . . . It is unnecessary to call your attention to these things because they do not exist. . . ."[27] Frank designed the crown-shaped lighting fixtures long used in the main dining room.

The Baums settled into a routine of leaving Chicago in January, when the boys returned to school, staying at the Hotel del Coronado until late March or early April, then moving to Macatawa, and in November returning to Chicago. As always, Baum continued to write busily wherever he was. He wrote to Emerson Hough from Santa Barbara on March 15, 1904, that since January he had completed *The Marvelous Land of Oz, Queen Zixi of Ix,* and five "Animal Fairy Tales."

Baum would write all morning until half past two in the afternoon and then play golf until half past four. "My one recreation is golf, and conditions here are ideal for the game. Every afternoon sees me out on the Coronado links." With all this practice, he commented, perhaps "I'll no longer be the worst golfist in America." Actually, he did not care much about his score; his main object was to knock the ball around in the right general direction, while thinking about a current or future story. But he was always punctilious about his dress, wearing "baggy knickerbockers buckled below the knee, wool hose, a red vest with a scarlet silk back, and a plaid cap with a long visor." In the evening there were parties or entertainment at the hotel.[28]

In November 1904, *Queen Zixi of Ix; or The Story of the Magic Cloak* began to appear in serial installments in *St. Nicholas,* the most prestigious children's magazine of the time. It ran through October 1905 and was published in book form on October I by the Century Company of New York, owner of the magazine. On September 4, 1904, Baum had written from Macatawa Park to W. W. Ellsworth, Secretary of the Century Company, about Frederick Richardson's illustrations, in which he found beauty but not enough humor. His point was taken, for

Richardson's Roly Rogues (the villains of the story) are delightfully funny. Frank added that he and Maud would be in New York about October 15 and looked forward to "meeting our good friends the Ellsworths."[29]

He dedicated *Queen Zixi* to his son Frank, inscribing on the flyleaf of his copy: "You are the last of my boys to have one of my books dedicated to you, but it was your own wish, and in waiting for this story perhaps you have not been unwise. In some ways *Queen Zixi* is my best effort, and nearer to the 'old-fashioned' fairy tale than anything I have yet accomplished."[30]

Queen Zixi of Ix is indeed the finest of Baum's fairy tales in the traditional mode. Its plot centers on a cloak that grants wishes within specified limits, and it features children abused by their guardian who are raised to high status, a throne given on an arbitrary condition, a witch who tries to steal the magic gift, villains who enslave the people, and withdrawal of the magic gift when it is not properly used. But Baum made all this his own by adding comic touches, realistic motivation, and moral complexity. The cloak is woven by fairies in the Forest of Burzee who, like Necile in *Santa Claus* and the fairy who became Prince Marvel, grew bored with their life of static perfection and relieved it by getting involved with struggling mortals. The cloak will grant one wish to its owner, and it is given to the most unhappy person that a fairy messenger can find.

This is a little girl, Fluff, who has been orphaned, along with her brother, Bud, and is now under the power of their severe Aunt Rivette; Rivette is not an evil woman, but she has been made harsh by years of hard work as a laundress and has no understanding of children. Fluff's wish is to be happy, and her resultant happiness makes her amiable. Bud becomes King of Noland because he happens to be the forty-seventh person to pass through the eastern gate one morning. He shows the selfishness and irresponsibility that is only natural in an inexperienced child given the privileges of kingship, although his older sister persuades him to behave tolerably.[31]

The cloak passes through the hands of a series of people unaware of its power, whose frivolous wishes are granted with amusing results. But Zixi, witch-queen of the neighboring country of Ix, seriously wants it. Although she is centuries old, she looks like a beautiful young woman; but her mirror shows her the truth, that she is a hideous crone. She desperately wants a beautiful reflection because it is the one thing she cannot have. On a deeper level, she hates the self-knowledge the mirror forces upon her; she longs to look in a mirror and not see the ugliness she knows is there. Like all of us, she wants to preserve her flattering illusions even when she sees herself clearly. "Zixi wanted to admire herself; and that was impossible so long as the cold mirrors showed her reflection to be the old hag others would also have seen had not her arts of witchcraft deceived them." Although Zixi is a good and wise ruler, she cannot resist trying to get the cloak by force or fraud. She finally succeeds, but it will not grant her wish. In the end the fairies take their gift back but allow the now maturer Bud to make one last wish, that he "may become the best king that Noland has ever had."[32]

While *Queen Zixi* was appearing in *St. Nicholas,* Baum's "Animal Fairy Tales" were serialized in the *Delineator,* a popular women's magazine, from January to September 1905. Baum's articulate animals living under a rule of law owe something to Rudyard Kipling's *Jungle Book* (1894–95) and *Just So Stories* (1902). But Baum developed his own theosophically inspired nature mythology, which relates the animals' law to the divine Law of the universe and gives animals guardian fairies just like people.

In "The Story of Jaglon," an orphaned tiger is raised by the Tiger Fairies to be noble, judicious, and law abiding; and he rightfully seizes the kingship of the jungle from a usurping lion. The morals are unusually explicit for Baum, and the imaginative level rather low. There are also some distressing lapses in natural history, such as endowing the chimpanzees in "The Forest Oracle" with tails.

Baum's most powerful Animal Fairy Tale, "The Tiger's Eye: A Jungle Fairy Tale," was not printed in the *Delineator,* probably because it was considered too frightening for small children. A letter in Reilly & Britton's files indicates that he intended it for a book edition of the tales, but the book never materialized, and the story remained unpublished during his lifetime. An evil magician is forced to take the form of an eye, which moves from animal to animal and corrupts each one it enters. It causes a tiger to slaughter every animal he sees, contrary to the law that forbids animals to "kill except for food" and condemns "the wicked sport of murder." It changes the chief's amiable son into a surly and cruel man. He suffers so from the conflict between this implanted cruelty and his naturally kind nature that he heroically plucks out the eye. It lands in the head of a deer and drives it to impale every animal it meets until the eye finally drops into water and is destroyed.[33]

Baum actually had three serials running in the summer of 1905— *Queen Zixi,* the "Animal Fairy Tales," and *The Fate of a Crown,* his first novel for adults, which was appearing (as *The Emperor's Spy*) in the *Philadelphia North American*. Reilly and Britton published it in book form in the same year. Baum wrote under the pseudonym Schuyler Staunton (the name of his mother's brother), which he also used in his second adult novel, *Daughters of Destiny* (1906). Both follow a popular formula of the time: the Graustarkian novel in which vigorous Americans fight for wholesome and enlightened values in a decadent monarchy. The hero of *The Fate of a Crown*, a young American businessman, becomes involved in the Brazilian revolution that established a republic in 1889; the plot is a maze of mysteries and reversals in which no one is what he or she seems. *Daughters of Destiny* has an even more complicated plot, involving conflicting claims to the throne of Baluchistan, a party of Americans trying to negotiate the building of a railroad there, and a young American who has confessed to embezzlement but turns out to be, not only an honorable man, but the rightful heir to the throne. Baum's conclusion adds a bit of interest: Howard Osborne/Hafiz, renounces the throne and returns to America because he realizes that the progress he would inevitably bring would destroy traditional values.

Reilly & Britton noticed the profit potential in teenage novels, which were quickly written and very popular. They asked Baum to write some, and he promptly started producing series aimed at girls and boys eleven to fourteen, which were to continue to the end of his life. The contract he signed with his publishers on October 6, 1905, shows his friendly relationship with them, as well as his astounding productivity in varied lines. He agreed to deliver (1) the manuscript of "Schuyler Staunton's," "The Girl in the Harem," (*Daughters of Destiny*) by October 15; (2) six complete children's stories of approximately four thousand five hundred words each "written by him under the pen name of 'Laura Bancroft' or some female appelation of equally dignified comprehensiveness" (the *Twinkle Tales*, six related stories that added up to book length) by November 15; (3) a novel for young folks, "the authorship to be ascribed to Maud Gage Baum, or to 'Helen Leslie' [Maud's sister] or to some other female" ("Suzanne Metcalf"'s *Annabel*) by January 1, 1906; (4) "the manuscript of a book for young girls on the style of the Louisa M. Alcott stories, but not so good, the authorship to be ascribed to 'Ida May McFarland,' or to 'Ethel Lynne' or some other mythological female" ("Edith Van Dyne"'s *Aunt Jane's Nieces*) by March 1, 1906; (5) "a story of adventure for boys, the authorship to be ascribed [to] Capt.

Arthur Fitzgerald, or some other mythical male" ("Hugh Fitzgerald"'s *Sam Steele's Adventures on Land & Sea*) by April 15; and (6) "material for a book to be entitled 'Father Goose's Foolish Calendar' by L. Frank Baum" (*Father Goose's Year Book*) on or about April 1, 1906.[34]

Reilly & Britton agreed to publish all these works by September 1, to copyright them in their own name except for the last (in Baum's), and to pay Baum a 10 percent royalty on all except the six Laura Bancroft stories, for which he would get two and a half cents on each copy sold. If they should ever cease to do business, all the copyrights would revert solely to Baum. They promised to promote the books "to the full extent of whatever ability God has given them." They also agreed "that in case said Baum shall at any time become hard up" they would advance him on his royalties "upon demand any sum or sums of money that he may wish to squander that will not total more than two thousand dollars, although they hope it will be less." Finally, Reilly & Britton agreed not to publish any other juvenile book except those mentioned without Baum's written permission during the season of 1906, except only for his fairy book *John Dough, the Baker's Man* (*John Dough and the Cherub*), covered under a previously executed contract.[35]

Probably about 1906, Reilly & Britton agreed to an unusual arrangement with Baum that would help him with his budgeting problems by giving him a steady income on which he could depend. Every month they would send him an advance on his royalties for the year, consisting of one-twelfth of 80 percent of his royalties for the previous year; whatever amount remained would be sent him the following January.[36]

The series books were published under pseudonyms because Baum, who took authorial pride in his fantasies for older children, did not want to impair his reputation with potboilers. Some of his quasi-realistic pseudonymous works have interest and merit, particularly when he used them to express views on current issues more directly than he could in his fantasies. But they were written with the primary aim of making money. In addition, this spreading of authorial responsibility ensured that failure of one series would not damage the fortunes of another. "Capt. Hugh Fitzgerald" was not successful with *Sam Steele's Adventures on Land & Sea* (1906) and *Sam Steele's Adventures in Panama* (1907). In 1908, the same books reappeared as *The Boy Fortune Hunters in Alaska* and *The Boy Fortune Hunters in the Panama* by "Floyd Akers," and they generated a successful series of four other books.

Baum produced an incredible six books in 1906—the first five mentioned in the contract and *John Dough and the Cherub.* In 1907, there were again six new books; in 1908, four; in 1909, three; in 1910, three; in 1911, five; in 1912, four; in 1913, three. In the years of illness before his death, his production declined to a mere two new books per year, except for three in 1916. On the side, he took a twenty-week tour abroad in 1906, developed projects for the stage and the movies, pursued gardening and other hobbies, and led an active social life.

Peter Hanff estimates that Baum could expect to sell approximately twenty thousand copies of the new fantasy he would produce each year, in addition to about forty thousand copies of his older titles and the pseudonymous series.[37] Assuming sales of twenty thousand copies of the new fantasy (priced at $1.25), twenty thousand copies of older fantasies (at $1.25), and twenty thousand copies of adolescent series books (at $0.60), a 10 percent royalty would have yielded Baum $6,200 a year. The *Aunt Jane's Nieces* series in its day sold as well as the Oz books.

Baum used five distinct personae in 1906 (not counting Suzanne Metcalf, who quickly merged into Edith Van Dyne). First there was Schuyler Staunton, author of adventure tales for adults with strong love interest. Then there was Laura Bancroft, whose books for small children were written in a consistently simple, straightforward style. Edith Van Dyne, who wrote for adolescent girls, was decorous and concerned with manners; she avoided violence and evil characters, toned down excitement, and sometimes expressed piety. Capt. Hugh Fitzgerald's boys' books are stereotypically masculine, full of action and shooting, and set in exotic places. Finally, of course, there was the humorous fantasy writer L. Frank Baum.

Nearly forty thousand copies of "Laura Bancroft"'s six little volumes of Twinkle Tales sold in their first year; Reilly & Britton reissued them in a single volume 1911 as *Twinkle and Chubbins* and twice again as individual books after 1916.[38]

Although written for young children, the *Twinkle Tales* are not sweetly insipid like *Dot and Tot.* For one thing, the adventures start not in pretty Rose Lawn but in Edgeley, a grim town on the Dakota prairie, which Baum describes realistically. It is the actual town where Julia Carpenter was so miserable, and Twinkle is modeled on her bright, outspoken daughter, Magdalena. The school picnic must be held in the only bit of shade that can be found outside, under the bridge that crosses a muddy little stream "which they called a 'river,' but we would call only a brook." Edgeley is so called "because it is on the edge of civilization."[39] Beyond it is a great prairie, where Oz-like wonders can occur.

The most popular of the tales proved to be *Bandit Jim Crow*, a strangely grim story of the crimes and punishment of a wicked crow who robbed the nests of other birds. Under the leadership of Policeman Blue Jay, the little birds mobbed him and pecked out his eyes. "Crows are tough, and this one was unlucky enough to remain alive," but he was afraid to leave his nest and had to depend on the charity of the birds he had wronged to bring him food and water. "So Jim Crow, blind and helpless, sat in his nest day after day and week after week . . . And I wonder what his thoughts were—don't you?"[40] Despite his public protestations, Baum recognized that children have a taste for bloody retributive justice.

Mister Woodchuck is the most imaginative of the stories. Twinkle fell asleep by the woodchuck hole where her father had set a leg-hold trap to catch the woodchuck that was eating his red clover. When she opened her eyes, she was woodchuck size, and a well-dressed Mr. Woodchuck dragged her into his handsomely furnished house. He railed against human beings for destroying woodchucks; she protested that a woodchuck that destroyed people's clover and vegetables had to be stopped. He retorted that humans were selfish and cruel to torture "poor little animals that can't help themselves and have to eat what they can find, or starve"; and "Twinkle felt a little ashamed." Killing is not so bad, he said; for "Death doesn't last but an instant. But every minute of suffering [in a trap] seems to be an hour." Just as the woodchuck Judge Stoneyheart was about to make her step into a leghold trap, Twinkle woke up. That night she persuaded her father not to set any more traps, for "surely, papa, there's enough to eat in this big and beautiful world for all of God's creatures."[41]

By giving a woodchuck a voice, Baum makes a powerful case for animal rights and against human self-centeredness. His questioning of conventionally accepted moral attitudes is a heavy, even disturbing, message for a children's story. Baum may have been moved by his son Bob's accounts of visits to Edgeley, when he went hunting with his cousin Harry. They used to hunt prairie dogs, which brought a one-cent bounty because they ate people's crops, shooting them when they had bullets and smashing the animals when they had no more.[42]

Annabel, Baum's first book for teenage girls, is a flat, Horatio Alger–type story in which a virtuous, hard-working young vegetable peddler discovers that his supposedly dead father is alive and rich, and marries the daughter of the local steel magnate. Baum introduced an uncharacteristically pious note into this potboiler for young people: Considering the wonderful coincidences that brought about the restoration of justice in *Annabel,* the steel magnate "bowed his head reverently" and said, "perhaps my little girl is right, and it is the hand of God!"[43] Apparently this book did not catch on, for its author, "Suzanne Metcalf," produced no more.

However, Baum's next novel for girls, "Edith Van Dyne"'s *Aunt Jane's Nieces,* is genuinely original and interesting. It focuses on three adolescent girls, two of whom combine basic good character with ugly traits not usually found in fiction for young girls. Baum starts with a trite situation that could occasion prosy moralizing—three nieces competing to prove who is most worthy to inherit their aunt's legacy—and gives it several original twists. First, rich old Aunt Jane Merrick is too selfish and unpleasant to deserve any devotion. Second, Baum shows sympathy for the two mercenary nieces who are willing to scheme and dissemble for the money. Third, the ideal niece is neither pretty nor decorous.

As the story opens, fifteen-year-old Elizabeth (Beth) De Graf, the daughter of a weak, unsuccessful music teacher and his sour wife, has been peremptorily invited to visit her ailing Aunt Jane, her mother's sister. Openly disregarding her mother and father, Beth cold-bloodedly considers whether it is worth her while to act a living lie and flatter Aunt Jane, whom the whole family justifiably hates, in order to escape from her shabby-genteel existence and constantly bickering parents. Seventeen-year-old Louise Merrick, a socialite whose late father's life insurance will not keep her and her mother in luxury much longer, is delighted with her invitation; for she has no problem with hypocritical flattery and is confident she can win the contest. The third niece, sixteen-year-old Patsy Doyle, daughter of a lovable comic Irishman, is a sort of grown-up Dorothy. Her total freedom from affectation wins all hearts; her wonderful blue eyes cause onlookers to forget her freckles and general plainness. Both she and her father work for their living, she as a hairdresser and he as a bookkeeper; and as the more responsible member of the family, she controls the money. Declaring they are already wealthy, "because we've health, and love, and contentment," she indignantly burns up Aunt Jane's invitation.[44]

Beth arrives at Aunt Jane's estate determined to be gracious but finds it hard to "curb her natural frankness" and conceal her resentment of her aunt's nastiness. Louise gushes affectionately over everyone. She takes hope from Beth's lack of charm and polish, Beth from Louise's obvious insincerity. Aunt Jane sees through both of them and per-suades Patsy to come. Patsy is the only niece to stand up to Aunt Jane, but she is also the only one to be touched by her suffering and to treat her with genuine kindness. Aunt Jane leaves her the estate, but Patsy refuses to accept what Aunt Jane had withheld from her mother, Jane's own sister, when she direly needed it. Patsy would like to "go to a girl's college, like Smith or Wellesley, and get a proper education. But not with your money, Aunt Jane."[45] It turns out that the estate was not Jane's to give, but fortunately Uncle John, her rich brother, turns up and provides generously for the whole family.

All of the nieces have interestingly mixed characters. Patsy is amiable and charming even though she is plain, forthright to the point of tact-lessness, and manifestly aware that she is more competent than her father. Unfortunately, her lovable simplicity becomes cloying. Intelli-gent, sullen, ruthlessly realistic Beth, tormented by doubts that she is worthy to be loved, is much more interesting. Even Louise is less sim-ply contemptible than she appears; Baum explains that her effusive gra-ciousness is not wholly false, for she genuinely wants to make people like her. Her superficiality and false cordiality, like Beth's bitterness and self-interest, are largely the fault of their selfish, worldly parents. How-ever, Louise, the most conventionally "feminine" of the nieces, is clearly Baum's least favorite.

Baum's situation and characters are potentially complex and inter-esting. However, his quasi-realistic fiction does not show the mastery of his fairy tales. His characters are not sufficiently developed to sustain interest within the realistic social situations in which they are placed. Unable to resort to magical solutions, Baum resolves difficulties with blatantly implausible events. Uncle John happens to show up while the nieces are competing for the inheritance; despite his artlessness and apparent poverty, he has a genius for business and has accumulated a vast fortune. In later books his endless supply of money will fill an analogous function to magic in Oz.

Baum's fourth persona was Capt. Hugh Fitzgerald, author of *Sam Steele's Adventures on Land & Sea*. Baum's boys' series lacks the character interest of *Aunt Jane's Nieces*, for the central figure, Sam, is a stereotyped ideal: a capable, brave, enterprising, likable, manly sixteen-year-old

American. He starts off as a penniless orphan and is rescued by his Uncle Naboth, who closely resembles Uncle John and anticipates Trot's friend Cap'n Bill. Uncle Naboth, a shrewd trader, takes on Sam as purser of his Pacific schooner. Two South Pacific islanders, Nux and Bryonia, are among the crew; devoted to Uncle Naboth because he saved their lives, they are versatile and loyal helpers. Unfortunately, they act the parts of comic darkies. Uncle Naboth plans to take advantage of the Alaska Gold Rush (1897) by selling provisions to the miners. In the climactic adventure, Sam, aided by the serviceable Nux and Bryonia, pursues and foils some robbers who are stealing a community's gold.

Finally, Baum published a fantasy, *John Dough and the Cherub*, under his own name. It was serialized in several newspapers from mid-October through December 1906 and published in book form in the same year. It is one of his weaker fantasies, perhaps because he could not have had much time for it with all the other books he was writing. In addition, he seems to have written it with plans for a musical comedy in mind, although this never materialized. This would account for the episodic nature of the book, its underdeveloped characters, and its plethora of puns, spoonerisms, and topical references.

In the opening chapter of *John Dough and the Cherub* Baum moved with his usual skill from everyday life to magical wonder. A mysterious Arab enters an ordinary high-class French bakery in America and gets the baker's wife to hide his vial of the Great Elixir of Life. When the baker makes a life-sized gingerbread man to advertise his shop and celebrate July Fourth, he unwittingly moistens his dough with water containing the Great Elixir, with the result that as soon as John Dough comes out of the oven, he sits up and remarks on the heat of the room.

John is accidentally sent up with a rocket at a July Fourth fireworks display and comes down on the Isle of Phreex. One inhabitant is Chick the Cherub, the Incubator Baby; premature babies actually were displayed in their incubators in sideshows at the time. Chick proves to be an amiable, cheery child, who immediately makes friends with John.[46] Most of the other inhabitants are crank inventors like those in Swift's Laputa, whose inventions include a Power of Revulsion that sends raindrops back up into the sky and a noiseless music box. There is one nonconformist among them, who has invented a flying machine that actually works; he is threatened with execution as an unsuitable citizen. When the Arab arrives in pursuit of his Elixir, which he plans to recover by eating John Dough, John and Chick escape in the flying machine.

They stop briefly at Pirate Island, where they meet a nasty character called Sport, whose body is composed of sporting equipment—a football head, a punching-bag body, and so forth. Finally they arrive at the beautiful island of Hiland and Loland, which is divided by a high wall. In Hiland everyone is tall and slight and convinced that their country and people are the most "great and wonderful...in all the world" and that those on the other side of the wall are "miserable creatures." The short, fat Lolanders are equally convinced of their superiority to the "poor barbarians" on the opposite side. These views can never change because the laws of both countries forbid the citizens to question foreigners. The island is leaderless because neither nation will accept a king from the other, but they ultimately agree to accept the stranger John Dough.[47]

Although there are some successful fantastic elements in *John Dough*, the story suffers from a lack of structure. It is a succession of unrelated oddities, most of which are too vaguely sketched to evoke much interest or feeling. Sport, who could have been an effective satire on the American infatuation with athletics, is left insufficiently developed to make any definite point.

In the course of production, Reilly & Britton noticed that Baum had left Chick the Cherub's sex ambiguous in his manuscript; and they pressed him to say whether Chick was a boy or a girl. He coyly refused to commit himself, even when Reilly told him his child readers would demand to be informed. "I wrote the story as I felt it," Baum insisted. "I can't remember that Chick the Cherub impresses me as other than a joyous, sweet, venturesome and lovable child. Who cares whether the Cherub is a boy or a girl?"[48] Baum was no doubt having fun teasing his publishers, but he was also making his usual point that girls can have the same qualities as boys. The frank, adventurous Cherub would have been male in a conventional story.

Ultimately Reilly & Britton made the best of the situation by sponsoring a competition to determine Chick's sex. They bound a contest blank into each copy of the book, encouraging readers to express their opinion and the reason for it in twenty-five words or less, and they offered prizes for the best answers.[49]

In the first half of 1906, Frank and Maud took their only trip abroad. They sailed from New York on January 27 and spent about five weeks in Egypt, six and a half in Sicily and the vicinity of Naples, three in northern Italy, and two in Switzerland and France. They returned in the middle of June. At the first cataract on the Nile, Baum was gratified to come upon a South African child reading *The Wizard of Oz*.[50]

Maud wrote the letters home because Frank was busy writing stories for publication. She reported on March 23 that they had to stay in Taormina for three weeks so that Frank could finish a book, and again on April 28 from Sorrento that he was finishing a book. Maud later recalled that Frank "always wrote...wherever he was....I remember when we were at Taormina, Sicily, we used to sit outdoors with Mount Etna in front of us, he writing, I reading or needle work. He wrote a friend of his in the U.S. that Mount Etna smoked nearly as much as he did."[51] It is impossible to identify the book or books, in view of the number that Baum was writing at this time, except that it was probably not one of the *Aunt Jane's Nieces* series.

When they returned, the Baums published Maud's letters in a very small edition for the family and friends under the title *In Other Lands Than Ours* (1907). At her request, Frank lightly edited the letters, as well as adding a preface and sixteen photographs he had taken. The frontispiece shows a handsome, square-faced woman who looks firm and self-assured. In other pictures she and Frank appear as a tall and striking couple. Frank's preface praised Maud's "simple, straightforward and expressive language," "her observation of details," and her true "artistic instinct." Her letters also demonstrate intellectual curiosity and a sense of humor. She commented on the limited range of subjects on view in the Uffizi Gallery: "Raphael painted only about ninety Madonnas because he died young, but some of the 'old masters' were old when they died, and what an industrious lot they were!"

"L.F. grieves me," she went on. "He says 'he can tell one old master from another as soon as he reads the name on the frame,' and makes other slighting remarks when I grow enthusiastic; but he seems as eager to study the pictures as I am, and so surely are we being educated by observation that we can both detect now the peculiarities of style and color effects of most of the great masters." It is clear that the Baums assiduously visited museums and other cultural sites and appreciated what they saw. They liked Egypt even more than Europe: "never have we enjoyed anything more or been so intensely interested," Maud wrote.[52]

Probably Frank edited Maud's letters at the same time that he was writing the sequel to *Aunt Jane's Nieces, Aunt Jane's Nieces Abroad*, published late in 1907.[53] Baum organized his novel around a European tour, so that he could thriftily use his travel experiences to fill out the story. (He saved the Egyptian experience for two other novels.) Uncle John takes his nieces to Europe, and they closely follow the Baums' itinerary and have many of the same experiences, down to staying at the same hotels and enjoying the hospitality of a charming Colonel Angeli in Naples. As the Baums had, they witness the major eruption of Mount Vesuvius on April 7—all except Louise, who remains below in her berth to avoid losing her beauty sleep. Maud's letters were invaluable in reminding Frank of the details that filled out his pictures of what the nieces see; for example, he closely followed her description of the destruction wrought by the eruption.[54]

Baum had only to add a melodramatic adventure to the travel account. Near Taormina, Uncle John and a young American (Louise's suitor, Arthur, following her under an alias) are kidnapped and held for ransom by bandits, led by a gentlemanly chief with an engaging tomboy daughter. The nieces manage to rescue the two men without paying a ransom, which is not remarkable considering they are Americans. As Beth informs the local authorities, who are helpless to deal with the bandits, "being Americans, we have decided to assist ourselves." Of course we didn't pay your ransom, Patsy assures Uncle John. "Did you think your nieces would let you be robbed by a bunch of dagoes?"[55]

Such chauvinism was unfortunately a stock and expected element in contemporary teenage novels about adventures abroad. Baum, however, refreshingly qualified it with a surprise ending to his story. When the bandit chief is dislodged from his fortress, he asks Uncle John and the nieces to take charge of his daughter and teach her to be respectable and refined. They magnanimously agree and think she is reforming under their good influence until one day they find she has disappeared, complete with the ransom money. The "dagoes" have outsmarted the self-satisfied Americans.

Baum as the artist Hugh
Holcomb, leading man
in *The Maid of Arran,*
1882.

Baum in his house on Homboldt Park Boulevard, where he wrote *The Wizard of Oz,*
with his sons: Robert, Frank Junior, Harry (holding the family cat), and Kenneth, c.
1899.

Portrait of Maud Baum and the four boys: Robert, Harry, Kenneth, and Frank Junior, 1900.

Portrait of Baum, aged fifty-six, taken in Los Angeles, c. 1912.

The trial of Ojo from Baum's film *The Patchwork Girl of Oz* (1914). A frightened Ojo stands beside the Woozy in the center, with the jury on the left and Ozma and the Wizard, flanked by the Hungry Tiger and the Cowardly Lion, on the right.

The first meeting of the Scarecrow and the Tin Woodman with the Cowardly Lion from Baum's film *His Majesty, the Scarecrow of Oz* (1914).

Baum, aged fifty-eight, working in his garden at Ozcot, c. 1914.

Baum during his final illness, aged sixty-three, 1918 or 1919.

seven

ROYAL HISTORIAN OF OZ,

1907–1910

When Maud and Frank returned from Europe in June 1906, Frank Junior was twenty-two and had started his military career, Robert was twenty and studying engineering at Cornell, and Harry and Kenneth, aged sixteen and fifteen, were away at school. By November, the senior Baums had moved from their big house to a second-floor apartment at 5243 South Michigan Avenue. They continued to go to Macatawa in the summer, but they spent many winter months in warmer parts of the country, looking for a new place to settle. In 1907, they spent about four months in Coronado, their longest visit so far.

In 1907, the Baums celebrated their twenty-fifth wedding anniversary, probably in Chicago. Frank sent out the invitations without Maud's knowledge. They included a facetious record of their married life that shows how thoroughly successful the marriage was:

> Quarrels: Just a few. Wife in tears. Three times (cat died; bonnet spoiled; sore toe).
> Husband swore: 1187 times; at wife, 0.
> Causes of jealousy: 0. (Remarkable in an age of manicured men and beauty doctor women.)
> Broke, occasionally; bent, often.
> Unhappy, 0.[1]

In the same year, "Laura Bancroft" published her best work, *Policeman Bluejay*. Twinkle and Chubbins get lost in the woods and close their eyes; they open them to see a tuxix that turns them into larks when they refuse to do its bidding. Policeman Bluejay (from *Bandit Jim Crow*) befriends them and finds them an old nest. They meet Wisk the squirrel, tenant of the second-floor hollow in their tree, and some other birds. All have stories of human cruelty. One tells how a hunter shot Susie Oriole's husband just when she had a nest of four eggs. She followed him home and found a room filled with stuffed birds, including her husband, as well as an egg collection, including the contents of her nest. A bobolink points out the irony: "how greatly these humans admire us birds. They make pictures of us, and love to keep us in cages so they can hear us sing, and they even wear us in their bonnets after we are dead." Robin Redbreast adds: "Mankind . . . is the most destructive and bloodthirsty of all the brute creation. They not only kill for food, but through vanity and a desire for personal adornment. I have even heard it said that they kill for amusement, being unable to restrain their murderous desires." In contrast, kind Mrs. Hootaway the owl, who occupies the top hollow of the child-larks' tree, kills only her natural prey, which is compatible with "the Great Law of the forest," namely Love. Even though animals like owls must kill and eat others in order to live, they practice love and tenderness for their own kind and for their neighbors as well.[2]

The child-larks are rudely awakened the next morning by a loud bang, shouts, barks, and screams of pain. Hunters have shot Mrs. 'Possum, the occupant of the first-floor burrow, and their dogs are tearing her babies apart. Then they shoot the owl, whose last words are, "Remember that—all—is love." Finally the squirrel pokes his head out and is shot. Twinkle drops beside the owl's body and orders the man off, but her voice comes out as chirping. Just as his dog is about to grab her, the Eagle seizes the two child-larks and takes them to his nest. The home of the monarchs of the bird world occasions Baum's usual scorn for high society. Mrs. Eagle is "larger and more pompous even than her husband. . . . Neither the nest nor the eagles appeared to be very clean, and a disagreeable smell hung over the place."[3]

Immediately after the slaughter in the tree and the visit to the Eagle's nest, where the child-larks were in imminent danger of being eaten, Policeman Bluejay takes them to the Land of Paradise in the center of the forest, which is, appropriately, populated exclusively by birds of paradise. This happy country is totally free of the dangers and suffering that dominate life on the outside. Policeman Bluejay leaves his nightstick at home when he takes the child-larks there because the Guardian Bird of Paradise does not "like to see anything that looks like a weapon. In his country there are no such things as quarrels or fighting, or naughtiness of any sort; for as they have everything they want there is nothing to quarrel over or fight for."

Only "one race" lives in Paradise, "every member of which is quite particular not to annoy his fellows in any way. That is why they will admit no disturbing element into their country. If you are admitted my dears, you must be very careful not to offend any one that you meet." Paradise is, indeed, perfect: it is bathed in rosy light, the flowers are always full of nectar, the fruits regrow constantly, and there is a Lake of Dry Water, where the birds can play and come out dry. The King Bird of Paradise, who is even more magnificently plumed than his subjects, welcomes the child-larks graciously, but immediately asks them to admire his beauty. In a metal forest (sterile, like the Nome King's in *Tik-Tok of Oz*), the King and the other male birds dance while admiring their reflections in the silver leaves. The brown females sit in the background admiring them and occasionally rush forward to smooth a disarranged feather.[4]

This land without need, evil, or conflict is indeed a Paradise in its sharp contrast to the stressful life of the forest. By referring to "a legend that man once lived there, but for some unknown crime was driven away," Baum clearly relates it to the biblical Garden of Eden. But he does not portray it as the ideal place of orthodox Christian doctrine. Baum's unfallen creatures are vacuous and complacent. The Birds of Paradise do no evil because they have no temptation: everything they need for a comfortable life is constantly provided, and conflict cannot exist in a society that has bound itself to bland conformity. As the Owl pointed out, they "are not obliged to take life in order to live themselves; so they call us savage and fierce. But I believe our natures are as kindly as those of the Birds of Paradise."[5] They have not sinned, but they have not done any good either; it is scrappy Policeman Bluejay who helps the child-larks and the predatory Owl who maintains that all is love even as she is being murdered.

Perhaps Baum intended an even more daring allusion, for Paradise can also mean Heaven. The King Bird of Paradise, who exists solely to be perfect and to be admired by his beautiful and sinless subjects, does bring to mind God surrounded by the heavenly hosts who sing hosannas all day long. This is very different from the theosophist heaven, where souls actively strive for improvement of themselves and the world. Paradise and the forest outside are both undesirable extremes; Baum implies that some evil and conflict are necessary if we are to live. Existence in Paradise contrasts strongly with the rich variety of Oz, where every human, animal, or machine is accepted for what s/he is, where females are equal, where conflicts arise because people express their differing opinions, where adventures are possible because evil exists, even though good always wins.

In the end Twinkle and Chubbins are disenchanted, and they can no longer talk with the big blue bird they see in a tree. The *Twinkle Tales* had been presented as dreams, presumably because they were supposed to have happened in America. In his Preface to *Policeman Bluejay*, Baum dismissed this evasion by declaring that it really made no difference whether the children's experience was a "real" magic adventure or a dream; both are real in the world of imagination, which has its own validity.

Policeman Bluejay is surprising fare for small children, and it does not hold together like the Oz stories, where disparate elements are subordinated to a consistent atmosphere. But its discordant elements make it a powerful and fascinating story: without leaving the level of fairy tale, it moves us to question accepted practices and beliefs, from our exploitation of animals to our assumptions about the nature of virtue, the necessity of evil, and the moral superiority of a perfect being that demands admiration.

Although the book was not successful by Baum standards—its first edition evidently did not go into a second printing—his publishers considered it worthwhile to reprint it under other guises. In 1911, it reappeared as *Babes in Birdland*, capitalizing on *Babes in Toyland* (1903). In 1917, they reprinted it under Baum's name. He suggested they enhance it further by calling it "An Oz Tale," but they vetoed the suggestion.[6]

Edward Stern, a Philadelphia publisher, had met the Baums when they were touring Egypt and asked Frank for a book. It became *The Last Egyptian: A Romance of the Nile*, published anonymously on May 1, 1908. Baum's best novel for adults, it is an exciting adventure story in the Rider Haggard manner, set in contemporary Egypt. Kāra, a man of Coptic (pure Egyptian) stock descended from Ahtka-Rā, the vizier of Rameses II, has been raised by his evil grandmother to take revenge on the entire family of the English lord Roane, who seduced and betrayed her. Using treasure from his ancestor's tomb, Kāra gets Lord Roane and his son government appointments in Egypt and secures himself a place in upper-class Cairo society. He ingratiates himself with the Roanes: the old lord, whose only redeeming trait is love for his granddaughter;

the young lord, who is totally worthless; and the granddaughter Aneth, who is the only decent member of the family.

Kāra ruins the young lord through his weakness for gambling and inveigles the old lord into embezzling a thousand pounds from the Egyptian government. He blackmails Aneth into accepting his proposal of marriage by threatening to expose her grandfather. She is saved by Winston, the English Egyptologist who loves her, and her strong-minded older friend Mrs. Everingham, who declares: "No right-minded girl would ruin the life of the man she loves to save her grandfather from the consequences of his own errors. If she is in the mood to sacrifice, we will let her sacrifice Lord Roane instead of herself or you."[7] Kāra is shut up in his ancestor's tomb and dies there.

This book, like Maud's letters from Egypt, makes a point of the distinction between pure native Egyptians (Copts or "Fellahin Egyptians") and Arabs or Turks. Both the Baums were fascinated by ancient Egyptian antiquities, partly because much of the occult wisdom prized by theosophists was traced to Egypt; Madame Blavatsky called her textbook *Isis Unveiled*. With the help of Maud's letters, Baum skillfully used the background he picked up on his Egyptian tour—the awful heat, the contemporary natives, and the tombs and treasures—to give color and plausibility to his novel. The architecture and contents of Ahtka-Rā's tomb are described in detail and appear to be authentic.

On November 19, 1906, Baum had hopefully mentioned the novel to Ellsworth, who had encouraged him to show him his work: "It's based on material I picked up in Egypt and I'm sure it has the right 'atmosphere,' whatever other merit it may chance to possess. It will have to be published under a pen name (if it has the luck to be published at all) because I cannot interfere with my children's books by posing as a novelist. But I wanted to write this Egyptian Tale, so I'm hard at it. I wonder if you will read the MS when it's ready, and *if* you find it good bluff the Century Company into printing it."[8] Apparently Ellsworth was not interested, for Stern published it in May 1908, and it is dedicated to "Mr. Edward Stern, A Fellow Traveler in the Wilds of Egypt."

The Egyptian trip also inspired *The Boy Fortune Hunters in Egypt*, although that work has little distinctive local color. Egypt influenced Oz in more subtle ways. After seeing Egyptian chariots, Baum gave Ozma a chariot covered with gold, like one he had seen in the Cairo Museum. A relief on a wall at Medinet Habu showing Rameses III "in battle, with his trained lion running beside his chariot" may have suggested that her chariot be drawn by the Cowardly Lion. The travelers' climb up through Pyramid Mountain in *Dorothy and the Wizard in Oz* might have been inspired by the Baums' climb at the temple at Edfu, where they mounted 242 steps, in relays of 14, with a chamber cut into solid masonry, lighted by small windows, at each landing. The half-submerged Temple of Isis at Philae, its upper part "apparently rising from the bosom of a placid lake," could have been in Baum's mind when he envisioned the half-submerged Island of the Skeezers in *Glinda of Oz*.[9]

Aunt Jane's Nieces at Millville, one of the four books Baum published in 1908, shows the understandable strain of his work schedule, for it is heavily padded. Uncle John takes his nieces to spend the summer in Millville, a backward town in upstate New York; and the substance of the book is humor at the expense of the local yokels.

Its sequel the following year, *Aunt Jane's Nieces at Work* (1909), is misleadingly titled: *work* refers to the nieces' amateur electioneering in their friend Kenneth's campaign for the New York State Legislature. He hopes "to defeat a bad man who now represents Kenneth's district." But it appears that he will be crushingly defeated because his opponent, Hopkins, is an unscrupulous demagogue. Hopkins is a Democrat, but Baum takes care to have Kenneth's wise mentor point out that "There is no difference of importance" between the parties, although both are needed to keep the nation going properly and to watch each other.[10] Baum was always more interested in the quality of candidates than in their party affiliation.

Uncle John suggests the nieces go to Elmhurst and help Kenneth with their "shrewdness and energy," and after some debate about whether women should get involved in politics, they do. Patsy plans the campaign, Louise goes around charming the farmers' wives (who can be counted on to "tell their husbands how to vote"), Beth will write campaign literature, and Uncle John buys the support of the local newspaper by paying the editor more than Hopkins had.[11] Hopkins, who oppresses his wife without even realizing that he does so, retaliates by railing against female influence in politics. His illiberal arguments backfire, and Kenneth wins by a good margin. The next book in this series, *Aunt Jane's Nieces in Society* (1910), develops a favorite theme of Baum's, the emptiness and artificiality of fashionable life.

All this while, Baum was regularly producing his Sam Steele books for boys. In *Sam Steele's Adventures in Panama* (1907), Baum enriched his conventional swashbuckling adventure with imaginative invention in the manner of *The Master Key*. Sam, now captain of a rickety ship heading around South America to California, carries with him the dreamy inventor Duncan Moit with his wonderful Moit Convertible Automobile. This super-automobile, which would be magic if its mechanism were not so plausibly explained, can travel equally well on land and water; it is made of a mysterious aluminum-like alloy and powered by compressed air, which can be obtained wherever there is air. Cars were still novelties in 1907, although the Baums had had one since 1905.

A storm forces them to land on the coast of Panama, which is populated by the Techla Indians, descended from Aztecs who fled the Spaniards. These Indians hate white people and bar them from their domains; they have large supplies of gold and diamonds, but refuse to trade or use them because of the damage done by white people's greed. Sam and his party resolve to get some diamonds, so they use Moit's automobile to take them over the swamps to the Indian king, who sees right through the Americans' attempts to fool him. Meanwhile, his daughter and heir, Ilalah, has fallen in love with Moit and agrees to go away with him. Sam "noticed that while she had abandoned all—her life, her prejudices, and her kingdom—for her white lover, Duncan Moit had promised nothing in return except that they would not be separated. The thought made me sorry for the poor maid; but it was none of my affair."

Ultimately the king accidentally blows up the automobile and himself with it, making Ilalah queen. Moit has not got the heart to build another automobile, so he gives up his ambition and decides to live with Ilalah as her consort. He willingly gives his share of the diamonds to his comrades and resolves to destroy all the gold and diamonds he can find, for the Techlas can only retain their territory if they "own nothing that will arouse the cupidity of the outside world." Sam wonders whether this shows the "streak of madness" he has always suspected in Moit.[12]

Baum's attitude toward the Indians is ambivalent throughout. The Techlas do not practice the bloodthirsty customs of their Aztec ancestors, and their laws are just and humane. Their dignity, disdain for treasure, detestation of falsehood, and simple directness suggest noble savages. On the other hand, through much of the plot the Indians are the standard hostile natives, to be shot or blown up because they do not cooperate with the Americans. Baum seems to have been torn between presenting a different point of view to make us question our assumptions, as he did in his fairy stories, and patronizing or routing non-white characters to conform to the conventions expected by his publisher and readers.[13]

In 1908, Reilly & Britton reissued the two *Sam Steele's Adventures* books as *The Boy Fortune Hunters in Alaska* and *The Boy Fortune Hunters in the Panama* by "Floyd Akers," together with Floyd Akers's *The Boy Fortune Hunters in Egypt*. Sam acquires two boy comrades to fit the new title. Both are stock characters: Joe, a pathetic runaway cabin boy who turns out to be a skilled wrestler and heir to a fortune, and Archy, a spoiled but redeemable rich boy. Baum used local color from his recent trip to Egypt to give this formula work such individuality as it has. Sam's ship is carrying American-made Oriental carpets and Egyptian antiques to sell to American tourists in the Middle East. Again Baum emphasized the distinction between true Egyptians and later invaders, as the fortune hunters rationalize taking the treasure of Karnak from Egypt on the grounds that the descendants of its ancient Egyptian owners cannot regain it anyway, and it does not belong to the Arabs and Turks who now rule the country.[14]

In the foreword to *The Boy Fortune Hunters in China* (1909), the author makes a spurious claim to have "penetrated far into the Chinese Empire" and drawn his Chinese characters from life. The book actually does contain some authentic-sounding details, perhaps reflecting the younger Frank's observations on his way to Manila in 1904. In his letters home, he described being graciously entertained by high-ranking Chinese, one of whom was very Americanized, and seeing the ancestral treasures of a distinguished family.[15] In his father's book, Sam and his friends (including Nux and Bry, "our faithful blacks") are directed by a dying young Chinese man, who is attractive and amiable because he is so Westernized, to go across China to collect a great treasure. They are opposed by Chinese superstition and a crafty Chinese villain and aided by a very sympathetically presented eunuch.

In *The Boy Fortune Hunters in Yucatan* (1910), the usual conflict between Americans and hostile natives is complicated by the fact that the natives are a highly superior (and white) race. Sam and his friends decide to help Lieutenant Allerton on his expedition to the forbidden city of the Tcha, descendants of survivors of Atlantis, where he hopes to trade modern inventions for their gold and rubies. Allerton has brought along devices invented by his brilliant Uncle Simeon, who must have touched the Master Key: gas-jackets with wings to fly through the air, electric stun guns, and garments of protection.

In this book Baum borrowed heavily from his Oz fantasies: the Tcha are red-haired and blue-eyed like Glinda the Good, and they live in a beautiful city built of white marble. More significantly, their society resembles the utopia that Baum was developing in his Oz books from 1907 to 1910. The Tcha are socialists, with everyone working and everyone receiving what they need; gold is their most common metal, for they can render it as hard as steel; they are law-abiding and courteous; "the women were considered the equals of men in all ways, and their superiors in many"; and their ruler is the High Priestess of the Sun, who is a seventeen-year-old "embodiment of grace and beauty."[16] Nevertheless, no people can remain superior to Americans in a conventional boys' adventure story, so the Tcha have to be destroyed by earthquakes that send them into a superstitious frenzy.

During these years, Baum's major creative work—his fantasies for children—finally came to focus on Oz. Both sales and readers' letters made clear to him and to his publishers that Oz fantasies sold better than anything else he could write. Readers clamored to hear more of Dorothy, and one suggested he have her meet Ozma so they could "have a good time together." On June 28, 1906, Baum signed a contract with Reilly & Britton to deliver the manuscript for *Ozma of Oz* by December 1 and to supply two additional Oz books in 1909 and 1911.[17]

Ozma of Oz: A Record of Her Adventures with Dorothy Gale of Kansas, the Yellow Hen, the Scarecrow, the Tin Woodman, Tiktok, the Cowardly Lion and the Hungry Tiger; Besides Other Good People Too Numerous to Mention Faithfully Recorded Herein appeared in 1907. He dedicated it "To all the boys and girls who read my stories—and especially to the Dorothys." As his subtitle indicates, he took care to include most of the characters beloved in *The Wizard of Oz*.

Probably Baum had not envisioned a sequel to *The Land of Oz*. Its ending suggests closure; for example, "Jack Pumpkinhead remained with Ozma to the end of his days; and he did not spoil as soon as he had feared, although he always remained as stupid as ever." At the end of the new book, Baum left the way open for Dorothy to return to Oz. Oz is more clearly an ideal place than it was in *The Wizard of Oz* or *The Land of Oz*, so it is natural that American characters would want to remain there; Dorothy returns to the everyday world only out of consideration for Uncle Henry.[18]

Dorothy is several years older than she was in *The Wizard of Oz* and consequently more self-aware and articulate, more ready to formulate her feelings and evaluate others' behavior. We are more aware of her distinctive personality than in *The Wizard*, which deals more with universal experience.[19] The book opens with a vivid description of a storm at sea, in which Dorothy is blown overboard, clinging to a chicken coop. As in *The Wizard*, she is not thrown into panic or despair by this catastrophe, but she articulates her reaction as the younger Dorothy would not have done: "You're in a pretty fix, Dorothy Gale . . . and I haven't the least idea how you're going to get out of it!"[20]

This shift to a more sophisticated point of view subtly shifts the tone of this and the succeeding Oz books. Motivation and social interactions become more complex, and plots can introduce social and political issues. Older children often find the Oz books from *Ozma* on to be more absorbing than the first two books. But although Dorothy has outgrown her childish simplicity, she retains her matter-of-fact acceptance of things as they come and her unselfconscious egalitarianism: she will soon be talking as an equal to a hen, a robot, and a princess.

After his realistic opening, Baum brings us into fairyland with his usual masterful casualness: Dorothy asks a rhetorical question, and the yellow hen that shares her coop answers it. Billina, the engaging result of Baum's lifelong interest in chickens, is a realistic hen that examines objects first with one eye and then the other. But she is also an enhanced Ozian animal with her own distinctive point of view, arguing vigorously that live bugs are more wholesome food than the dead meat preferred by humans. Like many Ozian females, she displays qualities conventionally reserved for males. Her original name was Bill (sex being impossible to determine in chicks), and she lives up to it when she is locked in a chicken house and beats up the dominant rooster: "Do you think I'd let that speckled villain of a rooster lord it over *me*, and claim to run this chicken house, as long as I'm able to peck and scratch?"[21] In later books she will become a matriarch over many chickens (proceeding, apparently, from her skirmish with the rooster in Ev). She will retain her disdain for males, hopefully naming all her chicks Dorothy and changing this to Daniel only if they grow into "horrid roosters."[22]

In a cave at the top of the hill, they find Tiktok, the copper machine man, who "thinks, speaks, acts, and does everything but live."[23] Thus

Baum introduces yet another type of creature into his Oz world. What differentiates Tiktok from the Tin Woodman, who is also made of metal? The Tin Woodman is a naturally formed human personality who happens to be embodied in metal, while Tiktok has been manufactured by clever mechanics (Americans, judging by their names, who protected their invention by patent) and therefore has no self or consciousness of his own. Live things are endowed by nature with their own consciousness, whether they are humans, animals, immortal spirits, or dummies that come to life.[24]

Consciousness entails feelings, needs, interests, and aspirations, which Tiktok knows nothing of. He does only what he is wound up to do, so that he cannot make free choices like a living being. He is limited, as he freely admits—for being a machine he thinks clearly and is free of vanity. But in some ways he is more perfect than a living being. He reliably does what he is wound up to do, whether it is telling the truth or serving his owner. His thinking is not clouded by prejudice or emotion, and his unswerving courage and loyalty to Dorothy contrast very favorably with the behavior of the human officers of Ozma's army. He can only do what he is wound up to do, but his machinery is such that he can only be wound up to do the right thing.

In Ev, Dorothy and her group meet Ozma, who is leading a party from Oz to persuade Roquat, the Nome King, to release the Queen and Princes of Ev, whom the King of Ev sold to him and he has changed into ornaments for his palace.[25] Roquat rules the mineral world underground; his immortal subjects are rock fairies (or, in theosophical terms, elementals of the earth). On meeting Tiktok, the Scarecrow and the Tin Woodman boast ungenerously of their constantly functioning brains and heart; he modestly admits his inferiority, but actually performs as well as they do. In industrialized countries in this world, human workers are reduced to machines; in Oz, a machine is humanized. Potentially frightening technology can be benign, and, just as animals are brought close to humans, machines are brought close to living things. Tiktok contrasts totally with Smith & Tinker's other creation, the cast-iron Giant with the Hammer, who is a horrible illustration of the machine as mindless, untiring power. Only another machine, Tiktok, can admire his efficiency. The Giant unceasingly pounds the road to block the way to the Nome Kingdom.

From here on, suspense builds. After they pass under the Giant's hammer, the Oz party must travel over a darkening, silent path where the mountains block out the sunshine and there are no birds or squirrels because there are no trees. They hear jeering laughter as they come to a blank rock wall at the end of the path and can barely see the rock-colored forms that flit over its surface. Roquat himself looks like a rock-colored Santa Claus and is disarmingly jolly and avuncular. But he absolutely refuses to give up his prisoners, and he shows Ozma his huge army—equipped with bronze axes, steel armor, and electric lights on their foreheads.[26] Only evil powers have effective armies in the Oz books, for Baum advocated pacifism.

Then the Nome King seemingly relents and makes a deceptively fair offer: the Oz people may go in one by one and guess which ornaments are the enchanted Ev people; if they succeed, he will release them; if not, the guessers will become ornaments themselves. The ordeal is just sufficiently harrowing to build up agreeable suspense. Ozma makes her guesses, and when she is finished the Nome King's magnificent rooms are "quite empty of life" and there is a new emerald grasshopper on a table.[27] All the others fail except Dorothy, who by lucky chance changes a statue of a purple kitten back into a Prince of Ev. The King laughs pleasantly as each person disappears.

It is the hen Billina who saves the situation. Sitting unseen under the King's throne, she overhears the clue to the transformations, enters the palace, and undoes them all. When the restored characters return to the throne room, they find a horribly changed Roquat, transported with rage, who has called out his army to keep them imprisoned forever. But the resourceful hen, who has also learned that eggs are poison to Nomes, supplies eggs to defeat them. It is appropriate that eggs, symbols of new life, are poisonous to Nomes, whose kingdom is lifeless. Eggs are also, of course, the quintessential female product. Every Nome who appears is male, and the values of their kingdom—accumulation of wealth and militarism—are associated with the lack of female influence. It is typical of Baum's whimsical inventiveness to use a barnyard hen, and a hen who is quite realistic apart from her cleverness and power of speech, to save the situation.

Dorothy and the Wizard in Oz (1908), dedicated to Baum's sister Harriet, is the first of Baum's books to use an explicitly Californian setting; the action is set off by the great San Francisco earthquake of 1906. It is an unpleasant book, flouting Baum's own criteria for children's stories and lacking his usual exuberant imagination, humor, and genial morality.

In the first two-thirds of the story, Dorothy and her friends—the

Wizard, the boy Zeb, the old horse Jim, and her kitten Eureka—barely escape from an unrelenting succession of threatening magical countries, populated by emotionless vegetable people, invisible bears, aggressive gargoyles, and hungry dragons.[28] Dorothy is a helpless little girl, given no opportunity to show her resourcefulness. When the travelers finally arrive in Oz, it proves to be a goody-goody place where the only events are the punishment of Jim and Eureka for not being nice.

Jim, a broken-down horse who uses his new magical power of speech to express the pessimism produced by a lifetime of abuse, is a touching character. In Oz, Baum sets him up for humiliation: considerate treatment is such a novelty to Jim that it goes to his head, and he becomes conceited and triumphs over the Sawhorse. The pampered wooden horse behaves perfectly, while Jim, like a disfavored child, asserts himself obnoxiously and is a sore loser when his rival defeats him in a race. His humiliation, however well deserved, illustrates a judgmental morality that is one of the things we should be free from in Oz, where it is usually understood that people or animals behave badly because they are unhappy and where bad behavior is handled with loving understanding. Normally Baum, like his own Santa Claus, did not insist on strict retributive justice. Santa brought toys to the children, not because they were good, but "because they were little and helpless, and because he loved them. He knew that the best of children were sometimes naughty, and that the naughty ones were often good."[29]

The harsh condemnation of Jim is reinforced by the trial of Eureka for following Nature's law for cats by allegedly eating a tiny piglet; this is the culmination of a hostility to cats that has been evident throughout the book. Eureka's indifference and perversity are true to feline nature and an appropriate comment on the absurd, self-righteous proceedings; but Baum reprehends her an unrepentant criminal.[30]

Baum now had three successful series going—his Oz books for children, his Aunt Jane's Nieces books for teenage girls, and his Boy Fortune Hunters books for teenage boys. He and Maud had as comfortable a lifestyle as they could wish and could have maintained it indefinitely. But, alas, Baum could not keep away from the stage. He needed contact with an enthusiastic audience and the possibility of greater profits than could be obtained from book royalties. So he devised a novel way to bring his works to the stage, one that had the further appeal for him of using the new media of slides and film. Baum's "Fairylogue and Radio-Plays" was a two-hour mixed media show that dramatized his fairy stories by means of narration by himself, enactment by live actors, slides, and short films. Baum coined the word *fairylogue* on the pattern of *travelogue*, meaning a trip to fairyland. *Radio* did not have its modern sense, but referred to the process invented by Michel Radio by which the movies were hand-colored (which Baum may have investigated when he and Maud had visited Paris).[31]

The first half of the show ran through fourteen scenes from *The Wizard of Oz, The Land of Oz*, and *Ozma of Oz* in an hour and ten minutes. The seven scenes of the forty-minute second half realized Baum's hopes of staging *John Dough and the Cherub.* The intermission featured slides advertising the just published *Dorothy and the Wizard in Oz.*

Baum, dressed in white, introduced the show by explaining how a fairy approached him in a clover field and took him on a visit to the Land of Oz, so that he came to write the Royal History. Then he would go off into the wings, and a red velvet frame would open to reveal a small stage and screen. A movie would come on to show him, dressed in the same white suit, leading characters out of the illustrations of a giant book. These were actors dressed as Oz characters— Dorothy, the Scarecrow, Jack Pumpkinhead, the Nome King, and so forth. The story would be told through short films and slides, while Baum narrated from the wings. In addition, a live orchestra played twenty-seven instrumental numbers composed by Nathaniel D. Mann.[32] Baum proudly described some of the special effects in an interview he gave in New York. For the scene with Dorothy in the chicken coop from *Ozma of Oz*, moving pictures were taken of a storm at sea; then Dorothy was filmed in the studio balancing in her coop, which was moved by rockers, casters, and wires to simulate the motion of waves; finally this film was superimposed on the storm film. It took seven attempts to make the coop "follow the roll of the waves."[33]

Baum, assisted by his son Frank, who was the projectionist, presented the first shows in Grand Rapids, Michigan, from September 24 through September 26, 1908. From there they did three-day stands in Chicago, Saint Louis, Milwaukee, Saint Paul, and Minneapolis. They returned to Chicago on October 24 and stayed until November 6. Then they spent a day each in Rockford and Rock Island, Illinois; in Burlington, Iowa; in Peoria, Illinois; two days in Syracuse; and one in Auburn, New York. They finished their tour in New York City from

December 14 through 31, when Baum had to admit that the show was losing money.[34] In less than three months, he had made fourteen stops and staged over forty performances.

The Radio Plays must have been delightful to see, and the reviewers admired some of the scenes as "marvels of beauty," mentioning the one in which John Dough is sent up in a fireworks display and falls to earth uninjured and the one that showed Dorothy adrift in the chicken coop, "the waves rolling and the spray flying." They also praised Baum's "wonderfully musical voice," platform presence, and boyish manner, "despite his rather fierce mustache." Adults as well as children appreciated the show, but it still lost money because it was so expensive to mount. Baum had to have twenty-three film clips made in the Selig Polyscope studios in Chicago and sent to France to be hand tinted, to have 114 slides made from Neill's illustrations, to have twenty-seven musical numbers composed by Mann, to engage actors and an orchestra to play the musical score in each city, to transport a heavy projector and other equipment from place to place every few days, and to hire handsome theaters, such as the newly decorated Orchestra Hall in Chicago.[35] Far from making his fortune, as he had hoped, Baum lost his comfortable security and found himself badly in debt to his friend Harrison Rountree, who had financed many of the expenses, and to various contractors.

Fortunately, Baum was able to keep on writing regardless of financial worries. *The Road to Oz* (1909) is dedicated to his first grandson, Frank Junior's son, Joslyn Stanton Baum, born in 1908.[36] The entrance into fairyland in this book is particularly captivating. Dorothy sets out on the road to Butterfield in Kansas; after walking fifteen minutes from her home, she realizes she no longer sees any familiar landmarks, and before long she has reached a city of civilized foxes who recognize her as a friend of Ozma of Oz. At no point is there an obvious break between ordinary reality and magical country. It makes us feel that wonderful things are right next door to our daily lives if only we use our imagination or look at things the right way.

The story opens with a shaggy man asking directions of Dorothy outside her house. The "shaggy man" is an Ozian view of a tramp— "shaggy" accurately describes his ragged clothes and unkempt hair, but suggests humorous eccentricity rather than poverty and slovenliness. He may derive from James W. Riley's kindly, fanciful "Raggedy Man" and romanticized tramps in contemporary writers like Jack London, who presented the tramp not as a derelict but as a carefree nonconformist who refused to fit into a proper social role and despised money.[37]

Once the shaggy man arrives in the Emerald City, Baum brings out the distinctiveness of Oz by reminding us how it is with tramps in our world. The shaggy man cannot believe that he will be welcome in Ozma's palace: "He had never been a guest in a fine palace before; perhaps he had never been a guest anywhere. In the big, cold, outside world people did not invite shaggy men to their homes." Yet in Oz he is accepted for his good heart and outfitted with splendid shaggy clothes that make it possible to "be finely dressed and still be the Shaggy Man," to be true to himself without being disreputable.[38]

Halfway to fairyland, Dorothy and the shaggy man meet Button Bright by the road. He is curly haired, blue-eyed, adorable, stupid, and passive—a typical fairy-tale girl, but in Baum's fantasy he is a boy. Flouting the older-boy-protecting-younger-girl convention, Baum always makes the girl the more competent of the two and the leader.[39]

After leaving Foxville, where the king expresses predictable opinions of Aesop's representation of foxes, the travelers meet the engaging cloud fairy Polychrome, the Rainbow's Daughter, who has carelessly slipped off her father's bow. As usual in Baum, all the adventurers quickly adapt to their unprecedented circumstances and optimistically await whatever new experiences may come. Dorothy, Button Bright, and Polychrome are lost children; Button Bright has been given a fox head in Foxville and the shaggy man a donkey head in the next village of Dunkiton, and yet: "None of the party was really unhappy. All were straying in an unknown land and had suffered more or less annoyance and discomfort; but they realized they were having a fairy adventure in a fairy country, and were very much interested in finding out what would happen next."[40]

Their confidence is challenged, however, by their encounter with the truly horrible Scoodlers, creatures with reversible bodies and heads that may be removed and used as missiles, who intend to make the travelers into soup. Like many of Baum's fantasies, the Scoodlers were a heightened form of a familiar everyday object. They were modeled on a common toy, a wooden jumping jack that could be worked by strings to walk or to leap up from a crouching position. Its round head, attached by a string to the torso, could be made to leave the body and shoot upward by a quick jerk of the string. One side of the figure was black

The Road to Oz. The Scoodlers threaten to make soup of Dorothy, Polychrome, Toto, Button
Bright (with a fox's head), and the Shaggy Man (with a donkey's head). Note the varied
symbols on the Scoodlers' heads. John R. Neill.

and the other white, and the operator could twist the strings to make it
flap back and forth.[41]

Baum again blurs the boundary between fairyland and the everyday
world when the shaggy man brings in Johnny Dooit to get his party

across the deadly desert. Johnny Dooit is "an American wizard":[42] that is, he carries American ingenuity, craftsmanship, and hard work just a little further than a first-class handyman we might meet in America. He arrives with his box of tools, with which he builds a sand boat with runners and sails that will be blown across the desert. It is left a mystery how he heard the shaggy man call him and how he came from America to the edge of Oz.

Once in Oz, the shaggy man and Button Bright get rid of their animal heads by plunging into the Truth Pond, which reverses transformations that falsify reality.[43] Bathing in the pond also makes people face the reality about themselves; it forces the shaggy man to confess that he stole the Love Magnet in order to gain the love he could not get otherwise, and in *The Lost Princess of Oz* it will force the Frogman to confess that he is nothing more than a big frog. Baum will not let his characters live a lie. The same zeal for genuineness produced his repeated insistence that Dorothy charmed everyone "because she was a simple, sweet and true little girl who was honest to herself and to all whom she met."[44] It would have been better, of course, if Baum had let these valuable virtues emerge from his story.

In the preface to *Dorothy and the Wizard in Oz*, Baum playfully complained that "The children won't let me stop telling tales of the Land of Oz," even though he knew "lots of other stories" and hoped "to tell them." He repeated this plaint in the preface to *The Road to Oz* and hinted that his next Oz book would be his last. At the end of *The Emerald City of Oz* (1910) he announced that Oz was forever closed off from the outside world. To celebrate its farewell appearance, the publishers put out an especially handsome book. Normally, the coloring of Neill's plates was left to the printers; but the color plates in *The Emerald City* were beautifully reproduced from watercolors done by the artist. The book was dedicated to Cynthia II of Syracuse, daughter of Baum's brother Harry and born in 1909.

Baum laid the groundwork for sealing off Oz by subjecting it to a truly frightening threat from genuinely evil characters. The Nome King, who was a good-humored if unscrupulous antagonist in *Ozma of Oz*, has lost all his geniality from stewing over his defeat and the capture of his Magic Belt. His constant anger has destroyed his own happiness as well as that of his subjects: "To be angry once in a while is really good fun, because it makes others so miserable. But to be angry

The Road to Oz. Dorothy and Toto are amused by Denslow's rendition of them. John R. Neill.

morning, noon and night, as I am, grows monotonous and prevents my gaining any other pleasure in life."

Baum set up the situation with a perfect balance of menacing evil and comic relief. The Nome King, like all too many historical rulers, is an irresponsible tyrant who has given himself over to malice. At the same time, he is a naughty child who works himself up into impotent rages and whose own subjects tell him he is ridiculous. As the story opens, "the King stormed and raved all by himself, walking up and down in his jewel-studded cavern and getting angrier all the time."[45] He punishes subjects who disagree with him by throwing them away. The unexpected application of this phrase to people instead of scrap paper is ludicrous, though it is at the same time mysteriously horrible. It also seems the perfect punishment for certain people in every reader's life.

Ultimately the King finds a bold and clever Nome who will undertake to lead his army through a tunnel they will dig under the deadly desert, conquer Oz, and recapture the Belt. General Guph (guff?) hates good, happy, contented people: "That is why I am so fond of your Majesty." He goes off to enlist some allies more thoroughly evil than the Nomes—the brainless Whimsies, who love fighting of any kind, the thuggish Growleywogs, who amuse themselves by sticking pins in

Guph, and the frightful Phanfasms, whose immeasurable powers include the ability to disable people by controlling their perceptions. Since they can get anything they want by their magic powers, they can be tempted to join the Nomes only by "the exquisite joy" of destroying happiness.[46]

The Nome Kingdom, supplemented by the other evil nations, is a convincing dystopia. There is no good feeling anywhere; every encounter bristles with threats and insults, and no one will help anyone without a bribe. Each ally is plotting to betray the others—the Growleywogs plan to enslave the Nomes, Guph to overthrow Roquat, the Whimsies and the Phanfasms to destroy their allies, and the Nomes to cheat them all. All these nations have mighty armies, and they excel in fighting rather than any kind of constructive activity. Even the peacetime work of the Nomes consists only of accumulating gems and precious metals. They are brutally regimented; the few who emerge as individuals in a total of four Oz books are individualized only in terms of their roles in serving Roquat. Their kingdom is rich in minerals, but nothing lives there except Nomes. Similarly, "All living things kept away from the [Phanfasms'] mountain."[47] Finally, these seem to be exclusively male societies, since females are not mentioned in any of them.

All these negative values serve to set off Oz as the ideal. In *The Emerald City of Oz*, just before he finished with Oz (as he thought), Baum characterized it as a full-scale utopia. Oz was a wonderful, magic-filled country in *The Wizard* and *The Land of Oz*, but it was not an ideal society. It began to take on utopian aspects in *The Road to Oz*, where the Tin Woodman explains that money is not known in Oz. People give others what they want for love and kindness rather than money, so that "We have no rich, and no poor." The necessary work is done by everyone's working half time. No one dies in Oz, unless he is condemned and executed for a crime.[48]

In *The Emerald City* Baum developed his ideal society more systematically, even to the point of providing statistics on the population of Oz. There is no disease in Oz, so no one dies except from some rare accident; the possibility of execution for crime has been eliminated. All people, both men and women, produce "for the good of the community" and freely give their neighbors what they require for use, "which is as much as any one may reasonably desire." The economy has become explicitly socialist: all property belongs to the Ruler, who distributes it fairly to her people, as a parent does to her children. "If by chance the

The Emerald City of Oz. The first and foremost of the Phanfasms terrorizes the Nome, General Guph. John R. Neill.

supply ever ran short," so that everyone's needs could not be met by free, unorganized giving, "more was taken from the great storehouses of the Ruler, which were afterward filled up again when there was more of any article than the people needed." "Every one worked half the time and played half the time, and the people enjoyed the work as much as they did the play, because it was good to be occupied and have something to do" and because they were never watched by cruel or fault-finding overseers.[49]

Freed from repression and from social and economic problems, the Oz people are nicer than those outside because they are happier. Although they are governed by an absolute monarch, she is wise and benevolent and therefore lets them express themselves as eccentrically as they like, so long as they do not harm others. Free, happy people do not want to harm others and cheerfully obey the few laws that are necessary; hence, there are no law courts or prisons. Love and friendliness are the rule in Oz, and they always elicit a positive response. The weather, now "always beautiful,"[50] reflects that of Baum's new home, Southern California.

Baum's Oz reflects the thinking of progressive contemporaries who were appalled by the misery produced by exploitative big business, industrialization, and wide class distinctions. Many writers preached the need for a system that would distribute wealth more fairly and would thereby eliminate poverty and a criminal class, as well as the distraction of destructive competition to acquire unlimited wealth. In the America of 2000 described in Edward Bellamy's *Looking Backward 2000–1887* (1888), wealth is fairly distributed because capital is controlled by a great national trust, rather than greedy and irresponsible private corporations. War no longer exists, but all citizens work during their middle years in the government's "industrial army," in jobs best suited to their natural aptitudes; in return, all their physical and mental needs are provided for throughout their lives. "Buying and selling is considered absolutely inconsistent with the mutual benevolence and disinterestedness which should prevail between citizens and the sense of community of interest which supports our social system." All work is equally respected, and all citizens have the same income. With equal wealth and equal opportunities for culture, all citizens belong to one class, corresponding to the most fortunate class in the present society.[51]

Freed from burdensome housework by electrical devices and communal laundries and kitchens, women work in the industrial army like men, in whatever occupation they are best suited to, and they also take part in government. "Our girls are as full of ambition for their careers as our boys. Marriage ... does not mean incarceration ... nor ... [does it] separate them ... from the larger interests of society," although mothers of small children do retire temporarily from outside work. Since all, including mothers who work at home, get credit cards just like men, they are not dependent. Therefore they are happier than they were in traditional society and also more able to make men happy.[52]

Bellamy's utopia would have been too regimented for Baum and is deficient in imaginative appeal and warmth. William Morris's *News from Nowhere* (1891), a utopian vision of later twentieth-century England, is more satisfying in these respects. "We live as we like," a citizen says. There is no central government; decisions are made in local meetings where everyone votes and the majority carries. Even the best prison would be a disgrace to the Commonwealth because a crime is regarded as the error of a friend. Adults retain their love of fairy tales, because "it is the child-like part of us that produces works of imagination." Costumes and architecture are picturesquely medieval, and most work is done by hand. All signs of industrialization have disappeared.

As in Bellamy, there are no class distinctions because no job is considered inferior to any other and, in the absence of destructive competition and greed, there are plenty of comforts and luxuries to go around. Everyone works because work is its own reward. Money is not used, for each person does his work for anyone who needs it. Everyone has "a happy and friendly expression," and they address each other as "Neighbor."[53]

Baum shared these two writers' ideals of fair distribution of goods and freedom from repression and class snobbery, Bellamy's belief in equality for women, and Morris's value for individualism, hand craftsmanship, and unspoiled nature. But he did not believe that the more radical ideals could be implemented in a society of people made imperfect by imperfect institutions. Such ideals work finely in Oz, but Baum does "not suppose such an arrangement would be practical with us."[54] He believed the populist and socialist parties of his day were too impractical to be effective.

Oz and most of Baum's other fairylands are absolute monarchies partly because that seems to be the appropriate government for a fairyland. But in the case of utopian Oz, there is a better reason: Oz is modeled on the institution closest to child readers, the family, which is (generally speaking) ruled by parents with tender concern for their children's well-being. Ozma's awesome power, backed by Glinda's and made omniscient by the Magic Picture and the Book of Records, is not threatening because it is as benevolent as the supervision of a loving parent. Also, as he was to make clear in *Glinda of Oz*, Baum was not convinced that democracy would promote the people's welfare better than enlightened monarchy.

Evil creatures and their evil plots shadow the first half of *The Emerald City of Oz*, but they do not weigh it down too heavily for an Oz story, as do the grim adventures in *Dorothy and the Wizard in Oz*. Even the most gruesome details are lightened by comic incongruity: Roquat tells his servants, "Please take General Crinkle to the torture chamber. There you will kindly slice him into thin slices." " 'Anything to oblige your Majesty,' replied the servants, politely."[55] Even the wickedest Nomes are periodically reduced to naughty children, and children know that naughty children cannot seriously hurt them, while the traditional fairy-tale villains, ogres and evil stepmothers (bad fathers and mothers), can.[56]

More important, Baum used a double plot, effectively counterbalancing one against the other. The happy, light second plot relieves the grimness and suspense produced by the first. It, too, starts off grimly; for the Gale family is in the very situation that animated the protests of the Populists and of reforming writers like Bellamy. No matter how hard he works, Uncle Henry cannot pay off the mortgage he had to put on his farm; it will be foreclosed, and the family will be thrown out of their home and livelihood. His plight was not unusual: sixty percent of the farm acreage of Kansas was mortgaged in the years of agricultural depression around 1890. But the situation is promptly relieved by the removal of the whole family to Oz, which is comforting to child readers who would not like to stay in Oz if it meant leaving their beloved family outside.

The mood changes to broad comedy with Em's and Henry's difficulties in adjusting to fairyland. They are neither children nor outsiders like the carnival Wizard and the Shaggy Man, but respectable farmers with settled ideas who have never had to deal with an unfamiliar situation. Baum dramatizes their discomfort as realistically as if they were working-class people suddenly displaced into high society in our own world. Then he sends them off with a party of Ozians to tour some odd communities in Oz, such as the jigsaw-puzzle people in Fuddlecumjig. The casual structure of this plot provides welcome relief from the relentless purposefulness of the projected invasion of Oz, yet all the while suspense is building in the reader's mind from the opening chapters of the book.

The situation is resolved happily and without violence when the invaders are induced to drink from the fountain of the Water of Oblivion, forget their evil impulses, and peacefully return home. But the relieved reader is soon saddened by the news that Oz has been forever closed off from the world outside: Tiktok, with his perfect mechanical logic, has pointed out that, if the Nomes could tunnel under the desert, so could other enemies.

Oz books following *The Wizard of Oz* did not receive so much critical attention, as perhaps should be expected in the case of sequels. The number of reviews tapered off, from ninety-seven or ninety-eight for *The Land of Oz, Ozma of Oz,* and *Dorothy and the Wizard in Oz* to seventy-three for *The Emerald City of Oz;* and the reviews tend to be in midwestern and less prestigious newspapers. The *New York Times* reviewed no Baum book after *The Land of Oz.*[57] Nevertheless, reviews were generally favorable, although often very brief. The end of the Oz series was generally lamented.

eight

A NEW LIFE IN CALIFORNIA,

1909–1914

It took the Baums years to recover from the financial disaster of the Radio Plays. Money was so short in 1909 that they ran into debt with numerous small merchants in Chicago. They economized by moving to rented quarters in Los Angeles and selling their cottage at Macatawa.[1] Even so, Frank was unable to pay his debts and was forced to take a more painful measure. On August 1, 1910, he signed a contract acknowledging that he was unable to settle his year-old debt to Rountree, his major creditor, and would therefore sign over to him his copyrights and royalties on all his books published by Bobbs-Merrill—*The Wizard of Oz*, his most popular work, and nine others. By a later contract with the four other creditors for whom he was acting, Rountree agreed that the Bobbs-Merrill royalties would be disbursed proportionally to the sums owed them. The total was $6,335.70 (over $3,000 due Rountree, about $2,500 due two printing companies, and two smaller debts). The royalties from 1910 to 1916 amounted to $10,000, which should have more than covered the debt, but Baum never got any more money from his Bobbs-Merrill titles.[2]

Although it was certainly cheaper to live in California than to maintain two homes in Chicago and spend months in hotels, the main motive for the Baums' move was love of the area. Southern California has consistently fine weather, like Oz; many plants grow there, they grow fast, and they grow throughout the year. The travelers in *Aunt Jane's Nieces and Uncle John* are amazed and delighted when they reach California and see fields of splendid wildflowers and roses growing in midwinter. The bountiful orchard in *The Lost Princess of Oz*, where the trees bear all kinds of ripe fruit at the same time, was not too different from California. A nineteenth-century publicity brochure for Los Angeles makes it sound as wonderful as Oz: "The purity of the air . . .

is remarkable. Vegetation dries up before it dies, and hardly ever seems to decay. Meat suspended in the sun dries up, but never rots. The air, when inhaled, gives to the individual a stimulus and vital force which only an atmosphere so pure can ever communicate."[3]

In 1910, Maud used part of an inheritance from her mother to buy a large corner lot in Hollywood, then a quiet, sparsely settled suburb with orange trees on the main street. They borrowed money to build a house at number 1749 Cherokee Avenue, a block north of Hollywood Boulevard, and named it Ozcot.[4] The house was large and comfortable, with an immense living room on the first floor, as well as a solarium, a library completely lined with books, a large dining room, a kitchen with a three-oven range, and maid's quarters. Baum's library included children's books, Kipling, Voltaire, Stevenson, Dickens, and Scott. On the second floor were four large bedrooms and a railed-in sunporch, and there was also an enormous attic. Baum himself made the center lighting fixture and the four corner lights in the dining room. "He sketched the intricate design, traced it on large sheets of copper and cut it out with a jeweler's saw. He then formed and soldered the fixtures, after which he cut and fitted thick pieces of emerald glass behind the copper so that the light came through, softly tracing his design in green." On December 18, 1910, Frank wrote to Robert that their house was nearly completed and they hoped to move in at the end of the month.[5]

Their comfortable home life continued to be shadowed, however, by financial worries. Baum still owed money to creditors whom he could not pay, and some of them were pressing him for satisfaction. The only escape was to go into bankruptcy. On June 3, 1911, when he was living in Ozcot, Baum filed for bankruptcy in the Federal District Court in Los Angeles. His debts totaled $12,600 and consisted of loans he was unable to repay, outstanding bills from contractors for the Radio Plays such as the Selig Polyscopy Company (who had received only half what was due), and numerous small debts accumulated while the Baums must have been living largely on credit, ranging down to $2.78 due Munger's Hyde Park Laundry. As assets, Baum listed two suits of clothing, one "in actual use and another kept in his room" at home (worth $50), eleven second-hand reference books (worth $10), and a five-year-old typewriter (worth $25)—all of which he claimed to be exempt property because they were "used by Bankrupt in his vocation as a writer and necessary for making his living."[6] This bizarre statement was more or less true because by this time Maud held title to the family assets, including their new house and Frank's royalties from Reilly &

Britton. Because her property was not touched by his bankruptcy, it humiliated them but did not reduce them to poverty.

Maud had been managing the family finances since their early years in Chicago. After Baum's incompetence as a businessman became apparent, she insisted that he assign her his copyrights as they were issued; probably this arrangement dated from his move to Reilly & Britton in 1904. She received his royalty checks from books and plays and deposited them in her personal account, from which she paid all the household expenses. Frank "kept a small checking account under an arrangement with the bank that he was to be notified when it was overdrawn. When the money was depleted Maud would deposit enough money to keep her husband in funds for a while." In this way, he did not even have to keep a record of his expenditures.[7] It is indeed fortunate that Maud was able to supply practical business sense in the Baum marriage; without her competent management, Frank would probably have been too oppressed by financial worries to create imaginative works. Harry Baum confirmed that "Father was a creative man with glorious ideas—but a poor businessman—enthusiastic—imaginative—but unreal and impractical—I always said it was a good thing that Mother managed the family finances instead of Father."[8]

It is also fortunate, and more remarkable, that Frank was obviously comfortable with Maud's managing role, which did not interfere with his romantic devotion to her. He "covered a wall of Ozcot . . . with his favorite pictures of Maud taken throughout her life, and christened them his 'yard of Maud.' " She, in turn, remained devoted and encouraging through all his financial vicissitudes. During one of these, she wrote to him: "We will come [out] all right. Trouble comes to us all but when met bravely and together surely we can stand it. You have always been able to earn a living. For all time and through all things, Your sweetheart and wife."[9]

Once, while she was visiting her sister Helen in Duluth, Frank sent her a despondent letter about the poor reception of the first movie produced by his Oz Film Manufacturing Company. Her reply was so sympathetic and encouraging that he cheered up immediately:

> My dear old Sweetheart, I got your sweet letter today . . . and it was just the letter I would have expected you to write. Aside from the fact that I reproached myself with making my dear wife share my bothers, I got such a heart-warming through that letter that the sweet cheering words will keep me happy for many days to come. Yes, sweetheart,

nothing can dismay us while we have each other and while the old love, which has lasted and grown stronger during all these years, remains to comfort and encourage us.

He immediately regained hope in the movie, and he signed himself, "Always your lover, Frank."[10]

If Frank was the more charming and amiable partner in the Baum marriage, Maud supplied the necessary firmness and hardheaded practicality that he lacked. Together, they maintained a joyful and stable family life. She maintained faith in him and appreciated his warmth and humor even during the long years when there was little evidence that he would ever amount to much. Each could appreciate the other's fine qualities, and they remained devoted for over thirty-six years of marriage.

Frank generated the fancy and fun that animated the Baum household, but Maud was lively and keen to see the humor in things, according to her niece Matilda Gage. She "was a symbol of what an older person should be . . . something always struck her funny. She never was somber. . . . She was one of the people all during my life I *really* had fun with." Maud's granddaughter Ozma (Kenneth's daughter), who was an infant when Frank died, remembered her grandmother fondly. She found her interesting, well-informed, and amusing. Maud "was a strong, independent and intelligent woman," who inspired Ozma "to believe in my strength as a woman and to think about what I would do with my life." Even as an old lady, "she still kept up her reading and her knowledge of the world . . . continued to have flowers in the house and a dog named Toto at her side." Ozma also remembered her father and uncles laughing at each other's "terrible jokes and puns," and supposed that this was what used to go on between her grandfather and his sons around the table.[11]

The Baums' financial problems did not prevent them from establishing a prosperous lifestyle in their new home. Frank developed the garden at Ozcot into a showplace and became a prize-winning gardener. There was a large backyard, 100 feet wide and 125 feet deep (183 feet, according to Maud), enclosed by a 6-foot redwood fence. It was filled with flower beds, in half of which Baum raised show dahlias and chrysanthemums. He planted each of the other beds with a single variety of flowers, creating a brilliant pattern recalling the formal gardens of Rose Lawn. A long summer house divided the garden lengthwise, and near it stood a concrete pedestal with a copper sundial that Baum had marked himself. He indulged his love of birds with a circular aviary almost 12 feet in diameter. There he kept forty birds, chosen for their brilliant coloring or lovely songs, which "were so tame that they would take food out of his mouth, sit on his shoulder and hand." There was a large goldfish pond at the rear of the lot, behind which were a chicken yard and a two-car garage. To the side of the garden, Baum had an archery range.[12]

He would get up at about eight o'clock and eat a hearty breakfast of fruit, meat or fish, eggs, potatoes, and four to five cups of strong coffee with sugar and heavy cream. All his life, Baum ate three substantial meals a day; dinner was typically a thick cream soup, roast meat with gravy, potatoes and vegetables, and a rich dessert.[13] After breakfast, he would go into his garden, change into work clothes, and cultivate his flowers. He devoted painstaking study to his gardening, including mixing his own fertilizer according to a formula that he did not disclose to anyone. A gardener did such heavy work as digging beds and weeding, but Baum did everything else.[14]

After lunch at one o'clock, he would write, in the garden when the weather was fine. As always, he wrote his first draft of a book in longhand on a clipboard. "He would make himself comfortable in a garden chair, cross his legs, and with a cigar in his mouth, begin writing whenever the spirit moved him ... When he had finished an episode or adventure, he would get up and work in his garden. He might putter around for two or three hours before returning to his writing; or it might be two or three days or a week before the idea he was seeking came to him. " 'My characters just won't do what I want them to,' he would explain."[15] Once, after he started writing again, Maud "asked him how he settled the matter. He replied, 'By letting them do what they wanted to.' "[16] When the book was completed, Baum would go after lunch to his study, a converted bedroom, where he would type it himself with two fingers, revising as he went.

Baum described the interplay of spontaneous inspiration and deliberate planning in his writing when he explained in a letter to Britton why *The Patchwork Girl of Oz* was not ready to be sold as a serial.

> I said I had it written, and that doubtless misled you. A lot of thought is required on one of these fairy tales. The odd characters are a sort of inspiration, liable to strike me at any time, but the plot and plan of adventures takes me considerable time to develope [sic]. When

I get at a thing of that sort I live with it day by day, jotting down on odd slips of paper the various ideas that occur and in this way getting my material together. The new Oz book is in this stage. I've got it all—all the hard work has been done—and it's a dandy, I think. But laws-a-massy! it's a long way from being ready for the printer yet. I must rewrite it, stringing the incidents into consecutive order, elaborating the characters, etc. Then it's typewritten. Then it's revised, retypewritten and sent on to Reilly and Britton. By close application there's about six weeks work on it. If I took my time I'd devote two months to getting it ready for the press.

He sent in the manuscript on March 8 and completed it—presumably, meaning that he made final revisions in response to his publishers' suggestions, on April 20; it was published the following year.[17]

Baum would accumulate ideas as they came to him, gradually shape them into a plot, and then revise his entire manuscript once or twice— a process that took many months. Reilly approved the basic plot of *The Tin Woodman of Oz* on August 10, 1916, and Baum sent him the corrected galley proofs eighteen months later, on February 14, 1918. The first official map of Oz, which appears in the front endpapers of *Tik-Tok of Oz* (1914), indicates how long ideas incubated in Baum's mind; for it includes the Yip country of *The Lost Princess of Oz* (1917), Mount Munch of *The Tin Woodman of Oz* (1918), and the Skeezers' country of *Glinda of Oz* (1920). (When he later decided to place the Skeezers on an island in a lake, he had to give Glinda a line to explain why only a river is shown on the map.[18])

Busy as he was, Baum did not mind being called from his writing to meet children. He would soon have them laughing and climbing into his lap. Once he welcomed a stranger and his young son, who loved the Oz books and had got the idea that Baum could answer any question. The father made an appointment, and Baum received them as very important visitors. He and the child "were at home immediately and every question was understood, solved and answered to fullest satisfaction."[19] These visits and letters from children kept Baum in touch with his readership and may have been vital in stimulating his creative efforts. He needed personal contact to sustain his writing— one reason, perhaps, that he was so eager to write for the stage and to make authorial appearances at productions of his plays. In addition, the children's enthusiastic responses supported his confidence in the value of his work when critics ignored it or sales were disappointing.[20]

After dinner at six, the Baums would listen to music from the player piano or phonograph for a while if they were alone. They entertained frequently, "for both enjoyed conversation and a game of cards. After the guests had left and the family had gone to bed, Baum would seat himself in a large leather-covered club chair placed in a corner of the library and pencil the next series of episodes in his current story."[21]

He occasionally played golf at Griffith's Park in Los Angeles, although not every afternoon as in earlier years at Coronado. Matilda Gage, who visited often, played golf with Frank; and Maud was grateful there was someone else to do so. In 1915, the three of them drove to San Diego to see the Pan-American Exposition and to have lunch at the Hotel del Coronado. Matilda spent many months with the Baums in 1916, the last time she saw Frank. She ultimately made a career in a bank in Aberdeen.[22] Since she shared Frank's interest in gardening, he sent her dahlia tubers with detailed advice for their planting and care. In a postscript to his letter of April 29, 1917, he expressed his feelings on America's entry into World War I on April 6: "Damn the Kaiser and King George. Why in mercy didn't we let the Germans and English eat each other?"[23] This opinion was to appear in *Mary Louise and the Liberty Girls*, written at about this time; but Baum put it in the mouth of an injudicious German-American merchant.

The Baum sons soon followed their parents to Southern California. Frank Junior had an advertising business and also continued to assist in his father's work. At some periods, "I worked with him daily—typing his plays and making extra copies of his stories for children. . . . We were closely associated in the Oz Film Manufacturing Company, of which I eventually became general manager." They also played golf together and chess in the evenings, "a game he especially enjoyed." Both Robert and Kenneth were married at Ozcot in 1914.[24] Robert had graduated in engineering from Cornell, and he married Edna Ducker, whom the Baums had known at Macatawa since she was fourteen. Shortly afterwards, Robert and Edna established an orange ranch in Claremont, about fifty miles from Hollywood.[25] Harry married Mary Niles in 1910. He had health and financial problems, and his parents brought him to California.[26] But he was unable to succeed in business there, and he and Mary eventually returned to Chicago, where he went into advertising. Harry "resembled his father in face and figure more closely than his three brothers, and had the same gentle disposition and literary tastes." He wrote three history books for children, as well as "Edith Van Dyne" 's *Mary Louise Solves a Mystery*.[27] Kenneth moved to Hollywood in 1910, worked as a reporter for a while, and then started an advertising agency, specializing in automotive advertising. He shared his father's love for making things, organizing social events, gardening, and keeping birds.[28]

Shortly after the Baums moved to California, Frank joined the Los Angeles Athletic Club. He would not have felt his life complete if he were not a member of a prestigious men's club. As a young man, he had been an enterprising businessman with creative impulses. As a mature artist, he created fantasy worlds where imagination was unrestrained by everyday probability, worldly values, or conventional thinking; but at the same time he pursued materialistic, conventional success. His best friends were prosperous businessmen, and he loved card parties, golf, and convivial meetings. He was ever ready to throw his energies into a scheme that he hoped would make him rich. He would readily cheapen his own creations in order to make a profit, as he was to reduce Tiktok into a clown in his dramatized version of *Ozma of Oz* and cheerfully let Sam Steele and his friends demolish the Oz-like society of the Tcha in *The Boy Fortune Hunters in Yucatan.*

On the other hand, Baum's conventional, convivial businessman's side contributed to the distinctive quality of his fantasy. His respect for plain common sense and his assumption that people naturally feel good fellowship with one another represent the American businessman at his best. His practical orientation produced the solid quasi-realistic foundations of his imaginative worlds. His tolerance for commercial trickery produced his engaging humbug Wizard of Oz. Graham Greene snobbishly dismissed *The Wizard of Oz* (the movie, rather than the book) as an "American drummer's [traveling salesman's] dream of escape," material and fettered by literalism.[29] Possibly so, but this dream is the basis for a uniquely believable, approachable imaginary world.

Baum was an enthusiastic charter member of the Lofty and Exalted Order of Uplifters, an inner group of Athletic Club members organized in 1909 by Harry Marston Haldeman, a pipe company executive from Chicago. Meeting every Saturday over lunch, the Uplifters enjoyed songs and lively conversation, followed by a talk on current affairs. The group meant a great deal to Baum, as he explained in the Athletic Club magazine: "I am a busy man and not wholly carefree; but that one hour each week within the Uplifters is more sweet and restful than any recreation I can indulge in, and I must admit that this band of 'good fellows'—good in every sense of the word—has brought joy into my life and made me happier."[30]

Most of the Uplifters were rich businessmen; actors and artists contributed their talents instead of paying dues. Baum created jokes, verses, skits, and celebrations for the Uplifters' boyish moments as enthusiastically as he created fantasies for children. As might be expected, these are mildly clever but not in any way extraordinary. He made up the titles for the officers: the president, Haldeman, was the Grand Muscle, "because the chief requisite in uplifting is muscle"; the board of governors were called the Excelsiors, "because Excelsior means higher." Baum remained an Excelsior until his death, played the bass drum in the orchestra, organized the versifying at the "Spring Poets Dinner," wrote shows and acted in them.[31]

From 1914, the Uplifters held annual outings with shows written by Baum. The first, with music by Louis F. Gottschalk, another member, was "Stagecraft, or The Adventure of a Strictly Moral Man," produced on January 14. For the second one, held in Santa Barbara in 1915, Baum wrote "The Uplift of Lucifer or Raising Hell" again with music by Gottschalk, and for the third, at Del Mar, he wrote "The Uplifters' Minstrels," with music by Byron Gay.[32] Baum dedicated *The Scarecrow of Oz* (1915) to " 'The Uplifters' . . . in grateful appreciation of the pleasure I have derived from association with them, and in recognition of their sincere endeavor to uplift humanity through kindness, consideration and good-fellowship. They are big men—all of them—and all with the generous hearts of little children."

"The Uplift of Lucifer, or Raising Hell," the only one of these farces to be preserved, was performed by the Uplifters on October 23, 1915. It must have delighted the club members with its topical old-boy jokes and fantastic humor. The Grand Muscle of the Uplifters (played by himself) goes to Hell to uplift it and demands to see King Lucifer. Imp olite tells him Lucifer is busy putting the children to bed, because "Mrs. Lucifer has been to the Woman's Club all afternoon and returned late." Of course there's a woman's club in Hell: "Hell and Women's Clubs are synonymous." Lucifer shows the Grand Muscle the horrors of Hell, and the Grand Muscle lists those of earth: "You ought to attend a meeting of the Common Council . . . or eat in a cafeteria; or go to a church sociable . . . or hear your wife beg for a new hat . . ." Lucifer abdicates, since his punishments are minor compared to these.[33]

In 1917, Baum attended the Uplifters' Convention at the Hotel del Coronado, for which he wrote "The Orpheus Road Show," with music by Gottschalk. The Uplifters' outings were discontinued when America entered World War I, and Baum died before they were resumed.[34]

Thus the Baums managed to live very pleasantly despite Frank's bankruptcy. On the other hand, they were chronically worried about money; apart from debts that could not be paid, their income declined. Frank had lost the royalties on his Bobbs-Merrill books, and his new series of major fantasies, *The Sea Fairies* (1911) and *Sky Island* (1912), were not selling well. Even the Oz books were not doing as well as they had in previous years, although sales of the six *Aunt Jane's Nieces* books jumped to 22,569 in 1911. Baum was still borrowing to make ends meet, usually from his publishers, and was grateful when they let a loan of several hundred dollars stand to the end of the year.[35]

Baum's need for more money is a constant theme in his correspondence with Reilly & Britton, much of which has survived from December 27, 1911, through December 27, 1912, and from December 16, 1914, through December 26, 1916, with a few letters from 1918. On January 1, 1912, Baum facetiously asked Britton for his annual statement of royalties "so we will know if we can eat three times a day this year." By November 6, he was optimistically looking forward to better sales the next year so that he could "smoke 5c. cigars instead of twofers." On December 11, he explained to Britton that he could not repay the $200 he had borrowed to bring Harry to California. "Our present income is so much less than our needs that I sometimes despair of pulling through each month, and to save this $200. has been impossible." He has received $135 from his publishers for some serialization rights, and he asks them to make up the difference in advance of their settlement for the year in January.

Repeatedly, disappointing sales prompted Baum to reproach his publishers for not promoting his books energetically enough. But then he had to acknowledge that they had consistently treated him fairly; he assured Britton on December 27, 1912: "I'd rather—far rather—feel that I was earning less with you than be with some stranger where I positively knew I could earn more. . . . I believe in your future; I trust your good will; I am quite certain that the coming year we're both going to make a lot of money from our combination. So forgive me if anything I said stirred your bile. Remember that Baum is nervous and restless, that inadequate finances render him dissatisfied at times, because his needs are greater than his income." Despite his financial problems, his more pleasant environment in California has enabled him to write "the two best books of my career—'Sky Island' and 'The Patchwork Girl.' "

Fortunately, with Maud's support and his own remarkable ability to concentrate, Frank was able to write industriously through all his financial worries and distractions. Every year, he produced an addition to each of his series for teenagers, as well as a major fantasy. But his hard work could not clear his debts any more than Uncle Henry's could avert the foreclosure on the Gales' farm in *The Emerald City of Oz*.

He tirelessly thought up additional publishing projects. Something called "Our Married Life," with illustrations by Neill, was to have come out in 1912 (but did not). He attached high hopes to a novel, "Johnson," which (unlike his other novels for adults) he wanted to publish under his own name. It failed to impress Reilly & Britton, even though, the author insisted, "Some quite experienced critics out here think it is a great book, so distinctive and appealing that it ought to sweep the country." On September 19, Britton told Baum that *Cosmopolitan* had rejected "Johnson." Baum asked about it on October 15, but it is not mentioned thereafter. He also kept writing short stories, but for the most part was unable to sell them.

Meanwhile, despite his experience with the Radio Plays, he determined to try again for a lucrative stage success. He wrote a comic opera, "Peter and Paul," with music by Arthur Pryor, and a musical comedy called "The Pipes o' Pan," with Tietjens, probably based on their "King Midas" of 1901; it is a burlesque of the classical story of Apollo clapping ass's ears on Midas when he misjudges Pan to be the better musician. In 1909, Baum sketched out two versions of a musical extravaganza based on *Ozma of Oz*. An interview published in *The Theatre Magazine* that August displays his wishful thinking about these projects. "The Pipes o' Pan" was "practically finished"; "Peter and Paul" was already written and was to star Montgomery and Stone. "An extravaganza that will go either by the name of 'Ozma of Oz' or 'The Rainbow's Daughter,' will be put on the first week in October by Montgomery and Stone at the Studebaker Theatre in Chicago"; it will have remarkable mechanical effects and music by Manuel Klein. Actually, only the last of these plays was to reach production—"Ozma of Oz," rewritten as "The Tik-Tok Man of Oz"—and that four years later. The others were presumably not written, since only a fragment of "The Pipes o' Pan" survives, and nothing at all of "Peter and Paul." It is unlikely that Montgomery and Stone, who had refused to star in "The Woggle-Bug," would have touched another Baum show. Yet another theatrical project was an attempt, with Edith Harrison and other society women, to organize a children's theater, "the only playhouse of its kind in the world," in New York City, which "will probably be opened early in the coming season... for the production of fairy plays." This, too, never materialized.[36] The whole interview displays Baum's ability, remarked on by his friends, to imagine things so vividly that he came to believe them true.

Baum did not mention "The Girl from Oz," a musical comedy he wrote at about this time, probably because it differed from the other works: it had a unified plot, a rather bold theme, and no spectacular effects. Beautiful young Elile arrives at an American army base from Oz, which is identified as a Pacific island ruled by an exiled Russian princess and is generally called Delcapan in the play. The main connection between Oz and Delcapan is that both are matriarchies: in Delcapan, a stuffy elderly major explains, "The women have the ascendancy. They're the politicians, the shop-keepers, the dominating sex. They usurp all the rights of men. They make love to the fellows and flirt with them." Elile practices this assertive approach, and the two young leading men, as well as every other man in the play, fall in love with her.[37]

Reilly & Britton were helping to market "The Girl from Oz" and several other Baum plays to producers, and on November 6, 1912, Baum shared with Britton the good news that Oliver Morosco, a major West Coast producer, had agreed to stage "The Tik-Tok Man of Oz" as a lavish extravaganza. The show would open in Los Angeles, move to San Francisco, and then "go straight to New York for an extended run." "It means a lot to all of us," Baum rejoiced—a big theatrical comeback for him and a big advertisement for his books. "It means getting my nose away from the grindstone and a little ease-up for me financially. It will also mean that Morosco will produce "The Patchwork Girl" when we are ready for it." He had not yet mentioned The Patchwork Girl to Morosco, he admitted; but he felt "assured that Morosco can be induced to follow this play with another on the Patchwork Girl.... It is logical." This, of course, would do much to promote the forthcoming book. Baum's vaulting optimism is apparent, as well as his probably correct belief that he could earn incomparably more from a theatrical hit like "The Wizard of Oz" than from writing, however industriously.

Throughout these hard times, only Baum's *Aunt Jane's Nieces* books continued to sell as well as ever. They were particularly popular as gifts to girls graduating from grammar school, Britton wrote to Baum on November 15, 1912. In 1911, Baum capitalized further on this market by launching two new series for adolescents with *The Daring Twins* and *The Flying Girl.* It is understandable why his *Aunt Jane's Nieces* and *Boy Fortune Hunters* books for that year are thin and flat.

The Boy Fortune Hunters in the South Seas (1911) is the last of its series. It combines two scrappy plots and uses much material recycled from *The Boy Fortune Hunters in the Panama.* Sam Steele's ship is grounded on the South Sea island of Faytan, where the people are hostile because they do not want greedy white people to despoil them of their pearls. Sam and his friend Joe are captured and taken to the King, also a boy. Sam has to admire the King for his royal air, intelligence (he "was remarkably intelligent for a savage"), and noble simplicity, and has "always regretted that Joe had to kill" him.[38]

In *Aunt Jane's Nieces and Uncle John* (1911), Uncle John takes Patsy and Beth on an automobile trip through the Southwest. The book is padded with travelogue based on the Baums' tour of 1904, contrived adventures, and repeated character routines, such as friendly sparring between the dear old eccentrics Uncle John and Major Doyle. Ultimately the party arrives at "the magnificent Hotel Del Coronado, which is famed throughout the world."[39]

The book for the following year, *Aunt Jane's Nieces on Vacation* (1912), draws on Baum's newspaper experience and is more substantial. Uncle John and his nieces arrive in Millville and find there is no local newspaper. Patsy suggests they start one, and Uncle John encourages her, over the objections of conventional Arthur Weldon, now married to Louise. Uncle John is "educating my girls to be energetic and self-reliant" and is sure they "will rise to every occasion and prove their grit." Patsy announces that she will be managing editor and that everyone must be very professional so that "the columns of the *Millville Daily Tribune* will be quoted by the New York and Chicago Press." Louise wants to put her inane "Ode to a Mignonette" on the front page and is aggrieved when the others point out its obvious flaws, which were never mentioned by the big publishing houses that rejected it.[40] This seems an unkind cut at Baum's sister Mary Louise, an unsuccessful aspiring poet and author of this poem, which Frank had published in the *Rose Lawn Journal.* Arthur, as advertising manager, appeals to businessmen with the disarming candor Baum had used in the *Aberdeen Saturday Pioneer* and, this being fiction, gets many clients with this approach.

The young journalists get in trouble when, reporting on an ostentatious party given by a prosperous but uncultivated local farming family, they misprint the hostess's "roguish smile" as a "roughish smile." Her brother comes to thrash Arthur, the nominal editor-in-chief, but is luckily persuaded to challenge him to a duel instead. The brother runs away when he realizes he might be killed; Arthur, who was himself sensibly running away, is informed of the situation, comes back, and is cheered by the crowd. This anecdote has been repeated with Baum as the hero, but it is probably a humorous fiction inspired by a mildly embarrassing misprint he had made in the *Pioneer.* At first the nieces' work is "woefully amateurish," but gradually it becomes reasonably competent. When they return to New York City, they sell their paper to Hetty, a gifted cartoonist with a drinking problem whom they had generously given a chance to rehabilitate herself.[41]

In the next year's offering, *Aunt Jane's Nieces on the Ranch* (1913), Uncle John, Beth, and Patsy go to visit Louise, Arthur, and their baby at their fruit ranch in California. It is a thin, far-fetched mystery involving rivalry between an American trained nurse and a Mexican nursemaid over care of the baby; many melodramatic apprehensions arise, but everything turns out to have an innocent explanation. Despite its inanity, Baum was pleased with the book and it sold well.[42]

For the more interesting of his new series, "Edith Van Dyne"'s *The Flying Girl* (1911), Baum exploited his abiding interest in new technology by making his heroine an aviator. His new home was a major center for aviation, and the Dominguez Air Meet held near Long Beach in January 1910 had attracted thousands of spectators. Baum constantly insists on seventeen-year-old Orissa Kane's competence in supposedly masculine areas. Though Stephen "posed as the head of the family" (their father was dead and their mother helpless), it was his sister, Orissa, who "had inherited her father's clear, business-grasping mind" and who raised the capital for Stephen to develop his design for an improved airplane. By studying his plans and questioning him, she came to understand thoroughly the airplane he was building. When a villain copied Stephen's machine and then removed him from competition by engineering a disabling accident, Orissa volunteered to replace Stephen, noting that she had "a clear head and a quick eye" and had "personally tested all the working parts time and again, except in actual flight." Stephen seconded her, predicting that "The most successful aviators of the future . . . are bound to be women," who are generally "lighter than men, more supple and active, quick of perception and less liable to lose their heads in emergencies." Predictably, Orissa succeeded brilliantly in showing off her brother's airplane, even though she had never flown before; furthermore, the exhilaration of controlling an aircraft inspired her to resolve on a career as an exhibition pilot.

Nevertheless, "Edith Van Dyne" took care to make her a model of young womanhood by giving her "feminine" modesty: far from taking pride in her achievements, she "basked in the reflected glory of her brother's inventive genius."[43]

In *The Flying Girl and Her Chum* (1912) Orissa has become famous all over America for her daring and skill. Moreover, her success is based on a thoroughly professional attitude that is usually associated with men: "Everything I do is figured out with mathematical precision and I never take a single chance that I can foresee."[44] Demonstrating her brother's newly invented Hydro-Aircraft in San Diego, she sets out with her friend Sybil to fly out over the Pacific, touch down, and return with the plane acting as a motor boat; but their instruments are accidentally damaged so that Orissa loses control and they cannot stop until their gasoline runs out. They come down at an unknown island and deal with the emergency with the usual courage and resourcefulness of Baum girls. Their adventures continue on another island occupied by villainous Mexicans, but Baum had to tone down some violent scenes such as he used in his boys' series. Britton told him on May 9, 1912: "you have made the story too thrilling . . . Mrs. Van Dyne . . . has a fine standing, and it wouldn't do to risk her reputation as an author." He reminded Baum that he was writing for eleven to fourteen year olds and the books had "to pass muster with their parents, teachers and librarians."

The Daring Twins: A Story for Young Folk (1911), which for some reason Baum published under his own name, is a wholesome and moderately ingenious, but ordinary, mystery story. The sixteen-year-old twins, Phil and Phoebe, are the oldest of five orphaned children. Phoebe is the more practical and responsible twin and the one who takes the initiative to prevent Phil from being framed for theft from the bank. Their father, a successful manufacturer of beet sugar, was ruined when he refused to join other manufacturers to form a monopoly, on the grounds that such a trust was "unjust and morally unlawful."[45] Baum was probably remembering the way the Standard Oil Trust had blocked his father's enterprise in the Pennsylvania oil fields.[46]

Occasionally Baum managed to place one of his short stories in a magazine. One of the most interesting is "Aunt Phroney's Boy," which appeared in *St. Nicholas* in December 1912. It is a thinking man's reworking of "Aunt Hulda's Good Time," which turns the pleasant sentimental tale of 1899 into a pointed criticism of male selfishness. In the earlier story, a rich boy stops at a poor farm and finds an old woman who is home alone because she and her husband are so poor they have to alternate going on an annual outing, and he gives her the most wonderful day of her life with just part of his birthday money. In the revision, Aunt Phroney always sits home alone because her husband, who considers all the family property his own, is too stingy to take her with him to the county fair. "She hadn't left the old farm-house except to go to church for nearly two years, and days at a time she never saw a human being other than her silent, morose husband. Yet she was not lonely—not really lonely—only at times did her isolation weigh upon her spirits." The boy persuades Aunt Phroney to go to the fair with him, where they see her husband (who is named after Martin Luther) squandering his money in an obviously rigged game. Then they watch the rooster she has raised win a blue ribbon, while Martin Luther's produce wins nothing.[47]

Baum's major creative efforts were still, of course, his fantasies for children. Having closed off Oz, he tried to interest his readers in a new little girl, Trot, and a new fairyland located under the sea. He published *The Sea Fairies* in 1911, dedicated to Judith of Randolph, Massachusetts, evidently one of his devoted readers. He got his initial idea from the caves along the shore at La Jolla (near Coronado), which people could enter at high tide to observe sea life.[48] Trot lives on the California coast; her father is captain of a trading schooner, and her closest friend is wooden-legged Cap'n Bill, who had to retire when he lost his leg. The story opens with Cap'n Bill's claim that mermaids lure and destroy humans. Trot is unconvinced and wishes she could see one. Sure enough, when she and Cap'n Bill go to explore an ocean cave, some mermaids appear. They invite the two mortals to visit their ocean kingdom and fit them with tails so they can swim nimbly. Then the mermaids take Trot and Cap'n Bill to their beautiful palaces at the bottom of the sea, made of coral with a ceiling of magically created glass and lit by electricity long before humans knew about this force.

They are introduced to King Anko, a friendly sea serpent, whose enormous power and size are incongruously combined with a mild expression and comical features. They go on to meet a variety of actual sea creatures, such as unsociable hermit crabs and an octopus that is overwhelmed with shame when he discovers that his name has been applied to the Standard Oil Company: "Just because we have several long arms, and take whatever we can reach, they accuse us of being like—oh, I cannot say it!"[49]

Baum used the mackerel for one of his sly satires on the orthodox view of the afterlife. The fish think that when one of them is jerked out of the water and disappears "he has gone to glory—which means to them some unknown, but beautiful sea." And so they eagerly take the bait and the hook. When a mackerel laments that another got the hook before him and Trot tells him his friend "will be fried in a pan for someone's dinner," the stupid fish insists "Flippity has gone to glory!" Trot worries that "It seems wicked to catch such pretty things," but a mermaid tells her that they are needed to feed other creatures and would soon clog the oceans if none were destroyed, so "it is just as well they are thoughtless and foolish."[50]

Eventually the travelers and their mermaid escort are driven by the terrible sea devils (large spidery cephalopods) into the palace of Zog the Magician, the evil power of the sea. He is served by many human slaves whom he has saved from drowning and fitted with gills, all of whom profess a zombie-like contentment. Zog is a hybrid creature, "and such a monstrosity could not be otherwise than wicked. Everybody hates me, and I hate everybody." The Mermaid Queen uses her magic to fend off his various attempts to destroy his prisoners, but they cannot escape until Anko kills Zog. Finally the Queen escorts Trot and Cap'n Bill back to the Giant's Cave and asks her to speak "well of the mermaids when you hear ignorant earth people condemning us."[51]

The book is thin: neither its main plan nor its individual ideas have the gripping power of good Oz fantasy, and there is padding in the form of uninspired descriptions and strings of puns. Many of the marvels are nothing more than representations of undersea life, which may be exotic to land dwellers but do not transport them into a wonderful new world. The story is excessively leisurely; almost half the book consists of the two mortals' sightseeing in the sea. It did not do well for a Baum fantasy, selling only 12,401 copies during its first year, as compared to about 20,000 for *The Emerald City of Oz*.

Sky Island: Being the Further Adventures of Trot and Cap'n Bill after Their Visit to the Sea Fairies (1912), dedicated to Baum's sister Mary Louise Brewster, is a much richer fantasy; it is related to its predecessor only by the two central characters. To make this new series more popular, Baum introduced Button Bright and Polychrome from *The Road to Oz*. The story opens when Button Bright is carried by a magic umbrella to Trot's home. Fortunately he has matured since *The Road to Oz* and become a competent, plucky child. The children and Cap'n Bill attach themselves to the umbrella and direct it to take them to an island out in the Pacific that they call Sky Island because "it looks as if it was half in the sky," as islands on the horizon line actually do look from Coronado. Instead, the umbrella takes them to the real Sky Island in the sky.

They land in a disagreeable country where everything, including the people's skins, is blue; it is ruled by a tyrannical Boolooroo, and everyone hates them on sight because creatures with their "horrid white skins" do not belong. Trot is given as a slave to the Six Snubnosed Princesses, who, if they can find no other use for her, will make her into a living pincushion. The Boolooroo is as small-minded as Jonathan Swift's Lilliputians: just as they assume their own and the neighboring tiny island are the two great empires of the universe, the Boolooroo knows that no one can live on the Earth "because it's just a round, cold, barren ball of mud and water," and scorns the ignorance of the Americans who "know nothing of Sky Island, which is the Center of the Universe and the only place anyone would care to live."[52]

The Boolooroo has devised a particularly hideous punishment called patching: two offenders are split in half (Blues cannot die before their life span ends at six hundred years), and the halves are mismatched. The more ill-sorted they are, the more fun the Boolooroo has. He gloats over the prospect of patching Trot with Cap'n Bill. Baum probably derived this idea from the political projector in Swift's Academy of Lagado in *Gulliver's Travels* who proposes to reconcile factional differences by splitting politicians' brains and interchanging the halves, so that each head contains half a brain from each party and the two half brains can debate and settle issues within their skull. Interestingly, it is Baum who made this conception vivid and therefore horrible. As a victim says, "there you are, patched to someone you don't care about and haven't much interest in. If your half wants to do something, the other half is likely to want to do something different, and the funny part of it is you don't quite know which is your half and which is the other half."[53] Can two people be a person? What would happen to consciousness, ego, and integrity in such a situation?

The Blues are hostile to all strangers, but they particularly loathe the inhabitants of the other half of their island, the Pink Country. In *Sky Island* Baum fully developed his satire on neighboring nations that despise each other for no reason, first advanced in Hiland and Loland of *John Dough.* The Blues and the Pinks are convinced that each other's color is disgusting, and they are impassably separated by the Great Fog Bank.

The Pink Country is altogether more attractive. The people are happy and good-natured, in contrast to the joylessness of the Blues; they are puzzled by the first foreigners they have ever seen but treat them nicely. While the Blue Country is apparently a patriarchy, the Pink "women seemed fully as important as the men, and instead of being coddled and petted they performed their share of the work, both in public and private affairs . . . exactly as the men did." The Pinkies are, however, as color conscious as the Blues. One remarks of Trot: "How strangely light her color is! And it is pink, too, which is in her favor. But her eyes are of that dreadful blue tint which prevails in the other half of Sky Island, while her hair is a queer color all unknown to us. She is not like our people and would not harmonize with the universal color here."[54] It sounds exactly like the reasons why certain people are excluded from country clubs. The modest little Queen is sympathetic to the strangers, but reluctantly forced to condemn them to death because she must obey the law and follow the advice of her counselors, for it would be impolite to ask for their advice and not take it. Fortunately, Polychrome comes off her rainbow just in time to figure out a way around the law. *Sky Island* was far superior to *The Sea Fairies*, but even so, it sold even fewer copies in its first year: 11,749.[55]

These disappointing sales, together with the loss of his Bobbs-Merrill royalties, meant that Baum's income declined by about a third from that of his prosperous years. Meanwhile, his readers were clamoring for more books about the Land of Oz.[56] Even before *Sky Island* was published, Baum yielded and started writing a new Oz book. The Royal Historian reopened communications with Oz by setting up a wireless telegraph connection with Dorothy. He and his publishers thought of publishing Oz and "Trot" books in alternate years, but gave up the idea when *The Patchwork Girl of Oz* proved much more successful. Britton suggested on January 15, 1912, that the new Oz book should be serialized and asked for the manuscript the following month so that he could start negotiations. But Baum explained on January 23 that it required at least six more weeks of work. He could proceed faster only if he dropped work on *The Flying Girl and Her Chum*, for which he had just been doing research by attending an aviation meet.

By March 3, he was seriously considering the requirements of serialization. He consulted Britton about the length of his book: he could "make it anywhere from 40,000 to 50,000 words . . . or even carry it to 60,000 . . . if we syndicate it [in newspapers], or sell the serial rights to a monthly, like the Ladies' Home Journal, I would make it into 24 or 36 chapters—the latter preferred, so that two or three chapters could be published each month." (In 1912, the *Ladies' Home Journal* was the largest and most prestigious women's magazine in the country; it turned down *The Patchwork Girl* in May.) The book finally came to almost 60,000 words in 28 chapters. Britton received the manuscript on April 22. On February 9, Baum had suggested "The Ozites" and "Adventures in Oz" as possible titles; on March 3, he asked Britton which he thought best—"The Patchwork Girl of Oz," "Miss Patchwork," or "Princess Dorothy of Oz."

In his letter of January 15, Britton had promised that Reilly & Britton would publicize Baum's return to Oz with a large "promotion of L. Frank Baum and all of his books" during 1913. Baum prepared the way with six little books under the general title, *The Little Wizard Stories of Oz* (1913, published in one volume in 1914). The best of these six short tales written for younger children give a slightly different view of familiar Oz characters by putting them in situations that Baum could not accommodate in a full-length novel. In "The Cowardly Lion and the Hungry Tiger," the animals become bored by their job of unnecessarily guarding Ozma in her throne room and go outside to satisfy their natural appetites, the Tiger to eat a fat baby and the Lion to show everyone his power by springing on a man and making "chop suey of him." Of course they soon discover they are too kind to hurt anyone. In "Little Dorothy and Toto," the Wizard teaches Dorothy not to be so reckless in seeking adventures.[57] Reilly & Britton advertised *The Patchwork Girl of Oz* intensively and issued cut-out figures and models of the characters. The book appeared in 1913 and is dedicated to Sumner Hamilton Britton, Britton's youngest son.

As the story opens, Ojo and his Unc Nunkie come to visit Unc Nunkie's friend, the magician Dr. Pipt, just as the magician is about to animate a patchwork doll his wife, Margolotte, has made to be her servant. By a terrible accident, when the Patchwork Girl is brought to life, the Liquid of Petrifaction spills on Unc Nunkie and Margolotte and turns them to marble. Ojo, with the Patchwork Girl and the Glass Cat, a vain creature also brought to life by the magician, set out to collect the five ingredients of a charm to reanimate the victims, including a six-leaf clover and the hairs from a Woozy's tail. The Woozy (befuddled one) turns out to be an engaging animal constructed of squares and rectangles; he was inspired by cubism, particularly as expressed in Marcel Duchamp's *Nude Descending a Staircase* (1911). This painting was copied and circulated in the United States in 1912, where it aroused attention and controversy. Baum described the Woozy as blue, but Neill colored him brown, like the nude in the picture.[58]

Scraps, the Patchwork Girl, is the most emancipated character in the whole Oz series. She is free of inhibitions, of self-doubt, and of concern for what other people think. She brazenly flouts the conventional virtues of her sex and class. Margolotte had deliberately constructed her of a patchwork quilt so that she would be ugly and humble, and planned to give her only the utilitarian mental attributes of obedience, amiability, and truth—a limitation that some have considered appropriate to women as well as servants. But the boy Ojo thinks it is "unfair and unkind to deprive her of any good qualities that were handy," so he adds all the humanly desirable qualities on the magician's shelf of Brain Furniture—cleverness, judgment, courage, ingenuity, learning, poesy, and self-reliance.[59] The result is a creature who is exuberantly pleased with herself and totally self-confident; she brashly announces her opinions and is the only character in Oz to scoff at the authority of the perfect Ruler, Ozma. She simply ignores class distinctions—the best way to deal with them.

She lacks even the "feminine" qualities of Baum's realistic girls, being conspicuously devoid of modesty, propriety, and tenderness of heart. She rejoices that the magician's wife forgot to give her a heart, which "must be a great annoyance," as it "makes a person feel sad or sorry or devoted or sympathetic—all of which sensations interfere with one's happiness."[60] In a country where everybody's love for every single creature can become cloying, she refuses to profess concern for butterflies or unfortunate people she does not know.

Despite her lack of tender feeling, Scraps is irresistibly likable and attractive. From the moment she comes to life, she delights in every experience, from the incongruity that she is alive while the woman who made her for a slave is dead marble, to the beauty of the trees and wildflowers in the forest, which is dreary and dull to Ojo and the Glass Cat. Scraps's happiness with herself keeps her constantly cheerful and well-disposed toward others. She is a warm friend to Ojo and boldly tries to conceal his guilt when he is accused of the crime of picking a six-leaf clover (although she forgets all about him as she gazes at the wonderful Emerald City, where she promptly announces she is going to live). Only the rigid and stupid dismiss her uninhibited exuberance as crazy (like the quilt she is made of); the wiser authorities in Oz come to value her cleverness and good temper and decree that she may "live in the palace, or wherever she pleases, and be nobody's servant but her own."[61]

If Scraps shows how a positive attitude leads to happiness and success, Ojo the Unlucky, Baum's first boy hero in a fantasy book, shows

The Patchwork Girl of Oz. The Patchwork Girl meets the Scarecrow. John R. Neill.

how a negative attitude nourishes itself. Brought up in isolation by silent Unc Nunkie who never laughs, Ojo naturally starts out depressed. This causes him to seize on every pretext for discouragement. It must somehow be his fault that Unc Nunkie has been turned to marble by the Liquid of Petrifaction—a thought that Scraps promptly rejects as nonsense. But Ojo persists in attributing every misfortune to his Unlucky destiny. When the Scarecrow is stuck on a fence picket, Ojo laments that "because I am Ojo the Unlucky ... everyone who tries to help me gets into trouble." Dorothy rejoins, "You are lucky

to have anyone to help you." When Ojo finds more evidence for
unluckiness in his being left-handed, the Tin Woodman reminds him
that "Many of our greatest men are that way"—a sly allusion to Baum
himself.[62] Finally Ojo manages to rid himself of his "Un," and in the
end he is persuaded that he is Ojo the Lucky.

Defeatism is satirized metaphorically when the travelers are stopped
by what appears to be an iron-barred gate across the yellow brick road.
The Shaggy Man tells them to close their eyes and covers Scraps's button
eyes with a handkerchief, and they pass right through. The discouraging

illusion is so plausible that they must block their normal method of seeing in order to recognize that it is not real and proceed on their course.

Anyone who reads about certain beautiful plants bordering the road must doubt Baum's protestations that he would never introduce anything frightening into a children's story. The huge leaves bend to scoop up Ojo, Scraps, the Glass Cat, and the Woozy and immediately wrap tightly around them. Ojo, swathed in a leaf, waits for hours, wondering "how long one could live in such a condition and if the leaf would gradually sap his strength and even his life, in order to feed itself." Then, remembering that no one could die in Oz, he feared "that he would always remain imprisoned in the beautiful leaf and never see the light of day again."[63] This being Oz, the leaf is ultimately forced to relax by the Shaggy Man's whistling.

Baum originally planned to develop this idea even more horribly in a later chapter called "The Garden of Meats." The chapter itself is lost, but its title, Neill's illustrations, and their captions survive in Reilly & Britton's files. Neill's pictures are very disquieting indeed. One shows a crowd of anthropomorphic vegetables viewing human heads, fully developed and most belonging to children, growing on stems rooted in the ground. Another shows a beet pouring water from a can into the mouth of a little girl plant, with the caption: "He put the spout to the mouth of the girl and gave her a big drink."[64]

When he sent Baum the galley proofs on November 23, 1912, Reilly tactfully wrote: "We are inclined to believe that it would be best to omit Chapter XXI, 'The Garden of Meats.' As we see it, this chapter is not at all essential to the movement of the story, and we do not think that the ideas therein are in harmony with your other fairy stories. If this chapter remains in the book we should fear (and expect) considerable adverse criticism."

Baum graciously accepted their judgment, replying on November 27: "I am glad you objected to the 21st. chapter of *The Patchwork Girl*, for I do not like it myself." He offered to send a replacement, "a meeting with the Marshmallow Twins, who are to appear in another story." He concluded by declaring his "premonition that this book is destined to be my greatest success . . . if you boost it along as we have arranged." Neither version of the chapter was used; Reilly had written on November 23 that he did not want to add a new chapter since Neill had already completed his illustrations. "The Garden of Meats" carried to a horrible extreme Baum's concept, introduced in *Dorothy and the Wizard in Oz*, of repellently heartless vegetables with human powers. It is fortunate that his publish-

The Patchwork Girl of Oz. The travelers face Mr. Yoop. John R. Neill.

ers persuaded him to drop it; the animal-eating plants of chapter 10 provide quite enough vegetable horror for the book.

There were at least sixty-three favorable reviews. The Saint Louis *Times* of October 4, 1913, praised *The Patchwork Girl of Oz* and particularly noted that it had a rare quality for a children's book—"an air of earnestness—as if the author really believed in the mythical land he depicts."

The reviewer in the Burlington, Iowa, *Hawk Eye* of September 23, 1913, found *The Patchwork Girl* "the most unique character creation from Mr. Baum's pen" and related her to contemporary emancipated women: "She represents the spirit of this day and age, and is quite the liveliest girl ever put into a story." *The Patchwork Girl* sold 17,121 copies, not so many as *The Emerald City of Oz*, but significantly more than the Trot books.[65]

Seeking a reason for the disappointing sales that kept him anxious about money, Baum unfairly blamed the poor sales of the Trot books on Neill's illustrations. Baum actually urged his publishers to find another illustrator for the *Little Wizard* stories, but fortunately they refused. Baum then demanded a meeting with Neill to make sure he did justice to the eccentric characters in the forthcoming *Patchwork Girl.* So in August 1912, Neill came to Syracuse, where Baum was visiting his sister Harriet. Perhaps this was the occasion when Reilly & Britton met a request from a representative of an Eastern publisher to meet "Edith Van Dyne." They suggested he meet her at a tea in a hotel in Syracuse, her supposed home, and arranged for a woman author on their list to pose as Miss Van Dyne after reading all of the *Aunt Jane's Nieces* series. Frank and Maud attended the tea under assumed names and greatly enjoyed the joke.[66]

The meeting with Neill gave Baum his first opportunity to go over the illustrator's interpretations with him. He found Neill's drawing of the Patchwork Girl on the half-title page stiff, and Neill redrew her face. He made the same criticism of Neill's Woozy and wrote on his drawing: "The Woozy is not made of wood. He is an animal . . . alive but not brought to life by any magical means. Skin like a hippopotamus, and while carrying out the square idea in build give him more of an animal appearance—less wooden." Despite the meeting, Baum remained ungracious: he told his publishers that he thought the book would be a great success "in spite of Neill's pictures."[67]

Meanwhile, Baum continued to work on his extravaganza loosely based on *Ozma of Oz*, which was finally to be produced as "The Tik-Tok Man of Oz." This script has been lost, but its earlier versions survive in two variants, a detailed synopsis of "The Rainbow's Daughter," which Hearn dates February 23, 1909, and a script of *Ozma of Oz*, including dialogue and songs, dated April 15. Both were to have music by Manuel Klein and scenic effects by Arthur Voegtlin. Both open with a storm at sea and a girl floating in a chicken coop, although she is Betsy

Baker rather than Dorothy. She meets Shaggy Man and goes with him to the cavern of the Gnome King (renamed Ruggedo in "Ozma") to force him to release Shaggy Man's relatives (his wife and ten children in "The Rainbow's Daughter," his brother in "Ozma of Oz"). On the way they meet Polychrome and Tiktok. They are joined by Queen Ann of Oogaboo and her army of sixteen officers and one private, a variant on Ozma's army in *Ozma of Oz.*

Baum added the usual ingredients when he prepared his book for the stage. The Chorus appears as Vegetables (Roses in "Ozma of Oz"), who throw Betsy out of their kingdom when she is stranded there, then as Field Flowers, then as Nomes (who become female for the occasion), and finally as fireflies. Betsy is attended by Hank the Mule, the stock clown in an animal suit. Shaggy Man's Love Magnet precipitates innumerable farcical romantic entanglements as it passes from character to character. When Betsy takes the Magnet in "Ozma of Oz," Shaggy Man, Tiktok, and Hank immediately fall in love with her. Tiktok tells Shaggy Man to stop his "kid-ding," Shaggy says he can't because he is Captain Kidd, and this provokes a totally irrelevant pirate chorus that includes a sarcastic reference to the Standard Oil trust.[68] Shaggy Man fights with Tiktok and causes him to fall to pieces, so that he can later be reassembled on stage in a reprise of the reassembly of the Scarecrow in "The Wizard of Oz" extravaganza. Tiktok becomes a clown who constantly runs down rather than the well-imagined machine man of the Oz books. The dialogue is filled with puns, and the songs with worldly wisdom. Ruggedo falls in love with Polychrome, and together they sing "When in Trouble Come to Papa," about the financial advantages of being an old man's darling.

There were some enthralling special effects. Act II is set in the Gnome King's Underground Cavern, with a background of irregular rocks and the girls' chorus, now costumed as working Gnomes, perched among them. They beat on anvils "tuned so that the blows of the hammers play an anvil accompaniment to the Opening Chorus, and as each blow is struck the different anvils light up electrically, showing flashes of different colors. The face of the rock is everywhere set with colored jewels ... made by setting imitation cut-glass saucers, with rounding sides out, in the scenery, coloring them with transparent colors, and placing an electric light behind each one."[69] In the final scene, the Rainbow descends and turns the common rocks in the Valley of Gold into gold nuggets. Ruggedo is ecstatic, but when he grasps the nuggets they change back into rocks, because Rainbow gold turns to dross if touched by a profane hand. (This effect was retrieved from Baum's unfinished farce "The King of Gee Whiz.")

"The Tik-Tok Man of Oz" opened in Los Angeles on March 31, 1913, with music by Louis Gottschalk. The star comedians were James Morton and Frank Moore, as Tik-Tok and Shaggy Man; but the hit of the show was Fred Woodward as Hank the mule. The show also had short but profitable runs in San Francisco and Chicago and went on tour, but its success did not compare to that of "The Wizard of Oz." Critics in Los Angeles were enthusiastic, but those in Chicago contrasted it unfavorably with "The Wizard." Amy Leslie in Chicago was devastating: she said "Tik-Tok" was practically a revival of "The Wizard," "almost letter for letter, scene for scene, spectacle for spectacle and chorus girl for chorus girl." She did find Gottschalk's melodies beautiful.[70] Baum remained involved in the show throughout its run, making personal appearances before and after performances.

Living in Hollywood, Baum could watch the rapid developments in the movie industry and imagine what he could do with this exciting new medium.[71] He used his current *Aunt Jane's Nieces* book, *Aunt Jane's Nieces Out West* (1914), to express his interest and his hopes. Beth, Patsy, and Uncle John are spending the winter in Hollywood; and the two girls have been filmed, unawares, as extras in a disaster movie. This leads to an acquaintance with two actress sisters and their script reader aunt, to scenes on movie sets, and to debates over the social value of movies. Beth and Patsy propose to build a Children's Picture Theater and "have some fairy tales made into movies." The script reader encourages them: "The various manufacturers have made films of the fairy tales of Hans Andersen, Frank Baum . . . and other well-known writers," which were quite successful.[72] Unfortunately, her words proved to be no more than wish-fulfilling fantasy.

Some of Baum's friends in the Uplifters organized the Oz Film Manufacturing Company to make movies of his stories, and one hundred thousand dollars' worth of stock was soon subscribed to by Uplifters and other members of the Los Angeles Athletic Club. Fortunately, Baum did not put any of his own money into the venture: he gave the company exclusive movie rights to his books in exchange for a block of stock. He was to write the scripts and Gottschalk to write original music for the Oz pictures (which would be sent along with them to be performed in the theaters), also in return for stock in the company. Baum was made president, Gottschalk vice president, Clarence H. Rendel secretary, and Harry M. Haldeman treasurer. They bought a seven-acre site just south of Hollywood and built a large, elaborate studio, which Baum designed. Under the 65 × 100 foot stage there were a large concrete tunnel, a large concrete tank, and eight smaller tanks. These could be filled with water to represent ponds or a river, and the big tunnel could be used for illusions and transformations; actors could appear or disappear through trap doors on the stage opening into the tunnel. The original plan was to film all of Baum's twenty-eight fairy stories, followed by his musicals.[73]

Production started on the first film, a five-reel version of the recently published *Patchwork Girl of Oz*, in mid-June 1914. This was a superior film for its time, with some clever special effects like walking through an illusory wall. Baum made his usual alterations of a book for theatrical production. The Patchwork Girl was played by a male acrobat, Pierre Couderc, who greatly exaggerated her tendency to awkward comic capers. Fred Woodward, the mule in "The Tik-Tok Man of Oz," played the Woozy and an added mule character. Ojo was represented by a pretty young woman. The plot more or less follows the book, except that Dr. Pipt has a daughter, Jesseva, with a lover, Danx. Danx is accidentally turned to marble along with Unc Nunkie and Margolotte, but even as a statue, he causes humorous romantic complications. The Patchwork Girl and the Scarecrow have several courtship scenes.

"The Patchwork Girl of Oz" was completed in one month (by July 18), but problems developed with distribution; for most movie theaters were monopolized by the big producers. The Oz Film Manufacturing Company established an office in New York City, managed by Frank Junior, to arrange distribution of the films. After much negotiation, he got Paramount Pictures to book "The Patchwork Girl" into the Strand Theatre in New York City in September. More trouble developed when the Motion Picture Patents Company, which claimed to be the owner of Edison's patents, sued the Oz film company and several others for patent infringement. The suit was settled out of court, and the Oz company went on to make another five-reeler, "The Magic Cloak of Oz," finished in early September. They expected Paramount to distribute it, but Paramount refused because "The Patchwork Girl" was not doing well. The market for children's films had not yet been recognized; patrons resented paying to see a "kid" picture. Meanwhile, the Oz company had made "His Majesty the Scarecrow of Oz," finished at the end of September, which was released in October but did not earn enough even to cover production costs. "It is conceded to be the best trick picture ever made," Baum wrote Reilly on January 10, 1915, "full of interest and produced with wonderful scenic and costuming effects by a cast that includes 130 people. . . . [It] cost the Oz Film Co. $23,500 to make."[74]

But no major distributor would touch either "His Majesty the Scarecrow" or "The Magic Cloak." The latter is a drastically curtailed version of *Queen Zixi of Ix.* Bud as well as Fluff are played by young women, and they have a cavorting mule played by Fred Woodward. There is a lot of action involving clowns in animal suits. The villainous Roly-Rogues are effectively costumed and presented, and other clever special effects include the reassembling of the cut pieces of the magic cloak. Ultimately the Oz company cut the picture and tried to market it as two two-reelers, still without success.

"His Majesty the Scarecrow of Oz," also in five reels, is more plot heavy even than the earlier two films. It combines elements from several Oz books, including the rescue of the Scarecrow and the Tin Woodman from *The Wizard of Oz* and the finding of Button Bright from *The Road to Oz.* In addition, Baum for the first time invented an original main plot for his film. King Krewl asks the witch Mombi to destroy the love of his niece, Gloria, for Pon, the gardener's boy. Mombi summons some assistant witches and freezes Gloria's heart. From then on, Gloria wanders among the characters, cold, aimless, and indifferent to whatever is going on; her icy presence makes an effective contrast to the frantic action. There is a good special effect when the Wizard, who happens along driving a wagon, reduces Mombi's size and imprisons her in a can of Preserved Sandwitches. He lets her out on condition that she unfreeze Gloria's heart. She does, the lovers are reunited, and the Scarecrow replaces King Krewl on the throne. As usual, Woodward was on hand to play a burlesque mule and various other animals. Baum may have directed all three films, although most sources credit J. Farrell MacDonald for the first two.

Unable to distribute its children's films, the Oz company made a five-reel version of *The Last Egyptian* that closely follows Baum's book, begun in September or October and released in December 1914; but they could not get it booked into theaters because the distributors would no longer touch any film from the Oz company. The same thing happened with four one-reel children's films called "Violet's Dreams," filmed at the same time to use the stars of the children's movies. For a while the company kept the studio open by handing over the selection of subjects for production to the Alliance Company, with Baum pushed into a subordinate position. It is not known whether he had any hand in "The Gray Nun of Belgium," a war film that went into production in April 1915. The distributors turned it down sight unseen. By summer the Oz company had to close altogether.[75]

Baum had put an enormous amount of effort, as well as creative thought, into the Oz Film Manufacturing Company. A reporter described him in the studio when they were about to start filming "The Magic Cloak of Oz" as "Probably the busiest man" of the whole company. "He is there at 8 and in overalls, and he stays on duty until the 5:30 whistle blows, when they all shut up shop. He personally designs and makes the intricate mechanism connected with his freak animals and supervises all the sets. . . . He never rested a moment."[76] Although Baum lost no money in this venture, the waste of a year's work and creative efforts must have been painful.

nine

A WRITER TO THE END,

1914–1919

In 1913, Baum was promoting "The Tik-Tok Man of Oz," and in 1914, he was working full-time to keep the Oz Film Manufacturing Company going. In addition, he published an Oz book and an *Aunt Jane's Nieces* book each year. On December 16, 1914, he wrote to Reilly that he had set aside *The Scarecrow of Oz* in order to begin work on *Aunt Jane's Nieces in the Red Cross.* He finished the first draft of *The Scarecrow* at midnight, December 31. As soon as he got the *Aunt Jane's Nieces* book off his hands, he wrote on January 28, 1915, he would revise and type *The Scarecrow.* "I am not wasting any time on either story, but I want them to be as good as I can make them." He sent the completed manuscript of *The Scarecrow* to Reilly & Britton on March 15.

In addition to all this work, he was suffering from serious health problems. His lifelong defective heart began to give him distressing and constant symptoms—irregular heart rhythm and difficulty in breathing, leading ultimately to congestive heart failure. In addition, he developed severe attacks of angina pectoris, probably caused by a narrowing of the coronary arteries, aggravated by decades of a cholesterol-laden diet and heavy smoking. These attacks forced him to stop whatever he was doing and seek relief by pacing the floor. They may have been connected, as his son Frank believed, with his overwork and stress in trying to keep the Oz Film Manufacturing Company in business. In 1914, Baum also began suffering excruciating attacks of tic douloureux, which recurred unpredictably for the rest of his life; as much as possible, he resisted taking morphine lest he become addicted.[1] A portrait photograph of 1915 shows him looking significantly older and more worn than in the preceding years; his expression suggests an effort to control pain. In the preface to *Tik-Tok of Oz,* he raised the possibility that he might not be "permitted to write another Oz book." It is not remarkable that he cut some corners on *Tik-Tok* and the next two Oz books.

Tik-Tok of Oz (1914) was dedicated to Louis F. Gottschalk, who had composed the music for "The Tik-Tok Man of Oz." The book was based on the show and accordingly has puns (though not nearly so many) and a love interest.[2] Even when Baum reused elements from the play, however, he developed them with an incomparably more delicate touch. Instead of multiple wild infatuations, there is only a quietly developing fondness between Files and the outcast Rose Princess. (In the book as in the play, her brainless, heartless subjects rejected her because they insisted on having a male ruler.)[3] Files's suggestion that she get directions to the Nome Kingdom from her cousins the wild flowers does not engender heavy-handed personifications and choral numbers as in the show. Instead, when she diffidently asks the flowers to help, their stems bend to the right and their heads nod three times in that direction, and Files assures her there was not a breath of wind to stir them. It is a subdued, appealing, almost believable bit of fantasy. Ruggedo's enchantment with Polychrome is not the stock old man's dotage on a young woman that it was in the show, but vivid evidence that the sky fairy's shimmering beauty and freedom can affect even a hardened tyrant. Hank is an endearing realistic mule, not a clown in an animal suit. Although Baum's animals are humanized in the Oz books, they are never demeaned by the clownish human antics that are so tedious in his movies. They keep some essentials of their animal nature, and they are as much respected as the human characters.

Ann Soforth of Oogaboo (bugaboo) and her army are broadly ridiculed, but not through slapstick military drills, as in the show. Instead, Baum cleverly reduced their motives to fairy-tale versions of the motives that he was seriously to ascribe to the makers of World War I in *Aunt Jane's Nieces in the Red Cross*. Queen Ann is inspired to conquer the world by her discontent with ruling a petty kingdom and her ambition to enslave people and enrich herself with their property. She persuades the officers to join her by promising them gold epaulets and swords. Her original private, Files, does genuinely want to become a hero, but even his idealistic ambition is questionable: "to slash and slay the enemy" so that he can have a marble statue of himself "for all to look upon and admire." Being a decent man, he resigns when he is ordered to make war on girls. He is replaced by Tik-Tok, who is the

Tik-Tok of Oz. The Rose Princess asks directions of her cousins the field-flowers. John R. Neill.

perfect private because, being a machine who does what he is wound up to do, he obeys without questioning. The officers, who maintain that fighting is only for privates, run away from any danger that appears.[4]

Despite its recycled elements, *Tik-Tok of Oz* is lively and amusing. There is a charming, chatty sky blue dragon called Quox. The Nome

Kingdom is developed with further delightful detail. King Ruggedo (who had to take a new name when he forgot his original one in the Fountain of Oblivion) is as flamboyantly evil and comic as ever. He has trouble amusing himself when the Nomes behave well and there is no one to punish, and he becomes even more provoked when Kaliko, his High Chamberlain, will not stand still to have a scepter hurled at his head. With the folly of a child, Ruggedo chooses to destroy himself rather than give in and yield up a prisoner: "I don't want him. . . . But I won't allow anybody to order me around. I'm King of the Nomes and I'm the Metal Monarch, and I shall do as I please and what I please and when I please!"[5]

Tik-Tok was less handsomely produced than the earlier Oz books, with twelve colored plates instead of sixteen, because World War I pushed up the costs of book production. It sold 14,216 copies,[6] 3,000 less than *The Patchwork Girl.* Reilly lamented on December 14, 1914, that fall orders and repeat orders for the book were "way off," despite an outlay of $1,000 on advertising. He also informed Baum that *Sky Island, The Sea Fairies, Baum's Own Book for Children,* and *John Dough* would be "absolutely dead as money earners for either you or us" unless he agreed to let the publishers sell them at radically reduced prices, with proportionally reduced royalties for him.

Baum replied on December 21; "Your report of poor sales is the more disappointing inasmuch as it is likely to reduce my income for next year, which will prove a hardship because I have obligations to meet in 1915 that I had depended on taking care of from my monthly remittances." He hoped for dividends from his stock in the Oz Film Manufacturing Company, but could not expect any for at least eighteen months. The situation was aggravated by the activities of M. A. Donohue, a cheap publisher who had bought out Baum's early titles from Rountree and Bobbs-Merrill and was selling them at cut-rate prices. Reilly argued on December 31 that "the average buyer" who could purchase *The Wizard of Oz* for 35 cents "can't see why he should be expected to pay 75 cents for Tik-Tok of Oz."

On January 10, 1915, Baum urged Reilly to find a way to "give new impetus to the Baum line," perhaps by using publicity obtained from the film *His Majesty the Scarecrow of Oz,* which would, Baum optimistically but wrongly expected, "be shown quite generally throughout the U.S. for six or eight months to follow."

In the preface to *The Scarecrow of Oz* (1915), Baum suggested hopefully that his child readers might someday want a change from

Oz books. It may be that the first half of *The Scarecrow* was originally intended as material for a third Trot book, although of course Baum must have decided to give up on that series when he brought Trot to Oz.

The book starts well, with Trot and Cap'n Bill sucked down by a whirlpool to a cavern beneath the sea. Trot, a brave, enterprising little girl, sensibly calms her adult friend's apprehensions over a risky escape plan by pointing out that "nobody can stay alive without getting into danger sometimes, and danger doesn't mean getting hurt, Cap'n; it only means we *might* get hurt." The story picks up when the Ork arrives in the same cavern. The Ork, who is large and friendly like the traditional stork, is not quite a bird: he has four legs and flies with a propeller tail like a helicopter, and he despises the "horrid feathered things" that also fly.[7]

From then on, Baum's imagination flagged. He drew on his own earlier invention the Land of Mo and on the conventional stock of fairy tales. The travelers pass through Mo, where they find Button Bright (who has been using his magic umbrella again) in a heap of popcorn snow.[8]

Their next stop is Jinxland in an isolated corner of the Land of Oz, which is an undistinguished fairy-tale country with the standard cruel king, wicked witches, and beautiful princess who is being coerced to marry an ugly old courtier instead of the poor young man she loves. When Princess Gloria persists in her love, the king hires the chief witch to freeze her heart. Baum took this romantic plot directly from his film "His Majesty the Scarecrow," where he was aiming at an adult as well as a child audience. He justified the new element of romance in a letter to Reilly on January 17, 1916: "In the Scarecrow I introduced a slightly novel theme, for me, in the love and tribulations of Pon the gardener's son [sic] and the Princess Gloria. It smacked a bit of the Andersen fairy tales and I watched its effect upon my readers. They accepted it gleefully, with all the rest, it being well within their comprehension." It was an intentional departure from his usual formula, he claimed, as was his next book, *Rinkitink in Oz*, because the one after that ("Three Girls in Oz," which became "Adventures in Oz" and then *The Lost Princess of Oz*) "was exactly in line with the style of the first four Oz books, and I could see an advantage in so varying the subject matter that the little ones would have no cause to tire of my stories."

This looks like a rationalization after the fact, but Baum did adapt

the Pon-Gloria romance to the Oz world by subjecting it to comic criticism. Pon, the romantic hero, is a pathetically inadequate youth,
always crying and never able to defend Gloria or resist those who mis-
treat him. Trot tries to console lovelorn Gloria by telling her, "Pon isn't
any great shakes, anyhow, seems to me. . . . There are lots of other people you can love." Of course Gloria should not marry old Googly-Goo,
but she should "Hunt around, and I'm sure you'll find someone worth
your love. You're very pretty, you know, and almost anyone ought to
love you." Gloria explains that when Trot is older she "will realize that
a young lady cannot decide whom she will love, or choose the most
worthy. Her heart alone decides for her, and whomsoever her heart
selects, she must love, whether he amounts to much or not." Trot,
understandably, "was a little puzzled by this speech, which seemed to
her unreasonable." The humans politely congratulate Pon when he
wins Gloria at the end, "but the Ork sneezed twice and said that in his
opinion the young lady might have done better."[9]

When Baum sent the manuscript to Reilly & Britton on March 15,
he noted that his wife "thinks this is the best of the Oz series and, next
to Sky Island, the cleverest fairy tale I have ever written. So I hope it
will help all of us to big sales this fall." Nevertheless, sales continued
disappointing. *The Scarecrow* sold 14,349 copies, only a few more than
Tik-Tok of Oz had, although it went on to become one of the best selling Oz books.[10]

Reilly and his staff thought the problem might be "a slight tendency . . . to get away from the youthful viewpoint" in the most recent
Oz books (January 12, 1916). This suggestion stung Baum into a rare
display of anger. "I honestly believe I am doing right now the very best
work of my career," he retorted on January 17; and this is amply confirmed by the children's letters. "As against the judgement evidenced in
these letters . . . the judgement of your 'staff' doesn't amount to a row
of pins. You are not obliged to print my books, if you do not wish to,
but let me ask you where you could find another juvenile author as dear
to the American children as Baum, or one whose books have a demand
so firmly established." He went on to justify the romantic element in
The Scarecrow (also found in *Tik-Tok*). Nevertheless, he did not touch this
theme in subsequent Oz books except *The Tin Woodman of Oz*, where he
presented it as a child might see it.

Baum blamed Neill's illustrations, which he found persistently lacking in humor, although "his fanciful drawings are excellent." Baum
demanded an artist "who could infuse new life and a spirit of fun into

the Oz characters, which in Mr. Neill's hands are now perfunctory and listless." His displeasure was aggravated when he discovered Neill's *The Oz Toy Book* listed in Reilly & Britton's Fall 1915 catalogue. He considered Neill's cutouts an infringement of his copyrighted characters and was not mollified when the publishers claimed (with probable truth) that they were intended primarily as a promotion of *The Scarecrow* and the other Oz books.[11]

Later Baum recognized his unfairness to Neill. He also conceded, in a letter to Reilly on October 25, 1915, "perhaps no author is ever satisfied with his illustrator and I see my characters and incidents so differently from the artist that I fail to appreciate his talent. Mr. Neill is good, and perhaps we could find no better." By June 23, 1916, when his income began to improve, he declared he was "quite delighted" with the illustrations to *Rinkitink in Oz*. And he praised Neill's "exceptionally clever and attractive" illustrations for *The Lost Princess of Oz*, although he did spot one of Neill's very rare slips in rendering Baum's text: drawing two peaches on a tree where there was only one in the plate facing page 156. He invited Neill to visit him in Hollywood: "I'm sorry not to have met you personally for so many recent years . . . as I remember our former foregatherings with real pleasure and think we could harmonize if we were jailed together in the same cell." But Baum died before Neill visited.[12]

Searching about for a source of easy money, Baum proposed to Reilly on August 10, 1915, a book called "Father Goose's Party" that would present his characters "with an appropriate nursery rhyme accompanying each and interspersed with the well known characters of Mother Goose and the best known fairy tales, the idea being to establish the Baum characters with the older classics of the nursery." Fortunately he was persuaded to write *Rinkitink in Oz* instead and sent Reilly & Britton the manuscript on October 25. It appeared in 1916 and is dedicated to his new grandson, Robert Alison Baum, Robert's first child.

This book also is based on old material, a traditional fantasy Baum had written in 1905. The 1905 story reflects his discovery of California in its emphasis on the sea, which had not figured significantly in his earlier works, even in *The Enchanted Island of Yew*. *Rinkitink* is similar in spirit to *Queen Zixi of Ix*, written shortly before. It has a medieval setting and does not include the nonhuman eccentrics that distinguish the Oz books.[13] Like *Zixi*, it centers on a fairy gift that has certain limitations and therefore produces exciting complications. The peaceful, prosperous island of Pingaree is ravaged by northern warriors from Regos and Coregos, who carry off its king, queen, and citizens as slaves. By chance, Prince Inga and two visitors, jolly King Rinkitink and his surly talking goat Bilbil, are left on the island. Inga must rescue his parents and people with the help of three magic pearls: a pink pearl, which makes him invulnerable; a blue pearl, which gives him enormous strength; and a white pearl, which gives him unerring advice. At various times, he loses or parts with one or two of the pearls and must manage with what he has left.

As usual in Baum, Queen Cor of Coregos is far more capable than her blustering husband, King Gos of Regos. When Inga conquers their countries with the aid of his pearls, her husband collapses in panic, but she forms a plan to block Inga's advance by taking his parents to the Nome King and bribing him to keep them as hostages. Inga, Rinkitink, and Bilbil must go to the Nome Kingdom to rescue them. Kaliko, made king after Ruggedo was deposed for offending Tititi-Hoochoo in *Tik-Tok*, refuses to release the prisoners and tries to destroy Inga and his party when they persist in demanding them. Rinkitink is protected by the pink pearl, which Inga has lent him; but this means that Inga has to get past a huge giant, a wide gulf, and a floor covered with burning coals aided only by the strength given by the blue pearl.[14]

In order to turn his independent fantasy of 1905 into the 1916 volume of the Oz series, Baum had to bring in Oz characters and to adapt his presentation of the Nome King, whom the plot required to do evil things, even though he was now Kaliko, a good Nome. Baum managed the latter very plausibly. Kaliko is not sadistic or violent like Ruggedo, but he is unscrupulous because that is Nome nature. He accepts unlawfully taken prisoners for a bribe and he will not give them up, but he has no interest in making them suffer, as Cor recommends. He tries to destroy Inga and his comrades only because they will not go away and leave him alone, and, after his attempts fail, he is pleasant and friendly. He is aggrieved by Dorothy's insistence "on the nomes being goody-goody, which is contrary to their natures," and puzzled to hear that she is coming to see him, "for I've been behaving very well lately." She does force him to give up his prisoners, but leaves him merely with a warning "not to be wicked any more if he could help it."[15]

Baum was not so successful in incorporating Oz into the story. He brought in Dorothy gratuitously, over five-sixths of the way through the book, solely to connect the story with Oz. *Rinkitink* does not succeed as an Oz book, but the complications involving the magic pearls and the adventures in the Nome Kingdom make it a delightful fantasy nevertheless.

As Baum told Reilly, *The Lost Princess of Oz* (1917) was in the style of his early Oz books; and it is one of his best. It is a well-plotted book, full of fine inventions; and it displays some of the most engaging of the familiar Oz characters, as well as a new one, the Frogman. Baum sent in the manuscript on September 6, 1916, complete with a map of the search, which he definitely wanted included, because the maps on the endpapers of *Tik-Tok* had been a big success. The book was dedicated to his granddaughter, Ozma.

Baum used his preface to reaffirm the importance of fairy stories in developing imagination, the essential source of all creativity. Imagination has led us to every discovery we have made, from the New World to electricity to the automobile, "for these things had to be dreamed of before they became realities.... The imaginative child will become the imaginative man or woman most apt to create, to invent, and therefore to foster civilization."

The story opens arrestingly with the theft of precious things from all over Oz—the Wizard's tools, Ozma's Magic Picture, and Ozma herself from the Emerald City; Glinda's Book of Records and magic compounds and tools from her castle in the south; and, incongruously, the magic dishpan of Cayke the Cookie Cook from her home in the remote Yip Country. The dishpan enables her to bake perfect cookies—which seems a far-fetched connection even for a Baumian fantasy—and turns out to have other magical properties as well. Parties go out in search of the thief, who now holds all the important magic in Oz except for the Magic Belt, which he did not know about because it originated in another country.

Baum focuses on Dorothy's party, consisting of Dorothy, Betsy, Trot, Button-Bright, the Wizard, the Patchwork Girl, the Cowardly Lion, the Woozy, Hank the mule, the Sawhorse, and Toto, going west from the Emerald City, who meet Cayke and the Frogman, going east from the western border of the Winkie Country. The Frogman, an ordinary frog who acquired human size and intellect from eating skosh in a Yip pond, had been received as an oracle by the Yips. "They had never seen a frog before and the frog had never seen a Yip before, but as there were plenty of Yips and only one frog, the frog became the most important." The Frogman starts out as one of Baum's conceited pretenders to extraordinary wisdom, but after he swims in the Truth Pond, he has to confess he knows no more than anyone else; and he then becomes a useful member of the search party. Having divested himself of his intellectual pretensions, he can encourage the others by sensibly pointing out that even a great magician is "an ordinary man" who has "learned how to do magical tricks," and "surely there are ways in which a man may be conquered."[16]

The mixed search party illustrates the democratic Baumian pattern of a group of equals where everyone is respected and everyone contributes something. The Wizard knows the trick that will dispel an apparent wall of fire, the Frogman jumps over a high wall, Dorothy thinks to bring along the Magic Belt, the thick-skinned Woozy carries the Lion over a field of thistles. It is the Patchwork Girl who supplies most of the ideas, tossing off solutions to problems as she dances around or walks on her hands. Unlike the helpful Scarecrow, she has to be coaxed to provide solutions, protesting she doesn't "want to wear my brains out with overwork." She doesn't seriously mean this, of course; she just wants to remain free of obligations of any kind. She tells the normal humans: "Such brains as you have are of the common sort that grow in your heads, like weeds in a garden. I'm sorry for you people who have to be born in order to be alive."[17] This cotton-stuffed doll *is* more alive than many humans—always thinking, always moving, seeking interesting experiences, and enjoying every bit.

The advantages of diversity are spelled out one evening in a debate among the animals. The Woozy remarks on Hank's big ears and scraggly tail, and Hank sneers at the Woozy's squareness. Finally, the four meat animals refer to the Sawhorse to decide which is most beautiful, and the Sawhorse declares his superiority to all creatures who must sleep and eat. Then the Lion settles the matter: it is far better to be a group of distinct individuals, "various enough to enjoy one another's society," than to be a mere herd of mules or of sawhorses.[18]

About the middle of the book, the story begins to point to Ugu the Shoemaker as the villain who has stolen Ozma and the magic of Oz. Button-Bright eats a peach and is warned by a bluefinch and a rabbit that Ugu will not like what he has done. Dorothy's group learns that Ugu was an ordinary citizen who taught himself to be a great magician and went off to live in a solitary castle lest his neighbors discover his secrets. There is a climactic contest of magic, in which Ugu holds most of the advantages and the search party must make do with natural wit and bits of magic Ugu does not know about.[19] Dorothy saves the situ-

The Lost Princess of Oz. The Woozy carries the Cowardly Lion over the field of thistles. John R. Neill.

ation by using the Magic Belt to turn Ugu into a dove, on which the Wizard cheerfully remarks, "We have conquered the wicked magician." Scraps corrects him: "Don't say 'we'—Dorothy did it!"[20] In the end Ugu, who was not totally wicked but had merely let his ambition and pride blind him to the rights of others, repents and decides he would rather be a good dove than a bad man.

In the intervals of creating these fantasies, Baum was regularly turning out his series books for girls. *Aunt Jane's Nieces in the Red Cross*
(1915) is more interesting than most because he used it to express
his feelings about World War I, feelings similar to those he had
expressed fantastically in *Tik-Tok of Oz*. His foreword (an innovation
in his Edith Van Dyne books) sets forth a serious purpose: "I wish I
might have depicted more gently the scenes in hospital and on battlefield, but it is well that my girl readers should realize something of
the horrors of war, that they may unite with heart and soul in
earnest appeal for universal, lasting Peace and the future abolition of
all deadly strife." (Actually, in keeping with his Van Dyne persona, he
kept his descriptions mild.) Both Patsy and Beth are keenly interested
in and distressed by the war, especially because the Germans have
won two days running; Uncle John reminds them that America is
supposed to be neutral. All agree with Patsy that "This great war is
no manly struggle. . . . It is merely wholesale murder by a band of
selfish diplomats." Beth wishes she could do something to help the
"poor victims of the war's cruelty, the wounded and dying."[21] They
turn a yacht into a hospital ship and go to the battlefields of Europe,
together with their movie star friend, who is a trained nurse, and Dr.
Gys, an eccentrically independent and hideously scarred American
who, like the Cowardly Lion, trembles at danger but finds courage
when he needs it.

The girls perform bravely and competently at their first battle scene
and remark on the courage of all the soldiers, Allied and German.
Their Belgian chauffeur speaks for them all when he says,

> We do good to both sides, because the men who do the fighting are
> not to blame for the war, at all. The leaders of politics say to the gener-
> als: "We have declared war; go and fight." The generals say to the sol-
> diers: "We are told to fight. . . . We do not know why, but it is our duty,
> because it is our profession. So go and die, or get shot to pieces, or lose
> some arms and legs. . . ." The business of the soldiers is to obey; they
> must back up the policies of their country, right or wrong. But do
> those who send them into danger ever get hurt?

Our friends' sympathy is with the Allies, but they encounter gentlemanly and admirable German officers, as well as bullies.

This book makes explicit what Baum repeatedly expressed figuratively in his fantasy tales: quarrels between nations are unnecessary because they are based on illusory differences. Dr. Gys dies heroically on the battlefield, Patsy is injured but recovers, and they all go home. Having demonstrated their competence and courage and having "unselfishly devoted . . . three strenuous months to the injured soldiers of a foreign war," the girls leave and let other women fill their places as nurses.[22]

Although the *Aunt Jane's Nieces* series was "one of your—and our—bread-and-butter winners," Reilly & Britton told Baum on October 7, 1915, that "Edith Van Dyne" should start something new, while they continued to promote the profitable older books. He was glad to make a change and proposed a series on "Mary Louise" (named after his favorite sister), promising the first book by January 1 and the second by July 1.[23] However, America's entry into World War I, which meant that two of his own sons were fighting the Germans, so changed Baum's attitude toward the war that he left his new series to rewrite the ending of *Aunt Jane's Nieces in the Red Cross*.

He wrote four new chapters and spliced them into the original ending for the 1918 edition. This gave him room to side definitely with the Allies as well as to formally close down the series. Baum now presented the war not as a tragically unnecessary folly, but as a momentous conflict between the forces of right and of wrong. Uncle John speaks of "stricken countries devastated by German cruelty" and sees "that the great war was destined to alter the social, political and economic conditions of the world . . . and that all the Merrick money and energy must be expended in defeating the menace of the Central Powers." Action on the battlefield is presented more graphically, with an American cameraman's right arm reduced to "a pulp of mangled flesh and bone."[24] Instead of casually bringing the Americans home after three months, Baum leaves them to continue their vital work. They take on another doctor, who turns out to be a brilliant plastic surgeon and succeeds in restoring Dr. Gys's original looks. Beth becomes engaged to Dr. Gys, now good-looking and affable, and Patsy's engagement is expected.

In his new series, Baum evidently planned to focus on character: the interest would lie not in adventures, as in the Aunt Jane books, but in the heroine's development from a mischievous, irresponsible twelve year old into a thoughtful fourteen year old, he wrote to Reilly on January 8, 1916; she would mature further in each subsequent book.

Baum sent in his manuscript on December 22; to his amazement, Reilly found it unacceptable, presumably because the heroine was not sufficiently idealized. The publishers and their readers felt "it would be harmful . . . to publish over the name of Edith Van Dyne a book which we believe would have little of [if] any chance of a sale," he wrote on January 3.

Mortified and displeased, Baum explained his aims, noted that whatever publishers' readers might say his "stories *delight the girls* and sell," but agreed to provide a replacement with a "quite different," fifteen-year-old Mary Louise, which followed the plan of the *Aunt Jane* stories (January 8). Baum did manage to deliver his new manuscript on February 26. It is no wonder the result is flat. *Mary Louise* is a routine girls' mystery story with a tiresomely perfect fifteen-year-old heroine, who is distinguished for mature judgment and makes her first appearance justifying the teacher's refusal to let her fellow students to go to the movie in town. This is explained by the immoral content of so many movies—an obvious dig at the industry that refused to distribute the amusing, wholesome offerings of the Oz Film Manufacturing Company. Mary Louise's world collapses when her beloved grandfather appears to be guilty of some major crime. There is a mildly interesting surprise when Detective O'Gorman, who is pursuing her as she flees to her grandfather's hideout, turns out to be sympathetic. She reminds him of his daughter, Josie, who is an apprentice detective. The book was published in late June or early July, and its sequel a few months later.

Mary Louise in the Country (1916) is full of mysteries, principally involving an eccentric old man who lives in utmost penury but somehow disposes of large sums of money. It turns out that he is working for the Cause: that is, the liberation of Ireland from English rule. He is criticized for his excess devotion to the Cause, which has made him self-centered and neglectful of his family, but respected for his "lofty philanthropy, his self-sacrifice, his dogged perseverance." Although his activities are technically illegal because of America's treaty with England, Detective O'Gorman will not pursue him: "it's no work for an O'Gorman." Josie O'Gorman becomes prominent in this book, and more is made of the career of female detective. O'Gorman declares that he is "promoting the interests of both my daughter and the public safety by training Josie to become a good detective," for more women are needed in the profession.[25] Josie is a tough, aggressive character who makes a welcome contrast to sweet Mary Louise.

All Baum's series books for girls suffer because he was caught between his publishers' demand for mystery stories "full of thrills and surprises" and the constrictions of his refined Edith Van Dyne persona. A mystery cannot hold attention unless it involves serious evildoing, yet "Edith Van Dyne" was reluctant to bring real villains and wickedness into her stories. The result is that the solutions are flat and contrived. In *Mary Louise*, Mary Louise's honorable, patriotic grandfather looked like a traitor because he had accepted blame for a misdeed of her mother's, caused by her mother's weak love for a worthless husband. In *Mary Louise in the Country*, an old man's criminal exploitation of his granddaughter is explained away as thoughtlessness resulting from his self-sacrificing devotion to his Cause.

When it came time to write the next book, Baum's worsening health made it impossible to meet his heavy publishing commitments. *Mary Louise Solves a Mystery*, the potboiler for 1917, was apparently written by his son Harry, in a plausible imitation of Frank's manner.[26] But Frank did exert himself to write *Mary Louise and the Liberty Girls* (1918) in order to deal with an issue of real importance to him: the venomous anti-German feelings in this country after America entered World War I. He remembered that his own ancestors had emigrated from Hesse, even though it was back in the eighteenth century. Moreover, as several of his fairy tales show, he deplored reflexive ethnic hostility. He again gave "Edith Van Dyne" a preface, where she explained that the story aimed not only "to show what important tasks girls may accomplish when spurred on by patriotism," but to encourage "charity to all and malice toward none." Mary Louise's grandfather, a civic leader, urges the citizens at a town meeting to buy government bonds "that all may participate in our noble struggle for the salvation of democracy and the peace of the world" and personally help "to defeat Civilization's defiant and ruthless enemy." Jake Kasker, a German-American merchant, is the first to step forward; but at the same time he declares his opposition to the war. The grandfather thanks him coldly and rebukes him for his "traitorous" words.[27]

Since the results of the appeal are disappointing, Mary Louise organizes a group of girls, the "Liberty Girls," to collect more money, using feminine charm, picturesque costumes, and, if necessary, tears. Her campaign is successful, but she discovers that someone is sending circulars around that urge people not to buy bonds and that attack the draft as unconstitutional. Mary Louise suspects Kasker, who complains that his only son has just been drafted "off to a war there's no good excuse for"; but Kasker disavows the circulars and insists that he and his boy will stand by the flag no matter what: "I'm for America first, last and all the time. . . . I don't like the Germans and I don't like the English, for Jake Kasker is a George Washington American." Mary Louise remains positive that Kasker is the traitor, but her grandfather points out that "Germans came to America to escape the militarism and paternalism of the Junkers." Josie O'Gorman arrives and discovers that the traitor is a home-grown local politician.[28] Baum was careful to emphasize his patriotic support of the war and to criticize Kasker as a foolish loud-mouth, but it was brave of him to defend German-Americans and risk offending the public in a book that was supposed to "sell and not be adversely criticized." His publishers discouraged references to the war or politics on the grounds that they might antagonize some readers or their elders. The Liberty Girls' enthusiasm and effectiveness is feminist as well as patriotic propaganda: suffragists cited women's contributions to the war effort as evidence of their public spirit and right to the vote.[29]

Looking for some additional means to increase his income, Baum kept trying to publish short stories. Strangely, this proficient and well-known author could not apparently write stories salable to magazines. On September 11, 1915, he appealed to Reilly: "If you hear of any chance for me to place any stories anywhere, please give me the tip, as I'd like to get hold of a little extra money. It seems that this year, when my own income is smaller, I have had more than the usual number of calls on my purse by those I am bound to assist, and the consequence is that I'm devilish hard up and need money."

It is not remarkable that "The Diamondback" was rejected. It is a strange though powerful story, narrated by a sympathetic rattlesnake, that illustrates nature's law that all animals "are doomed to periods of intense suffering to compensate the pleasures they have enjoyed." But "Chrome Yellow," returned without comment by the *Saturday Evening Post*, is a conventional and reasonably effective tale of retribution set among orange growers in California.[30]

Occasionally Baum hinted that he might do better with another publisher. Reilly sent William Lee to Los Angeles to conciliate him. Lee reported to Reilly on April 2, 1916, that he had convinced Baum to stay with Reilly & Britton, and he passed on Baum's request for an increase in his monthly payments when his contract was renewed at the end of December. Baum wanted one hundred dollars a week; Lee replied that "his average earnings hardly justified it" and offered four hundred dollars a month, which Baum accepted. On June 17, Reilly agreed to this, provided business conditions were good enough to warrant it, but offered to advance more if Baum had particular need.

Lee's description of Baum at this luncheon meeting shows that he was not always as sweet as his family and friends remembered him. "I found Baum in a flexible frame of mind," Lee wrote, "and easy to handle with a little tact. . . . He has the author's ego well developed, but like all humans he particularily wants the cash to keep up the standard of living he thinks he is entitled to." Lee figured that Baum's average earnings from 1910 through 1915 were $5,300, with a low of $4,963 in 1915.[31] Oz book sales were still disappointing in 1917.

While Baum was writing *The Lost Princess of Oz*, he was struck by acute illness, gall bladder attacks so severe that they threatened his ability to continue writing. Fearing the consequences of an operation on his damaged heart, he resisted his doctor's advice to have his gall bladder removed and treated himself with patent medicines. He resolutely continued to work, but he completed *The Lost Princess* in a state of constant pain. Only when he could no longer write did he agree to the surgery. On January 1, 1918, he apologized to Reilly for not being able to deliver *Mary Louise and the Liberty Girls* on time and said he was awaiting his January statement "with unusual interest"; for he could not arrange for the operation until he had the money. When he returned the galley proofs of *The Tin Woodman of Oz* on February 14, he had to ask in addition for a loan of $350 in order to secure a first-class doctor, nurse, and hospital room.

He added, with heartbreaking conscientiousness, that he was meeting his obligations to his publishers: "I want to tell you, for your complete protection, that I have finished the writing of the *second* Oz book—beyond the 'Tin Woodman of Oz'—which will give you a manuscript for 1919 and 1920. Also there is material for another book, so in case anything happens to me the Baum books can be issued until and including 1921. And the two stories which I have here in the safety deposit I consider as good as anything I have ever done, with the possible exception of 'Sky Island,' which will probably always be considered my best work." Baum was optimistically extending the truth, as he often did. He must have meant that he had first drafts of *The Magic of Oz* and *Glinda of Oz*. Nothing is known about the notes for a third book; *The Royal Book of Oz*, the first book to continue the series after his death, was written entirely by Ruth Plumly Thompson.[32]

On February 17, right before he entered the hospital, Baum finished the first draft of *Glinda of Oz* and wrote a one-sentence will that left everything to Maud. His estate consisted of one thousand dollars in cash, since the major assets were already in her name. The witnesses were her sister and niece, Julia and Magdalena Carpenter, who were evidently at Ozcot to sustain the Baums during this crisis.[33]

The Tin Woodman of Oz: A Faithful Story of the Astonishing Adventure Undertaken by the Tin Woodman, assisted by Woot the Wanderer, the Scarecrow of Oz, and Poly-chrome, the Rainbow's Daughter (1918) is dedicated to Frank Junior's second son, Frank Alden Baum. In his preface Baum proudly responded to a query about the age level for which his books were intended by quoting enthusiastic readers from five to seventy. He concluded, "my books are intended for all those whose hearts are young, no matter what their ages may be."

The book opens with one of Baum's characteristic bits of realism, a scene between old friends. The Scarecrow was visiting the Tin Woodman and they were talking over the many adventures they had shared. "But at times they were silent, for these things had been talked over many times between them, and they found themselves contented in merely being together, speaking now and then a brief sentence to prove they were wide awake and attentive." Nevertheless, they were glad when the stranger Woot "arrived at the castle, for this would give them something new to talk about."[34]

Woot asks the Tin Woodman how he came to be made of tin, and the Woodman tells the familiar story from *The Wizard of Oz*, giving more details about the Munchkin girl he loved, including her name, Nimmie Amee. Nimmie Amee actually preferred the Woodman in his tin form, because she would not be obliged to cook for a man who did not eat or make the bed of one who did not sleep. "All day long, while you are chopping wood in the forest, I shall be able to amuse myself in my own way—a privilege few wives enjoy. There is no temper in your new head, so you will not get angry with me." For the Tin Woodman, whose conception of romantic love is obviously limited, this picture of "the best husband any girl could have" "shows that Nimmie Amee was as wise as she was brave and beautiful." However, because his new tin body contained no heart, the Woodman no longer loved his fiancée, and so he left her in servitude to the witch. Even when he got a heart from the Wizard, it was "a Kind Heart instead of a Loving

Heart, so that I could not love Nimmie Amee any more than I did when I was heartless."[35]

Woot objects that the Tin Woodman's much prized heart could not really be kind, or he would not have abandoned the girl who had shown such devotion to him. This point has never occurred to the Tin Woodman, but, once reminded, he immediately resolves to find Nimmie Amee, marry her, and make her Empress of the Winkies; for "Surely it is not the girl's fault that I no longer love her." "Nick Chopper . . . is a man who never shirks his duty, once it is pointed out to him." Woot, a typical sensible Baumian child, suggests that marrying "a nice girl through kindness, and not because he loves her . . . somehow . . . doesn't seem quite right." But the Tin Woodman can think only of his virtue in seeking Nimmie Amee and her forthcoming delight when he rewards her love by making her an Empress in a gorgeous tin costume, "for all girls are fond of finery."[36]

This passionless pseudo-romance becomes even more absurd when the Tin Woodman meets a Tin Soldier, who has become tin in the same way he did and also once loved Nimmie Amee but no longer does. Both these slaves to duty are ready to marry her, although each hopes she will prefer the other. Nevertheless, they have no doubt that she will be enraptured to marry one of them. But when they finally find her, they discover she has married Chopfyt, a composite of the discarded body parts of the two tin men.

Through this character Baum further developed the question he had raised in *The Wizard of Oz* about the location of identity. The tin men, who retain no part of their original bodies, are their likable, integrated original selves, while Chopfyt, who actually consists of their physical parts, has no self to speak of. For unlike them, he retains no memory of his past life. In *The Wizard of Oz* Baum suggested that the sense of self is developed or retained by remembered experience, and in *The Tin Woodman of Oz* he imagined a character who had lost this memory. As psychologist Janet Feigenbaum explains: "When memory goes . . . the person ceases to be 'themselves.' . . . With the loss of memory we lose not only our sense of personal identity but also our ability to relate to others." Baum might have explained the situation in terms of theosophical doctrine, according to which one's true self, the continuing "I," exists separately from the physical body, which it acquires on being born into the physical world. The tin men have retained their "spiritual body," which is not changed or lost in birth or death, while poor Chopfyt is left with nothing but the material body.[37]

Nevertheless, to the discomfiture of the two self-satisfied tin men, Nimmie Amee prefers Chopfyt to them. As she once preferred a tin man who would make few demands on her time, she now prefers a man she has already trained to hoe the cabbages and dust the furniture. She advises her suitors "to go back to your own homes and forget me, as I have forgotten you."[38]

Her crass utilitarianism ludicrously deflates the sentimental assumptions of the tin men—which richly deserve to be deflated because they are, in fact, self-centered. Relying on their own preconceptions rather than observing their beloved one, the tin men assumed that she must be idealistic because she was beautiful, that she was so dependent on her man that she would pine away when deserted, and so completely ruled by her heart that she could never think of marrying for a practical reason like securing a comfortable lifestyle. The tin men's courtship is broadly comic because even children can see the incongruity in their resolution to marry for duty alone, their confidence about the feelings of a girl they have forgotten for years, and their blissful unawareness that their attitude is inappropriate. Adults can perceive a similarity between these absurdities and attitudes that have been seriously presented in romantic literature. Baum pokes fun at men who are so preoccupied with their idealistic love for a woman that they remain unaware of her feelings or who retain illusions about her that they would never have formed had they listened to her in the first place.

Counterpointing this comedy is a really frightening experience in the castle of the giant Mrs. Yoop. She is a terrifying figure, in striking contrast to her husband, Mr. Yoop, who appeared in *The Patchwork Girl of Oz*. Mr. Yoop was ferocious and hungry and posed a real threat to the travelers who had to rush through a narrow passage within his reach. But like most Baum villains, he was both ineffectual and ridiculous: he was locked behind bars and was easily outwitted, and he wore a pink velvet suit.

Mrs. Yoop is beautiful, self-possessed, and pleasant, living comfortably in Yoop Castle and not missing her husband at all. She never blusters, just quietly does what she likes without the least sympathy or scruple. She can do almost anything because she is a Yookoohoo, whose magic is more awesome because it is done without benefit of chants, potions, or instruments; she can and does transform people by simply pointing her finger at them. Yookoohoos specialize in transformations, a suspect branch of magic in Oz. For transformation violates the integrity and dignity of a living being by turning him or her into something else, as Mrs. Yoop will transform the boy Woot into a ludicrous green monkey or the Nome King transformed people into ornaments in *Ozma of Oz.*

When Mrs. Yoop found Polychrome asleep, she turned her into a caged canary in the expectation that she would sing and talk and they would have good times together. Disappointed when the canary moped instead, she told the Tin Woodman, the Scarecrow, and Woot, "I mean to keep you here as long as I live, to amuse me when I get lonely" and reminded them that "in this valley no one ever dies." "In the morning I will give you all new forms, such as will be more interesting to me than the ones you now wear. Good night, and pleasant dreams."[39]

The Tin Woodman affords a rare opportunity to trace Baum's working methods, because his handwritten draft of the book has been preserved, as well as a later draft of chapters nineteen and twenty, which narrate the travelers' passage through the invisible country on their way to Nimmie Amee's home on Mount Munch. Comparison between the two earlier and the final versions shows that Baum revised minutely despite his speed in producing books. He added or deleted words, replaced vague words with more precise ones, inserted phrases to make a situation absolutely clear, and adjusted sentence structure for emphasis or clarity. He frequently added details to enhance emotional effect or humor. For example, in both the earliest version and the book, the Tin Woodman tells how he boldly defied the Witch when she told him to keep away from Nimmie Amee; but in the book he adds, "not realizing that this was a careless way to speak to a Witch." He added the Tin Woodman's fatuous comment that Nimmie Amee's explanation of why she preferred a tin fiancé showed she "was as wise as she was brave and beautiful." He amplified the Tin Woodman's self-congratulation on resolving to fulfill his duty and marry Nimmie Amee by adding to his speech, "I'd like you to know that Nick Chopper, the Tin Emperor of the Winkies, is a man who never shirks his duty, once it is pointed out to him."[40]

Baum added numerous phrases to increase sinister effect in the travelers' frightening encounter with Mrs. Yoop, which I have italicized in the following quotations. When they entered her dining room, she "smiled *in a curious way* as she looked at them. Woot noticed that the door had closed silently after they had entered, *and that didn't please him at all.*" Her narrative of what she did to Polychrome is amplified to emphasize her heartlessness: "before Poly wakened, I stole out and transformed her into a canary-bird in a gold cage studded with diamonds. *The cage was so she couldn't fly away.*" After Mrs. Yoop's announce-

The Tin Woodman of Oz. The travelers face Mrs. Yoop. John R. Neill.

ment that she would keep the travelers with her as long as she lived, Baum inserted her chilling reminder that "in this Valley no one ever dies." He changed "her prisoners found *no chance* to leave" the giant's hall to *not the slightest chance.* Adding that on going to bed Mrs. Yoop hung her magic apron "where it was within easy reach of her hand" increases the suspense of whether Woot will succeed in stealing it. When they manage to escape from the castle, Polychrome does not say, "We're safe now," as she did in the manuscript, but, "I believe we are safe now."[41]

Most important, Baum originally called Mrs. Yoop a Whisp; when he wrote his final version, he had thought of the infinitely more effective term Yookoohoo.

Several of Baum's additions enhance his depiction of Polychrome, who is even more delightful than usual in this book, as free a spirit as the Patchwork Girl and graceful as well. The Scarecrow thinks hard, boasts of his finely working brains, and produces an unworkable scheme for restoring Woot to his proper form; Polychrome dances around, apparently without a thought in her head, and tosses off the solution to the problem. In revision, Baum further enhanced her spirit, giving her a love of adventure like that of his mortal heroines: while her proper sisters take care never to dance off their rainbow, she is always slipping off to find exciting new experiences.[42]

Chapter 19 in the original manuscript does no more than fill the gap between the travelers' departure from Ku-Klip's workshop to their arrival at Nimmie Amee's house at the foot of Mount Munch. They pass through pleasant farming country, visit with hospitable farmers, and spruce themselves up for the climactic reunion. Baum saw the need for something more and wrote two new incident-filled chapters, taking the principal characters through the invisible country, where they meet the Hip-po-gy-raf, a huge beast who wants to eat the Scarecrow's straw stuffing, and to the house of Professor and Mrs. Swyne, a self-important pig couple.

These chapters, too, he revised to enhance the vividness and humor of his final version. He added twenty-six lines describing the damage a collision in the invisible country did to the tin men, several details emphasizing the conceit of the adult males in the party, phrases revealing the actual timidity of Professor Swyne that belies his wife's boast of his fierceness, and a tribute to Polychrome, whose perpetual motion no one minded "because to them she was like a ray of sunshine."[43]

With *The Tin Woodman of Oz* in 1918, Baum at last recaptured the best-selling success that had been eluding him for the past eight years, when he had not been able to write a new fantasy that was really profitable and sales also declined on his old ones. Not only did *The Tin Woodman of Oz* sell 18,600 copies, almost as many as *The Emerald City of Oz* had, but sales on all the Oz books rebounded to their previous levels. Eight of them sold about 3,000 copies each, and *The Land of Oz* and *The Lost Princess of Oz*, about 4,000. In the following year, all but *The Tin Woodman of Oz* sold significantly more copies, double the number in most cases; and the 1919 story, *The Magic of Oz*, sold 26,219. In addition, each title in the *Aunt Jane's Nieces* and *Mary Louise* series sold about 1,500 copies. *John Dough and the Cherub* sold 1,562 copies, but *The Sea Fairies* only 611.[44]

Baum got a 10 percent royalty on sale prices of $1.50 for *The Tin Woodman of Oz*, $1.35 for *The Lost Princess of Oz*, $1.25 for the earlier Oz books, $0.75 for the *Mary Louise* books, and $0.60 for the *Aunt*

Jane's Nieces books. This meant that in 1918 he would have made $6,742.52 on his Oz books, $900 on the *Aunt Jane's Nieces* series, and $450 on *Mary Louise*—a total of $8,092.52, in addition to what he earned on his other titles. (As a comparison, the average annual income of a clerical worker in 1918 was $941.) In 1919, Baum's income would have been considerably higher, since almost twice as many Oz books were sold and the prices of all of them had been raised to $1.50.[45] There had been no financial disasters after the Radio Plays. "The Tik-Tok Man of Oz" made moderate profits, and the movie venture did not involve any of Baum's money. In his last years, Baum regained the secure upper-middle-class lifestyle he had enjoyed just before the Radio Plays.

Unfortunately, however, he was no longer healthy enough to enjoy it. Although his operation was successful, the strain of four hours on the operating table further weakened his heart. It pumped less and less efficiently, causing difficulty in breathing and easy fatigue. He developed kidney trouble, and the doctors could not predict whether he would live. After spending five weeks in the hospital, he was ordered to stay in bed for six weeks after he returned home. For some time he could not even sit up; all he could do was lie in bed and think of ideas for stories. In April, he could be propped up in a sitting position and was allowed to write for a few hours a day.[46] He kept himself going by will and a resolutely positive attitude. Fortunately, as Maud wrote to Reilly on June 17, "the amount of vitality he has has been a source of wonder to everyone."

Baum managed to shape and revise *The Magic of Oz* from his bed and was able to send Reilly & Britton the manuscript on October 29. He made transformation the central theme in this book, but presented it as more imaginatively appealing than terrible. Kiki Aru, the dissatisfied, no good son of a magician, accidentally discovers his father's greatest magical secret. One who correctly pronounces the word **Pyrzqxgl** can transform anybody into anybody or anything he or she chooses. Kiki Aru transforms himself into a hawk and flies away from his native mountaintop to Ev, lest he be caught unlawfully practicing magic in Oz. There he meets Ruggedo, the vengeful deposed Nome King, who enlists him in a plan to conquer Oz. They will take the form of beasts and incite the wild animals of the forest to attack the Oz people. The simple boy with powerful magic forms a partnership with the Nome King, who has nothing but his abundant natural cunning. Even from the outset they are plotting against each other: Kiki plans to turn Ruggedo into a marble statue once they have conquered Oz, while Ruggedo is trying to learn the magic word so that he can turn Kiki into a bundle of faggots and burn him up.

Kiki transforms the two of them into composite beasts called Li-Mon-Eags, and they fly to the largest forest in Oz. As usual in Baum's fantasy world, the animals live under their own laws and government, ruled by a great leopard named Gugu. The Li-Mon-Eags try to inflame the animals by telling them the Oz people mean to invade their forest and enslave them, and to tempt them by promising to change them all into humans so they can enjoy human luxuries—the familiar demagogue's technique of provoking discontent that can be exploited to advance himself. William Hollister points out a particular reference to the Russian Revolution of March 1917, when radical leaders used similar arguments to inspire peasants and workers to revolt against the privileged classes.[47] Through Ruggedo the Li-mon-eag, Baum implies that the revolutionary leaders were using spurious ideology to promote their private ends: peasants would be no more happy as aristocrats than wild beasts would be as civilized humans. As the revolutionary leaders professed comradeship with the peasants they were soon to dominate and exploit, Ruggedo the Li-mon-eag addresses the animals as "Brothers."[48]

Gugu is wisely suspicious, but he calls together all the forest animals to vote on their course of action. While they are debating, Dorothy, the Wizard, the Cowardly Lion, and the Hungry Tiger come into the clearing. Kiki panics and transforms the Wizard into a fox, Dorothy into a lamb, the Lion into a little boy, the Tiger into a rabbit, and Gugu into a fat woman. The effects are devastating to all the victims. The Lion and Gugu are as upset and mortified to be humans as the humans are to be animals. The situation is saved when the Wizard-fox learns the magic word, restores the victims to their proper shapes, and transforms the Li-Mon-Eags into a hickory nut and a walnut, so that they will not be able to say a word.

A contrasting, lighter plot involves getting inventive birthday presents for Ozma; Dorothy and the Wizard entered Gugu's forest to persuade twelve of the monkeys to allow themselves to be reduced in size, taken to the Emerald City, trained to do tricks, and hidden in Ozma's birthday cake to leap out when it was cut and amuse the company. (They would, of course, be restored to their proper size and homes after the party.) There is suspense in the birthday present plot as well as the conquest plot, for Trot and Cap'n Bill are trapped on an island where they have gone to get a wonderful plant for Ozma, which blooms with constantly changing flowers. Once on the island, their feet take root in the ground and they begin to shrink; and the Wizard fears that he cannot get them unrooted in time.

Reilly asked for and got one revision in this story. On their way to the island, Trot and Cap'n Bill are attacked by a Kalidah, which Cap'n Bill impales on a stake. Baum had left the beast there, but Reilly remonstrated that leaving it "staked out on the sand indefinitely" was too horrible. Baum admitted this was an oversight "and I'm glad you caught it. In a day or two you'll get a paragraph or so fixing up the matter to the satisfaction of the youngsters." The exchange shows the happy cooperation between Baum and his publishers: they made helpful suggestions, and Baum was willing to listen to them.[49]

Baum had alluded to his poor health in the prefaces of every Oz book from *Tik-Tok of Oz* on. He made Cap'n Bill remark, when trapped on the island: "If somethin' would 'most stop your breath, you'd think breathin' easy was the finest thing in life. When a person's well, he don't realize how jolly it is, but when he gets sick he 'members the time he was well, an' wishes that time would come back."[50] When it came time to revise the manuscript of *The Magic of Oz*, Baum was no longer able to use his customary method of making changes as he typed his handwritten manuscripts; for, of course, he could not manage a typewriter while lying in bed.

Accordingly, he did not revise *The Magic of Oz* with anything like the thoroughness of *The Tin Woodman of Oz*. He made small verbal changes to improve precision or eliminate repetition and dropped a few unnecessary sentences, but his only significant changes were adding two pages to narrate the escape of the impaled Kalidah and three pages to reintroduce the Lonesome Duck, thus prolonging suspense about Trot and Cap'n Bill's fate and further developing the bird's self-congratulatory isolation. He left infelicities that he would not have passed in earlier books. In the manuscript, when Dorothy asked whether they should take the Sawhorse on their journey, "The Wizard did not answer that at once. He took time to think of the proposition." Baum replaced the last word with the more appropriate "suggestion," but he did not revise the flat, wordy sentence structure. Had he felt up to it, he would probably have devised some happy invention to replace the padding in chapter 22, "Ozma's Birthday Party."[51] On the whole, however, the manuscript as originally written was good enough to satisfy without much revision. When Reilly received the final version, he congratulated Baum on "one of the cleverest books you have written."

The Magic of Oz: A Faithful Record of the Remarkable Adventures of Dorothy and Trot and the Wizard of Oz, Together with the Cowardly Lion, the Hungry Tiger and Cap'n Bill, in Their Successful Search for a Magical and Beautiful Birthday Present for Princess Ozma of Oz (1919) is dedicated to "the Children of our Soldiers, the Americans and their Allies, with unmeasured Pride and Affection."

As the Oz series continued, the books got less critical attention. There were still some very favorable reviews, however, though rarely in prestigious newspapers. The number ranges from fifty-eight for *Rinkitink in Oz* to sixteen for *The Magic of Oz* and only one for the last book, *Glinda of Oz* (both published when Baum was no longer alive to collect reviews). The reviewer for the *Chicago Post* wrote of *The Lost Princess of Oz*: "There are few characters in fiction that one could wish would go on forever—Sherlock Holmes is one. Certainly the inhabitants of Oz are among that few elect." One reviewer of *The Magic of Oz* appreciated the irresistible appeal of a magic word that can transform anything (1919). Another, Frank Parker Stockbridge, wrote prophetically in the *New York Sun*: "There is a Wonderland in which American boys and girls have roamed in never-ending delight for twenty years or so, a Wonderland in the memories of which men and women of twenty years from now will find common meeting places and the keys to unlock the gates that keep them apart. This is the Wonderful Land of Oz ... alas, the wonderful land will yield no more of its magical secrets...."[52]

Baum had already drafted *Glinda of Oz*, however; and by November 2, four days after sending in *The Magic of Oz*, he had started revising it.[53] *Glinda of Oz: In Which Are Related the Exciting Experiences of Princess Ozma of Oz, and Dorothy, in Their Hazardous Journey to the Home of the Flatheads, and to the Magic Isle of the Skeezers, and How They Were Rescued from Dire Peril by the sorcery of Glinda the Good* was to appear in 1920. This book, which Baum must have realized would be his last, is dedicated to his son Robert. There is no preface, such as Baum wrote shortly before publication of a fantasy book.

One day when Dorothy is browsing through Glinda's Book of Records, she notices that the Skeezers and the Flatheads, living in a far corner of the Gillikin country, are on the brink of war. Ozma recognizes that her duty as ruler is to keep all her people contented and settle their disputes, and she believes she can best deal with the situation by going in person and alone to persuade them to make peace. Dorothy asks to go with her on the grounds that "Whatever happens it's going to be fun—'cause all excitement is fun—and I wouldn't miss it for the world!"[54]

They find that the Skeezers are ruled by an arrogant, tyrannical Queen and that the Flatheads are no better off, even though they elect their ruler democratically. Every year the Flatheads have the opportunity to elect a new Su-Dic, or Supreme Dictator; but since the present incumbent counts the votes himself, he always wins. He keeps his subjects from protesting by flattering their self-importance: "Everybody here is a dictator of something or other." A democratic form of government does not necessarily represent the people's will, in Oz or America. Corrupt leaders and ignorant voters can produce political results contrary to justice and the general welfare, as Editor Baum and Mrs. Bilkins noted in the South Dakota elections of November 1890. No form of government guarantees the essentials: that is, respect for citizens' rights and concern for their welfare. It takes a conscientious ruler, like Ozma; and it does not matter whether she rules by right of birth or election. Queen Coo-ee-oh and the Su-Dic have dragged their naturally peaceful peoples into war because of a personal quarrel, as Baum believed political leaders had dragged their nations into World War I.[55]

In this last book, Baum systematically used different types of magic to suggest the various routes to knowledge in this world. The power of all the magic workers (except possibly for Red Reera the Yookoohoo) is subject to limits, for, in accordance with Baum's belief in egalitarian cooperation, no one can (or should) have the power to do everything. As in the real world, people must pool their various abilities to solve problems, and even the most talented people have to tax their ingenuity to meet unfamiliar challenges. The only difference is that in Oz there are more wonderful powers to draw on.

Fairies like Ozma are endowed by nature with magical powers that they can use by simply wishing or waving a wand, comparable to extraordinarily sensitive intuition; but because these powers are delimited by nature, they cannot be extended. The Adepts, a direct import from theosophy, have acquired supernatural powers through studying the secret laws of nature. The Sorceress Glinda proceeds like a modern scientist, working with instruments, carefully prepared compounds, and reference books that sometimes do "not give as many details as one could wish." When Glinda learned that she had to raise Skeezer Island and could find no useful information in her library, she "made a little island, covered by a glass dome, and sunk it in a pond near her castle, and experimented in magical ways to bring it to the surface. She made several such experiments, but all were failures." Therefore she had to go to Skeezer Island to work with the actual machinery.[56]

The Krumbic Witch Coo-ee-oh is practically an engineer; her elaborate mechanical inventions present insoluble puzzles to the less technically oriented magic workers typical of Oz. Her technological magic raises and lowers Skeezer Island by means of a steel column under its base, using the authentic physical principle of the force of expanding steel, a force that is in fact strong enough to raise an island, although only by a few inches. Others of her discoveries have actually been realized through modern technology. As she makes her mass of interlocking cogwheels and pulleys run by magic words, we work machinery by voice-controlled computer. Even her mysteriously powered submarines, inspired by the U-boats of World War I, anticipate the nuclear-powered submarines of today.

At the opposite extreme is Red Reera the Yookoohoo, who works wonderful magic with no more than a silent wish and a handful of powder. She is a true Artist in Transformations, constantly changing herself and her zoo of pet animals in order to produce new and interesting experiences. Her transformations are not presented as heartless domination of others, in accordance with Baum's usual interpretation, but rather as playful inventions; she is like a fantasy writer imagining variations on reality. Reera has the same self-centered independence as Baum's other Yookoohoo, Mrs. Yoop, but she is simply indifferent to others rather than cruel; her cool moral neutrality makes her unique in Baum's work. She "cannot be bribed with treasure, or coaxed through friendship, or won by pity. She has never assisted anyone, or done wrong to anyone."[57] She acts to amuse herself, and she does not want to be bothered by requests to oblige others. Yookoohoos are set off from all other creatures by their utter self-sufficiency and their undefined powers. It is significant that Baum made both of them female.

Baum underlined Reera's untouchable independence by leaving her to do as she likes, regardless of Ozma's law against unauthorized magic; but all the other transformations are righted at the end of *Glinda of Oz*, with one exception. The selfish witch Coo-ee-oh remains a beautiful diamond swan because this transformation has not really changed the subject's nature: a vain, self-centered woman has become a vain, self-centered bird. As a bird she is disabled from hurting others, for she has lost all her knowledge of magic, and at the same time she is more happy with herself, for she now has more beauty than she had originally. In a typical Baumian ending, evil is neutralized without violence or repression.

By November 1918, when Baum started revising the manuscript of *Glinda of Oz*, he was very ill indeed. Although there are more small differences between this manuscript and the published book than there are in *The Magic of Oz*, it seems probable that many changes were made by someone in Reilly & Lee's office rather than by Baum himself, and that some would not have been left standing had he been able to oversee them.

Baum's own revisions in earlier drafts of *The Tin Woodman of Oz* and *The Magic of Oz* are consistently improvements, as one would expect from the author. Many of the revisions of the *Glinda of Oz* manuscript, on the other hand, are inconsequential, seeming to reflect no more than different personal preferences between author and editor. Word order is sometimes reversed (*have never* to *never have*). Transitional words are often dropped from the manuscript text, especially at the beginning of sentences.[58]

On several occasions, the changes actually garble Baum's meaning. In the manuscript, Glinda's maids of honor look at the approaching Sawhorse and red wagon *curiously;* obviously these model young women would not have looked *enviously,* as they do in the printed text. When Ozma and Dorothy went to the Skeezer country and left the Scarecrow in charge in the Emerald City, Baum wrote in his manuscript that "only the Scarecrow [of characters in the Emerald City] knew they were going until after they had gone, and even the Scarecrow didn't know what their errand might be." The published book replaces the Scarecrow with Glinda, even though she had just discussed Ozma's errand with her. Obviously Baum would not have contradicted his own story line. I suspect it was an editor who dumbed down the vocabulary in Baum's manuscript, changing *broke the monotony* to *added to the beauty, deplorable* to *serious, arrogant* to *wicked,* and so forth.[59]

It is impossible to tell whether it was Baum or an editor who cleared up occasional unclarities in the manuscript text and removed some superfluous words and phrases. The manuscript's "magic arts are only comparative" is not clear; in the book, "magic arts are divided, some being given to each of us" spells out an important theme. Baum carelessly referred to Reera as a Witch in the manuscript; in the final text she is always a Yookoohoo—an essential distinction in the context of this book. Coo-ee-oh's magic boats, underwater or subaqua boats in the manuscript, become submarines in the book. Repeatedly, the weaker word is removed from a duplicative pair: "Interested and much impressed" becomes "much impressed"; "violet, or purple," "violet."[60]

There is only one substantive change from the manuscript to the printed book: Red Reera the Yookohoo, who in the book first appears to the Skeezer Ervic as a gray ape, appeared as an animated skeleton in the manuscript. The skeleton is graphically described—naked bones wired together, with eye sockets that "seemed to have two live coals burning in them." A gray ape in a lace cap and apron is, of course, a ludicrous image rather than a frightening one. Probably Baum was responding to a remonstrance from his publishers about an excessively gruesome invention, as he had removed the Garden of Meats from *The Patchwork Girl of Oz*.[61]

As Baum had explained to Britton in connection with *The Patchwork Girl of Oz*, his fairy tales started with spontaneous inspirations for odd characters and ideas, which he then had to develop into a coherent plot. *Glinda of Oz* includes fine imaginative inventions, but it appears that Baum did not have health and time to shape them into as sustained and effective a story as usual. The central problem of raising the sunken island is implausibly drawn out, the long description of Ozma's Counsellors in chapter 14 is obvious padding, and the ending is flatly moralistic. Ozma congratulates herself on having put herself out to relieve two obscure groups of her subjects of their war and their oppressive rulers—"Which proves that it is always wise to do one's duty, however unpleasant that duty may seem to be."[62]

Still, it is wonderful that Baum was able to produce four Oz books, not to mention two *Mary Louise* books, during these years of painful illness. Even more wonderful than the amount of writing he accomplished was his ability to sustain the vitality and optimism of the Oz stories. *Glinda of Oz* does seem to be perceptibly flattened, but *The Lost Princess of Oz, The Tin Woodman of Oz*, and *The Magic of Oz* are consistently lively, joyful, and funny.

On September 18, 1918, while he was completing his revision of *The Magic of Oz*, Baum wrote to his son Frank on a battlefield in France: "I have lately been much improved in health and trust that before many weeks the doctors will allow me to leave my bed and at least move about the house."[63] Perhaps he was just taking a positive view to boost his son's morale; in any case, his hopes were disappointed. He never left his bed again.

In his preface to *The Magic of Oz*, Baum apologized that "a long and confining illness has prevented my answering all the good letters sent me." But even on his deathbed he answered some of them. On March 6, 1919, two months before he died, he responded to nineteen-year-old Edward Wagenknecht: "I am very glad my books have given you pleasure, both in your childhood days and also now you are older. I have quite a few readers of mature years, who being children at heart still enjoy my tales." Recently a Church of England clergyman wrote to tell him that, "When tired and discouraged with this war-worn world, he could let himself be taken to Oz and for a time forget all else. It is things like your letter and his as well as the children's letters that make one feel they have done a bit to brighten up a few lives."[64]

In early May, Baum's heart action became even more erratic and his breathing more difficult; and "on May 5 he lapsed into unconsciousness. In the evening he opened his eyes and smiled at his wife, who was sitting at his bedside." He told her, " 'I'm going to slip away in a few hours. I feel this is my last farewell.' For a moment he struggled for breath and she begged him not to talk. 'I'm all right. There is little pain now. And there is something I want you to know—and remember. All my life, since I first met you and fell in love with you—I've been true to you. There has—never been—another woman in my life—or thoughts.' His breathing quieted a bit and he lay still with eyes closed. Maud thought . . . he had again lapsed into unconsciousness. But presently he opened his eyes and said: 'This is our house, Maud. I would like to think you are staying here where we have been so happy. The royalties will last for many years. You should have plenty to live on without worry.' 'I shall stay here as long as I live,' she replied. He smiled faintly. His eyes closed." He became unconscious again, but in the morning, on May 6, his lips moved. He murmured something indistinct and then clearly spoke his last words: "Now we can cross the Shifting Sands."[65]

Maud wrote to her sister Helen on May 16; "For nearly thirty-seven years we had been everything to each other, we were happy, and now I am alone, to face the world alone."[66]

The Reverend E. P. Ryland, a personal friend, conducted Baum's funeral at Forest Lawn Memorial Park, where he is buried. *The Magic of Oz* was on the press, so the children would get it for Christmas. The following Christmas, they had *Glinda of Oz*.[67]

ten

BAUM'S ACHIEVEMENT:
THE WORLD HE CREATED

Despite the enormous popularity of the Oz books ever since the first one of them appeared in 1900, Baum has only recently been recognized as a major children's author. In his own day, high-prestige publications treated him as a run-of-the-mill writer whose books happened to sell well. The *Dial* and the *Nation* included only a few Oz titles in the long lists of recommended holiday books for children in their December issues—*The Wizard of Oz* and *The Land of Oz* in the *Dial; Dorothy and the Wizard in Oz* and *The Emerald City of Oz* in the *Nation*. Baum's books were only briefly noted, while other now-forgotten books got relatively long, enthusiastic reviews.[1] *The Ladies' Home Journal* rejected the wonderful *Patchwork Girl of Oz* for serial publication. For decades after his death, Baum's books were excluded from libraries and courses in children's literature. It is hard to understand how anyone could dismiss Baum as an inferior artist. His writing is at least adequate in all respects and truly outstanding in the most important.

Baum's characterization is lively, inventive, and amusing. His characters are what humours characters ought to be—vivid and true to nature. If they were more complex, they would be less colorful and the story would not move so briskly. They are convincing because they are consistent and their actions are satisfactorily motivated. Baum's inventiveness in creating diverse characters seems boundless—the Scarecrow, the Cowardly Lion, Jack Pumpkinhead, the Nome King, Tik-Tok, the Patchwork Girl, Quox the dragon, the Ork, Red Reera the Yookoohoo. In book after book, we recognize delightful old acquaintances and meet new ones. Attebery compares the Scarecrow and the others to Dickens's amiable eccentrics, "a perfect blend of the grotesque and the lovable," who "demonstrate Baum's ability to assume the viewpoint of even the oddest creature."[2] The central human characters, while less interesting, are adequate to their function as the necessary realistic foil to the others. Like Dickens, one of his favorite authors, Baum excelled in creating eccentrics who are more lively than real living people around a less colorful central character.

Much of Baum's humor comes from his deflation of pretentious self-delusions: the King of Bunnybury longs to return to nature, but cannot part with a single one of his civilized luxuries; the tender-hearted Tin Woodman has forgotten all about Nimmie Amee, but assumes she has been pining for his return. Often contrasting characters set off each other's absurdities. The war between the Hoppers and the Horners in *The Patchwork Girl of Oz* shows that leaden literal-mindedness and the compulsion to make jokes about everything are equally tiresome. Baum concluded this episode by giving the Scarecrow a pun and slyly leaving it uncertain whether he was poking fun at the Horners' taste in jokes or indulging his own. The Scarecrow, taken down from a fence on which he had been impaled, remarked, " 'I prefer not to do picket duty again. High life doesn't seem to agree with my constitution.' And then they hurried away to escape the laughter of the Horners, who thought this was another joke."[3]

Other characters amuse by baldly declaring familiar, recognizable sentiments that seem odd because conventionally they are concealed. Guph volunteers to lead the Nome King's army against Oz because, "I hate good people; I detest happy people; I'm opposed to any one who is contented and prosperous."[4] The King of Bunnybury announces he will tell Dorothy all his troubles, which are "a great deal more interesting than anything you can say about yourself."[5] King Dox of Foxville explains that his foxes wear clothes because they are civilized: "to become civilized means to dress as elaborately and prettily as possible, and to make a show of your clothes so your neighbors will envy you, and for that reason both civilized foxes and civilized humans spend most of their time dressing themselves."[6] This is another bit of self-mockery, for Baum took much care with his appearance.

Objections that Baum's plots tend to be loose and episodic are beside the point, since tightly constructed plots are not desirable in all novels, especially those written for children. Baum's usual aim was to present a series of wonderful experiences rather than to drive purposefully toward a climax.

Nor is it relevant to point out that his style is not poetic or beautiful or especially distinctive. Such qualities would have detracted from the impression he wished to create of plainly narrating events that happened. His style is what it needs to be—clear, direct, and lively. A measure of his success is that not one of the four authors who continued the Oz series succeeded in recapturing his style. In all their books, we feel the presence of a self-conscious adult narrator between reader and story, as we never do in Baum's mature fantasies.

Baum never appears to be writing simply so as to be understood by simple minds. As Harry Baum said, "Father never 'wrote down' to children. They were his friends and companions, and he always treated them as such. . . . If he felt the need of a word, he used it whether it was one syllable or five."[7] In fact, Baum delighted in introducing esoteric words. The meaning is always as clear as it needs to be, and yet the child reader's knowledge is agreeably stretched. The new and perhaps imperfectly understood word has imaginative appeal from its strangeness. It is interesting to learn the scientific name for seahorse or a whole array of specialized names for shades of blue and pink in *The Sea Fairies* and *Sky Island.* "A gill of water from a dark well," one of the ingredients of the reanimating charm that Ojo seeks in *The Patchwork Girl of Oz,* sounds much more magical than a quarter of a pint. Baum's readers have never heard of a gill, but they understand it must be a small measure and feel good about acquiring the word.

Although critics can pick at instances of sloppy style, such as trite, repetitive effusions on the lovely girl ruler Ozma and sweet, unaffected Princess Dorothy, the only really annoying feature is Baum's attempts at dialect. He was not skilled at rendering dialect, yet he evidently believed it added to the humor and appeal of his stories. The most obvious example, often mentioned, is the excessive colloquialism he inflicted on his children from *Ozma of Oz* on. In her first conversation in *Ozma of Oz* Dorothy constantly drops syllables—"comfor'ble," "poss'bly," "[ex] 'spected," while the barnyard hen she is conversing with speaks perfect English.[8] Dorothy continues to talk this way throughout the series, as do Betsy and Trot. This is not really baby talk (although Baum used that too in some other stories), but rather a heavy-handed rendition of colloquial speech. His attempts to reproduce Rinkitink's laughs and chuckles are a running irritation in *Rinkitink in Oz.*

Baum's greatest gifts were the two most important ones for a writer of fantasy: he could create a wonderful world, and he could make it believable.[9] In Oz you can come into a town filled with live jigsaw-puzzle pieces, put the cook together, and have him cook you a delicious meal. You can be threatened by a twenty-one-foot giant in a pink velvet suit (and, of course, you will outwit him). You can be delighted by an animated bit of the rainbow dancing around you in the form of the fairy Polychrome.

A fantasy world must be convincing as well as inventive, for if we cannot believe in it for the time, it provides no escape from the humdrum, limited world in which we live. Oz is believable. First of all, Baum wrote as if he believed in it himself: he did not make a world so sweet and bland as to be obviously false, nor did he drop hints that he was more sophisticated than his readers. Second, his fantasy world is filled with familiar details from actual everyday life—a bag of tools, the job of washing dishes, a terrier that loves to bark. Finally, his world is internally logical and consistent. Even in Oz, mortals must eat and sleep at regular intervals. The Scarecrow and the Patchwork Girl are magically alive and highly intelligent, but their ability to manipulate is limited by their clumsy stuffed fingers. The air of reality given by homely details and attention to logic makes the Oz stories more satisfying than traditional fairy tales. Moreover, the Oz protagonists are neither victims nor princesses, but normal children who confront magical situations just as readers imagine they would do themselves.[10]

Magic working in Oz is governed by clearly defined laws. It is analogous to science and technology in our world, and a magician does not have unlimited power any more than a scientist does. Even the great sorceress Glinda must work with her proper tools and within the limits of her knowledge. When they are robbed of their equipment in *The Lost Princess of Oz*, neither she nor the Wizard can find the thief by magical means. Glinda sets about replacing her equipment, and the Wizard joins one of the search parties physically seeking the thief.

Although it is a fairyland, Oz clearly came out of Baum's actual place and time. The humbug showman-politician, the carved pumpkin face of Jack Pumpkinhead, and the crazy quilt that Scraps is made of are characteristically American. So is Baum's delight in clever contrivances, from the makeshift Gump to the marvelous robot Tik-Tok. Baum celebrated inventiveness and workmanlike skill in making things, and, unlike many fantasy writers, he appreciated technological advances. (One of his friends said that Baum could have been a successful technical writer if he had not chosen juvenile fiction instead.)[11]

The same imagination and effort that is supposed to produce magical wonders in Oz was actually producing technological wonders in Baum's America—glass-walled skyscrapers, automobiles, airplanes,

Edison's electric light, phonograph, and motion picture. Advances in canning technology, an enthusiastic promoter wrote, have given "the American family—especially in cities—a kitchen garden where all good things grow, and where it is always harvest time.... A regular Arabian Nights garden, where raspberries, apricots, olives, and pineapples, always ripe, grow side by side with peas, pumpkins, spinach; a garden with baked beans vines, and spaghetti bushes, and sauerkraut beds, and great cauldrons of hot soup, and through it running a branch of the ocean in which one can catch salmon, lobsters, crabs, and shrimp, and dig oysters and clams."[12] It would have been inappropriate to transpose the new inventions directly into a nonindustrialized fairyland, but they make Oz wonders like the magic picture and dinner-pail trees seem more plausible.

It is magic, rather than technology, that solves practical problems in Oz; for Baum wanted to preserve old-fashioned American rural values there. Most of the people are farmers, and things are made by hand; Glinda's ladies-in-waiting occupy themselves with spinning and embroidery. There are no automobiles in and around Oz (except for the Rak in *Tik-Tok of Oz*); people travel by walking or riding on animals' backs or in vehicles drawn by animals, as they still did between farms and towns in rural America. When the Wizard must get an urgent message to Glinda in *The Lost Princess of Oz*, he rides the Sawhorse—who does, it is true, gallop tirelessly and with miraculous speed.[13]

Oz is an American version of the pastoral ideal: people are basically good; and moral, social, and economic issues are simple and straightforward. Manners in Oz are those of rural America at its best—pleasant and friendly to everyone one meets, but disregardful of decorum or deference to rank. Dorothy speaks politely to a hen and outspokenly defies Princess Langwidere. Her unconsciousness of conventional status distinctions is the prevailing attitude in Oz. Everyone is treated with consideration because everyone is respected for what he or she is. The egalitarian acceptance of animals and machines like Tik-Tok signifies humans living "in complete harmony with nature and technology."[14]

When problems appear in the Oz books, the characters apply their traditional American self-reliance and practical common sense to solving them. If a group is involved, everyone contributes something: human adults and children, stuffed or metal people, animals, robots. They discuss the problem logically, everyone is free to give his or her opinion, everyone is listened to. When anyone thinks of a promising suggestion, the rest of the group agrees to follow it. It is spontaneous democracy, without a formal structure. Very often it is the least prestigious member of the group who comes up with the best ideas. In *Glinda of Oz* the Adepts laughed when the Patchwork Girl suggested a solution to the problem of getting into the Skeezer city submerged under the lake: "If the Great Sorceress and the famous Wizard and the three talented Adepts at Magic were unable as yet to solve the important problem of the sunken isle, there was little chance for a patched girl stuffed with cotton to succeed."[15] But, of course, she did.

Children in the Oz books are reasonable, responsible, and deserving of the respect they get; many grown-ups, on the other hand, are humbugs, like the Wonderful Wizard and the wise-sounding Frogman, or, like the Nome King, "are transparently childish in their greed, their self-centeredness and their temper tantrums."[16] Over and over, Baum's work deflates self-important adult authority figures—which, for obvious reasons, is a common theme in literature that is genuinely for children. The self-assurance and independence of Baum's children was particularly characteristic of American literature, as well as life, and was often noted by British observers.[17]

At the same time that children in Oz get wonderful opportunities for adventure, they retain the security of a family. As Russel Nye put it, Oz "is simply the perfect family, built on love, permeated by happiness. . . . In Oz you do enjoyable duties, live in cooperation and affection with brothers, sisters, neighbor children, and pets, find your wants satisfied" by your parents, and "play in the happy security and harmony of the ideal home . . . everything in the house is alive, helpful, friendly, and full of fun. . . . Beyond the neighborhood lie thrillingly unknown lands of adventure . . . where things and people may be bad or good, but always strange and exciting."[18] In Oz the loving concern that is expected within a family is extended to everyone in the whole society.

A remarkable feature of Baum's version of the perfect family is the predominance of females. His relationship with his forceful and beloved wife and her mother must have contributed to his faith in female rule. His observation of politics as an editor in South Dakota convinced him that women were oppressed and slighted in America and that the country would be better with more female influence on government. His contrasting presentations of little girls and little boys may reflect his and Maud's longing for a girl, as well as the greater idealization possible when one brings up four boys and no girls.

Whatever the reason, Baum's fantasy world contains many mother figures, most of them good, and no father figures.[19] Glinda is the perfect good mother and the wicked witches are bad ones. Mrs. Yoop, the ultimate bad mother, is not only much bigger than the sympathetic characters but can read and control their thoughts. Older men in Baum's world are either naughty children, like the Nome King, or friends and equals, like the Wizard (in later books), Cap'n Bill, and Rinkitink. Considering that Baum was devoted to his four boys and delighted in playing and joking with them, it is odd that his fictional boys are not more lively; there are no Huck Finns or Jim Hawkinses in Oz. Girls are the heroes of ten of the fourteen Oz books; they are sweet and well-behaved like proper girls, but their salient qualities are courage, enterprise, and love of adventure. Of the boys, Ojo is easily discouraged, Woot is chronically apprehensive, Inga could do nothing without his magic pearls, and Tip is really a girl. Like Gage and other feminists of the time, Baum seems to be endorsing feminine values that are suitably broadened to include virtues that patriarchs restricted to men.

The Oz books appeal to children and adults alike because they convincingly affirm positive, optimistic views: in his life and his fiction, Baum always hoped for the best and both saw and brought out the best in other people. Reading about Oz provides the escapist pleasure of entering a better and more exciting place than the world we live in. It satisfies desires that can only be satisfied in fantasy— that novel adventures can always be found, that all problems can be solved, that effort is always rewarded, that social groups can function without status discrimination, that the loving concern that is normal within a family can be extended to everyone in society. But at the same time, the Oz books make us more alert to the goodness and interesting possibilities that in fact exist around us. We are readier to see the good in people and the probability that everyone has some contribution to make. We have more hope that a seemingly impassable obstacle may turn out to be an illusion and even a catastrophe like a cyclone need not necessarily lead to ruin. We have more confidence that problems can be solved with good will and common sense, that right behavior and helpfulness to others will be rewarded, and that evil people will destroy themselves and each other. We are

more aware of the magic in the processes of nature and the achievements of science. We are more disposed to expect that new experiences will be enjoyable and interesting.

Baum's presentation of the world is optimistically one-sided—but it
is not false. As C. S. Lewis explained, a children's story may be "the
best art-form" for what an author has to say; "this form permits, or
compels" him to leave out things he might want to leave out and "to
throw all the force of the book into what was done and said." Subtle,
complex motives, for example, and moral ambiguity are out of place in
children's books. Characters in Baum's fantasies are clearly either good
or bad, the right course of action is always apparent, and it is never
necessary to use questionable means to achieve a good end. "Where the
children's story is simply the right form for what the author has to say,"
Lewis declared, it will appeal to readers of any age; "the children's story
which is enjoyed only by children is a bad children's story." Baum
rightly made the same claim for his own work. Like Lewis, he wrote
"for children out of those elements in [his] own imagination which
[he] share[d] with children: differing . . . not by any less, or less serious,
interest in the things [he] handle[d], but by the fact that [he had] other
interests which children would not share."[20]

Oz retains validity for adults as well as children because it is not a
fatuously perfect utopia; it is not purged of evil and conflict like the
ironic Paradise of Birds in *Policeman Bluejay*. It contains characters that
are simply no good, like Kiki Aru, the disgruntled boy who caused so
much trouble in *The Magic of Oz* and whom Baum characterized with
blunt contempt: "No one paid any attention to Kiki Aru, because he
didn't amount to anything, anyway."[21] Good characters have failings—
conceit in the Scarecrow, hard-heartedness in the Patchwork Girl, fatu-
ity in the Tin Woodman. People (and animals) are realistically
presented as self-centered, and nature can be threatening and unpleasant. Normally the tendency of things to spring to life in Oz demonstrates the richness of life there,[22] but there are also some very
disturbing animations, such as Fighting Trees that suddenly activate to
seize people with their branches. Baum transmuted the Scarecrow that
haunted his childhood nightmares into one of the most lovable characters in Oz. But his Scoodlers, outsize jumping jacks that throw their
heads as missiles, are horrid indeed. Alongside his basically positive
outlook and sunny imagination, Baum had a sardonic streak that produced gruesome fantasies (the dismemberment of the Tin Woodman,
the patching on Sky Island) and exposed the cruelty of man (the

slaughter of the residents of the tree in *Policeman Bluejay*) and the harsh realities of nature: a lovely mermaid explains that it is fortunate mackerel are stupid and easily caught, since they are needed to feed others and if their numbers were not checked they would clog the sea.

Both children and adults enjoy entering a world where friendliness and respect can be expected, where everything comes out right in the end and every day may bring a wonderful new adventure. But adults also find engaging morsels of sophisticated wisdom or philosophical speculation that are above the heads of children, tidbits that children can simply pass over or accept on a literal level until they are old enough to understand them. The Scarecrow consoles the Gump on its disorientation in its new body by telling it, "To 'Know Thyself' is considered quite an accomplishment, which it has taken us, who are your elders, months to perfect."[23] A mature reader will recognize the reference and pick up the ironic undertone that none of these elder characters truly know themselves either, perhaps because they expected to achieve self-knowledge in a matter of months.

Baum introduced complex philosophical questions into his children's books, taking advantage of the potential of fantasy to present "the clash of ideas and issues in simple and concrete form";[24] with great skill, he translated abstract ideas into concrete terms that are meaningful even to a child. He examined the nature of human identity from many angles. Where do consciousness and personality come from? (In Oz, they are somehow imparted to stuffed dummies.) Where in the body do they reside? (The Tin Woodman remains himself even though he has lost all parts of his body.) What happens if an integrated personality is split into two (like the High Ki of Twi in *The Enchanted Island of Yew*)? or two personalities are forcibly put together into one person (like the Boolooroo's victims in *Sky Island*)? Transformations are evil magic because they destroy or pervert the victim's identity, and every creature's identity is respected in Oz.

Long before chess-playing computers were thought of, Baum explored the boundary between machines and humans with the marvelous robot Tik-Tok. What is the difference between the copper man Tik-Tok, designed and constructed by humans, and the Tin Woodman, who started off as a human being? Among these questions of intellectual interest is one of the greatest practical consequence: why do groups who are next-door neighbors so often seize every pretext to hate and despise each other? The absurdity, which has failed to prevent bitter warfare throughout history, is apparent to any child who reads about the loathing of the color pink on one half of Sky Island and the equal loathing of blue on the other.

Once readers have accepted the Oz world as real, they can delight in its unending novelty. We are interested to learn, and we do not doubt, that the Patchwork Girl saw nothing one morning until Aunt Em sewed on her button eyes, which the Woozy had scraped off in a tussle the night before.[25] We accept Oz values as well. Later in the same book there is an Unhappy Ferryman who has been punished for cruelty to animals by being deprived of the ability to understand what they say or to make them understand him. Because we have grown familiar with this society in which animals converse with humans on an equal basis, we appreciate the weight of this punishment. At the same time, as so often in Baum, we are inspired to see that here, too, in the world we know, we impoverish ourselves by cutting ourselves off from our animal kin.

After Baum's death, his publishers chose a young Oz devotee, Ruth Plumly Thompson, to continue the series.[26] Thompson proved to be an excellent choice: she produced nineteen Oz books between 1921 and 1939 that were inventive, amusing, and sufficiently authentic to delight children who wanted to hear more about Oz.[27] *Kabumpo in Oz* (1922), one of her best, introduces the self-important and testy but likable court elephant Kabumpo, takes the characters through ingeniously imagined countries like dry Rith Metic, convincingly develops Ruggedo after he reformed and settled in the Emerald City (at the end of *The Magic of Oz*), and exploits the contents of a wonderful box of Mixed Magic. However, while Baum imagined his own fairylands and adventures, Thompson drew heavily on the stock elements of fairy tale and romance. The main plot in *Kabumpo* concerns a charming prince who must find and marry the proper princess in order to save his kingdom.

More important, Thompson undermined the credibility and seriousness of her fiction by using the voice of a knowing adult omniscient author who did not give the appearance of believing her own story. Baum wrote from the viewpoint of his child protagonists and narrated events directly, as his characters experienced them. Thompson often commented on her situations, sometimes using exclamation points to draw attention to her inventiveness. In *The Cowardly Lion of Oz* (1923), she described a doorknob reaching out from a door and dragging two characters through its keyhole: "Yes, it really did! . . . Whether the keyhole had stretched as they went through or whether they had shrunk, I cannot say."[28] There is no child among the central characters of *Kabumpo*, and the protagonist of *The Cowardly Lion of Oz* is an adult clown, not the pallid, passive orphan boy Bob Up. As an adult writing down to children, she indulged in consciously cute style, such as giving her characters quaint exclamations like Glinda's "Great gooseberries!"[29] Although the contagious negativity of the sky island of Un in *The Cowardly Lion* expresses psychological insight worthy of Baum himself, such significance is rare in Thompson's work. Generally she merely invented fantastic adventures to entertain.

After Thompson retired from writing Oz books, Reilly & Lee chose the illustrator Neill to succeed her; and he wrote three Oz books from 1940 to 1942. Despite his marvelous skill in catching the spirit of Baum's Oz in his illustrations, Neill completely missed it when he tried storytelling. Most disastrously, he ignored Baum's concern with logic and plausible motivation: instead, he piled one wild, pointless invention upon another without attempting to make them believable. In *The Wonder City of Oz* (1940), Jenny Jump, an ordinary girl in New Jersey, finds a leprechaun in her kitchen and forces him to give her fairy powers. She jumps to Oz and proposes an election ("ozlection") to determine whether she or Ozma will rule the country; and the conscientious Ozma, for no reason, agrees.

After Neill's death, Jack Snow contributed two Oz books in 1946 and 1949. His *Shaggy Man of Oz* (1949) is more credibly plotted and developed than Neill's books, but it is deficient in Ozian exuberance and humor. Its central fantasy is an elaborate and confused allegory on false romance versus love, in which the Shaggy Man and other people are reduced to automata to act out an endlessly repeated romantic play and are restored by looking at the Love Magnet and realizing what genuine love is.

Rachel Cosgrove's *The Hidden Valley of Oz* (1951) recaptures the humor and inventiveness of Thompson. A biologist's son, Jam, is carried off by his kite, along with a white rat and two guinea pigs, and lands in the Gilliken country. The animals immediately begin to talk; the brash and clever rat, Percy, the personality kid, is particularly engaging. Sadly, Reilly & Lee rejected Cosgrove's second attempt. *Merry Go Round in Oz* (1963), by Eloise Jarvis McGraw and Lauren McGraw Wagner, also presents some engaging animals, but in general fails to recapture the Oz spirit. Its Land of the Fox-Hunters and Kingdom of

Halidom are heavy-handed burlesques that do not fit in Oz. This was the last attempt to prolong the Oz series by a commercial publisher.

Various novelists have been inspired by *The Wizard of Oz* to make Baum's vision meaningful in the real world: in a way these must be taken as tributes, but the authors carry revision to the point of debasement. In Philip José Farmer's *A Barnstormer in Oz* (1982), the pilot Hank Stover, who is Dorothy's son, accidentally flies from Kansas into the alternative world of Oz. He has to save the country from a new wicked witch, Erakna, and from the U.S. Army, who have learned how to pierce the barrier into Oz and want to colonize the country and exploit its gems. Farmer makes engaging use of the articulate animals of Oz, but right overcomes wrong in an orgy of blood-soaked violence utterly opposed to the spirit of Oz. Geoff Ryman's *Was* (1992) rewrites Dorothy's story so that Aunty Em kills Toto, Uncle Henry sexually abuses Dorothy, and Dorothy consequently becomes psychotic. Baum makes a brief endearing appearance at Dorothy's school, and his *Wizard of Oz*, inspired by sympathy for her, provides a transitory release from the deadly world the characters live in; but grayness overpowers life and joy in the "real" world of *Was.* Gregory Maguire's *Wicked: The Life and Times of the Wicked Witch of the West* (1995) imposes on Oz the guilt, repression, and torture of actual history; thus the Wicked Witch can be sympathetic because she is rebelling against an unjust order. Glinda appears as a goody-goody simpleton.

Perhaps these authors' perverse need to "tell the truth" about Oz sprang less from Baum's book than from the moving picture of 1939, which is more emphatically affirmative of the virtues of middle American farm life and of home. Maguire's two witches are modeled on the characters as portrayed in the film.

Certainly it was the film that brought Oz back to a central place in American culture. Although it was not an immediate success, it has been replayed on television so often since 1956 that almost all American children and their families have seen it.[30] The film made everyone aware of Oz as a wonderful place, technicolor in contrast to the sepia real world, in which the yellow brick road leads to the Emerald City, where wishes are fulfilled. The live scarecrow, the tin man, and the cowardly lion, who long for the brains, heart, and courage they already have, became familiar, beloved characters.

It was the movie that suggested Oz as a theme to political cartoonists. On August 30, 1939, shortly after its release, Herblock published a cartoon captioned "In the Not-So-Merry Land of Oz," which depicted Hitler as the wicked witch, Mussolini perched on his shoulder in the form of a Winged Monkey, and Dorothy and her friends as the European countries that opposed Hitler. Presidents Carter, Reagan, the senior Bush, and Clinton have all been drawn as the Wizard of Oz exposed to be a humbug. During the presidential campaign of 1980, Stephen Sack drew Carter as the Scarecrow without brains, Reagan as the Tin Woodman without a heart, third-party candidate Anderson as the Lion singing, "If I Only Had a Chance," and Dorothy as the voters groaning, "If I Only Had a Choice."[31]

Some of the folklore of Oz is clearly traceable to the movie rather than the book. It was the film that gave us the term *Munchkins* for ridiculous little people. (In Baum's book all the inhabitants of Oz were the size of Dorothy, a child of about six; and the effect was to give her a comfortably child-proportioned world. In the film, all the characters, including Dorothy, tower over the Munchkins.) The Wicked Witch of the West became more pervasive in the story and more stereotypically witchy in character and appearance than Baum-Denslow's homely, marginally comic character. It is the green-faced Margaret Hamilton of the film who has become the archetypal witch in our culture. When a wag wrote "Surrender, Dorothy" on a bridge that crosses the Washington Beltway just as the rising towers of the Mormon Temple come into view, he was obviously recalling an episode in the movie and its view of the Emerald City rising from the Munchkin plain. The streetwise black musical *The Wiz* (1975) took off from the film rather than the book.

The film is a fine imaginative creation and undoubtedly would have delighted Baum. Something has been lost, however: worldly adults have taken over a straightforward story of a child's marvelous experiences, seen from a child's point of view. Judy Garland, a mature fifteen year old, could not plausibly convey a child's point of view. She is not a small child who is accidentally transported to a strange land and instinctively longs for the security of home, but a dissatisfied teenager who is so critical of home that she runs away and has to learn that "There's no place like home"—a moral lesson that is not an issue in the book. Baum's cowardly lion is anthropomorphic, but he is a real lion—not a clown in an animal suit like Bert Lahr. The makers of the film—like the makers of the "Wizard of Oz" extravaganza—felt the need to make Baum's story acceptable to adults, although they went about their task with infinitely finer imagination and more subtlety.[32]

Their ultimate falsification was to turn Dorothy's journey into a dream, a mere projection of her wishes and fears that could not possibly be mistaken for reality. The film constantly emphasizes the unreality of Oz, starting with the stiff outsize flowers and the polished yellow brick road. This is false to Baum's view that the world of imagination—whether represented by dream, fairy tale, or actual innovative invention or discovery—has its own validity. Baum's Oz can be said to exist; it should not be dismissed as a dream. Devotees of Oz can be glad that the film *Wizard* popularized Baum's imaginative world, but they do not want to see the film supplant the greater work.

NOTES

Introduction

1. Gillian Avery, *Behold the Child: American Children and Their Books 1621–1922* (Baltimore: Johns Hopkins University Press, 1994), 144–45. Ruth Plumly Thompson, Baum's successor, described a publicity party given in her honor on August 10, 1955: "Critics and librarians turned out in force, also the booksellers. The latter were fine, but the others tried in every way (subtle and blunt) to impress upon me their low opinion of Baum, R.P.T., and Oz. As the drinks progressed, they grew ruder *and* ruder." (*Baum Bugle* 28 [Autumn 1984]: 7).

   Cornelia Meigs's 624-page *Critical History of Children's Literature* (1953) includes not one mention of Baum. Nor does he appear in the first three editions of May Hill Arbuthnot's *Children and Books*. In the fourth edition (1972), revised by Zena Sutherland, *The Wizard of Oz* is grudgingly included among "Books That Stir Controversy," only to be dismissed as "flat and dull" in style (Glenview, IL: Scott, Foresman, 1972), 263. Even feminist specialists in children's literature have remained oblivious to Baum. Kathleen Odean's *Great Books for Girls: More than 600 Books to Inspire Today's Girls and Tomorrow's Women* (1997) does not include any of his works.

1: Early Life: Actor, Playwright, Oil Salesman 1856–1888

1. Henry Demarest Lloyd, *Wealth Against Commonwealth*, cited by John L. Thomas, *Alternative America: Henry George; Edward Bellamy, Henry Demarest Lloyd and the Adversary Tradition* (Cambridge: Harvard University Press, 1983), 290–92.
2. Frank Joslyn Baum and Russell P. MacFall, *To Please a Child: A Biography of L. Frank Baum* (Chicago: Reilly & Lee, 1961), 20–21. Baum and MacFall say that Benjamin bought Rose Lawn in 1860, when Frank was four, but Susan Ferrara found the deed of sale, dated Nov. 10, 1866, in Deed Book 169, in the Clerk's Office, Onondaga County Courthouse, (*The Family of the Wizard: The Baums of Syracuse* [Xlibris 2000], p. 81–82).
3. L. Frank Baum, *Dot and Tot of Merryland* (Indianapolis: Bobbs-Merrill, 1901), 16.

4. Interview in the *North American,* October 3, 1904, cited in *Baum Bugle* 29 (Spring 1985): 13.

5. Baum and MacFall, 21–22.

6. Copies of census and business directory records, article by Clara Houck in *Chittenango Bridgeport Times* in Baum collection at Syracuse University; Baum genealogy and life of Benjamin Baum by Frank Joslyn Baum, newspaper clippings, letter of Benjamin Baum to a state lobbyist in Baum collection at Onondaga Historical Society.

7. Baum and MacFall attribute Baum's symptoms to congenital heart disease, but the rheumatic fever hypothesis seems more consistent with the evidence. According to Dr. Alan R. Sheff, a person born with a heart so defective as to cause severe symptoms in childhood would not survive to lead an active life in the days before effective treatment for heart disease; and Baum led a very active life. Rheumatic fever, on the other hand, would cause acute illness and prolonged weakness; but then the disease could naturally go into remission, and there would be no symptoms until the consequences of childhood heart damage caught up with the patient in middle age.

8. Baum and MacFall, 23–24.

9. Ibid., 25–26.

10. Michael Patrick Hearn, *Baum Bugle* 30 (Spring 1986): 11–18.

11. Ibid.

12. Baum and MacFall, 29–32.

13. Michael Patrick Hearn, *Baum Bugle* 30 (Autumn 1986): 23–24.

14. L. Frank Baum, *The Book of the Hamburgs, A Brief Treatise upon the Mating, Rearing, and Management of the Different Varieties of Hamburgs* (Hartford, Connecticut: H. H. Stoddard, 1886), 8–9, 58–59. Flock at Ozcot from Baum and MacFall, 22.

15. Baum and MacFall, 32–34.

16. Baum collection, Syracuse University; Baum and MacFall, 35.

17. Harry Neal Baum in *Baum Bugle* 10 (Spring 1966): 4.

18. "The Maid of Arran," unpublished script in the Theater Collection at the New York Public Library, 4. The same collection holds a program for its New York performances. Evidently Baum thought Arran was an Irish, rather than a Scottish, island.

19. Baum and MacFall, 36–37.

20. Ibid., 42–43, 45.

21. Ibid., 45.

22. Elizabeth Cady Stanton, Susan B. Anthony, and Matilda Joslyn Gage, *A History of Woman Suffrage* (New York: Fowler & Wells, 1881) Vol. I: 466, 529.

23. Katherine Devereux Blake, daughter of a coworker in the women's movement, in Leila R. Brammer, "The Exclusionary Politics of Social Movements" (Ph.D. dissertation, University of Minnesota, 1995), 1.

24. Annie Besant, *The Ancient Wisdom* (Adyar, Madras: Theosophical Publishing House, 1966), 198–201, 269–71; Annie Besant, "Theosophical Society," *Encyclopedia of Religion and Ethics* 12 (1921): 302.

25. *Baum Bugle* 40 (Fall 1996): 25.

26. *Baum Bugle* 26 (Winter 1982): 9, 4.

27. Baum and MacFall, 43–44.

28. Letter of January 26, 1887, in Gage papers in the Schlesinger Library, Radcliffe College (Woman's Suffrage. National Leaders).

29. Baum collection at Syracuse University. Baum and MacFall give a different route, but Maud's letter provides decisive evidence. Baum's troupe was in Omaha in November, and they were going to Sioux City, Council Bluffs, Atchison, Topeka, Saint Louis, various points yet undecided, and Chicago for three weeks in April.

30. Baum and MacFall, 46.

31. Ibid., 50–51.

32. Interview in the *Washington Post*, May 16, 1965.

33. Baum and MacFall, Foreword, 46, 48–50.

34. Robert Baum's recollection, in *Baum Bugle* 14 (Christmas 1970): 17; Harry's, ibid., 29; (Autumn 1985): 9.

35. Maud's recollection in *Baum Bugle* 27 (Spring 1983): 5; Harry's, ibid., 29 (Autumn 1985): 6; Frank Junior's, ibid., first issue.

36. Baum and MacFall, 47–48.

37. Interview in *Washington Post*, May 16, 1965.

38. Baum and MacFall, 47–48.

39. *Syracuse Standard*, April 21, 1884; November 19, 1899.

40. Baum and MacFall, 52–54.

41. Syracuse city directories; Baum and MacFall, 54; bulletin of Onondaga Historical Association.

42. *Syracuse Journal*, October 24, 1885.

43. Baum and MacFall, 54–56.

44. Letter in Alexander Mitchell Library, Aberdeen, SD.

45. Diary at University of North Dakota, 85–86.

46. Baum and MacFall, 54–57.

47. Elizabeth Hampsten, *Read This Only to Yourself: The Private Writings of Midwestern Women, 1880–1910* (Bloomington: Indiana University Press, 1982), 202.

48. Diary (March 16, 1884): 53, 59.

49. *South Dakota: A Guide to the State.* Compiled by the Federal Writers' Project of the Work Projects Administration, 2d ed. (New York: Hastings House, 1952), 94–96.

50. Matilda Gage, in *Baum Bugle* 10 (Spring 1966): 6.

51. *Baum Bugle* 15 (Spring 1971): 7.

52. Letter of July 30, in Alexander Mitchell Library.

53. Letter to Clarkson in Baum collection, Syracuse University.

2: Frontier Storekeeper and Newspaper Editor 1888–1891

1. Matilda J. Gage, "The Dakota Days of L. Frank Baum," *Baum Bugle* 10 (Spring 1966): 6–7.

2. Frank Junior's draft biography, in Baum collection, Syracuse University.

3. "Dakota Days of LFB," in Alexander Mitchell Library.

4. After this season, Baum was only a fan of baseball, rooting for the Chicago Cubs. Many years later, in *The Road to Oz*, the Shaggy Man is able to save his party from

the head-throwing Scoodlers by neatly catching their heads—able to do so because he'd played baseball as a boy (123). See Michael Patrick Hearn, "The Wizard Behind the Plate," in Nancy Koupal, *Baum's Road to Oz: The Dakota Years* (Pierre:
South Dakota State Historical Society Press, 2000), 4–5, 12–18, 22, 30–33,
37–39, 42.

5. Baum and MacFall, 62.
6. L. Frank Baum, *Our Landlady*, Nancy Koupal ed. (Lincoln: University of Nebraska Press, 1996), 6.
7. Newspaper interview of c. 31 March 1913, cited by Koupal in Baum, *Our Landlady*, 159.
8. William Allen White, *Autobiography* (New York: Macmillan, 1946), 279.
9. *Baum's Road*, 55.
10. *Aberdeen Saturday Pioneer*, July 5, September 27, October 4. There is a persistent
tale, repeated by Baum and MacFall as a "tradition still alive in Aberdeen," that
Baum was involved in a duel as a result of a misprint in his social column in *The
Pioneer*. Meaning to print that a bride had a "roguish smile," Baum printed
"roughish smile"; her groom, outraged at the supposed insult, challenged him to
a duel. There were no serious consequences because both duelists ran off as soon
as they were out of sight and later peacefully made up (65). Since Baum was a
sensible man and Aberdeen was a civilized community, this was probably a tall
tale. A South Dakotan newspaperman plausibly accounts for it as a Dakotan's
mockery of Eastern illusions about the Wild West: "Baum was probably delighted by the Eastern idea that Dakota was a country populated by Indians and
gunfighters," and he was playing on the credulity of an artist friend, probably in
Chicago (Max Cooper, *Aberdeen American-News*, May 21, 1961).
    Baum did tell the tale about a character in *Aunt Jane's Nieces on Vacation*
(165–79), but it is much more likely that he was heightening life, as he often did,
than that he was relating an actual experience of his own. The real-life basis for
this story is probably a misprint that actually occurred in the *Pioneer* on April 19,
1890. Baum tells how he wandered into a rehearsal of an operetta in Aberdeen
and was told by a Miss McBride, "with a roughish smile," "As long as your [sic]
here, we must make the best of it" (5).
11. *Baum Bugle* 40 (Fall 1996): 25.
12. Dorinda Riessen Reed, *The Woman Suffrage Movement in South Dakota*, 2d ed. (Pierre:
South Dakota Commission on the Status of Women, 1975), 41, 45.
13. Koupal, ed., *Our Landlady*, 220.
14. Koupal points to a series of columns that ran briefly in 1884 in Baum's home-
town newspaper the *Syracuse Standard*, in which a landlady gives her opinions on
the new-fangled invention of electric lights and the doings of local politicians
and businessmen; these are similar enough to "Our Landlady" that they might
possibly have been written by Baum, although they are greatly inferior (*Our
Landlady*, 7–9).
15. Koupal, ed., *Our Landlady*, 75–76.
16. Ibid., 98.
17. Ibid., 42–43. Readers of "Our Landlady" were constantly reminded of developments in the suffrage campaign. Like more sophisticated local suffragists, Mrs.

Bilkins is too easily persuaded to throw her support to an Independent candidate (October 18), 127.

18. Ibid., 108–10.

19. Ibid., 73–74. Baum's review appeared on the same day, May 31.

20. Ibid., 133–34, 136.

21. Ibid., 153.

22. Ibid., 154–57. Koupal cites the parallel to page 236 of *The Master Key* (189–90).

23. Ibid., 164–65.

24. Ibid., 166–68.

25. Ibid., 104, 186–87.

26. Cecilia M. Wittmayer, "The 1889–1890 Woman Suffrage Campaign: A Need to Organize," *South Dakota History* 11 (Summer 1981), 220.

27. This fear of Indians prompted Baum to a truly shocking editorial on December 20, 1890. Prompted by his own and his neighbors' terror at the thought of an Indian invasion of their homes, he said the noble Indians had degenerated into "a pack of whining curs," who should be totally exterminated to preserve the safety of the frontier. Then "history would forget these latter despicable beings, and speak, in latter ages of the glory of these grand kings of the forest and plain that Cooper loved to heroise."

28. Onondaga Historical Society collection.

29. Koupal, ed., *Our Landlady*, 172.

30. *Ibid.*, 168–72, quoting interview with Maud Baum.

31. Barbara Cloud, *The Business of Newspapers on the Western Frontier* (Reno: University of Nevada Press, 1992), 178.

3: Becoming a Writer in Chicago 1891–1900

1. Hamlin Garland, *A Son of the Middle Border* (New York: Macmillan, 1956), 456–57.

2. Harold U. Faulkner, *Politics, Reform and Expansion: 1890–1900* (New York: Harper & Row, 1959), 32–33.

3. Thomas J. Schlereth, *Victorian America* (New York: HarperCollins, 1991), 115, 169–70, 172; H. W. Brands, *The Reckless Decade* (New York: St. Martin's, 1995), 43–45.

4. L. Frank Baum, *The Annotated Wizard of Oz*, ed. Michael Patrick Hearn (New York: W. W. Norton, 2000), 176, n. 1.

5. *Baum Bugle* 29 (August 1985): 9. Baum and MacFall tell a slightly different and less pointed version of this story: they do not mention an appointment with Maud and the children and have Baum recognized by his business friend, the sales manager of Pitkin and Brooks, 80–81.

6. Baum and MacFall, 76–77.

7. Ibid., 76–77, 81; Robert Baum in *Baum Bugle* 14 (Christmas 1970): 18.

8. Baum and MacFall, 78; Harry Baum in *Baum Bugle* 29 (Autumn 1985): 8.

9. Letter in Arents Collection, New York Public Library.

10. Robert Baum in *Baum Bugle* 14 (Christmas 1970); 18–19.

11. Matilda Gage's letters to Clarkson and Helen, June 1894, September 19, February 18, March 12, 1897, February 24, 1898, in Gage papers in Schlesinger Library.

12. Harry Baum in *Baum Bugle* 29 (Autumn 1985): 8.

13. Robert Baum in *Baum Bugle* 14 (Christmas 1970): 19; Baum and MacFall, 83–84.

14. Letter to Helen, November 3, 1897, in Schlesinger Library.

15. Robert Baum in *Baum Bugle* 14 (Christmas 1970): 18–19.

16. Harry Baum in *Baum Bugle* 9 (Christmas 1965): 3; Joslyn in *Baum Bugle* 28 (Spring 1984): 16.

17. Letters to Clarkson, May 25, and Helen, February 18, 1897, in Schlesinger Library.

18. Baum and MacFall, 93.

19. Letter of November 15, in Schlesinger Library.

20. Robert Baum in *Baum Bugle* 14 (Christmas 1970): 18.

21. Letter to Leslie Gage, December 29, 1896, in Schlesinger Library.

22. Testimony of two close friends in Baum's obituary in the *Mercury*, in Baum Collection, Columbia University; newspaper clipping of August 13, 1939, at Onondaga Historical Society.

23. Note by Frank Junior in Baum papers, Syracuse University.

24. A surprising number of distinguished American intellectuals shared the Gage-Baum interest in spiritualist psychic phenomena. William James tirelessly attended seances, "investigating claims by various mediums that they could communicate with the dead.... He brought his laboratory scepticism, to be sure, but he was forever hoping" that some medium would succeed (Mark Edmundson, review of Linda Simon's *Genuine Reality: A Life of William James, Washington Post* Book World [Sunday, February 1, 1998], 5).

25. Besant, *Ancient Wisdom*, 72–75; "Theosophical Society," 301. Gage, too, identified fairies as one type of the elementals who were real to theosophists. See *Woman, Church and State* (New York: Arno Press, 1972), 239.

26. Hearn, ed., *Annotated Wizard of Oz*, xcii.

27. L. Frank Baum, *Tik-Tok of Oz* (Chicago: Reilly & Britton, 1914), 161–62.

28. Paul Oltramare, "Theosophy," *Encyclopedia of Religion and Ethics* 12 (1921): 304.

29. Besant, *Ancient Wisdom*, 77–78.

30. *Baum Bugle* 27 (Spring 1983): 5.

31. It is true that many of her sources are now discredited and her argument is distorted throughout by its extreme anti-Christian (especially anti-Roman Catholic) bias. Although much of her information is true, and the churches have undoubtedly oppressed women, she weakened her case by exaggeration and by her willingness to seize upon any evidence, valid or not, to prove her point.

32. Gage, 14–15.

33. Ibid., 233.

34. Ibid., 234, 236.

35. Matilda to Clarkson, June 9, 1893, in Schlesinger Library.

36. Douglas G. Greene, "The Periodical Baum," *Baum Bugle* 19 (Autumn 1975): 3. Baum was able to sell some of these previously unsalable stories after he became an established writer, although he had surprisingly limited success even then (see chapter 8).

37. L. Frank Baum, *By the Candelabra's Glare* (Delmar, New York: Scholars' Facsimiles and Reprints, 1981), 39.

38. *Baum Bugle* 20 (Autumn 1976): 16–17.

39. In the *Times-Herald*, cited by Hearn in a letter to the *New York Times* (January 1, 1992).

40. In these years he also published in the *Times-Herald* the comic verses "Farmer Benson on the Motocycle" (August 4, 1895), "The Latest in Magic," on the discovery of X rays in 1895 (1896), and "Two Pictures," which contrasts the atmosphere in Chicago when Anson has won a game and when he has lost (May 5, 1896), as well as a thin supernatural story, "Who Called 'Perry'?" (January 19, 1896). He sold "My Ruby Wedding Ring" (a slight ghost story) and "How Scroggs Won the Reward" (now lost) to the Bacheller Syndicate in 1896 and 1897. "The Extravagance of Dan" and "The Return of Dick Weemins," two rather crass success stories, appeared in the *National Magazine* in May and July of 1897. "Jack Burgitt's Honor," a sentimental tale of two villains' reform, did not find publication until 1905 in *Novelettes*, no. 68. "A Shadow Cast Before," another thin supernatural tale, appeared in *The Philosopher* in December 1897 (Greene, *Baum Bugle* 19 [Autumn 1975]).

41. In the Baum collection, Columbia University. Mary Louise shared Frank's interest in women's rights as well as writing: She was the president of a Political Equality Club in Syracuse (Matilda Gage to Clarkson, October 23, 1893, Schlesinger Library).

42. Matilda Gage to Helen, March 12, June 10, in Schlesinger Library; Baum and MacFall, 87–88).

43. Baum and MacFall, 94–95.

44. *Show Window* (December 1899), 251.

45. Ibid. (March 1900), 120.

46. L. Frank Baum, *The Art of Decorating Dry Goods Windows* (Chicago: The Show Window Publishing Company, 1900), 181.

47. *Show Window* (June 1900), 292; (June 1899); Stuart Culver, "What Manikins Want," *Representations* 21 (Winter 1988): 106.

48. Baum and MacFall, 94–95.

49. Robert Baum in *Baum Bugle* 14 (Christmas 1970): 20–21.

50. *Show Window* (October 1900), 170.

51. Baum and MacFall, 86; letter from Frank Junior to Ronald Baughman, Baum Collection, Columbia University.

52. Trees in Oz will grow cooked items like bread and cream puffs in *The Patchwork Girl of Oz* (and manufactured ones like guns in the next book, *Tik-Tok of Oz*). The Wise Donkey reappears in *The Patchwork Girl*: he was visiting Oz when it was shut off from the rest of the world and therefore had to remain there.

53. L. Frank Baum, *A New Wonderland* (New York: R. H. Russell, 1900), 7–8.

54. Ibid., 59–60.

55. Daniel P. Mannix, "Ozma, Tik-Tok, and the Rheingold," *Baum Bugle* 22 (Spring 1978): 3.

56. Baum, *New Wonderland*, 12.

57. Baum overindulged his taste for gruesome fantasy in these tales; for example, the ultimate fate of the Purple Dragon, whose body is stretched out long and thin

and cut up into fiddle strings, is far-fetched and a bit nauseating. In later books, Baum presented this type of material less graphically (like the dismemberment of Nick Chopper in *The Wizard of Oz*), so as not to detract from the benignly comic tone of the fantasy.

58. *Baum Bugle* 29 (Autumn 1985): 9.

59. L. Frank Baum, *Mother Goose in Prose* (Chicago: Way & Williams, 1897), 245–52.

60. Letter dated December 31. Robert A. Baum has kindly sent me copies of LFB's correspondence with Reilly & Britton.

61. *Baum Bugle* 28 (Autumn 1984): 5; Ferrara, p. 146.

62. In Baum collection, Syracuse University.

63. Letter of May 18, 1898, at Syracuse University.

64. Carpenter, 128; Michael Patrick Hearn, "When L. Frank Baum was 'Laura Bancroft,'" *American Book Collector* 8 (May 1987): 13.

65. Douglas G. Greene and Michael Patrick Hearn, *W. W. Denslow* (Mount Pleasant, MI: Clarke Historical Library, Central Michigan University, 1976), 80, 108, 129.

66. These included "The Mating Day," published in September 1898 in *Short Stories*, "the most important periodical in which Baum had published" so far; it is an experiment in exotic native fantasy in the manner of Rider Haggard. *The Youth's Companion*, in which "Aunt Hulda's Good Time" appeared on October 26, 1899, was also a well-regarded magazine; the story is agreeably sentimental and expresses the pitifully confined nature of a farm woman's life, in which a single day away from the farm is a holiday treat. "The Loveridge Burglary" (*Short Stories* [January 1900]), is a detective story suggesting simplified Sherlock Holmes, such as Baum would develop in his later juvenile novels. "The Real 'Mr. Dooley'" (*The Home Magazine* [January 1900]) a nonfiction article on the original of Finley Peter Dunne's character, includes a reference to the reporter Sam Steele, whose name Baum would later appropriate for the hero of a boys' series. "To the Grand Army of the Republic August 1900," in the *Times-Herald* on August 26, 1900, is a routine topical poem written to publicize Baum's *Army Alphabet* (Greene, *Baum Bugle* 19 [Autumn 1975]).

67. Greene and Hearn, 80.

68. Baum and MacFall, 85.

69. Letter in Schlesinger Library.

70. Baum and MacFall, 84–85.

71. Greene and Hearn, 82.

72. Ibid., 86–87.

73. *Baum Bugle* 29 (Autumn 1985): 10.

74. Greene and Hearn, 84.

75. David L. Greene and Dick Martin, *The Oz Scrapbook* (New York: Random House, 1977), 7.

76. *Baum Bugle* 31 (Autumn 1987): 22.

77. David L. Greene and Peter E. Hanff, "Baum and Denslow: Their Books," *Baum Bugle* 19 (Spring 1975): 9.

78. Greene and Hearn, 88–89, 94.

79. Ibid., 94–95.

80. Greene and Hanff, "Baum and Denslow: Their Books, Part 2," *Baum Bugle* 19 (Autumn 1975): 15.

81. Ibid., 15–16.
82. *Baum Bugle* 11 (Spring 1967): 19; 32 (Spring 1988): 21.
83. *Baum Bugle* 32 (Spring 1988): 24. Lewis Carroll's *Wonderland* was in everybody's mind because he had just died in 1898.
84. Letter in Arents Collection, New York Public Library. Evidently Frank Junior did not get an appointment to either academy, for he went to Cornell to study law. He dropped out to take a lieutenant's commission and sailed to the Philippines in 1904.
85. Syracuse *Post-Standard*, June 1.

4: *The Wonderful Wizard of Oz 1899–1900*

1. Hearn, ed., *Annotated Wizard of Oz*, 11, 18, 20.
2. Ibid., 20.
3. Hamlin Garland, *A Son of the Middle Border* (New York: Macmillan, 1956), 361, 398–99.
4. Hamlin Garland, *Main Travelled Roads* (New York: Harper and Brothers, n.d.), 32–36.
5. Garland, *Middle Border*, 376, 415–16.
6. Hearn suggests that Baum might have got the idea of countries being actually colored as they are on maps from Mark Twain's *Tom Sawyer Abroad* (1894). He also suggests that the different colors and geometric shapes of the Oz countries suggest the formal beds of an old-fashioned garden, such as Baum remembered from Rose Lawn, described in *Dot and Tot*, and recreated at Ozcot (*Annotated Wizard*, 61, n. 7).
7. Hearn, ed., *Annotated Wizard*, 35, note 4: 232.
8. Ibid., 24, 26.
9. Roger Sale, "L. Frank Baum, and Oz," *Hudson Review* 25 (Winter 1972–73): 585.
10. Michael O. Riley, *Oz and Beyond: The Fantasy World of L. Frank Baum* (Lawrence: University Press of Kansas, 1997), 54.
11. James R. Shortridge, *The Middle West: Its Meaning in American Culture* (Lawrence: University Press of Kansas, 1989), 6–8, 29–30.
12. Alison Lurie, "The Fate of the Munchkins," *New York Review of Books* 21 (April 18, 1974): 24.
13. Hearn, ed., *Annotated Wizard*, 45.
14. Frederick Jackson Turner, "The Significance of the Frontier in American History," "Contributions of the West to American Democracy," in *The Frontier in American History* (Tucson: University of Arizona Press, 1986), 2–3, 37–38, 259–61, 263.
15. Hearn, ed., *Annotated Wizard*, 181, 185.
16. *Baum Bugle* 15 (Christmas 1971): 5–7.
17. Hearn, ed., *Annotated Wizard*, 36.
18. This episode was whitewashed in the 1939 film, where Dorothy does not mean to throw water on the Witch; she is only putting out the blazing Scarecrow. Baum was more realistic.

19. However, we later find out in *The Emerald City of Oz* that Uncle Henry had to mortgage his farm in order to pay for the new house (21); he will be unable to meet the payments and the mortgage will be foreclosed.
20. Hearn, ed., *Annotated Wizard*, 52.
21. Balloons at this time were made of silk, coated with glue. Ibid., 286, n. 3.
22. Ruth Plumly Thompson in *The Wonderful Wizard of Oz*, Critical Heritage series, ed. by Michael Patrick Hearn (New York: Schocken Books, 1983), 176.
23. Harry Baum, interview in *Washington Post*, May 16, 1965.
24. Hearn, ed., *Annotated Wizard*, 76.
25. L. Frank Baum, *The Tin Woodman of Oz* (Chicago: Reilly & Britton, 1918), 30. In the same way, Jack Pumpkinhead remains the same person even though his pumpkin heads spoil and have to be replaced.
26. Martin Gardner, *The Whys of a Philosophical Scrivener* (New York: William Morrow, 1983), 315; "*The Tin Woodman of Oz*: An Appreciation," *Baum Bugle* 40 (Fall 1996): 15.
27. Hearn, ed., *Annotated Wizard*, 111, n. 4. There is another jokey reference to heart disease in *The Patchwork Girl of Oz*, 152.
28. Ibid., 171.
29. Ibid., 188.
30. Daniel Boorstin, *The Image: or, What Happened to the American Dream* (New York: Atheneum, 1962), 207–10; Karl A. Lurix, *Baum Bugle* 30 (Spring 1986): 19.
31. Daniel F. Mannix, *Baum Bugle* 25 (Summer 1981): 5; Baum, *Annotated Wizard*, 267, n. 9. In Baum's exposition of "The Man in the Moon" in *Mother Goose in Prose*, the Man was sent back home on "a big balloon . . . which belongs to the circus that came here last summer, and was pawned for a board bill," 115.
32. Martin Gardner, quoted in Hearn, ed., *Annotated Wizard*, 262, n. 5.
33. Ibid., 283.
34. Ibid., 285.
35. Baum papers, Syracuse University.
36. Baum and MacFall, 108, 111–12; Greene and Hanff, *Baum Bugle* 19 (Autumn 1975): 18.
37. Greene and Hearn, 89–92.
38. *Ibid.*, 89–90; Baum, *Annotated Wizard*, xxxviii.
39. *Baum Bugle* 19 (Autumn 1975): 14. Baum and MacFall give a much higher figure: an initial edition of ten-thousand copies, followed by twenty-five thousand more copies in October, thirty-thousand more in November, and twenty-five thousand more in January 1901—a total of ninety thousand copies. The smaller (though still impressive) figures, based on Denslow's account books, are undoubtedly more reliable. Baum, of course, received the same payments.
40. Greene and Hearn, 89–90, 104.
41. Baum and MacFall, 122–23; Baum, *Annotated Wizard*, I.
42. *Baum Bugle* 29 (Autumn 1985): 10.
43. Baum and MacFall, 107–10; Baum, *Annotated Wizard*, n. 17, 43; letter from Henry Brewster to Jack Snow in Baum papers, Syracuse University.
44. Frank Junior in *Baum Bugle* I (1957); Sally Roesch Wagner, "Dorothy Gage and Dorothy Gale," *Baum Bugle* 28 (Autumn 1984): 6.

45. *New York Times* review in Critical Heritage Series, *Wizard,* 136; Hearn, ed., *Annotated Wizard,* 11, 33–34; *Baum Bugle* 22 (Spring 1978): 10; *Dial* (December 1, 1900), 436. Baum regularly kept scrapbooks of the reviews of all his Oz books. His scrapbook for *The Wizard* contains 202 reviews, all but two of them favorable. Of course he might not have preserved unfavorable reviews, so all the scrapbooks prove is the number of favorable reviews a book received.

46. Baum evidently felt a need to insist on the innocuousness of his stories, despite evidence to the contrary in the Oz books, *Sky Island,* and *Policeman Bluejay.* This claim may have appealed to his American contemporaries, but it has been used against him by unsympathetic modern readers such as Avery. Reminiscences by some of his friends and relatives suggest that he may sometimes have presented himself socially as blander than he was. Frank Junior wrote that his father "never spoke harshly under any condition. Never critical of anyone" (notes for his biography, Syracuse University). A friend eulogized Baum: "His soul was too full of light to harbor one thing that was small or mean, and his love was so great that it put white arms around humanity" (obituary, Baum Collection, Columbia University). Baum was a sweet and gentle man, but not—fortunately—totally devoid of hostile feelings.

47. Hearn, ed., *Annotated Wizard,* 208.

48. Her destruction by water reflects the folk belief that this pure element is antipathetic to witches: They could not cross running water and would not sink if thrown in, because the water would not receive them. Baum evidently invented the idea that water melts a witch, adding the characteristic homely simile that she dissolved like brown sugar. Then Dorothy swept the messy remains away—evil is readily cleaned up in Oz.

49. Hearn, ed., *Annotated Wizard,* 215–16.

50. Ibid., 143.

51. There have been several allegorical interpretations of *The Wizard of Oz,* all of which seem to me far-fetched. In some cases, they involve contradictions of what is known about Baum's life and attitudes. Henry M. Littlefield's "The Wizard of Oz: Parable on Populism" was innovative and valuable in taking Baum seriously and recognizing his social criticism. However, Littlefield's political interpretation of *The Wizard* is belied by Baum's known political views. Far from supporting the Populist Party, Baum opposed it as detracting from the strength of the Republican Party, which he supported editorially in his newspaper and by his votes throughout his life, so far as is known; he opposed free silver as editor of the *Pioneer* and published pro-McKinley, pro–Gold Standard verses in the *Times-Herald* in 1896. Harry Baum said that his father "was sometimes independent politically but usually he favored the Republicans" (Baum papers, Syracuse University). Although one could say that workers had been reduced to machines as the Tin Woodman was changed from a man to a metal artifact, the tender-hearted Woodman cannot be taken as an example of dehumanization.

   John G. Geer and Thomas R. Rochon carry Littlefield's line of argument even further in "William Jennings Bryan on the Yellow Brick Road." They see Dorothy as representing Bryan, equally sincere and guileless, and the difficulties of her journey as representing those of Bryan in his presidential campaign in 1896; the

Wizard's initial refusal to help the travelers represents Bryan's loss of the election, and their ultimate success presages a victory for him in 1900. Actually, if anyone in the book represents Bryan, it would probably be the Wizard, a politician who successfully fooled the people and who also came from Nebraska. Michael Gessel's argument against Littlefield's thesis is more conclusive than any of these errors in detail: he asks why Baum would write a political parable into one of his tales and not into any other and points out that when Baum did make political allusions they were perfectly clear, like the Standard Oil octopus in *The Sea Fairies* (*Baum Bugle* 36 [Spring 1992]: 22).

John Algeo, in "The Wizard of Oz: The Perilous Journey" (*American Theosophist* 74 [1986]) and "Oz and Kansas: A Theosophical Quest," in Susan Gannon and Ruth Anne Thompson, eds. *Proceedings of the 13th Annual Conference of the Children's Literature Association*, May 16–18, 1986 [1988]) makes the book into "a theosophical allegory." Gray Kansas is desirable to Dorothy, he argues, because it "is that world from which we have come before we find ourselves in the perilous land of the separate self . . . where there is no differentiation—but only Oneness; no color, which is diversity, not even any black or white, which are opposites, but only the unity of gray." The uniform grayness of Kansas indicates "the comforting, reassuring world of Oneness from which we have all come and to which we are destined to return. Kansas is home—the Devachan of unchanging Reality. . . . Oz is samsara, the seductive world of earthly beauty," the manifold world of differentiation and becoming. Like Dorothy, we must "get home to the nirvana of permanent Truth." And so forth. ("Wizard," 292–4, "Oz and Kansas," 137–8). This theory disregards the tone of Baum's description of Kansas; furthermore, there is no evidence that he accepted theosophical mythology with such painstaking literalness.

Osmond Beckwith's psychoanalytic interpretation, "The Oddness of Oz," is equally bizarre and defamatory as well. Beckwith reduces Baum's imaginative creations to neurotic fantasies expressing his inadequacies as a male, citing as evidence his numerous "emasculated" male characters (the straw-stuffed Scarecrow, the Tin Woodman whose body was chopped up and who can no longer love a woman, the Cowardly Lion, a symbol of virility who lacks masculine courage, and, in later books, the one-legged Cap'n Bill). In addition, there is the sinister feminism of Baum's presentation of enterprising girls and matriarchal power. His unsentimental tomboy hen Billina is a particularly morbid and repulsive creation. The wicked witches in *The Wizard* are equated with mother; Glinda cannot represent mother because she is not married (!). "Father" comes out badly too, however; because the Wizard gets the child Dorothy to kill the Witch, he is a regular Moloch, "immolating children to placate the elements," as is indicated by his fourth appearance, as a ball of fire (Critical Heritage Series, *Wizard*, 236–244).

52. *Baum Bugle* 30 (Autumn 1986): 9. In a short essay in the *Chicago Evening Post* (November 27, 1902), Baum had explained that children demand wonders in their stories because the world is still new to them and therefore full of wonderful adventures. And "namby-pamby books" are no more suitable for girls than boys: "The girls as eagerly demand and absorb the marvelous as their brothers; aye, and need it as much" (Koupal, *Baum's Road*, 167–8).

53. In Critical Heritage Series *Wizard*, 138–40.

54. Hamlin Garland, *Crumbling Idols* (Cambridge: Harvard University Press, 1960), 44, 52–54.
55. Ralph Fletcher Seymour, *Some Went This Way* (Chicago: Ralph Fletcher Seymour, 1945), 9.
56. Suzanne Rahn points to Frank Stockton, a very well-known writer of fairy tales about twenty years before Baum, as "the first to give his fairy tales a consistently American flavor." Although Stockton's characters and settings are more European than Baum's, both writers portrayed widely assorted creatures democratically coexisting in harmony, both made their fanciful characters as "realistic" as possible, and both delighted in inventions and mechanical devices. In "Modern Fairy Tales" Baum highly praised Stockton's "The Floating Prince," in which a traveling prince gathers an assortment of followers who will aid him in their distinctive ways (31–32).

5: Successful Author 1901–1903

1. L. Frank Baum, "The Box of Robbers," *American Fairy Tales* (New York: Dover Publications, 1978), 17.
2. Ibid., 81, 92. Cf. Annie Besant, *Ancient Wisdom:* The Egos of the Masters dwell on the third region of the mental plane, "raining down noble ideals, inspiring thoughts, devotional aspirations, streams of spiritual and intellectual help for men. . . . A discovery flashes into the mind" of a scientist, a melody to a musician, "a new energy of hope and love suffuses the heart of an unwearied philanthropist," 131–32.
3. *Baum Bugle* 34 (Spring 1990): 19.
4. *Baum Bugle* 14 (Christmas 1970): 21; 15 (Spring 1971): 6.
5. Daniel Boorstin, *The Americans: The Democratic Experience* (New York: Random House, 1973), 539.
6. L. Frank Baum, *The Master Key* (Indianapolis: Bowen-Merrill, 1901), 2–4.
7. Ibid., 10–13, 15.
8. Ibid., 95.
9. Ibid., 99–100.
10. Ibid., 193, 213.
11. Ibid., 236–38.
12. Ibid., 241.
13. Greenes' introduction to *The Master Key*; Baum and MacFall, 156–57.
14. In fact, Santa Claus developed his present character in nineteenth-century America, where Washington Irving described him traveling through the skies in a wagon, Clement Moore portrayed "a right jolly old elf" who comes down the chimney, and Thomas Nast gave him his present familiar appearance in cartoons (Gardner, *Order and Surprise* 170–171). Santa Claus was always very important to Baum as the embodiment of the spirit of Christmas. Santa Claus is by far the most treasured guest at Ozma's birthday party in *The Road to Oz*, where Baum gathered together representatives from almost all his fairylands.
15. L. Frank Baum, *The Life and Adventures of Santa Claus* (New York: Penguin USA, 1986), 8, 28. The Knook in charge of deer was reluctant to let his animals pull a sled, for it is the nature of deer to be wild and free; but "Flossie and Glossie, being deer of much intelligence, had long wished to see the great world, so they

gladly ran over the frozen snow to ask the Knooks if they might carry Claus on his journey," 86–7. Baum approved of curiosity in deer as well as in girls and boys.

16. Ibid., 80.

17. L. Frank Baum,. *A Kidnapped Santa Claus* (Indianapolis: Bobbs-Merrill, 1969), 43.

18. Michael Patrick Hearn, David Greene, and Peter Hanff, *Baum Bugle* 18 (Autumn 1974): 5–9. The play survives in a typescript at the Chicago Historical Society and a printed scenario that differs from it in a few details.

19. L. Frank Baum, *The Enchanted Island of Yew* (Indianapolis: Bobbs-Merrill, 1903), 1–3.

20. Ibid., 52.

21. Ibid., 133, 139.

22. Ibid., 242. Baum had touched on the same issue in *The Life and Adventures of Santa Claus*, where he sketched the development of humanity from its dim medieval past, when people were few and lived in harmony with nature, to the present, complete with apartment houses. What will happen to the idyllic world of Burzee in a completely civilized world filled with humans who cut down forests? Ak suggests a saving compromise: he has guarded the trees to meet the needs of vulnerable humans, but he hopes that they will retain love and respect for Nature and "will not cut down all the trees, for mankind needs the shelter of the woods in summer as much as the warmth of blazing logs in winter" (134; Riley, 82–3).

23. Baum and MacFall, 135–36; Peter Hanff, *Baum Bugle* 17 (Spring 1973): 23–24.

24. Tietjens's diary, at Syracuse University.

25. *Baum Bugle* (Spring 1971): 5–6.

26. Tietjens's diary; Greene and Hearn, 105–6.

27. L. Frank Baum, typescript of original "Wizard" script, Syracuse University, 353; Daniel Mannix, *Baum Bugle* 12 (Christmas 1968): 5–7; Ethan Mordden, *Baum Bugle* 28 (Winter 1984): 8–11.

28. Mannix, 5–7; Mordden, 8–11; Mark Evan Swartz, *Oz Before the Rainbow: L. Frank Baum's "The Wonderful Wizard of Oz" on Stage and Screen to 1939* (Baltimore: Johns Hopkins University Press, 2000), 57.

29. Baum's typescript entered for copyright in the Library of Congress, 1903. The script was changed to a greater or lesser degree in performance. The script used when "The Wizard" played New York, on which Swartz bases his discussion, differs in minor ways from the one described here.

30. Baum and MacFall, 1–2, 9–10; Mordden, *Baum Bugle* 28 (Winter 1984): 8–11; Fred M. Meyer, *Baum Bugle* 6 (August 1962): 5.

31. *Baum Bugle* 38 (Winter 1994):18, 27.

32. Baum and MacFall, 15–16. According to one of Baum's sons, each got over one hundred thousand dollars; according to Tietjens's daughter, the figure was ninety thousand dollars.

33. Clipping in Baum collection, Columbia University.

34. Daniel Mannix, *Baum Bugle* 13 (Spring 1969): 9.

35. Frank Baum Jr., *Baum Bugle* 26 (Winter 1982): 6.

36. Baum and MacFall, 152–53; *Baum Bugle* 6 (Christmas 1962): 16; (Autumn 1972): 17; (Christmas 1973); Greene and Hearn, 44, 119–20, 129.

37. Hough papers in State Historical Society of Iowa; Peter Hanff, "L. Frank Baum's Success and Frustration," *Baum Bugle* 21 (Winter 1977): 25–70. In 1911, Hough sent Baum a sympathetic letter on his bankruptcy (Hanff, 30). Baum's letter of January 8 is misdated 1905.

38. Synopsis in *The Musical Fantasies of L. Frank Baum*, ed. Alla T. Ford and Dick Martin (Chicago: Wizard Press, 1958); *Baum Bugle* 35 (Winter 1991): 2–3.

39. Synopsis in Ford and Martin.

40. *Baum Bugle* 26 (Winter 1982): 6–7.

41. Hearn, ed. *Annotated Wizard of Oz*, xxxviii.

42. Magazine clipping of c. 1901; *Baum Bugle* 11 (Spring 1967): 9.

43. *Baum Bugle* 27 (Spring 1983): 5.

44. Robert Baum in *Baum Bugle* 15 (Spring 1971): 6–7; Baum and MacFall, 168–70.

45. *Baum Bugle* 12 (Autumn 1968): 5; quotation from Baum and MacFall, 168.

46. Baum and MacFall, 168–69.

47. *Baum Bugle* 30 (Spring 1986): 3, 6; (Autumn 1986): 10; letter in Alexander Mitchell Library, Aberdeen, South Dakota.

48. Baum and MacFall, 170–72; *Baum Bugle* 26 (Winter 1982): 7.

49. Ibid.

50. Baum and MacFall, 173. Doctors today would not prescribe resting the brain to cure Bell's palsy. Most patients spontaneously begin recovery in two or three weeks and are well in a few months. This apparently happened in Baum's case, although, according to Frank Junior, he always retained a slight paralysis on the left side of his mouth (Frank Junior's biography, Syracuse University).

51. Letter of 1939 at Yale University.

52. Tietjens's diary, Syracuse University.

53. Eunice Tietjens, *The World at My Shoulder* (New York: Macmillan, 1938), 14–15.

54. Maud Baum, *Baum Bugle* 27 (Spring 1983): 2.

55. *Philadelphia North American*, October 3, 1904, quoted in *Baum Bugle* 29 (Spring 1985): 12; 29 (Christmas 1985): 15.

56. Baum and MacFall, 174–75; Maud in *Baum Bugle* 26 (Winter 1982): 9; 27 (Spring 1983): 2, 6.

57. *Baum Bugle* 29 (Christmas 1985): 13–14.

58. Baum and MacFall, 176.

59. *Baum Bugle* 15 (Spring 1971): 9.

60. Michael Patrick Hearn, *Baum Bugle* 28 (Autumn 1984): 19.

61. L. Frank Baum, *Tamawaca Folks* (USA: Tamawaca Press, 1907), 7, 15, 123–24; note in Frank Junior's copy at Syracuse University.

62. Perhaps Baum's best short story of these years is "The Bad Man," published in *The Home Magazine (of New York)* for February 1901; it is a humorous domestic tale of a father left alone with his three children, which sounds like Baum making fun of himself. The father-narrator has a holiday and looks forward to spending the afternoon reading Emerson, but his wife leaves the children with him, assuring him they will be good and will give him no trouble. First Charlie almost chokes on a shell from his father's collection; then the father must brush off Kitty, who begs him to read them a fairy story, and Maebelle, who teases him to join in a game. He persists in reading Emerson, and finally Kitty tells the others a story

about a Bad Man who they decide should be put in a cage and kept there until he is sorry. Mother has no trouble managing the children and keeping them happy, too. Although Baum was an indulgent father, there must have been times when he wanted to rest quietly; Maud apparently was better at keeping the peace.

6: Reilly & Britton's Star Author 1904–1907

1. Letter of March 7, 1905, in Hearn, *Baum Bugle* 18 (Christmas 1974): 17.
2. *Baum Bugle* 17 (Spring 1973): 24.
3. Hearn, *Baum Bugle* 38 (Winter 1994): 4.
4. Letter of December 27, 1912.
5. This would seem to be one of the magical countries surrounding Oz, since it contains an enormous jackdaws' nest and magic pills work there; but the nest is filled with U.S. dollars. Riley, who emphasizes the development of Baum's fantasy world, points out many discrepancies between Oz in *The Wizard* and Oz in *The Land*, resulting from Baum's need to fit a new story into an existing fairyland. The Ozians are of normal size, rather than child-sized, as in *The Wizard*. In order to accommodate the new history of Oz, the Wizard must be changed from a harmless humbug to a villain who handed over young Ozma to a wicked witch (104–7).
6. L. Frank Baum, *The Marvelous Land of Oz* (Chicago: Reilly & Britton, 1904), 21, 49, 207, 226; Martin Gardner's introduction to Dover Edition.
7. Scott Olsen, *Baum Bugle* 20 (Winter 1976): 4.
8. Baum, *Land of Oz*, 160–61, 206.
9. Ibid., 79–80.
10. Ibid., 148–49.
11. Ibid., 202.
12. Ibid., 173; Stephanie Perrin, "The Works of L. Frank Baum: American Fantasy in Changing Times" (M.A. thesis, Carleton University, 1994), 49–50. Jinjur's love of candy is a playful joke at Maud's expense, for Maud loved candy, and Frank "bought her a box of the finest every week of their married life" (ibid.).
13. Baum, *Land of Oz*, 277. Alas, Ozma retains none of Tip's fun and humanity after she becomes the sweet little girl ruler of Oz; but again and again Baum presents girl protagonists who are as enterprising and have as many adventures as any boy.
14. Letter to Reilly, August 10, 1915; Hearn, *Baum Bugle* 38 (Spring 1994): 20–23, 27; Hearn, ed., *Annotated Wizard*, liii.
15. *Baum Bugle* 8 (Autumn 1964): 5.
16. *Baum Bugle* 23 (Spring 1979): 12–13.
17. Baum may have written some of the *Ozmapolitan* himself. In any case, the content is trifling. Two very similar issues appeared in 1904 and at least one in 1905. No more are recorded in Baum's lifetime. *Baum Bugle* (Christmas 1964), 5.
18. October 2, 1904 story in L. F. Baum Collection, Columbia University; January 22, 1905, in *Baum Bugle* 11 (Autumn 1967): 12–13.
19. Hearn, *Baum Bugle* 38 (Winter 1994): 9.
20. Typescript in the Library of Congress.
21. Hearn, *Baum Bugle* 18 (Christmas 1974): 17.

22. *Baum Bugle* 36 (Spring 1992): 13.

23. Hearn, *Baum Bugle* 18 (Christmas 1974): 19–23; Baum and MacFall, 240.

24. Maud's letters, in Carpenter's diary; L. Frank Baum, *Aunt Jane's Nieces and Uncle John* (Chicago: Reilly & Britton, 1911), 249.

25. Olsen, *Baum Bugle* 20 (Winter 1976): 2.

26. Hotel brochure at Syracuse University.

27. Reported in the *San Diego Union*, February 10; in Olsen, *Baum Bugle* 20 (Winter 1976): 3.

28. Letter to Hough at State Historical Society of Iowa; *Baum Bugle* 15 (Christmas 1971): 22–23; 16 (Spring 1972): 16; 20 (Winter 1976): 2–3, 6; 27 (Spring 1983): 3; 28 (Autumn 1984): 18; Kevin Starr, *Material Dreams* (New York: Oxford University Press, 1990), 65–66; Frank Junior's biography, at Syracuse University; Baum and MacFall, 266.

29. Letter at Columbia University.

30. Baum and MacFall, 165.

31. Fluff persuaded Bud to fulfill his duty of judging differences between the people and advised him how to settle a dispute between two women over the ownership of a cow. In a manner reminiscent of Solomon deciding between the two women who claimed a baby, he awarded the cow to the only one of the women who could milk her. Then, in a whimsical Baumian twist, he discovered that this woman had actually stolen the animal from the other; she just happened to be the one who understood cows. I am reminded of Jim's reaction to the story of Solomon's wise choice in *Huckleberry Finn*.

32. L. Frank Baum, *Queen Zixi of Ix* (New York: Century, 1905), 147, 301.

33. *Baum Bugle* 23 (Spring 1979): 14–18.

34. *Baum Bugle* 12 (Christmas 1968): 21. *Father Goose's Year Book: Quaint Quacks and Feathered Shafts for Mature Children*, one last attempt to capitalize on the success of *Father Goose*, was brought out by Reilly & Britton in 1907. This is a calendar with comic verses by Baum on one side facing a blank page on the other. The verses emphasize the worldly element that appealed to adults in *Father Goose*. The material for January is typical: a seasonal verse on skating, a take-off on a nursery rhyme, and a smart saying based on puns. The rhyme runs:

> Tom, Tom, the piper's son,
> Stole a pig and away he run;
> Which is proof enough, 'tis true,
> Tommy couldn't be a Jew.
> If a Coon, I'm sure that then
> He'd have gone and stole a hen;
> If in politics, you'd find
> He'd have stole the people blind;
> If a Parson, on my soul
> I believe he'd *wear* the stole!

Baum should not be severely blamed for the casual racial slurs that jar on us today, because they were thoughtlessly accepted in his time. There are several objectionably patronizing verses on Irish laziness in *Father Goose*, which are, however, good-humored. Similar slurs on various groups can be found in *Dot and Tot*, *American Fairy Tales*, *The Patchwork Girl of Oz*, *Rinkitink in Oz*, and several books in his teen series, as well as the egregious *Woggle-Bug Book*. These include a rather shocking piece of racism in *Rinkitink*, where Bilbil the goat, who turns out to be a prince transformed by an evil magician, is restored to his proper form. The enchantment is almost too hard for Glinda to break, but she manages by transforming the goat into a series of ascending forms—a lamb, an ostrich (two legs), a tottenhot ("a lower form of a man"), a mifket (one of a horrid group imagined in *John Dough*, but still "a great step in advance"), and finally the prince, 294–5. The Tottenhot that is pronounced subhuman is clearly a Hottentot. In *Mary Louise in the Country* Baum contrasted the racism of the local storekeeper with the more enlightened attitude of Mary Louise and her grandfather toward African Americans. They love their two devoted black servants, who are, however, stereotyped retainers like Nux and Bry. All of these references must be interpreted in terms of the sensibility of Baum's time, less enlightened in this respect than our own.

These are thoughtless lapses, in which Baum unthinkingly went along with contemporary attitudes. When he was applying his mind, he ridiculed ethnic prejudices—how absurdly stupid, as well as pernicious, it is to despise people because they are tall or short (Hiland and Loland), or do or do not appreciate puns (Horners and Hoppers), or have blue skins or pink *(Sky Island)*. The satire on color prejudice in the last book is very telling indeed. One of the few essential principles that members of the Theosophical Society had to accept was abjuring distinctions "of race, creed, sex, caste or colour" (Oltramare, 304).

Baum's editorial in the *Pioneer* that recommended extermination of the remaining Indians (December 20, 1890) is atypical; it may be explained—though not, of course, justified—by his depression at the time and the fears he shared with the other settlers in Dakota.

35. *Baum Bugle* 12 (Christmas 1968): 21.
36. Letters of Reilly to Baum, August 23, 1915, June 17, 1916.
37. *Baum Bugle* 17 (Spring 1973): 24.
38. Michael Patrick Hearn, "When L. Frank Baum was 'Laura Bancroft,' " *American Book Collector* 8 (May 1987): 11–14.
39. L. Frank Baum, *Prairie-Dog Town* (Chicago: Reilly & Britton, 1906), 5, 9.
40. L. Frank Baum, *Bandit Jim Crow* (Chicago: Reilly & Britton, 1906), 60–63. On its popularity, see Hearn, "When . . . Baum was . . . Bancroft," 12.
41. L. Frank Baum, *Mister Woodchuck* (Chicago: Reilly & Britton, 1906), 24–26, 61.
42. Hearn, "When . . . Baum was . . . Bancroft," 11–14.
43. L. Frank Baum, *Annabel* (Chicago: Reilly & Britton, 1906), 189. Indeed, only God or a desperate author could have produced these coincidences. For example, the villain is discovered because he keeps the papers that prove his guilt in an oak tree that he walks to and examines every day.

Edith Van Dyne's novels also strike occasional pious notes. In *The Flying Girl*, Orissa Kane never let her brother work on Sundays, even when there was a pressing need to complete his airplane. In *Mary Louise* there is a cheerful polio victim who is a model of pious resignation. When Myrtle saves her uncle from suicide

on three occasions in *Aunt Jane's Nieces and Uncle John,* it is solemnly attributed to the
hand of God, 265.

44. L. Frank Baum, *Aunt Jane's Nieces* (Chicago: Reilly & Britton, 1906), 32. In a later
book, Baum made explicit that Beth, as well as Patsy, was responding to her
poverty in a sensible, self-respecting way: both girls "had been energetically earning, or preparing to earn, a livelihood" (*Aunt Jane's Nieces Out West* [Chicago: Reilly
& Britton, 1914], 19–20). Their behavior contrasts pointedly with Louise's para-
sitic passivity.

45. Baum, *Aunt Jane's Nieces,* 69, 210, 216.

46. Baum told Britton on February 9, 1912, that the editor of the *Ladies' Home Journal*
had once offered him "$2,500 for the serial rights of a fairy book." He submit-
ted *John Dough* but "it was minus the Cherub. He refused the story unless I would
write in a child character, and I either had a grouch or the big-head and refused
to alter the text. I thought better of his criticism, however, and later wrote in the
Cherub and gave the book to you." Since the book is included in Baum's contract
with Reilly & Britton of October 1905, David Greene supposes it was submitted
to the *Journal* in 1904 (*Baum Bugle* 15 [Autumn 1971]:15).

47. L. Frank Baum, *John Dough and the Cherub* (Chicago: Reilly & Britton, 1906),
303–7.

48. Baum and MacFall, 214.

49. Ibid., 215.

50. Letter from Maud, 1939, at Yale University.

51. *Baum Bugle* 27 (Spring 1983): 5.

52. Maud Gage Baum, *In Other Lands Than Ours* (Delmar, NY: Scholars' Facsimiles
and Reprints, 1983), 12, 79, 141, 145.

53. Although *Aunt Jane's Nieces Abroad* is conventionally dated 1906, Edith and Warren
Hollister argue, in their introduction to *In Other Lands Than Ours,* that it came out in
1907. It could not have been the book he was writing in March and April of 1906
because much of *Aunt Jane's Nieces Abroad,* which features detailed travel description
of every site, is set in places Baum had not yet visited. He probably wrote it on his
return, using Maud's letters to refresh his memory on details. Its predecessor, *Aunt
Jane's Nieces,* was then reissued in a new binding to match the first edition of *Aunt
Jane's Nieces Abroad.* All this suggests that *Aunt Jane's Nieces* was finished before Baum
left and that he wrote *Aunt Jane's Nieces Abroad* after his return, 7–10.

54. Maud wrote: "The town of Bosco Trecase . . . was overwhelmed by a stream of
lava. . . . We walked on lava so hot that it burned my shoes . . . although the general surface looked like lumps of pumice-stone. . . . Houses went down like paper before the lava stream, and vineyards, gardens and fields were covered deep.
[In Naples] We walked . . . ankle deep in ashes, and the trees droop under their
weight," 101, 103. Frank modified this slightly to heighten the dramatic effect:
"With a deep groan of anguish the mountain burst asunder, and from its side
rolled a great stream of molten lava that slowly spread down the slope, con-
suming trees, vineyards and dwellings in its path and overwhelming the fated
city of Bosco-Trecase." He added: "The lava was still so hot that it was liable
to blister the soles of their feet unless they kept constantly moving," and "the
foliage of the trees and shrubbery drooped under its load. . . ." (*Aunt Jane's Nieces*

Abroad [Chicago: Reilly & Britton, 1906], 56, 59, 113; Hollisters' introduction to *In Other Lands*, 6–8).

55. Baum, *Aunt Jane's Nieces Abroad*, 286, 291.

7: *Royal Historian of Oz 1907–1910*

1. Sally Roesch Wagner, *Baum Bugle* 28 (Autumn 1984): 5.
2. L. Frank Baum, *Policeman Bluejay*, intro. David L. Greene (Delmar, NY: Scholars' Facsimiles and Reprints, 1981), 41–42, 53–54.
3. Ibid., 56, 61.
4. Ibid., 71. The book shows Baum's knowledge of, as well as love for, birds: Female eagles are larger than males, and male birds of paradise have fine plumage and gather in a group to dance and display while the drab females watch. He did misinterpret their motives, however, in order to satirize his recurrent target of patriarchy: Actually, the females are deciding which of the competing males to choose as a mate. Baum also erred in having the children transformed into larks, which are strictly grassland (not woodland) birds.
5. Ibid., 54.
6. Ibid., ix–x. In 1915, Baum told Reilly he had "always considered" the *Twinkle Tales* "among my best stories," and he hoped they would some day be combined with *Policeman Bluejay* in a volume called "Baum's Wonder Book." This never happened (Hearn, "Baum . . . Bancroft," 12).
7. L. Frank Baum, *The Last Egyptian* (Philadelphia: Edward Stern, 1908), 200.
8. Letter at Columbia University.
9. Maud Baum, *In Other Lands Than Ours*, 15 (Hollister's introduction), 68, 72, 74, 81–82; L. Frank Baum, *Ozma of Oz* (Chicago: Reilly & Britton, 1907), 103.
10. L. Frank Baum, *Aunt Jane's Nieces at Work* (Chicago: Reilly & Britton, 1909), 10, 50.
11. Ibid., 17, 74.
12. L. Frank Baum, *Sam Steele's Adventures in the Panama* (Chicago: Reilly & Britton, 1907), 178–79, 303–5.
13. Baum was capable of respecting and despising Indians at the same time, largely on the basis of whether they had been corrupted by contact with whites. At the end of *Sam Steele's Adventures in the Panama*, Sam and Uncle Ned feel no qualms about despising the Panamanian Indians who have been exposed to white people and rejoice that they will disappear when Americans move in after the canal is built. The same attitude rationalized his editorial on Indians in the *Aberdeen Saturday Pioneer*.
14. L. Frank Baum, *The Boy Fortune Hunters in Egypt* (Chicago: Reilly & Britton, 1908), 100–101.
15. In Carpenter, Diary.
16. L. Frank Baum, *The Boy Fortune Hunters in Yucatan* (Chicago: Reilly & Britton, 1910), 205, 224.
17. Baum, *Ozma of Oz*, 11 (Author's Note), 271 (Glassman's Afterword).
18. Baum, *Land of Oz*, 285; Riley, *Oz and Beyond*, 137. In *The Land of Oz*, money is used, 60, and understood (the dollar bills in the jackdaws' nest). The Gump has been shot for a trophy, and there is a death penalty for chopping leaves from the royal palm tree, 192, 194.

19. The other girl protagonists, Trot and Betsy, as well as all the boys except Button Bright in *The Road to Oz*, are also noticeably older than Dorothy in *The Wizard.* Neill drew Dorothy as an older child, presumably with Baum's approval; he also dressed her fashionably, unlike Denslow's country child. Neill achieved his flowing and graceful, yet comic and "realistic" style of Oz illustrations in *Ozma of Oz.* His first take on Toto, in *The Road to Oz*, turned him from a small, shaggy terrier to a French bulldog, a breed fashionable in 1909. (In *The Lost Princess* and *The Magic of Oz*, he became a spaniel mix.) On page 163 of *The Road*, Neill indulged in a delicious joke at Denslow's expense: Dorothy and Toto smile at statues of themselves in the Tin Woodman's garden, which represent them as Denslow had.

20. Baum, *Ozma of Oz*, 8.

21. Ibid., 123. Roger Sale finely appreciates the natural-seeming opening of *Ozma of Oz*. Baum "moves, totally without self-consciousness, from a real world to an improbable world to a magic world.... We do not classify each situation according to how realistic or magical it is because Dorothy and Baum do not; instead, they take each one as it comes" ("L. Frank Baum, and Oz," *Hudson Review* 25 [Winter 1972–73]: 578).

22. L. Frank Baum, *The Emerald City of Oz* (Chicago: Reilly & Britton, 1910), 71. This is barely possible, although it would not have been appropriate to spell out details. A hen can produce fertile eggs a month after impregnation, and Billina could have subsequently mated with her sons.

23. Baum, *Ozma of Oz*, p. 55. Tiktok becomes Tik-Tok in his own book, *Tik-Tok of Oz*. Similarly, the shaggy man in *The Road to Oz* becomes the Shaggy Man in *The Patchwork Girl of Oz* and Shaggy Man in *Tik-Tok of Oz*, and the Saw-Horse of *The Land of Oz* and *Ozma of Oz* becomes the Sawhorse in *Dorothy and the Wizard in Oz*. Baum did not always maintain consistency from book to book, and I have followed his usage in whatever particular book I am discussing.

24. Paul Abrahm and S. Kenter, "Tik-Tok and the Three Laws of Robotics," *Science-Fiction Studies* 5 (March 1978): 68.

25. Baum must have been making one of his jokes when he said he changed *gnome* to *nome* because the unpronounced *g* would confuse children. The author who named the Phanfasms (*Emerald City*) and the Arch of Phinis (*Sky Island*) was not worried about puzzling his child readers with spelling problems. Probably he just wanted to make his underground spirits distinctive.

    While the Queen and Princes of Ev are imprisoned by the Nome King, Ev is ruled by Princess Langwidere, a satire of one of Baum's favorite targets, the empty society woman. Better equipped than the ordinary woman of fashion, who can vary her appearance only by changing her clothes, Langwidere can change her face: She has thirty beautiful heads, which she distinguishes by their appearance alone. While the identity of an ordinary woman of fashion depends too much on clothes, Langwidere could be said to have given up her identity altogether. Oblivious to the fact that a head includes a brain as well as a face, she cannot see why Dorothy should object to exchange her head for one of Langwidere's thirty. Incidentally, this is another indication that Dorothy is older than in *The Wizard*, since Langwidere would not want the head of a small child. Langwidere is totally languid, except when her will is crossed, and wearied by the ten minutes a day she must spend governing the country.

26. The Nome army's wonderfully anachronistic equipment is another realization of the child's outlook: an electric light that could be worn, advanced modern technology for 1907, and bronze weapons, exotically antique, would seem equally magical to a child, and thus equally suitable to a race of supernatural beings.

The ineffective army of Oz (as well as Merryland, where the Queen has a guard of wooden soldiers that do nothing but drill) is partly a general satire on the military, but mostly an indication that a good government could not have an effective army because it would not settle its problems with military force.

27. Baum, *Ozma of Oz*, 180.

28. Even the episode of the Braided Man of Pyramid Mountain illustrates the dispirited level of this book. Instead of being presented as an engaging eccentric, he is flatly diagnosed as crazy, 108.

29. Baum, *Santa Claus*, 94.

30. Contrast the more sensible, less self-righteous attitude implicit in the *Animal Fairy Tales* and *Policeman Bluejay*, where animals are criminal only if they violate Nature's Law by going against the character Nature gave them.

31. Mark Evan Swartz, in *Oz before the Rainbow* (Baltimore: Johns Hopkins University Press, 2000), points out that many other lecturers of Baum's time illustrated their talks with films and slides; however, Baum's show must have been far more dramatic. Swartz questions Baum's explanation of the *radio* in Radio Plays, since Duval Frères were credited with the coloring and he found no evidence of Radio's existence, 162.

32. Ibid., 162.

33. *New York Herald*, September 26, 1909.

34. However, his giving an interview on the wonders of the Radio Plays to a New York newspaper in September of the following year suggests that he was hoping to revive them. Although MacFall said the show closed on December 16, Swartz gives the date as December 31, based on advertisements in the *New York Times*, 162.

35. Reviews from *Milwaukee News* and St. Paul *News* quoted Russell MacFall, *Baum Bugle* 6 (Autumn 1962): 3–4; Richard A. Mills, *Baum Bugle* 14 (Christmas 1970): 4–7.

36. Baum inscribed a charming fantasy in the copy of *The Road* he presented to his grandson on July 14, 1909, his first birthday. "Once upon a time the Storks brought a baby to Frank Joslyn and Helen Snow Baum, and the baby was so smiling and sweet and merry that he won his way to all hearts—those of strangers as well as of his doting relations. For, as the Stork was flying Earthward, it met the Love Fairy, who stopped to kiss the babe; and next the Laughing Fay tossed it in his arms; and then Glinda the Good blessed it and decreed it happiness. So on the Stork flew with its burden until it passed the Emerald City, where the Shaggy Man took the Love Magnet from the great gates and pressed it against the infant's brow," *Baum Bugle* 8 (Christmas 1964): 9.

37. Daniel Mannix, *Baum Bugle* 34 (Autumn 1990): 4, 7.

38. L. Frank Baum, *The Road to Oz* (Chicago: Reilly & Britton, 1909): 196, 199.

39. Fluff is older and more responsible than Bud in *Queen Zixi*, Dot is older than Tot in *Dot and Tot in Merryland*, Twinkle usually takes the lead over Chubbins, and Dorothy is more self-possessed than Zeb in *Dorothy and the Wizard*. Button Bright has matured somewhat in *Sky Island* and *The Lost Princess of Oz*, but he remains shiftless and irresponsible in contrast to the girls.

In "L. Frank Baum, and Oz," Roger Sale points out that the introduction of Button Bright in *The Road to Oz* is perfectly timed: we would not accept his strangeness if he were brought in before the confusion of roads, and it would mean less if he were brought in after the magical villages of foxes and donkeys, 583. The same might be said of the Shaggy Man's Love Magnet, introduced immediately after the confusion of roads, which bestows a mysterious magical aura on a man who had appeared to be an ordinary tramp.

40. Baum, *Road to Oz*, 91.
41. Daniel Mannix, *Baum Bugle* 34 (Autumn 1990): 4, 7. Similarly, as Hearn points out, the Kalidahs of *The Wizard*, with bodies like bears and heads like tigers, could have come from the children's picture books in which pages are sectioned so that figures' body parts can be mismatched by flipping sections back and forth.
42. Sale, "Baum and Oz," 576.
43. Hence, the good sorceress Glinda never deals in them (Baum, *Land of Oz*, 273).
44. Baum, *Emerald City of Oz*, 49–50.
45. Ibid., 11, 12.
46. Ibid., 42, 125. Phanfasms must be phantasms, something apparently seen but having no physical reality; their true forms can never be known because they control people's perceptions. The Phanfasms may be related to the hideous thoughts without physical body that Besant described on the theosophical astral plane.
47. Ibid., 116.
48. Baum, *Road to Oz*, 165, 172, 191.
49. Baum, *Emerald City of Oz*, 29–31.
50. Ibid., 127.
51. Edward Bellamy, *Looking Backward 2000–1887* (New York: Modern Library, 1951), 69, 125.
52. Ibid., 212.
53. William Morris, *News from Nowhere and Selected Writings* (New York: Penguin Books, 1984), 191–92, 221, 238, 270.
54. Baum, *Emerald City of Oz*, 31.
55. Ibid., 41–42.
56. Sale, "Baum and Oz," 585.
57. The *New York Times* did give Baum a laudatory obituary (May 11, 1919), although it is a little patronizing and not very discriminating. "Years from now, though the children cannot clamor for the newest Oz book, the crowding generations will plead for the old ones." Still, the writer found a weakness in Baum's fairy stories, resulting from his disbelief in fairies. This is true only in a narrow technical sense, for Baum certainly did believe in the validity of an imaginative world beyond this one, which is the essential requisite for fantasy.

8: A New Life in California 1909–1914

1. Their address was 2322 Toberman Street, Los Angeles.
2. Baum papers, Syracuse University. Baum wrote to Reilly on December 13, 1915,

that the copyrights were to return to him once the debt was cleared, but that one creditor had recently told him that he was getting only about the interest due. Baum suspected, probably rightly, that the creditors were "being swindled somewhere." Even in 1931, Maud could not get any satisfaction from Bobbs-Merrill. At least she got the profit when the motion picture rights in *The Wizard* were sold to Samuel Goldwyn in 1934, when a careful copyright search "indicated that the rights in the book were the property of Mrs. Baum" (Hanff, *Baum Bugle* 17 [Spring 1973]: 25; Baum papers, Syracuse University).

3. Daniel Boorstin, *The Americans: The Democratic Experience* (New York: Random House, 1973), 274.
4. The original address of the house was 149 North Magnolia Avenue, and so it remained at least until May 1912. By October it had been changed to 1749 Cherokee Avenue.

   Although Matilda Joslyn Gage had been chronically strapped for cash, she had owned thousands of dollars' worth of real property—land and houses—in Fayetteville, East Syracuse, and Dakota. Presumably this had recently been sold, providing the inheritance for Maud.
5. Baum and MacFall, 264–65; Maud in *Baum Bugle* 27 (Spring 1983): 4; letter at Syracuse University.
6. Copy of bankruptcy proceedings, Syracuse University.
7. Baum and MacFall, 276.
8. Letter to MacFall, Syracuse University.
9. Fragment of undated letter in Wagner, *Baum Bugle* 28 (Autumn 1984): 5.
10. Letter of October 12, 1914, Syracuse University.
11. Matilda's reminiscences from *Baum Bugle* 30 (Autumn 1986) 12; Ozma's from 38 (Winter 1994), 11, 13.
12. Baum and MacFall, 268–69; Maud in *Baum Bugle* 27 (Spring 1983): 4.
13. Frank Junior's biography, Syracuse University, 68, 300.
14. Maud in *Baum Bugle* 27 (Spring 1983): 4; Baum and MacFall, 268–69.
15. Harry Baum, "How My Father Wrote the Oz Books," *American Book Collector* (December 1962), 17.
16. *Baum Bugle* 26 (Winter 1982): 10.
17. Letter dated January 23, 1912. The dates come from a Reilly & Britton folder that holds the manuscript of *Glinda of Oz* at the Library of Congress. It was evidently used to hold Baum's manuscripts as they successively came into the office.
18. L. Frank Baum, *Glinda of Oz* (Chicago: Reilly & Lee, 1920), 20.
19. Letter from Guy Bogart, the father, at Syracuse University.
20. Baum's answers to letters also directly promoted sales of his books, because, from the autumn of 1916, he used stationery bordered by pictures of the covers of his fourteen most recent books. Children would see these, he pointed out, and demand the titles they did not already have (to Reilly, August 15, 1917, probably a slip for 1916).
21. Baum and MacFall, 266–68.
22. *Baum Bugle* 20 (Winter 1976): 5; 30 (Spring 1986): 3; (Autumn 1986): 11.
23. Letter in Alexander Mitchell Library. Before America entered the war, anti-British was as widespread as anti-German feeling (*TLS*, November 12, 1999).
24. Baum and MacFall, Foreword, 250.
25. *Baum Bugle* 12 (Autumn 1968): 10.

26. Letter from Baum to Britton, November 6, 1912.

27. MacFall, *Baum Bugle* 11 (Autumn 1967): 3.

28. Ozma Baum Mantele, "Kenneth Gage Baum," foreword to his *The Dinamonster of Oz.*

29. Hearn, ed., *Annotated Wizard of Oz*, 271, note 17.

30. Betty Lou Young, *Rustic Canyon and the Story of the Uplifters* (Santa Monica: Casa Vieja Press, 1975), 56.

31. A selection of verses given at the "Spring Poets Dinners" of 1914, 1915, and 1916 was edited by Baum, the "Poet Laureate of the Uplifters," and privately printed as *Songs of Spring.* Baum included five undistinguished verses of his own, of which the best is a graceful, upbeat epitaph on an Uplifter who had died of heart disease ("Claudius Raymond").

32. Baum and MacFall, 257–58.

33. L. Frank Baum, *The Uplift of Lucifer, or Raising Hell* (Los Angeles, 1963), 12, 40. Imp olite, Imp oster, Imp ashunt, Imp rudent were recycled from Imps Olite, Udent, and Ertinent in "Ozma and the Little Wizard" in the *Little Wizard Stories of Oz.* Four songs from *The Uplift of Lucifer, or Raising Hell* and other shows have been reprinted as *The High-Jinks of L. Frank Baum.*

   The old boys' jeer at women's clubs shows Baum thoughtlessly conforming to the male chauvinist humor that prevailed in old-fashioned men's clubs. He must have been aware that women's clubs such as the WCTU provided a major way for women to attain political influence, a cause that in serious moments Baum approved and considered very important.

34. Baum and MacFall, 257–58. Baum also, according to Olsen, played the role of the trainer of the "Educated Frog" in his playlet "Sim Crabill's Circus," *Baum Bugle* 20 (Winter 1976): 5.

35. Letter from Baum to Reilly, February 9, 1912.

36. *Baum Bugle* 15 (Christmas 1971): 22; Hearn, ed., *Annotated Wizard*, 372.

37. L. Frank Baum, "The Girl from Oz," 18, 22–23. The song "When in Trouble Come to Papa," later used in "The Tik-Tok Man of Oz," was written for this play. Frank Junior wrote an adaptation for film or television, but it was never accepted for production. Typescripts of both are at the University of Syracuse.

38. L. Frank Baum, *The Boy Fortune Hunters in the South Seas* (Chicago: Reilly & Britton, 1911), 182, 254. By January 28, 1915, Baum noticed that Reilly & Britton were no longer advertising these books and asked Reilly plaintively if they were "quite dead and out of print." Reilly confirmed this on February 2.

39. L. Frank Baum, *Aunt Jane's Nieces and Uncle John* (Chicago: Reilly & Britton, 1911), 223.

40. L. Frank Baum, *Aunt Jane's Nieces on Vacation* (Chicago: Reilly & Britton, 1912), 66, 71–72, 90.

41. Ibid., 104, 165–79. The title of this book seems inappropriate, and indeed Baum had named it *Aunt Jane's Nieces in Journalism.* Reilly & Britton changed his title without informing him, and Baum retorted with an angry letter on April 10, 1912.

42. *Baum Bugle* 32 (Autumn 1988): 24.

43. L. Frank Baum, *The Flying Girl* (Chicago: Reilly & Britton, 1911), 26, 154, 160, 161, 225.

44. L. Frank Baum, *The Flying Girl and Her Chum* (Chicago: Reilly & Britton, 1912), 21.

45. L. Frank Baum, *The Daring Twins* (Chicago: Reilly & Britton, 1911), 25.

46. A sequel published the following year, *Phoebe Daring: A Story for Young Folk*, also centers on a theft of which a good man is accused. Phoebe exerts herself to find the real culprit and succeeds in solving the mystery. In all this story the only touch distinctive of Baum is a gratuitous pitch for woman suffrage, 153. He wrote a third Daring book and envisioned an unending series, featuring the younger Daring children and then their children (letter to Britton, October 15, 1912). Two titles appear in Baum's correspondence with Britton, "Phoebe Daring, Conspirator" and "Phil Daring's Experiment," which was changed to "The Daring Twins' Experiment." It is not clear whether these titles refer to the same or two different books. The label on the binder that now holds the manuscript of *Glinda of Oz* indicates that it once held a manuscript called "Phoebe Daring, 'Conspirator.' " But evidently the series was not successful enough to warrant continuation beyond the second book.

47. P. 106, detached story in Baum Collection, Columbia University.

48. Baum and MacFall, 194.

49. L. Frank Baum, *The Sea Fairies* (Chicago: Reilly & Britton, 1911), 104–5. Apart from Baum's personal resentment against the Standard Oil Company, it had become the type of the unscrupulous monopoly ever since Henry Demarest Lloyd's expose in the *Atlantic Monthly* of March 1881, "The Story of a Great Monopoly," where he had pictured it as an octopus.

50. Baum, *Sea Fairies*, 88–90.

51. Ibid., 148, 236.

52. L. Frank Baum, *Sky Island* (Chicago: Reilly & Britton, 1912), 44, 58, 63–64; Jonathan Swift, *The Writings* (New York: W. W. Norton, 1973), 30.

53. Baum, *Sky Island*, 76–77; Swift, 161; Ruth Berman, *Baum Bugle* 8 (Christmas 1964): 12–13. Berman points out also that the Woggle-Bug's Tablets of Learning are modeled on the wafers with mathematical propositions written on them that a professor at the Academy of Lagado forces his students to swallow (159).

54. Baum, *Sky Island*, 147, 157. It later develops, though, that the ruler of the Pink Country is, by law, the person with the lightest skin. This produces the absurd result that Trot, a foreigner, becomes Queen of the Pinkies.

55. Hearn, *Baum Bugle* 38 (Spring 1994): 27.

56. Hanff, *Baum Bugle* 17 (Spring 1973): 24–25.

57. On receiving the last of the *Little Wizard* stories, Britton wrote on October 7, 1912, to remonstrate with Baum on what seemed to him excess violence; he seems overly timid, in view of what he passed in other books. *Little Dorothy and Toto* originally ended with Toto eating up the giant who reduced himself to miniature size, and Britton suggested that the giant increase in size just in time and turn into the Wizard, who he had been all along. Britton also objected to an apparent murder and ghost in *Tik-Tok and the Nome King* (which Baum had lifted from his script for "Ozma of Oz," later "The Tik-Tok Man of Oz"). Britton also tactfully suggested that *The Scarecrow and the Tin Woodman* was weak. Baum's reply, a week later, showed annoyance; but he replaced the ending of the first story as Britton advised; he thought Britton's comments on *Tik-Tok and the Nome King* absurd, but slightly revised the story; and he wrote an entirely new *Scarecrow and the Tin Woodman*, which is still poor, no doubt because of the haste with which it was written (October 15).

58. *Baum Bugle* 11 (Autumn 1967): 17.

59. L. Frank Baum, *The Patchwork Girl of Oz* (Chicago: Reilly & Britton, 1913), 40.

60. Ibid., 209.

61. Ibid., 68, 338.

62. Ibid., 280–81, 329.

63. Ibid., 119–20.

64. *Baum Bugle* 10 (Christmas 1966): 5. This chapter fit between the escape from the giant Yoop and the meeting with the Hoppers.

65. *Baum Bugle* 28 (Autumn 1984): 11–12; Hearn, *Baum Bugle* 38 (Spring 1994): 28.

66. Hearn, *Baum Bugle* 38 (Spring 1994): 27–28; Baum and MacFall, 232.

67. Letter of November 27; Hearn, *Baum Bugle* 38 (Spring 1994): 27–28.

68. L. Frank Baum, "Ozma of Oz," 96. The script of "Ozma," as well as synopses of "The Rainbow's Daughter" and "Ozma of Oz," are in the Theater Collection, New York Public Library.

69. "The Rainbow's Daughter," 5–6. Baum used the standard spelling, Gnomes, in his scenario; but they are the same as the Nomes of the Oz books. Mannix argues persuasively that Baum's special effects were inspired by a contemporary Metropolitan Opera production of Wagner's *Ring of the Nibelungs.* Wagner's gods entered Valhalla over a rainbow bridge in *The Rhinegold,* and the characters in *Tik-Tok* crossed a chasm on a rainbow that Polychrome asked her father to send down. As Siegfried beat out his sword on the anvil in *Siegfried,* a shower of variegated colored sparks appeared at every blow, like the anvils struck by the chorus of gnomes in the Gnome King's cavern. The Metropolitan Opera's dragon Fafner was a mechanical marvel: he had red searchlight eyes "that swept alarmingly over the stage and even breathed smoke and flames by a bellows arrangement... his breath smelt of brimstone." He moved very slowly, with a great grinding of gears. It would have been too expensive to include a dragon in Baum's show, but one is prominent in his book *Tik-Tok of Oz,* and slow, creaking dragons draw chariots in Thi in *The Lost Princess of Oz* (*Baum Bugle* 22 [Spring 1978]: 7–8).

70. *Baum Bugle* 39 (Spring 1995): 9.

71. In 1910, there were ten thousand movie theaters playing to a nationwide audience of over ten million weekly. At first, movies were simply motion-picture filming of actual life, such as waves rolling in on a beach or part of a prizefight. By 1900, films told simple stories, like the eleven-minute *Great Train Robbery* of 1903. By 1914, full-length dramas appeared, such as Mack Sennett's *Tillie's Punctured Romance,* with Marie Dressler and Chaplin. See Thomas J. Schlereth, *Victorian America* (New York: HarperCollins, 1991), 200–5.

72. L. Frank Baum, *Aunt Jane's Nieces Out West* (Chicago: Reilly & Britton, 1914), 151.

73. Baum and MacFall, 258–59; *Baum Bugle* 16 (Christmas 1972): 5.

74. Richard Mills and David Greene, *Baum Bugle* 17 (Spring 1973): 7, 11; (Autumn 1973): 5, 7–10, 14. Prints of *The Patchwork Girl, The Magic Cloak,* and *His Majesty the Scarecrow* exist in the Library of Congress. The adult films seem to have been lost, but there are synopses of all the full-length films in *The American Film Institute Catalog of Motion Pictures... Feature Films, 1911–1920* (Berkeley: University of California Press, 1988). There are copyright statements for two of *Violet's Dreams, The Magic Bonbons* (based on a story by Baum), and *The Country Circus* (centering on the same little girl), dated October and September 1915, which Hearn believes are probably by Baum.

   Baum was involved in one last theatrical project in December 1916, when

William Lee of Reilly & Britton reported an opportunity to rewrite the script for an extravaganza on Snow White, which was to be produced in New York with scenes and costumes designed by Maxfield Parrish. This, Lee told Reilly, "promises to let Baum get some of the cash he is clamoring for." Reilly & Britton were to publish the story, written by Baum and illustrated with Parrish's pictures. There was some negotiation about advances and royalty percentages, but ultimately the project came to nothing (letters from Lee to Reilly, December 7, 1916; Reilly to Baum, December 11; Baum to Reilly, December 16; Reilly to Lee, December 20; Reilly to Baum, December 26).

75. Frank J. Baum, "The Oz Film Manufacturing Company," *Films in Review* 7 (August–September 1956): 329–33; Mills and Greene, *Baum Bugle* 17 (Christmas 1973): 6–8.

76. Newspaper clipping reprinted in *Baum Bugle* 11 (Autumn 1967): 18–19.

9: *A Writer to the End 1914–1919*

1. Baum and MacFall, 269–70.

2. The many similarities between *Tik-Tok of Oz* and *Ozma of Oz*, mentioned in my discussion of the "Tik-Tok Man" show, result of course from the fact that the show was ultimately based on *Ozma*.

3. Although the roses are primarily unpleasant, because they have some animal powers but lack animal hearts, the detail with which Baum depicted them reflects his new interest in flowers after he became a serious gardener at Ozcot. The Rose Kingdom may have been inspired by Lewis Carroll's Garden of Live Flowers in *Through the Looking Glass.*

4. L. Frank Baum, *Tik-Tok of Oz* (Chicago: Reilly & Britton, 1914), 22–23. At one point the army of Oogaboo is terrified by the Rak, a monster that, as Harold Miner points out, has many similarities to an automobile (kar). It is a "terrible beast with a horrible appetite" with "a glowing furnace of fire" inside its body and two glowing eyes; it "breathes in air and breathes out smoke, which darkens the sky for miles around," and it "feeds on any living thing." See *Tik-Tok*, 32; *Baum Bugle* 19 (Winter 1975): 3.

5. Baum, *Tik-Tok*, 157.

6. Hearn, *Baum Bugle* 38 (Spring 1994): 28. Earlier Oz titles were also reissued in cost-cutting formats at this time.

7. L. Frank Baum, *The Scarecrow of Oz* (Chicago: Reilly & Britton, 1915), 54, 78.

8. Button Bright has lost the competence and enterprise he showed in *Sky Island*. While the Scarecrow asks Trot's advice as though she were an adult, 234, "no one thought of asking Button Bright's opinion," 118.

9. Baum, *The Scarecrow*, 152–53, 244.

10. Hearn, *Baum Bugle* 38 (Spring 1994): 29.

11. Letters from Baum to Reilly, August 10, July 15; from Reilly to Baum, July 20, August 23, 1915.

12. Hearn, *Baum Bugle* 38 (Spring 1994): 31.

13. Also, animals do not talk, as in Baum's later fairylands—Oz, Ev, and the Nome Kingdom. Bilbil is an exception, remarked on by several characters. The interplay

between relentlessly cheerful Rinkitink and his pessimistic goat is amusing in it-self and provides further evidence that Baum did not promote fatuous optimism in his stories. Whenever Rinkitink's good humor and positive thinking become too cloying, the goat Bilbil deflates him with a well-aimed sneer.

14. Baum first used the idea of the monarch of an underground kingdom holding a prisoner in the play *Prince Silverwings*. Then he developed it in his 1905 story about Rinkitink. When he put that story aside, he used the idea in *Ozma of Oz*, where the Nome King put the would-be rescuers to perilous trials and showed Ozma his enormous army as Kaliko showed Inga in "Rinkitink." Then the theme appeared in Baum's plays based on *Ozma* and in *Tik-Tok of Oz*, and at last in the fi-nal version of "Rinkitink," *Rinkitink in Oz*.

15. L. Frank Baum, *Rinkitink in Oz* (Chicago: Reilly & Britton, 1916), 283, 290.

16. L. Frank Baum, *The Lost Princess of Oz* (Chicago: Reilly & Britton, 1917), 42, 239.

17. Ibid., 117.

18. Ibid., 148.

19. At one point in this contest, Ugu turns the hall in which they are all standing up-side down; he remains in a cage secured to the floor, while all the others slide down into the dome of the roof. This episode was inspired by a trick in an amusement park in San Francisco, in which visitors were induced to believe they were turning upside down, when in fact it was the room around them that was turning. See Daniel Mannix, *Baum Bugle* 31 (Spring 1987): 15–6.

20. Baum, *Lost Princess*, 289.

21. L. Frank Baum, *Aunt Jane's Nieces in the Red Cross* (Chicago: Reilly & Britton, 1915), 5, 11–12.

22. Ibid., 115–16, 256.

23. In the same letter (October 25), Baum accepted Reilly & Britton's additional plan for raising money: four (ultimately six) small books for tots, called *The Snuggle Tales* and consisting of selections from *L. Frank Baum's Juvenile Speaker*, which itself con-sisted of reprinted material (1916, 1917). These were reissued as the *Oz-Man Tales* in 1920.

24. Baum, *Aunt Jane's Nieces in the Red Cross* (Chicago: Reilly & Lee, 1918), 258–59, 262, 269–70. Baum's attitude had changed amusingly since the days when he ed-ited the *Pioneer*. He had predicted that the new kaiser would lead the German people to glory and called Germany "the first among civilized nations of the World. Our grand-children may witness the decline of Germany's greatness—we or our children never will" (March 29, 1890, 4).

25. L. Frank Baum, *Mary Louise in the Country* (Chicago: Reilly & Britton, 1916), 152, 211, 261. Although Baum sympathized with Ireland's desire for independence, he believed it was a lost cause when the Easter Rebellion failed (263).

26. Baum had planned to write "Mary Louise on the Great Lakes" and "Mary Louise in the City" (to Reilly, November 23, 1916), but evidently was too ill to do so.

27. L. Frank Baum, *Mary Louise and the Liberty Girls* (Chicago: Reilly & Lee, 1918), 5, 10, 16.

28. Ibid., 78, 80, 82–83. The home-grown traitor in *Mary Louise and the Liberty Girls* is "Professor" Dyer, the Superintendent of Schools, who got his job by political in-fluence alone. Baum may have been recalling his campaign against the incompe-

tent, overpaid local school superintendent in the *Aberdeen Saturday Pioneer*. There are two other German-Americans in the book who are also suspected of treason and who also prove to be loyal Americans.

29. Letter to Reilly, January 8, 1916. *Mary Louise Adopts a Soldier* (1919), the last book in the series to be published in Baum's lifetime, is not by him; it may have been written by his son Harry (Hearn, ed., *Annotated Wizard*, 387).

30. "The Diamondback" was reprinted in the *Baum Bugle* 26 (Spring, 1982): 7–9; "Chrome Yellow" survives in manuscript at Syracuse University. Baum's letter to Reilly of October 25, 1915, reports the fate of these two stories and mentions two others, "Mr. Rumple's Chill" and "Bess of the Movies," now evidently lost, as is a novel called *Molly Oodle*. According to a notation on the Reilly & Britton folder that covers the manuscript of *Glinda of Oz*, *Molly Oodle* was a full-length novel (63,000 words) finished, and presumably sent to the publisher, on September 7, 1915.

31. Lee's letter is found with the Baum-Reilly and Britton correspondence, obtained courtesy of Robert Baum.

32. Thompson confirmed that the claim that she had written *The Royal Book of Oz* from Baum's notes "was a pleasant little fiction invented by the publishers to make the break between Baum's books and mine" (letter at Columbia University).

33. After living on Baum's royalties for over thirty years, Maud still left an estate of over eighty-five thousand dollars. Copies of both wills are at Syracuse University. I base my statement that he finished *Glinda* on February 17 on my reading of a garbled note accompanying the manuscript, which says it was "finished the night before L F entered histepal [?]."

34. L. Frank Baum, *The Tin Woodman of Oz* (Chicago: Reilly & Britton, 1918), 14, 15. See Martin Gardner, *Baum Bugle* 40 (Autumn 1996): 17.

35. Baum, *Tin Woodman of Oz*, 29, 31.

36. Ibid., 33–34, 38–39.

37. Janet Feigenbaum, review in *Times Literary Supplement* (October 30, 1998), 14. The Tin Soldier was particularly mortified by Chopfyt because Chopfyt had his original head, but the Tin Woodman was equally mortified by his own original head, which he found in a cupboard. The disembodied head could not feel because a head is "made to think," but it had not thought for years, because in a cupboard it had nothing to think about, 213. Baum may be suggesting that thinking is impossible without feeling. Like Chopfyt, the head has lost its memory.

38. Baum, *Tin Woodman of Oz*, 278.

39. Ibid., 75, 84.

40. Ibid., 23, 29, 34; manuscript draft, 5, 7, 10.

41. Ibid., 71, 74, 75, 102, 104, 108; manuscript draft, 29, 31, 43, 44, 46.

42. Ibid., 173–78, 283; manuscript draft, 113.

43. Ibid., 250. The manuscript draft of *The Tin Woodman of Oz* is at the Harry Ransom Humanities Research Center at the University of Texas; the intermediate draft of chapters nineteen and twenty, at Yale University. Some examples of small revisions Baum made in his draft of chapter nineteen are replacing *said* with the more precise *admitted*, adding a phrase to make explicit that Woot could hear the tin men even

though he could not see them, replacing *pushed* with the more emphatic *managed to push*, deleting the adjective *dancing* that describes Polychrome because it has been too often repeated (Yale ms. 3, *Tin Woodman of Oz*, 232, 234). Examples of male conceit that Baum inserted into his early draft include the Scarecrow's remark that the Hip-po-gy-raf is a philosopher because he eats what is available to avoid going hungry and the beast's deflating reply—"No, I'm just a Hip-po-gy-raf"—and the detail that, after his dent was healed, the Tin Woodman strutted "around to show his fine figure" (Yale ms. 10, 11, *Tin Woodman of Oz*, 243, 249).

It would be tedious to list the constant small changes and amplifications Baum made throughout his original manuscript. He changed one name for the sake of propriety: the balloon woman Sal Loon became Til Loon, perhaps at his publishers' suggestion. He toned down Ku-Klip's graphic description of what he did with the original body parts of the two tin men (ms., 98–9, *Tin Woodman of Oz*, 223–5). Baum added details to clarify the symbolic significance of the Tin Woodman's disembodied head (ms, 92–3, *Tin Woodman of Oz*, 210–6). He revised his account of the climactic final meeting to emphasize Nimmie Amee's un-friendliness, Chopfyt's disagreeableness, and his henpecked state: Nimmie Amee looked "at them in *cold* surprise"; her house was "neatly furnished *and well swept and dusted*"; instead of giving the visitors a short nod and looking away, Chopfyt glared at them and looked away with a scowl; Nimmie Amee explains that "he is now trained to draw the water and carry in the wood and hoe the cabbages and weed the flower-beds *and dust the furniture and perform many tasks of a like character*. A new husband would have to be scolded—*and gently chided*—until he learns my ways" (ms., 108–10, *Tin Woodman of Oz*, 273–8; italicized words were added).

44. Baum and MacFall, 234. Specifically, in 1918, 3,914 copies were sold of *The Land of Oz*, 3,138 of *Ozma of Oz*, 3,360 of *Dorothy and the Wizard in Oz*, 2,657 of *The Road to Oz*, 2,811 of *The Emerald City of Oz*, 2,839 of *The Patchwork Girl of Oz*, 2,774 of *Tik-Tok of Oz*, 2,926 of *The Scarecrow of Oz*, 2,731 of *Rinkitink in Oz*, 4,139 of *The Lost Princess of Oz*, and 18,600 of *The Tin Woodman of Oz*.

In 1919, 7,387 copies of *The Land of Oz* were sold, 6,398 of *Ozma of Oz*, 6,323 of *Dorothy and the Wizard in Oz*, 5,584 of *The Road to Oz*, 5,721 of *The Emerald City of Oz*, 6,205 of *The Patchwork Girl of Oz*, 5,564 of *Tik-Tok of Oz*, 6,071 of *The Scarecrow of Oz*, 5,821 of *Rinkitink in Oz*, 6,622 of *The Lost Princess of Oz*, 7,439 of *The Tin Woodman of Oz*, and 26,219 of *The Magic of Oz*. *The Wizard of Oz* is not in-cluded because after his settlement with Rountree, Baum no longer received the royalties on any of his Bobbs-Merrill titles.

45. The Prices of Baum's books come from his publishers' advertisements in *Publishers' Weekly*, 93 (Jan.–June 1918), 95 (Jan.–June 1919).

46. Baum and MacFall, 270–72.

47. Warren Hollister, *Baum Bugle* 14 (Spring 1970): 9–11. He adds that, when Ruggedo tells his troubles to Kiki Aru, he rationalizes that he was kicked out of his country because "it's the fashion to kick kings nowadays" and goes on to say he had to abdicate, which, he explains to Kiki, "means to be kicked out," 35, a probable reference to Czar Nicholas II, who was forced to abdicate in March 1917.

48. L. Frank Baum, *The Magic of Oz* (Chicago: Reilly & Lee, 1919), 88.

49. Letters of November 1 and November 5, 1918. Probably for the same reason, and perhaps at his publishers' urging, Baum added a few paragraphs at the end of chapter 14 of *The Tin Woodman of Oz*, to explain how Mrs. Yoop would manage to survive even in the form of a green monkey.

50. Baum, *The Magic of Oz*, 175.

51. Ibid., 79, 116–18, 202–6; manuscript draft, 35. Generally, Baum carefully removed repeated words when he revised his manuscripts. But in a paragraph on page 59 he twice used "curious" to describe the Glass Cat. On the other hand, he did replace a number of words with more precise ones (e.g., Trot and Cap'n Bill will carry the Magic Flower "home with you" instead of "home again") and removed excess words (e.g., the Lonesome Duck "swam gracefully around up the bend of [the] stream" became "swam gracefully away") and tautological statements (e.g., the last clause from the sentence: some of the forest animals "wanted to fight the Oz people, some wanted to be transformed, and some wanted to do nothing at all [so they could not agree]" (*Magic*, 103, 132, 182; ms., 48, 60, 90). In his manuscript he first wrote that Ozma looked only fifteen years old and then altered the number to twelve; he ultimately decided to avoid mentioning a specific age and wrote that she looked "as if she had lived but a few years" (*Magic*, 75; ms., 32). The original manuscript of *The Magic of Oz* is at the Harry Ransom Humanities Research Center at the University of Texas.

52. Reviews in *Chicago Post* (December 7, 1917), *New York Evening Post* (December 6, 1919), *New York Sun* (December 21, 1919), in *Baum Bugle* 29 (Autumn 1985): 18.

53. Letter to Reilly, written by Maud.

54. L. Frank Baum, *Glinda of Oz* (Chicago: Reilly & Lee, 1920), 26.

55. Ibid., 74. It made no difference to the peoples who suffered whether they were led into World War I by an absolute monarch, like the Germans or the Skeezers, or by a democratically elected leader, like the Flatheads or the British and Americans.

56. Ibid., 16, 152. Because fairy powers are given by nature, animals can be fairies, as they are in several of Baum's fantasies. In theosophy, Adepts are superior beings who have acquired supernatural powers through study of the secret laws of Nature and use them to "watch over and guide the evolution of humanity" (Besant, *Ancient Wisdom*, 41; cf. *Glinda*, 244). Accordingly, Baum's Adepts taught the Flatheads how to make the most of their mountaintop home and built the beautiful Skeezer city under its glass dome.

57. Baum, *Glinda of Oz*, 206.

58. E.g., *so* on ms., 12; *Glinda*, 35; *then* on ms., 15; *Glinda*, 42.

59. Ms., 1, 11, 19, 57, 83; *Glinda*, 14, 35, 54, 138, 194.

60. Ms., 18, 22, 27; *Glinda*, 49, 58, 68.

61. Ms., 89. Baum did not entirely complete his transformation of Reera's original appearance from skeleton to ape: the ape retains the skeleton's burning eyes, is noted as moving naturally (remarkable in a skeleton, not so in an ape), and has "the coolest sort of a form" for the heat of the day (appropriate for a skeleton, not an ape) (ms., 89, 92; *Glinda*, 208, 213). Other examples of neutral changes made in the manuscript include substitutions of Princess (Ozma) for Ruler, insertions of titles such as Princess (Ozma) and Queen (Coo-ee-oh), and fussy revisions such as dressed "simply in white muslin gowns" to "in simple white muslin gowns" (ms., 1; *Glinda*, 14). Other errors introduced into the manuscript

text (and not corrected) include replacing *to* with *from*, making nonsense of the sentence, "The Flatheads had to have a way from [sic] their mountain top from the plain below," and making Ozma answer a question instead of asking it (ms., 24, 28; *Glinda*, 64, 72). Other improvements in the manuscript text include removing an unnecessary clause that blocks the movement of a sentence—"Directly in the center of the great saucer stood a larger building which [when they had reached it] the Flathead informed the girls was the palace of the Supreme Dictator"—and increasing precision of language, as when "the people in the boat" become "the Skeezers in the submarine" (ms., 29, 53; *Glinda*, 73, 129). The Skeezers recognized the Adepts and "believed them to be friends" sounds inappropriately suspicious; this was revised to "welcomed them as friends" (ms., 113; *Glinda*, 256).

In the manuscript, Glinda consulted a spirit about the danger threatening Ozma and Dorothy, presumably as spirits were called on in seances such as the Baums had attended; in the published book this reference has disappeared (ms., 64).

The manuscript of *Glinda* is in the Library of Congress, in a binder issued by Reilly & Britton that evidently held successive Baum manuscripts. A label on this binder lists the dates when *The Patchwork Girl of Oz* was sent in and completed and when *The Scarecrow of Oz* was completed. It shows that there was less time between completion of manuscripts and publication for the stories for teenage girls: *Phoebe Daring* was sent in on May 1, 1912; *Aunt Jane's Nieces in the Red Cross* on January 3, 1915; and *Mary Louise [in the Country]* on June 15, 1916. Baum wrote on the title page of the *Glinda of Oz* manuscript that he had completed the book on February 17, 1917, evidently meaning the original draft. A note placed with the manuscript says he finished it the night before he entered the hospital, a year later; and the manuscript is dated February 1918.

62. Baum, *Glinda of Oz*, 279. The moral seems less trite in view of the recent carnage of World War I; probably Baum was wishing that some wise ruler could have stopped that war as soon as it started.

Although a little explicit moralizing comes into the later Oz books, remarks such as the Shaggy Man's on illusory evils and the Tin Woodman's on borrowing trouble (*Patchwork Girl of Oz*, 162, 330) are so unobtrusive they are hardly noticeable.

63. Letter at Syracuse University. In *To Please a Child*, Frank Junior quoted only one letter that his father had written him, an earlier one dated September 2. It consists mostly of praise and pious encouragement of his son. He praised his son's descriptive writing (presumably of battlefield scenes) as "far superior" to his own, and piously assured him that, despite apparent setbacks, "God was at all times on our side" and arranged everything for the best (272–73). The letter reveals more about the son than the father, and one wishes Frank Junior had not been so self-serving in his selection.

64. Edward Wagenknecht, *Utopia Americana* (Seattle: University of Washington Book Store, 1929), 39.

65. Baum and MacFall, 273–74.

66. Wagner, *Baum Bugle* 28 (Autumn 1984): 5–6.

67. Baum left two interesting manuscripts that are undatable because they are not mentioned in his surviving correspondence. "The Littlest Giant, An 'Oz' Story"

(not actually about Oz) is a grim tale of how the Littlest Giant, ostracized by the others because of his inadequate size, manages to seize the throne through cold-blooded scheming. But it is relieved by characteristic Baumian details of home life among the giants. Prince Kwa pesters his father by asking "fool questions," which are defined as questions "that cannot be answered" (*Baum Bugle* 19 [Spring 1975]: 2–5). An opening chapter of an Oz book, never developed further, is reprinted in the *Baum Bugle* 9 (Christmas 1965): 11. In its four and a half typewritten pages, Ozma finds a tall stranger from Hiland by the magic lake in her palace garden. His friend, Ahd, is caught in the pipe that feeds her lake.

10: Baum's Achievement: The World He Created

1. The *Dial* 29 (December 1, 1900): 436; 37 (December 1, 1904): 385; the *Nation* 87 (December 3, 1908): 550; 91 (December 15, 1910): 584. Both periodicals paid more attention to Baum's apprentice work than to the better books of his maturity. The *Dial* praised *Mother Goose in Prose* and the second-rate *Father Goose*, disparaged *A New Wonderland* and *The Master Key*, and mentioned *The Marvelous Land of Mo* (i.e., *Surprising Adventures of the Magical Monarch of Mo*) and *The Enchanted Island of Yew* (23 [December 16, 1897], 399–400; 27 [December 1, 1899]: 436; 29 [December 1, 1900]: 436; 31 [December 16, 1901]: 522; 35 [December 16, 1903]: 478).

   The *Nation* sneered at *Mother Goose in Prose, Father Goose,* and *American Fairy Tales* (65 [December 16, 1897]: 483; 69 [November 23, 1899]: 395; 87 [December 3, 1908]: 550).
2. Brian Attebery, *The Fantasy Tradition in American Literature* (Bloomington: Indiana University Press, 1980), 99.
3. Baum, *The Patchwork Girl of Oz*, 296.
4. Baum, *The Emerald City of Oz*, 42.
5. Ibid., 208.
6. Baum, *The Road to Oz*, 56.
7. *Baum Bugle* 29 (Christmas 1985): 15.
8. Baum, *Ozma of Oz*, 25–28.
9. It was Warren Hollister who first pointed out that, although Baum might not equal other fantasy writers in the standard criteria of plot, style, and characterization, he excelled them in believability. Later he estimated Baum more highly on the first three criteria as well. See *Baum Bugle* 15 (Christmas 1971): 5–8; 40 (Spring 1996): 5–6.
10. It is fun to show one's close reading by finding inconsistencies in Oz. Most of them result from Baum's speed in writing; evidently he depended on his memory of his past books rather than taking time to check them. For example, Dorothy is unfamiliar with the powers of the Magic Belt in *The Lost Princess of Oz*, even though she had both captured and used it back in *Ozma of Oz*. The Shaggy Man and Polychrome do not recognize each other in *Tik-Tok of Oz*, although they had traveled together in *The Road to Oz*. In some Oz books the dominant color of each country is universal; in others, it is simply the preferred and prevalent color. However, none of these discrepancies significantly impair a reader's pleasure, and

they are a small sacrifice to make for the sake of Baum's wonderful ease and spontaneity in writing.

11. E. P. Ryland, quoted in an unidentified newspaper clipping at the Onondaga Historical Society.

12. Daniel Boorstin, *The Americans: The Democratic Experience* (New York: Random House, 1973), 321–22. The actual date of this history of canning was 1924, but the wonders it describes had developed well before Baum's death.

13. Baum was interested in contemporary scientific and technological advances, but he did not use them directly in his children's fantasies, although they are prominent in *The Master Key* and his *Flying Girl* books. Despite Baum's fascination with electricity, electric lights appear only on Skeezer Island in Oz and in a few lands outside, namely the Nome Kingdom, Mo, and Tititi-Hoochoo's country.

   On one of the rare occasions when Baum introduced up-to-date science into Oz, he made an amusing mistake. The Horners, a mining people who live underground, mine radium and line their houses with it, so that the walls are a lovely silver color and emit a soft light that illuminates the rooms. Radium makes their homes "pretty and cosy. It is a medicine, too, and no one can ever be sick who lives near radium" (*Patchwork Girl*, 288). Radium was a wonderful new element in 1913. It was discovered by the Curies in 1898, and metallic radium was isolated in 1910. It was and is used for therapy; its dangerous properties did not become apparent until much later.

14. Russel B. Nye's introduction to L. Frank Baum, *The Wizard of Oz and Who He Was*, Martin Gardner and Nye, eds. (East Lansing: Michigan State University Press, 1957), 10–11.

15. Baum, *Glinda of Oz*, 247.

16. Kenneth Reckford, *Baum Bugle* 32 (Winter 1988): 12.

17. Alison Lurie maintains that parents, teachers, and librarians prefer children's books "in which children are helped by and learn from grown-ups," while children prefer books in which "a group of kids ... face dangers, have exciting adventures and help and instruct one another," with adults either appearing as villains or being ignorant of what is really going on ("Reading at Escape Velocity," *New York Times Book Review* [May 17, 1998], 51). Baum's fantasies, of course, belong in the latter group; but actually he blurred the distinction between children and adults. Children are placed in situations where they can act as mature individuals, sympathetic adults like the Wizard have retained a childlike approach to life, and one cannot say whether characters like the Scarecrow or the Patchwork Girl are children or adults. Perhaps Baum's subversiveness is one reason that Gillian Avery, who pointed out the difference between British and American children, did not approve of him. See *Behold the Child*, 1, 6.

18. Nye, ed., *Wizard of Oz and Who He Was*, 10–11.

19. The sea serpent King Anko in *The Sea Fairies* is the closest approximation to a powerful, benevolent father figure in Baum's fantasies.

20. C. S. Lewis, "On Three Ways of Writing for Children," in *Only Connect: Readings on Children's Literature*, Sheila Egoff, G. T. Stubbs, and L. F. Ashley, eds. (New York: Oxford University Press, 1969), 208–10, 213–15, 219.

21. Baum, *Magic of Oz*, 21.

22. Attebery, 105.

23. Baum, *Land of Oz*, 204.

24. Attebery, 3–4.

25. Baum, *Lost Princess*, 22.

26. Reilly & Lee also found it worth while to continue "Edith Van Dyne's" *Mary Louise* series. They hired Emma Speed Sampson to write (for outright sale rather than royalties) *Mary Louise at Dorfield* (1920), *Mary Louise Stands the Test* (1921), *Mary Louise and Josie O'Gorman*, *Josie O'Gorman*, and *Josie O'Gorman and the Meddlesome Major*.

27. She wrote one last, very short Oz book in 1972, called *Yankee in Oz* and published by the International Wizard of Oz Club.

28. Ruth Plumly Thompson, *The Cowardly Lion of Oz* (Chicago: Reilly & Lee, 1923), 77.

29. Ruth Plumly Thompson, *Kabumpo in Oz* (Chicago: Reilly & Lee, 1922), 146, 168.

30. Like Baum's books, the film was at first sneered at by the so-called experts. The critic at the *New Yorker* actually denied it any "trace of imagination, good taste, or ingenuity"; and the critic at the *New Republic* declared that it displayed no humor and only leaden fantasy. See Aljean Harmetz, *The Making of the Wizard of Oz* (New York: Knopf, 1977), 20–21.

31. *Fort Wayne, Indiana, Journal*; Carl Rexroad, *Baum Bugle* 41 (Spring 1997): 21–23. Like most of the cartoonists, Sack misread Baum's characters. Actually, of course, the Scarecrow, Tin Woodman, and Cowardly Lion are well endowed with brains, heart, and courage from the beginning; they only think they lack these qualities. This is clearer in the book than the movie, where Bert Lahr's Lion displays rampant cowardice throughout.

32. I saw the film when it first came out and, at the age of seven, was deeply disappointed. At the time I was upset because it did not literally follow the book, but in retrospect I think I sensed and was hurt by its refusal to take Baum's story seriously.

WORKS BY L. FRANK BAUM

The Aberdeen Saturday Pioneer, January 25, 1890–March 21, 1891 (editor).

American Fairy Tales (1901). Illus. N. P. Hall, Harry Kennedy, Ike Morgan, and Ralph Fletcher Seymour. Intro. Martin Gardner. New York: Dover Publications, 1978.

Animal Fairy Tales. Intro. Russell P. MacFall. Chicago: The International Wizard of Oz Club, 1969.

(Suzanne Metcalf). *Annabel, A Novel for Young Folk.* Chicago: Reilly & Britton, 1906.

The Army Alphabet. Illus. Harry Kennedy. Chicago: George M. Hill, 1900.

The Art of Decorating Dry Goods Windows and Interiors: A Complete Manual of Window Trimming, Designed as an Educator in All the Details of the Art, According to the Best Accepted Methods, and Treating Fully Every Important Subject. Chicago: The Show Window Publishing Co., 1900.

(Edith Van Dyne). *Aunt Jane's Nieces.* Chicago: Reilly & Britton, 1906.

(Edith Van Dyne). *Aunt Jane's Nieces Abroad.* Chicago: Reilly & Britton, 1906.

(Edith Van Dyne). *Aunt Jane's Nieces and Uncle John.* Chicago: Reilly & Britton, 1911.

(Edith Van Dyne). *Aunt Jane's Nieces at Millville.* Chicago: Reilly & Britton, 1908.

(Edith Van Dyne). *Aunt Jane's Nieces at Work.* Chicago: Reilly & Britton, 1909.

(Edith Van Dyne). *Aunt Jane's Nieces in the Red Cross.* Chicago: Reilly & Britton, 1915; second edition, Reilly & Lee, 1918.

(Edith Van Dyne). *Aunt Jane's Nieces in Society.* Chicago: Reilly & Britton, 1910.

(Edith Van Dyne). *Aunt Jane's Nieces on the Ranch.* Chicago: Reilly & Britton, 1913.

(Edith Van Dyne). *Aunt Jane's Nieces on Vacation.* Chicago: Reilly & Britton, 1912.

(Edith Van Dyne). *Aunt Jane's Nieces Out West.* Chicago: Reilly & Britton, 1914.

(Laura Bancroft). *Bandit Jim Crow.* Illus. Maginel Wright Enright. Chicago: Reilly & Britton, 1906.

Baum's American Fairy Tales: Stories of Astonishing Adventures of American Boys and Girls with the Fairies of Their Native Land. Illus. George Kerr. Indianapolis: Bobbs-Merrill, 1908.

Baum's Own Book for Children: Stories & Verses from the Famous "Oz Books," "Father Goose: His Book," Etc., Etc. Chicago: Reilly & Britton, 1912.

The Book of the Hamburgs: A Brief Treatise upon the Mating, Rearing and Management of the Different Varieties of Hamburgs. Hartford, CT: H. H. Stoddard, 1886.

(Floyd Akers). *The Boy Fortune Hunters in China.* Chicago: Reilly & Britton, 1909.

(Floyd Akers). *The Boy Fortune Hunters in Egypt.* Chicago: Reilly & Britton, 1908.

(Floyd Akers). *The Boy Fortune Hunters in the South Seas.* Chicago: Reilly & Britton, 1911.

(Floyd Akers). *The Boy Fortune Hunters in Yucatan.* Chicago: Reilly & Britton, 1910.

By the Candelabra's Glare (1898). Illus. W. W. Denslow et al. Intro. Peter E. Hanff. Delmar, NY: Scholars' Facsimiles & Reprints, 1981.

The Daring Twins: A Story for Young Folk. Illus. Pauline M. Batchelder. Chicago: Reilly & Britton, 1911.

(Schuyler Staunton). *Daughters of Destiny.* Illus. Thomas Mitchell Peirce and Harold DeLay. Chicago: Reilly & Britton, 1906.

Dorothy and the Wizard in Oz. Illus. John R. Neill. Chicago: Reilly & Britton, 1908.

Dot and Tot of Merryland. Illus. W. W. Denslow. Indianapolis: Bobbs-Merrill, 1901.

The Emerald City of Oz. Illus. John R. Neill. Chicago: Reilly & Britton, 1910.

The Enchanted Island of Yew—Whereon Prince Marvel Encountered the High Ki of Twi and Other Surprising People. Illus. Fanny Y. Cory. Indianapolis: Bobbs-Merrill, 1903.

(Schuyler Staunton). *The Fate of a Crown.* Illus. Glen C. Sheffer. Chicago: Reilly & Britton, 1905.

Father Goose: His Book. Illus. W. W. Denslow. Chicago: George M. Hill, 1899.

Father Goose's Year Book: Quaint Quacks and Feathered Shafts for Mature Children. Illus. Walter J. Enright. Chicago: Reilly & Britton, 1907.

(Edith Van Dyne). *The Flying Girl.* Illus. Joseph Pierre Nuyttens. Chicago: Reilly & Britton, 1911.

(Edith Van Dyne). *The Flying Girl and Her Chum.* Illus. Joseph Pierre Nuyttens. Chicago: Reilly & Britton, 1912.

"The Girl from Oz." Typescript at Syracuse University.

"Glinda of Oz," manuscript draft in Library of Congress.

Glinda of Oz: In which are related the Exciting Experiences of Princess Ozma of Oz, and Dorothy, in Their Hazardous Journey to the Home of the Flatheads, and to the Magic Isle of the Skeezers, and How They Were Rescued from Dire Peril by the Sorcery of Glinda the Good. Illus. John R. Neill. Chicago: Reilly & Lee, 1920.

The High-Jinks of L. Frank Baum: Being a Selection of Songs by the Author of The Wizard of Oz. As Sung by the Uplifters of Los Angeles. Chicago: Wizard Press, 1959.

John Dough and the Cherub. Illus. John R. Neill. Chicago: Reilly & Britton, 1906.

A Kidnapped Santa Claus (1904). Indianapolis: Bobbs-Merrill, 1969.

L. Frank Baum's Juvenile Speaker; Readings and Recitations in Prose and Verse, Humorous and Otherwise. Illus. John R. Neill and Maginel Wright Enright. Chicago: Reilly & Britton, 1910.

(Anonymous) *The Last Egyptian: A Romance of the Nile.* Illus. Francis P. Wrightman. Philadelphia: Edward Stern, 1908.

The Life and Adventures of Santa Claus (1902). Afterword by Max Apple. New York: Penguin USA, 1986.

Little Wizard Stories of Oz. Illus. John R. Neill. Chicago: Reilly & Britton, 1914.

The Lost Princess of Oz. Illus. John R. Neill. Chicago: Reilly & Britton, 1917.

"The Magic of Oz," manuscript draft in Harry Ransom Humanities Research Center, University of Texas, Austin.

The Magic of Oz: A Faithful Record of the Remarkable Adventures of Dorothy and Trot and the Wizard of Oz, Together with the Cowardly Lion, the Hungry Tiger and Cap'n Bill, in Their Successful Search for a Magical and Beautiful Birthday

Present for Princess Ozma of Oz. Illus. John R. Neill. Chicago: Reilly & Lee, 1919.

(Louis F. Baum). "The Maid of Arran," typescript in Theater Collection, New York Public Library.

The Marvelous Land of Oz: Being an Account of the Further Adventures of the Scarecrow and Tin Woodman and Also the Strange Experiences of the Highly Magnified Woggle-Bug, Jack Pumpkinhead, the Animated Saw-Horse and the Gump. Illus. John R. Neill. Chicago: Reilly & Britton, 1904.

(Edith Van Dyne). *Mary Louise.* Chicago: Reilly & Britton, 1916.

(Edith Van Dyne). *Mary Louise and the Liberty Girls.* Chicago: Reilly & Lee, 1918.

(Edith Van Dyne). *Mary Louise in the Country.* Chicago: Reilly & Britton, 1916.

The Master Key. An Electrical Fairy Tale, Founded upon the Mysteries of Electricity and the Optimism of Its Devotees. It Was Written for Boys, but Others May Read It. Illus. Fanny Y. Cory. Indianapolis: Bowen-Merrill, 1901.

Mister Woodchuck. Illus. Maginel Wright Enright. Chicago: Reilly & Britton, 1906.

Mother Goose in Prose. Illus. Maxfield Parrish. Chicago: Way & Williams, 1897.

"A Musical Extravaganza Entitled The Woggle Bug," typescript in Library of Congress.

The Musical Fantasies of L. Frank Baum, with Three Unpublished Scenarios. Alla T. Ford and Dick Martin, eds. Chicago: Wizard Press, 1958.

The Navy Alphabet. Illus. Harry Kennedy. Chicago: George M. Hill, 1900.

A New Wonderland: Being the First Account Ever Presented of the Beautiful Valley, and the Wonderful Adventures of Its Inhabitants. Illus. Frank Ver Beck. New York: R. H. Russell, 1900.

Our Landlady. Ed. Nancy Tystad Koupal. Lincoln: University of Nebraska Press, 1996.

"Ozma of Oz, A Musical Extravaganza," typescript in Theater Collection, New York Public Library.

Ozma of Oz: A Record of Her Adventures with Dorothy Gale of Kansas, the Yellow Hen, the Scarecrow, the Tin Woodman, Tiktok, the Cowardly Lion and the Hungry Tiger; Besides Other Good People too Numerous to Mention Faithfully Recorded Herein. Illus. John R. Neill. Chicago: Reilly & Britton, 1907.

The Patchwork Girl of Oz. Illus. John R. Neill. Chicago: Reilly & Britton, 1913.

Phoebe Daring: A Story for Young Folk. Illus. Joseph Pierre Nuyttens. Chicago: Reilly & Britton, 1912.

(Laura Bancroft). *Policeman Bluejay* (1907). Intro. David L. Greene. Delmar, NY: Scholars' Facsimiles & Reprints, 1981.

(Laura Bancroft). *Prairie-Dog Town.* Illus. Maginel Wright Enright. Chicago: Reilly & Britton, 1906.

(Laura Bancroft). *Prince Mud-Turtle.* Illus. Maginel Wright Enright. Chicago: Reilly & Britton, 1906.

Queen Zixi of Ix: or, The Story of the Magic Cloak. Illus. Frederick Richardson. New York: Century, 1905.

"The Rainbow's Daughter," or "The Love Magnet," typed scenario in Theater Collection, New York Public Library.

Rinkitink in Oz. Illus. John R. Neill. Chicago: Reilly & Britton, 1916.

The Road to Oz. Illus. John R. Neill. Chicago: Reilly & Britton, 1909.

(Hugh Fitzgerald). *Sam Steele's Adventures in Panama.* Chicago: Reilly & Britton, 1907. Reissued as Floyd Akers's *Boy Fortune Hunters in the Panama,* 1908.

(Hugh Fitzgerald). *Sam Steele's Adventures on Land & Sea.* Chicago: Reilly & Britton, 1906. Reissued as Floyd Akers's *The Boy Fortune Hunters in Alaska,* 1908.

The Scarecrow of Oz. Illus. John R. Neill. Chicago: Reilly & Britton, 1915.

The Sea Fairies. Illus. John R. Neill. Chicago: Reilly & Britton, 1911.

The Show Window: A Journal of Practical Window Trimming for the Merchant and the Professional, November 1897–October 1900 (editor).

Sky Island: Being the Further Exciting Adventures of Trot and Cap'n Bill After Their Visit to the Sea Fairies. Chicago: Reilly & Britton, 1912.

The Snuggle Tales: Little Bun Rabbit and Other Stories, The Magic Cloak and Other Stories, The Yellow Hen and Other Stories, Once Upon a Time and Other Stories. Illus. John R. Neill. Chicago: Reilly & Britton, 1916.

(Laura Bancroft). *Sugar-Loaf Mountain.* Illus. Maginel Wright Enright. Chicago: Reilly & Britton, 1906.

The Surprising Adventures of the Magical Monarch of Mo and His People (1903). Illus. Frank Ver Beck. Intro. Martin Gardner. New York: Dover Publications, 1968.

(John Estes Cooke). *Tamawaca Folks: A Summer Comedy.* USA: Tamawaca Press, 1907.

Tik-Tok of Oz. Illus John R. Neill. Chicago: Reilly & Britton, 1914.

"The Tin Woodman of Oz," manuscript draft in Harry Ransom Humanities Research Center, University of Texas, Austin.

The Tin Woodman of Oz: A Faithful Story of the Astonishing Adventure Undertaken by the Tin Woodman, Assisted by Woot the Wanderer, the Scarecrow of Oz, and Polychrome, the Rainbow's Daughter. Illus. John R. Neill. Chicago: Reilly & Britton, 1918.

(Laura Bancroft). *Twinkle's Enchantment.* Illus. Maginel Wright Enright. Chicago: Reilly & Britton, 1906.

The Uplift of Lucifer, in Which Is Included the Corrugated Giant and Some Other Baumiana, Mostly Photographic. Ed. Manuel Weitman. Los Angeles, 1963.

"The Wizard of Oz: A Dramatic Composition in Three Acts," type-script in Library of Congress.

The Woggle-Bug Book (1905). Illus. Ike Morgan. Delmar, NY: Scholars' Facsimiles and Reprints, 1978.

Books of Wonder has reprinted the handsome first editions of the Oz books, *The Sea Fairies,* and *Sky Island.*

Films

His Majesty, the Scarecrow of Oz. Directed and written by L. Frank Baum. Oz Film Manufacturing Company. December 7, 1914. Five reels.

The Last Egyptian: A Romance of the Nile. Directed (and written?) by L. Frank Baum. Oz Film Manufacturing Company. December 12, 1914. Five reels.

The Magic Cloak of Oz. Directed by L. Frank Baum or J. Farrell Mac-Donald. Probably written by L. Frank Baum. Oz Film Manufacturing Company. September 28, 1914. Five reels.

The Patchwork Girl of Oz. Directed by J. Farrell MacDonald. Written by L. Frank Baum. Oz Film Manufacturing Company. September 28, 1914. Five reels.

Violet's Dreams. Four one-reel films, including *The Country Circus* and *The Magic Bon Bons.* September 1915 and October 1915.

Prints of all these films except *The Last Egyptian* are at the Library of Congress.

BIBLIOGRAPHY

Aberdeen: A Middle Border City. American Guide Series. Compiled and written by workers of the South Dakota Writers' Project, WPA. Aberdeen, 1940.

Abrahm, Paul, and S. Kenter. "Tik-Tok and the Three Laws of Robotics." *Science-Fiction Studies* 5, no. 14 (March 1978): 67–80.

Algeo, John. "A Notable Theosophist: L. Frank Baum" and "The Wizard of Oz: The Perilous Journey." *American Theosophist* 74, no. 8, 9 (1986): 270–73, 291–97.

———. "Oz and Kansas: A Theological Quest." In *Proceedings of the 13th Annual Conference of the Children's Literature Association.* Eds. Susan Gannon and Ruth Ann Thompson. May 16–18, 1986. (1988).

American Book Collector. December 1962. Special issue on Baum.

The American Film Institute Catalog of Motion Pictures Produced in the United States. Feature Films, 1911–1920. Berkeley: University of California Press, 1988.

Arbuthnot, May Hill and Zena Sutherland. *Children's Books.* Glenview, IL: Scott, Foresman, 1972. 4th ed.

Attebery, Brian. *The Fantasy Tradition in American Literature: From Irving to LeGuin.* Bloomington: Indiana University Press, 1980.

Avery, Gillian. *Behold the Child: American Children and Their Books 1621–1922.* Baltimore: Johns Hopkins University Press, 1994.

The Baum Bugle, 1957 to present.

Baum, Frank J. "The Oz Film Manufacturing Company." *Films in Review* 7 (August–September 1956): 329–33.

Baum, Frank Joslyn, and Russell P. MacFall. *To Please a Child: A Biography of L. Frank Baum.* Chicago: Reilly & Lee, 1961.

Baum, Harry (?). (Edith Van Dyne). *Mary Louise Adopts a Soldier.* Chicago: Reilly & Lee, 1919.

————. *Mary Louise Solves a Mystery.* Chicago: Reilly & Britton, 1917.

Baum's correspondence with Reilly & Britton. Copies courtesy of Robert A. Baum.

Baum letters at Knox College, the Missouri Historical Society, San Diego State University, and the University of California, Berkeley.

Baum papers at Alexander Mitchell Library, Aberdeen, SD.

Baum papers at Columbia University.

Baum papers at New York Public Library.

Baum papers at Onondaga Historical Society.

Baum papers at Syracuse University.

Baum papers at Yale University.

Baum, Maud Gage. *In Other Lands Than Ours.* Ed. with preface and photographs by L. Frank Baum (1907). Intro. Edith and Warren Hollister. Delmar, NY: Scholars' Facsimiles & Reprints, 1983.

Bellamy, Edward. *Looking Backward 2000–1887.* Intro. Robert L. Shurter. New York: Modern Library, 1951.

Besant, Annie. *The Ancient Wisdom: An Outline of Theosophical Teachings* (1897). Adyar, Madras: Theosophical Publishing House, 1966.

————. "Theosophical Society." *Encyclopedia of Religion and Ethics* 12 (1921): 301–4.

Bettelheim, Bruno. *The Uses of Enchantment: The Meaning and Importance of Fairy Tales.* New York: Knopf, 1946.

Black, William. *A Princess of Thule* (1874). New York: John W. Lovell, 1882.

Bobbs-Merrill archives, Lilly Library, Indiana University.

Boorstin, Daniel. *The Americans: The Democratic Experience.* New York: Random House, 1973.

————. *The Image: or, What Happened to the American Dream.* New York: Atheneum, 1962.

Bradbury, Ray. "The Exiles." In *The Illustrated Man.* Garden City: Doubleday, 1951.

Brammer, Leila R. "The Exclusionary Politics of Social Movements: Matilda Joslyn Gage and the National American Woman Suffrage Association." Ph.D. dissertation, University of Minnesota, 1995.

Brands, H. W. *The Reckless Decade: America in the 1890s.* New York: St. Martin's, 1995.

Brown, William F. *The Wiz. Adapted from "The Wonderful Wizard of Oz" by L. Frank Baum.* Music and lyrics by Charlie Smalls. New York: Samuel French, 1974. Revised 1979.

Carpenter, Julia Gage. Diary at University of North Dakota.

Cloud, Barbara. *The Business of Newspapers on the Western Frontier.* Reno: University of Nevada Press, 1992.

Columbia University College of Physicians and Surgeons. *Complete Home Medical Guide.* 3d revised ed. New York: Crown, 1995.

Cook, Timothy E. "Another Perspective on Political Authority in Children's Literature: The Fallible Leader in L. Frank Baum and Dr. Seuss." *Western Political Quarterly* 36, no. 2 (June 1983): 326–34.

Cosgrove, Rachel. *The Hidden Valley of Oz.* Chicago: Reilly & Lee, 1951.

Culver, Stuart. "What Manikins Want: *The Wonderful Wizard of Oz* and *The Art of Decorating Dry Goods Windows*," *Representations* 21 (Winter 1988): 97–116.

De Luca, Geraldine, and Roni Natov, "Researching Oz: An Interview with Michael Patrick Hearn." *The Lion and the Unicorn* 11, no. 2 (October 1987): 51–62.

The Dial, 23 (Dec. 16, 1897), 27 (Dec. 1, 1899), 29 (Dec. 1, 1900), 31 (Dec. 16, 1901), 35 (Dec. 16, 1903), 37 (Dec. 1, 1904).

Edmundson, Mark. Review of Linda Simon's *Genuine Reality: A Life of William James. Washington Post* Book World, Sunday, February 1, 1998, 5.

Egoff, Sheila, G. T. Stubbs, and L. F. Ashley. *Only Connect: Readings on Children's Literature.* New York: Oxford University Press, 1969.

Erisman, Fred. "L Frank Baum and the Progressive Dilemma." *American Quarterly* 20, no. 3 (Fall 1968); 616–23.

Farmer, Philip José. *A Barnstormer in Oz: or A Rationalization and Extrapolation of the Split-level Continuum.* Huntington Woods, MI: Phantasia Press, 1982.

Faulkner, Harold U. *Politics, Reform and Expansion: 1890–1900.* New York: Harper & Row, 1959.

Feigenbaum, Janet. Review in *TLS* (October 30, 1998): 14.

Ferrara, Susan. *The Family of the Wizard: The Baums of Syracuse.* Xlibris, 2000.

Gage, Matilda Joslyn. *Woman, Church and State: A Historical Account of the Status of Woman Through the Christian Ages: With Reminiscences of the Matriarchate.* 2d ed. New York: The Truth Seeker Company, 1893.

Gage papers in the Schlesinger Library, Radcliffe College (Woman's Suffrage. National Leaders).

Gardner, Martin. Introduction to *The Marvelous Land of Oz.* New York: Dover, 1969.

———. *Order and Surprise.* Buffalo: Prometheus Books, 1983.

———. *The Whys of a Philosophical Scrivener.* New York: William Morrow, 1983.

————, and Russel B. Nye, eds. *The Wizard of Oz and Who He Was.* East Lansing: Michigan State University Press, 1957.

Garland, Hamlin. *Crumbling Idols: Twelve Essays on Art Dealing Chiefly with Literature Painting and the Drama.* Ed. Jane Johnson. Cambridge: Harvard University Press, 1960.

————. *Main Travelled Roads* (1891). New York: Harper & Brothers, n.d.

————. *A Son of the Middle Border* (1914). New York: Macmillan, 1956.

Geer, John G., and Thomas R. Rochon. "William Jennings Bryan on the Yellow Brick Road." *Journal of American Culture* 16, no. 4 (Winter 1993): 59–63.

Glassman, Peter, ed. *Oz: The Hundredth Anniversary Celebration.* New York: Books of Wonder, HarperCollins, 2000.

Greene, David L., and Dick Martin. *The Oz Scrapbook.* New York: Random House, 1977.

Greene, Douglas G., and Michael Patrick Hearn. *W. W. Denslow.* Mount Pleasant, MI: Clarke Historical Library, Central Michigan University, 1976.

Hampsten, Elizabeth. *Read This Only to Yourself: The Private Writings of Midwestern Women, 1880–1910.* Bloomington: Indiana University Press, 1982.

Hanff, Peter E. et al. *Bibliographia Oziana: A Concise Bibliographical Checklist of the Oz Books by L. Frank Baum and His Successors.* International Wizard of Oz Club, 1976.

Harmetz, Aljean. *The Making of the Wizard of Oz.* New York: Knopf, 1977.

Harrison, Edith Ogden. *Prince Silverwings and Other Fairy Tales.* Chicago: A. C. McClurg, 1902.

Hawthorne, Nathaniel. "Feathertop." In *The Complete Short Stories of Nathaniel Hawthorne.* Garden City, NY: Hanover House, 1959.

Hearn, Michael Patrick, ed. *The Annotated Wizard of Oz.* Centennial ed. New York: W. W. Norton, 2000.

————. "When L Frank Baum was 'Laura Bancroft.' " *American Book Collector* 8, no. 5 (May 1987): 11–6.

————, ed. *The Wonderful Wizard of Oz.* Critical Heritage Series. New York: Schocken Books, 1983.

Holley, Marietta. *Samantha Rastles the Woman Question.* Ed. Jane Curry. Urbana: University of Illinois Press, 1983.

Hough (Emerson) papers at the State Historical Society of Iowa.

Karr, Phyllis Ann. "The Two Endings of *Aunt Jane's Nieces in the Red Cross.*" *Library Review* 26 (University of Louisville): November 1977.

Koupal, Nancy Tystad. *Baum's Road to Oz: The Dakota Years.* Pierre: South Dakota State Historical Society Press, 2000.

Koupal, Nancy. "The Wonderful Wizard of the West: L. F. Baum in South Dakota, 1888–91." *Great Plains Quarterly* 9 (Fall 1989): 203–15.

Lanes, Selma G. *Down the Rabbit Hole: Adventures and Misadventures in the Realm of Children's Literature.* New York: Atheneum, 1971.

Leach, William R., ed. *The Wonderful Wizard of Oz by L. Frank Baum.* Belmont, CA: Wadsworth Publishing Company, 1991.

L. Frank Baum: The Wonderful Wizard of Oz: An Exhibition of His Published Writings, in Commemoration of the Centenary of His Birth, May 16, 1856. Arranged and described by Joan Baum and Roland Baughman. New York: Columbia University Libraries, 1956.

Luehrs, Robert B. "L. Frank Baum and the Land of Oz: A Children's Author as Social Critic." *19th Century* 6 (Autumn 1980): 55–7.

Lurie, Alison. *Don't Tell the Grown-ups: Subversive Children's Literature.* Boston: Little, Brown, 1990.

———. "The Fate of the Munchkins." *New York Review of Books* 21, no. 6 (April 18, 1974): 24–5.

———. "Reading at Escape Velocity." *New York Times Book Review* (May 17, 1998), 51.

MacDonald, George. *The Princess and the Goblin.* New York: Dell, 1986.

McGraw, Eloise Jarvis, and Lauren McGraw Wagner. *Merry Go Round in Oz* (1963). New York: Books of Wonder, 1993.

McMath, Robert C., Jr., *American Populism: A Social History 1877–1898.* New York: Hill & Wang, 1993.

McReynolds, Douglas J., and Barbara Lips. "A Girl in the Game: *The Wizard of Oz* as Analog for the Female Experience in America." *North Dakota Quarterly* 54 (1986): 87–93.

Maguire, Gregory. *Wicked: The Life and Times of the Wicked Witch of the West.* New York: Regan Books, HarperCollins, 1995.

Mantele, Ozma Baum. "Kenneth Gage Baum: An Appreciation." Foreword to his *The Dinamonster of Oz.*

Mazlish, Bruce. *The Fourth Discontinuity: The Co-Evolution of Humans and Machines.* New Haven: Yale University Press, 1993.

Moore, Raylin. *Wonderful Wizard, Marvelous Land.* Intro. Ray Bradbury. Bowling Green, OH: Bowling Green University Popular Press, 1974.

Morris, William. *News from Nowhere* (1890). In *News from Nowhere and*

Selected Writings and Designs. Ed. Asa Briggs. New York: Penguin Books, 1984.

The Nation 65 (December 16, 1897), 69 (November 23, 1899), 87 (December 3, 1908), 91 (December 15, 1910).

Neill, John R. *The Wonder City of Oz.* Illus. John R. Neill. Chicago: Reilly & Lee, 1940.

New York Times, September 8, 1900; September 10, 1904; May 8, 1919; May 11, 1919.

Odean, Kathleen. *Great Books for Girls: More Than 600 Books to Inspire Today's Girls and Tomorrow's Women.* New York: Ballantine Books, 1997.

Oltramare, Paul. "Theosophy." *Encyclopedia of Religion and Ethics* (1921): 12: 304–15.

Perrin, Stephanie. "The Works of L. Frank Baum: American Fantasy in Changing Times." M.A. thesis submitted to Carleton University, 1994.

Publishers' Weekly, 84 (Sept. 20, 1913), 86 (Oct. 17, 1914), 88 (Sept. 18, 1915), 95 (June 14, 1919); Reilly & Britton (later Reilly & Lee) advertisements in 85 (Jan.–June 1914), 93 (Jan.–June 1918), 95 (Jan.–June 1919).

Rahn, Suzanne. *The Wizard of Oz: Shaping an Imaginary World.* New York: Twayne, 1998.

Reed, Dorinda Riessen. *The Woman Suffrage Movement in South Dakota.* 2d ed. Ed. N. T. Koupal. Pierre: South Dakota Commission on the Status of Women, 1975.

Riley, Michael O. *Oz and Beyond: The Fantasy World of L. Frank Baum.* Lawrence: University Press of Kansas, 1997.

Ryman, Geoff. *Was.* New York: Alfred A. Knopf, 1992.

Sale, Roger. "Child Reading and Man Reading: Oz, Babar and Pooh." In *Reflections on Literature for Children.* Ed. Francelia Butler and Richard Rotert. Hamden, CT: Library of Professional Publications, 1984.

———. *Fairy Tales and After: From Snow White to E. B. White.* Cambridge: Harvard University Press, 1978.

———. "L. Frank Baum, and Oz." *Hudson Review* 25, no. 4 (Winter 1972–73): 571–92.

Schlereth, Thomas J. *Victorian America: Transformations in Everyday Life, 1876–1915.* New York: HarperCollins, 1991.

Seymour, Ralph Fletcher. *Some Went This Way: A Forty Year Pilgrimage Among Artists, Bookmen and Printers.* Chicago: Ralph Fletcher Seymour, 1945.

Shortridge, James R. *The Middle West: Its Meaning in American Culture.* Lawrence: University Press of Kansas, 1989.

Snow, Jack. *The Shaggy Man of Oz.* Chicago: Reilly & Lee, 1949.

————. *Who's Who in Oz.* Chicago: Reilly & Lee, 1954.

South Dakota: A Guide to the State. Federal Writers Project. South Dakota. 2d ed. New York: Hastings House, 1952.

Stanton, Elizabeth Cady, Susan B. Anthony, and Matilda Joslyn Gage. *A History of Woman Suffrage.* 2 vols. New York: Fowler and Wells, 1881.

Starr, Kevin. *Material Dreams: Southern California Through the 1920s.* New York: Oxford University Press, 1990.

Swartz, Mark Evan. *Oz Before the Rainbow: L. Frank Baum's "The Wonderful Wizard of Oz" on Stage and Screen to 1939.* Baltimore: Johns Hopkins University Press, 2000.

Swift, Jonathan. *Gulliver's Travels.* In *The Writings of Jonathan Swift.* Ed. Robert A. Greenberg and William Bowman Piper. New York: W. W. Norton, 1973.

Thomas, John L. *Alternative America: Henry George, Edward Bellamy, Henry Demarest Lloyd and the Adversary Tradition.* Cambridge: Harvard University Press, 1983.

Thompson, Ruth P. *The Cowardly Lion of Oz.* Illus. John R. Neill. Chicago: Reilly & Lee, 1923.

————. *Kabumpo in Oz.* Illus. John R. Neill. Chicago: Reilly & Lee, 1922.

Tietjens, Eunice. *The World at My Shoulder.* New York: Macmillan, 1938.

Turner, Frederick Jackson. *The Frontier in American History.* Tucson: University of Arizona Press, 1986.

Ulveling, Ralph. "R U on Freedom of Information." *Amer Lib Assoc Bull* (October 1957): 653–55.

Vidal, Gore. "On Rereading the Oz Books," *New York Review of Books* 24, no. 16 (October 13, 1977): 38–42.

————. "The Wizard of 'The Wizard,'" *New York Review of Books* 24:15 (September 29, 1977): 10–15.

Wagenknecht, Edward. *As Far as Yesterday.* Norman: University of Oklahoma Press, 1968.

————. *Utopia Americana.* Seattle: University of Washington Book Store, 1929.

Wagner, Sally Roesch. "That Word Is Liberty: A Biography of Matilda Joslyn Gage." Ph.D. dissertation, University of California, Santa Cruz, 1978.

West, Mark I., ed. *Before Oz: Juvenile Fantasy Stories from 19th Century America.* Hamden, CT: Archon Press, 1989.

White, William Allen. *Autobiography.* New York: Macmillan, 1946.

Wittmayer, Cecilia M. "The 1889–1890 Woman Suffrage Campaign: A Need to Organize." *South Dakota History* II (Summer 1981): 199–225.

Young, Betty Lou. *Rustic Canyon and the Story of the Uplifters.* Santa Monica: Casa Vieja Press, 1975.

INDEX

NOTE: "LFB" stands for Lyman Frank Baum. Women are listed under their married names, when known. Fictional characters are listed under their "first name," e.g. "Louise Merrick" under "L." Works by L. Frank Baum, his pseudonyms, or his successors, are listed alphabetically. Works by other authors are listed under those authors' names. Italic page references indicate illustrations.